The ACTS of the Apostles

An Exposition

Classic Biblical Reprints Series no. 1

Arno C. Gaebelein

Updated and Revised Edition

Edited by David E. Graves, Ph.D.

456 Fourth Avenue
New York City, 1912.

Electronic Christian Media

Toronto, Canada

2016

Unless otherwise indicated, all Scripture quotations are from the ESV® Bible (The Holy Bible, English Standard Version®), copyright © 2001 by Crossway Bibles, a publishing ministry of Good News Publishers. Used by permission. All rights reserved. Italics within Scripture quotations indicate emphasis added.

The Acts of the Apostles: An Exposition: Updated and Revised Edition.
Classic Biblical Reprints Series No. 1.
Includes bibliographic references and indexes.
Copyright © 2016 by David E. Graves
Revision 1, May 2016
Published by Electronic Christian Media
Toronto, Ontario, Canada M2J 4T4

    ISBN-13: 978-0-9948060-7-9
    ISBN-10: 0994806078
    1. Bible. N.T. Acts (book)-Commentaries I. Title. II. Series.

Interior Book Design: David E. Graves
Cover Design: David E. Graves

Front Center – Bouleuterion in Ephesus. Photo by David E. Graves.
Front Border – Mosaic pattern found in the sidewalk in Ephesus. Photo by David E. Graves
Front – Wax seal created by David E. Graves.

Picture Acknowledgements

Photographs
Todd Bolen/BiblePlaces.com: Nos. 31, 34.
Classical Numismatic Group, Inc. (CNG): No. 20
David E. Graves: Nos. 1, 3, 4, 5, 7, 9, 10, 11, 12, 16, 26, 33, 35, 37, 39, 44, 51.
Ferrell Jenkins/BiblicalStudies.info: Nos. 22, 30, 32, 41, 43.
Leen Ritmeyer Archaelogical Design No. 42.
David Steeves: No. 6.
Mark Wilson: No. 15.
Wikimedia Commons, CC-BY 2.5 the free media repository. Public Domain (PD). Nos. 2. Seetheholyland.net, 8. ברק אפי ידי על צולם
    Pikiwikisrael, 13. Luis García, 14. Gerhard Haubold, 17. Maderibeyza, 18. Berthold Werner, 19. David Stanley, 21. Andrew Bossi, 23., 24. Marsyas, 25., 27., 28. A. Savin, 29. O. Mustafin, 36. Magnus Manskke, 38. Horacio36., 40. Berthold Werner, 45. Matthias Kabel, 36. Matthias Kabel, 47. Berthold Werner, 48. Giorces Bardo, 49. Frank Vincentz, 50. Albert Krantz.

Maps
David E. Graves: Nos. 1, 2, 3.

All rights reserved. No portion of this publication may be reproduced, stored in a retrieval system, or transmitted in any form (i.e., electronic, scanning, photocopy or recording) without the written permission of the publisher. The only exception is brief excerpts for reviews.

Printed in the United States of America.

Table of Contents

TABLE OF CONTENTS XIII
INDEX OF IMAGES IX
FOREWORD XIII
ABBREVIATIONS XIV
    OLD TESTAMENT XIV
    NEW TESTAMENT XIV
    ANCIENT AND MODERN SOURCES XIV
PREFACE TO THE UPDATED EDITION 16
INTRODUCTION 17
    BY WHOM WAS THIS BOOK WRITTEN? 17
    THE CONTENTS AND SCOPE OF THE BOOK. 18
    THE DIVISION OF THE BOOK. 19
CHAPTER ONE 22
    1. EVENTS PRECEDING THE ASCENSION AND RETURN (VS. 1–11) 22
        Introduction to Theophilus (vs. 1–3). 22
        Promise of the Holy Spirit (vs. 4–11). 23
    2. MATTHIAS ADDED TO THE APOSTLES (VS. 12–26). 27
        The waiting company in prayer (vs. 12–14). 27
        Peter argues to replace Judas (vs. 15–20). 28
        Matthias replaces Judas (vs. 21–26). 29
CHAPTER TWO 31
    1. THE OUTPOURING OF THE HOLY SPIRIT (VS. 1–4). 34
    2. THE IMMEDIATE EFFECT OF HIS PRESENCE (VS. 5–15). 36
    3. PETER'S ADDRESS (VS 14–36). 42
    4. THE RESULTS OF THE DELIVERED TESTIMONY (VS. 37–41). 47
    5. THE GATHERED COMPANY IN FELLOWSHIP (VS. 42–47). 49
CHAPTER THREE 53
    1. THE HEALING OF THE LAME MAN (VS. 1–10). 53
    2. PETER'S SECOND ADDRESS (VS. 11–16). 56
    3. THEIR ARREST (4:1–3). 61
    4. THE RESULT OF THE TESTIMONY (4:4). 61
CHAPTER FOUR 62

1. Peter and John before the rulers (vs. 5–7)...62
2. Peter's Bold Witness (vs. 8–12)..63
3. The Astonishment of the Sanhedrin. and the Release of the Apostles (vs. 13–22)..65
4. With their own company; their praise and prayer (vs. 23–31).......................66
5. The saved multitude one heart and one soul (vs. 32–37).............................68

CHAPTER FIVE 70

1. The Manifestation of evil in the church; Ananias and Sapphira (vs. 1–11)...70
2. The Signs and Wonders done by the Hands of the Apostles (vs. 12–16)..73
3. The Second Arrest of the Apostles and their Miraculous Deliverance (vs. 17–25)..74
4. Their Trial and Witness before the Council (vs. 26–32)................................75
5. The Advice of Gamaliel (vs. 33–39)...76
6. The Release of the Apostles. Their Continued Testimony (vs. 40–42)..........77

CHAPTER SIX 79

1. The Murmuring of the Grecians against the Hebrews (vs. 1–7)....................79
2. Stephen, his ministry and arrest (vs. 8–15)..82

CHAPTER SEVEN 84

1. The address of Stephen (vs. 2–53)..84
   Abraham's History (vs. 2–8)..85
   Joseph and his brethren (vs. 9–16)..86
   Moses as Deliverer rejected (vs. 17–38)..87
   The Story of their Apostasy and Shame (vs. 39–53).................................89
2. The Martyrdom of Stephen (vs. 54–60)...91

CHAPTER EIGHT 94

1. The first great persecution (vs. 1–3)..94
2. The preaching of the scattered believers. Philip in Samaria (vs. 4–8)...........96
3. The Events in Samaria (vs. 9–13)..97
4. The Gospel in many villages of Samaria (v. 25).. 101
5. Philip and the Ethiopian Eunuch (vs. 26–40).. 101

CHAPTER NINE 105

1. The Vision of Glory on the road to Damascus (vs. 1–9).............................. 107
2. The call to Ananias (vs. 10–16).. 113
3. Saul filled with the Spirit, baptized and preaching Jesus, that he is the Son of God (vs. 17–22)... 115
4. Saul persecuted and back in Jerusalem (vs. 23–31)................................... 117
5. Further Acts of Peter (vs. 32–43)... 120

CHAPTER TEN 122

1. Cornelius of Caesarea and his Preparation to hear the Gospel (vs. 1–8).. 123
2. The trance-vision of Peter in preparation for his mission (vs. 9–16).......... 125
3. Peter with Cornelius at Caesarea (vs. 17–20)... 126

    4. Peter preaching the Gospel to the Gentiles (vs. 34–43). 129
    5. The interrupted Message (vs. 44–48). 131

CHAPTER ELEVEN 132

    1. Peter's defence in Jerusalem and its results (vs. 1–18). 132
    2. The Foundation of the Church in Antioch (vs. 19–21). 133
    3. Barnabas sent to Antioch (vs. 22–26). 134
    4. The Prophecy of Agabus (vs. 27–30). 136

CHAPTER TWELVE 137

    1. The great persecution of the church by Herod Agrippa I (vs. 1–5). 138
    2. The miraculous deliverance of Peter (vs. 6–17). 139
    3. The Presumption and Judgment of King Herod (vs. 18–23). 141
    4. Barnabas and Saul returning to Antioch (vs. 24–25). 142

CHAPTER THIRTEEN 143

    1. The divine choice and call. Barnabas and Saul separated to the
       work (vs. 1–3). 143
    2. The beginning of the journey. The first events in Cyprus (vs. 4–12). 146
    3. The Gospel in Galatia. Paul's address in the synagogue of Antioch
       (vs. 13–15). 149
    4. The Gospel rejected by the Jews; they turn to the Gentiles (vs. 42–
       52). 153

CHAPTER FOURTEEN 155

    1. The work in Iconium and the persecution of the Apostles (vs. 1–7). 155
    2. Their testimony in Derbe and Lystra: the healing of the impotent
       man (vs. 8–18). 156
    3. The stoning of Paul and further ministries (vs. 19–24). 158
    4. The Return to Antioch (vs. 25–28). 159

CHAPTER FIFTEEN 161

    1. The false teachers from Judea; Paul and Barnabas sent to
       Jerusalem (vs. 1–5). 162
    2. The Council in Jerusalem (vs. 6–21). 164
    3. The Result made Known (vs. 22–29). 167
    4. The Consolation brought to Antioch (vs. 30–35). 168
    5. Paul and Barnabas separate (vs. 36–41). 169

CHAPTER SIXTEEN 171

    1. In Derbe and Lystra: Timothy chosen and circumcised by Paul (vs.
       1–5). 172
    2. The Holy Spirit forbids the preaching of the Word in Asia (vs. 6–8). ... 173
    3. The Macedonian Call (vs. 9–12). 174
    4. The Gospel in Europe: the conversion of Lydia (vs. 13–15). 176
    5. Paul and Silas in Prison (vs. 16–24) 177
    6. The Philippian Jailer Converted (vs. 25–28) 179

CHAPTER SEVENTEEN 182

1. THE GOSPEL IN THESSALONICA (VS. 1–9) 182
2. THE GOSPEL IN BEREA (VS. 10–15) 185
3. PAUL IN ATHENS (VS. 16–21) 186
   The Introduction (vs. 22–23) 188
   Who the Unknown God Is (vs. 24–29) 188
   The Message From God (vs. 30–31) 190

CHAPTER EIGHTEEN 191

1. PAUL IN CORINTH WITH AQUILA AND PRISCILLA (VS. 1–8) 191
2. ENCOURAGEMENT FROM THE LORD IN A VISION (VS. 9–11) 193
3. PAUL AND GALLIO (VS. 12–17) 194
4. PAUL RETURNS TO ANTIOCH: THE SECOND JOURNEY ENDED (VS. 18–22) 195
5. ESTABLISHING DISCIPLES IN GALATIA AND PHRYGIA (V. 23) 196
6. APOLLOS THE ALEXANDRIAN (VS. 24–28) 196

CHAPTER NINETEEN 199

1. THE SECOND VISIT OF PAUL TO EPHESUS (VS. 1–7) 199
2. THE APOSTLE'S CONTINUED LABORS. THE SEPARATION OF THE DISCIPLES.
   THE PROVINCE OF ASIA EVANGELIZED (VS. 8–10) 201
3. THE POWER OF GOD AND THE POWER OF SATAN (VS. 11–20) 202
4. PAUL PLANS TO GO TO JERUSALEM AND VISIT ROME (VS. 21–22) 204
5. THE OPPOSITION AND THE RIOT AT EPHESUS (VS. 23–41) 205

CHAPTER TWENTY 209

1. PAUL IN MACEDONIA (VS. 1–2) 209
2. EUTYCHUS RAISED FROM THE DEAD (VS. 3–12) 209
3. THE JOURNEY FROM TROAS TO MILETUS (VS. 13–16) 212
4. PAUL'S ADDRESS TO THE ELDERS OF EPHESUS (VS. 17–38) 213
   1. A Rehearsal of his integrity and faithfulness in ministry (vs. 19–21) 214
   2. The announcement of his anticipated sufferings and his determination to endure (vs. 22–27) 215
   3. The charge to the elders and the warning (vs. 28–31) 216
   4. The final word (vs. 32–35) 217

CHAPTER TWENTY-ONE 219

1. PAUL'S JOURNEY TO TYRE AND PTOLEMAIS (VS. 1–7) 219
2. IN CAESAREA (VS. 8–14) 220
3. THE APOSTLE'S ARRIVAL IN JERUSALEM AND HIS VISIT TO THE TEMPLE (VS.
   15–26) 222
4. THE UPROAR IN THE TEMPLE: PAUL TAKEN PRISONER (VS. 27–40) 225

CHAPTER TWENTY-TWO 229

1. THE ADDRESS OF THE APOSTLE (VS. 1–21) 229
   Paul's Account of himself as a Jew (vs. 1–5) 229
   The Story of his Conversion (vs. 6-16) 231
   The Divine Commission (vs. 17-21) 231
2. THE ANSWER FROM THE MOB AND PAUL'S APPEAL TO HIS ROMAN
   CITIZENSHIP (VS. 22-30) 232

CHAPTER TWENTY-THREE 234

- 1. Paul before the Sanhedrin (vs. 1–10). 234
- 2. The vision of the Lord (v. 11). 236
- 3. The Plot to Kill Paul and its discovery (vs. 12–22). 237
- 4. Paul taken to Caesarea (vs. 23–35). 237

CHAPTER TWENTY-FOUR 239

- 1. The indictment of Paul (vs. 1–9). 239
- 2. The defence of the Apostle (vs. 10–21). 240
- 3. How Felix disposed of the case (vs. 22–23). 241
- 4. Paul addresses Felix (vs. 24–27). 241

CHAPTER TWENTY-FIVE 243

- 1. Festus and the Jews. Paul appeals to Caesar (vs. 1–12). 243
- 2. King Agrippa visits Festus (vs. 13–22). 244
- 3. Paul before the King (vs. 23–27). 245

CHAPTER TWENTY-SIX 246

- 1. The Address of the Apostle Paul (vs. 2–23). 246
  - *The Opening Words (vs. 2–3).* 246
  - *A Restatement of his Past Life as a Pharisee (vs. 4–11).* 246
  - *The Heavenly Vision (vs. 12–17).* 247
  - *The Gospel Message Declared (v. 18).* 248
  - *The Obedience to the Heavenly Vision (vs. 19–23).* 248
- 2. The Interruption by Festus and the Appeal to the King (vs. 24–29). 248
- 3. The Verdict (vs. 30–32). 250

CHAPTER TWENTY-SEVEN 251

- 1. From Caesarea to Fair Havens (vs. 1–8). 251
- 2. The Storm at Sea and Paul's Vision (vs. 9–26). 252
- 2. The Shipwreck (vs. 27–44). 254

CHAPTER TWENTY-EIGHT 257

- 1. In the Island of Melta (vs. 1–10). 257
- 2. The Arrival in Rome (vs. 11–16). 258
- 3. Paul in Rome (vs. 17–29). 260
- 4. The Apostle's Activity in Rome (vs. 30–31). 262

CHRONOLOGY OF PAUL'S LIFE 263

MAPS 268

- Map 1: The First Missionary Journey 268
- Map 2: The Second Missionary Journey 269
- Map 3: The Third Missionary Journey and Trip to Rome 270

BIBLIOGRAPHY 271

INDEX 274

INDEX OF IMAGES

1. The Church of All Nations. It is located on the Mount of Olives outside Jerusalem. This mount is where Jesus ascended into heaven. 26

2. Tradition locates the "upper room" in the Cenacle on Mount Zion. 27

3. Dice made of bone found in Jerusalem during the Temple Mount Sifting Project and date to the early Roman period. 29

4. Pool of Siloam (John 9:11), discovered in 2004. Currently over 20 steps have been excavated leading down into the Pool. Some scholars believe that this was used as a *mikvah* (ritual purity bath). This was one location where 3,000 people could easily be baptized on the day of Pentecost. 49

5. A reconstruction of the gate from a model of the temple in Jerusalem. The Golden Gate (the beautiful Gate) is indicated as the entrance to the outer court. 54

6. Solomon's Colonnade (Also called a Protico or Porch) was a covered hallway that ran along the inner side of the Court of the Gentiles outside the Temple. It had 27 foot-high columns with the roof made of cedar. 56

7. West gate at Masada, Herod's plateau fortress. Jewish Zealots occupied the site in AD 66, but the Romans attacked it in AD 73. Upon breaching the wall, Eleazer, the Zealot leader, convinced 960 Jews to commit suicide rather than face Roman slavery. Gamaliel's advice in Acts 5 proved true in the case of Masada. The Zealots failed in their plans to resist the Romans, as they were of human origin and not from God. 76

8. The "Seat of Moses" carved from a block of basalt and discovered in 1926 in the Synagoguge at Chorazin (Matt 11:21; Luke 10:13). According to Matthew the "Seat of Moses" was where the reader of the Torah sat (23:1-3). 77

9. Petra was the capital of the Arabian kingdom of the Nabataeans under Roman control until it became a Roman province in AD 106. Paul likely have visited it during his stay in Arabia, since the Nabataean king, Aretas IV tried to seize Paul (2 Cor 11:32). 118

10. Roman centurion (Lat. *centurio*; Gr.: κεντυρίων). These military officers usually commanded 80 men in their unit, although senior officers usually commanded cohorts. Tower of David Museum, Jerusalem. 123

11. Remains of the ancient Roman aqueduct at Caesarea Maritima. 124

12. An inscription on a theatre seat in the Miletus theatre that states "Place of the Jews, who are also called God-fearing." Cornelius is mentioned as a God-fearer (Acts 13:16; 26). 125

13. Imperial bronze portrait of Roman emperor Claudius (10 BC–54 AD; r. 41–54 AD). National Archaeological Museum of Spain, Madrid. 135

14. Salamis from southwest with a view of the remains of the gymnasium and Therme. It is believed that after Paul and Barnabas separated (Acts 15:36-40) that Barnabas remained on Cyprus until his death. 146

15. Inscription of Sergius Paulus, the proconsul in Paphos, Cyprus, housed in the Yalvac Museum, Pisidian Antioch. Some scholars suggest that: "L[ucius] Sergius Paulus the younger, son of L[ucius]" may be the son of the elder Sergius Paulus, the proconsul of Acts 13. The name of Sergius Paulus (*nomen*, name of tribe) was certainly known in Cyprus. 147

16. A colonnaded street in the ancient city of Perga of Pamphylia (in modern Turkey). 148

17. Ruins of ancient Pisidian Antioch. 149

18. Statue of St. Paul in front of the facade of the Basilica of Saint Paul Outside-the-Walls, Rome. 153

19. A Roman sarcophagus from Iconium (ca. 250-260 AD) depicting the labors of Hercules in the Archaeological Museum, in Konya. 156

20. Head of Mercury wearing winged petasus, on a bronze Semuncia coin (215–211 BC). 157

21. Marble statue of Jupiter (Late 1st cent AD). Drapings, cepter, Eagle, and Victory are made of painted plaster dating to the 19th cent. Hermitage, St Petersburg, Russia. 157

22. Inscription with the name Lystra. The inscription includes the full Roman name *Colonia Iulia Felix Gemina Lustra*. Konya museum. 158

23. The old harbor of Attalia (modern Antalya, Turkey). 159

24. Philippi's forum and basilica B seen from the acropolis. 175

25. The ancient theatre of Philippi, Macedonia. 177

26. Politarch inscription from the gateway in Thessalonica now displayed in the British Museum (BM Inscriptions 171). Older English versions obscure Luke's accuracy in using this specific term by tranlating it "Rulers of the city" (AV) and "City authorities" (RSV). 183

27. The imperial family at the sacrifice of thanksgiving, depicted on the Arch of Galerius in Thessalonica. The faces have been chiselled off possibly as a *damnatio memoriae*. 184

28. View of Athens (Attica, Greece) from Acropolis hill – Stoa of Athens where Paul likely stood before the Areopagus (city coucil) who were in charge of admission of new deities into the Athenian pantheon. 187

29. Mars Hill or Hill of Ares (Areopagus), Athens, Greece. 189

30. Synagogue inscription displayed in the Archaeological Museum of Ancient Corinth (ID 123). 192

31. The Gallio inscription from the Temple of Apollo in Delphi, Greece. 194

32. The *bema* or platform in the agora of Corinth. This is where Gallio, the Roman procounsul of Achaia, accused Paul in Acts 18 and dates to AD 44. 195

33. Drawing of a pillar in Ephesus with the name Tyrannius inscribed on it, dating from the first century AD. 201

34. Erastus inscription which some claim refers to the Erastus mentioned by Paul in Romans 16:23 and Luke in Acts 19:22. 204

35. Reproduction of the Ephesian Greek goddess Artemis (Roman goddess *Diana*). She was the goddess of the hunt, wild animals, childbirth, virginity, and twin of Apollo. Homer describes Artemis "of the Wilds" (*Agrotera*) and "Mistress of Animals" (*Potnia Theron*; *Il.* 21.470) and she is often depicted as a huntress carrying a bow and arrow (Ovid *Metam*. 3.251). The Ephesian depiction of Artemis was unique with multiple breasts, sometimes identified by scholars as bull testicles, pomegranates, or eggs and wearing a long cloak of bees. There seemed to be similar attributes with Cybele (an Anatolian mother goddess), including being served in the Temple by female slaves, young virgins, and eunuch priests. 206

INDEX OF IMAGES

36. Recreation of the Artemision, Temple of Artemis, as it would have looked at Ephesus. This model is at Miniatürk Park, Istanbul, Turkey. 207

37. Restored Library of Celsus, Ephesus. The relief in the foreground is reminiscent of the elements of armor given in Ephesians 6:13–17, including the belt, breastplate, greaves for the feet, shield, helmet and sword. While the Library was only completed in 135 AD and was not present in Paul's day, the relief may have existed earlier, as it was not attached to the structure. 208

38. Remains of the ancient bath (Therme) of Herodes, at Aleaxandria Troas. 210

39. The visible area of the synagogue in Miletus next to the colossal circular Harbor Monument (63 BC). Paul may have met the Ephesian elders here. 212

40. Caesarea maritima, Roman theatre where Herod Agrippa I received divine accolades. The God-fearer Cornelius was converted in the city of Caesarea. 220

41. One of two mosaics at Caesarea Maritima quoting Romans 13:3. This is the shorter version. The original mosaic is on display at the Kibbutz Sdot Yam Museum. 222

42. Jerusalem, Herod's Temple Mount at the time of Jesus. A reconstruction based on archaeological and historical evidence. This drawing illustrates the Herodian Temple Mount with associated structures and features, as seen from the southwest. This reconstruction is based directly on Leen Ritmeyer's own work at the Temple Mount (© Ritmeyer Archaeological Design. Labels by David E. Graves). 225

43. The Theodotus (priest and synagogue ruler) inscription, discovered by Raymond Weill in Jerusalem in 1914, preventing Gentiles from entering the sacred space (Heb. *soreg*) of the Temple. 226

44. Model of the Fortress Antonia, a military barracks built by Herod the Great near the Temple Mount and the Pool of Bethesda, in Jerusalem. Although this model displays four towers, Josephus described it as the Tower of Antoinia (*Ant*. 18:4:3). (See Fig 43, No. 3). 227

45. Roman soldier in *lorica segmentata* or *lorica laminata*. Photographed during a show of Legio XV from Pram, Austria. 229

46. Fragment of a Roman military diploma, or certificate of successful military service, granting citizenship to a retiring soldier and the dependents he had with him at the time. The key phrase is *"est civitas eis data"* where *civitas* means citizenship. *CIL* XVI 26 tabula II, Museum Carnuntum, Austria. 233

47. Aerial photo of Caesarea Maritima. 1. King Agrippas' palace, probably the place of Paul's imprisonment. 2. Hippodrome. 3. The theatre. 249

48. Mosaic of a Roman galley, Bardo Museum, Tunisia, 2nd century AD. 255

49. View of the Bay of St. Paul, Malta. 256

50. Marble relief of a soldier from the Praetorian Guard from Puteoli, Italy, now displayed in the Pergamum Museum, Berlin (Sk 887). 259

51. Mamertine prison (Italian *Carcere Mamertino;* right) in Rome, Italy. The arch of Septimius Severus is on the left. It is believed, by eighth cent. tradition, to be the prison of Peter and Paul during the persecution of Nero (*ca*. A.D. 64–67. Tacitus *Ann*. 15.44; Suetonius *Nero* 35; *1 Clem*. 5:2–5). 262

52. **MAP 1:** The First Missionary Journey. 268

53. **MAP 2:** The Second Missionary Journey. 269

54. **MAP 3**: The Third Missionary Journey and trip to Rome.. 270

FOREWORD

Judaism and Christianity; Legalism and Grace; the Kingdom and the Church; these are in contrast, at poles apart, and defy all attempts at reconciliation. Ishmael "the wild-ass man" untamed and untamable, the son of the bond woman, is unalterably opposed to Isaac "laughter" spontaneous and obedient, the son of the free woman.

These distinctions, known and observed, are of incalculable worth in Bible Study.

In *The Book of the Acts* there is revealed the passing of Judaism, and the incoming of Christianity: wherein we see how the old wine-skins of legalism are without strength to restrain the expansive spirit of the new wine of grace. This *Book of the Acts*, showing as it does the transition of Judaism to Christianity, is, therefore, of absorbing interest; and Mr. Gaebelein, whose oral teaching is so abundantly owned and blessed of God, has, in this volume of interpretative study, extended the sphere of his ministry to multitudes that may never come within range of the hearing of his voice.

The author's breadth of conception of God's plan of the Ages stamps the book with a peculiar value; while, at the same time, there is of the spiritual application of truth a thorough and clear perception that pervades and illumines the exposition of the text.

From the study of this book, so untrammeled by the yoke of traditional interpretation, so far removed from the feverish discontent with the supernatural, so different from the cold and critical analysis of the casuist, so reverent. and so unalterably loyal to the plenary inspiration of the Scripture, one rises in spirit refreshed, in faith strengthened and to new endeavor encouraged. It is a pleasure and a privilege to commend this book.

Ford C. Ottman
Stamford. Conn.

ABBREVIATIONS

This work will conform to the abbreviations and general format conventions set out by *The SBL Handbook of Style: for Ancient Near Eastern, Biblical and Early Christian Studies* by Patrick H. Alexander, *et al.* eds. second printing (Peabody, Mass.: Hendrickson, 2002) for general literary conventions, Bible translations, biblical books, Dead Sea scrolls, pseudepigraphical, early patristic books, targumic material, *Mishnah*, Talmud, other Rabbinic works, *Nag Hammadi* tractates, commonly used periodicals, reference works and serials. Unless otherwise indicated the references to the works of ancient sources reflect the Loeb Classical Library numbering system and Latin abbreviations.

OLD TESTAMENT

Gen	Genesis
Exod	Exodus
Lev	Leviticus
Num	Numbers
Deut	Deuteronomy
Judg	Judges
Josh	Joshua
1–2 Sam	1–2 Samuel
1–2 Kgs	1–2 Kings
1–2 Chr	1–2 Chronicles
Neh	Nehemiah
Esth	Esther
Job	Job
Ps/Pss	Psalms
Prov	Proverbs
Eccl	Ecclesiastes
Isa	Isaiah
Jer	Jeremiah
Lam	Lamentations
Ezek	Ezekiel
Dan	Daniel
Obad	Obadiah
Jonah	Jonah
Mic	Micah
Nah	Nahum
Hab	Habakkuk
Zeph	Zephaniah
Mal	Malachi

NEW TESTAMENT

Matt	Matthew
Rom	Romans
1–2 Cor	1–2 Corinthians
Gal	Galatians
Eph	Ephesians
Phil	Philippians
Col	Colossians
1–2 Thess	1–2 Thessalonians
1–2 Tim	1–2 Timothy
Phlm	Philemon
Heb	Hebrews
Jas	James
1–2 Pet	1–2 Peter
1–2–3 John	1–2–3 John
Rev	Revelation

ANCIENT AND MODERN SOURCES

1 Clem.	*1 Clement*
Acts Paul	*Acts of Paul*, Hone, ed. *The Apocryphal NT*
Ann.	Tacitus, *Annales, Annals*
Ant.	Josephus, *Antiquitates judaicae,*

Abbreviations

	Jewish Antiquities	i.e.	*id est*, that is
AV	Authorized Verison	Lat.	Latin
ca.	Lat. *circa*, "around, about."	LXX	The Septuagint (the Greek OT)
cent.	century	*Nat.*	Pliny the Elder, *Naturalis historia*, *Natural History*
ch.	chapter (s)		
Cl.	Suetonius, *Divus Claudius*, *The Deified Claudius*	*Nero*	Suetonius, *Lives of the Caesars*, *Nero*
ESV	English Standard Version	RSV	Revised Standard Version
etc.	et cetera, and the rest	v./vs.	verse/verses
Gr.	Greek		
Heb	Hebrew		

Preface to the Updated Edition

Arno C. Gaebelein first published this work in 1912 and was translated into many foreign languages, to quickly became one of the most popular commentaries on Acts. Gaebelein, a noted Methodist pastor, has carefully crafted a doctrinally sound and reliable commentary on the book of Acts, that will provide invaluable insight into the life and work of Peter and Paul. It has now been updated and revised, leaving the majority of the original material intact.

Photocopies of the original work have been published in the past, but there was a need to update it with a newer translation of the Book of Acts. Crossway Bibles have kindly granted permission to use the the English Standard Version (ESV) as a modern translation of scripture for this work.

Like most commentators I do not agree with every word of Gaebelein, but the majority of the comments are beneficial and theologically sound. While maintaining the main body of the work precisely as Gaebelein himself made available, several improvements have been made to this new edition of *The Life of Saint Paul* including:

- Entirely reset in a modern and easy-to-read typeface.
- All scripture quotations are updated to the English Standard Version (ESV) and scripture references were added.
- Arabic numbers were replaced with Roman numerals.
- Modern photographs were added to improve the reading experience.
- A new "Appendix A: CHRONOLOGY OF PAUL'S LIFE" was added.
- New maps were added.
- A Table of Content, Index of Subjects and Bibliography of works were created to assist in finding material in the book.

It is the prayer and hope of this editor that the present work will continue to assist Bible students and scholars in a clearer understanding of the Book of Acts. *Sola Deo Gloria.*

David E. Graves, PhD
Toronto, Canada
October 1, 2015

INTRODUCTION

The book known by the name "The Acts of the Apostles"[1] follows the four Gospel records. This is its proper place. The books of the New Testament have been correctly divided into five sections, corresponding to the first five books, with which the Bible begins, that is the Pentateuch. The four Gospels are the **Genesis** of the New Testament. Here we have the great beginning, the foundation upon which the subsequently revealed Christian doctrines rest. The Book of Acts is the **Exodus**, God leads out from bondage a heavenly people and delivers them. It is the great historical book of the New Testament describing the beginning of the church on earth. The Pauline Epistles are the **Leviticus** portion. Holiness to the Lord, the believers separation and standing in Christ, what believers have and are in Christ by whose blood they have redemption, is the core truth of these Epistles. The Epistles of Peter, James, John and Jude, known by the name of the Catholic Epistles, are for the wilderness journey of God's people, telling us of trials and suffering; these correspond to the Book of **Numbers**. The Book of Revelation in which God's ways are rehearsed and a review is given of the entire prophetic Word concerning the Jews, the Gentiles and the Church of God has the same character as **Deuteronomy**.

BY WHOM WAS THIS BOOK WRITTEN?

There is no doubt that the writer of the third Gospel record is the one whom the Holy Spirit selected to write this account of the establishment of the Church on earth and the events connected with it. This becomes clear if we read the beginning of that Gospel and compare it with the beginning of Acts. The writer in the third Gospel says: "It seemed good to me also, having had perfect understanding of all things from the first, to write to thee in order, most excellent *Theophilus*, that thou mightest know the certainty of those things, wherein thou hast been instructed" (Luke 1:3–4). The Acts of the Apostles begin: "In the *first* book, O *Theophilus*, I have dealt with all that Jesus began to do and teach." The former treatise known to Theophilus is the third Gospel, called the Gospel of Luke. The writer of that Gospel is also the penman of the Book of Acts. Though we do not find Luke's name mentioned in the Gospel nor in the second Book he was entrusted to write, there is no doubt that he wrote them both. We find his name mentioned a number of times in the Epistles and these references give us the only reliable information we have. In Colossians 4:14 we read of him as "the beloved physician." In the Epistle of Philemon he is called a fellow laborer of the Apostle Paul, and from the last Epistle the

---

[1] The oldest Manuscript, the *Sinaiticus* dating from the 4th century gives the title simply as "The Acts" which is, no doubt, the better name for the book.

great Apostle wrote, the Second Epistle of Timothy, we learn that Luke was in Rome with Paul and was faithful to him, while others had forsaken the prisoner of the Lord. From Colossians 4 we also may gather that he was not a Jew, but a Gentile, for with the eleventh verse Paul had mentioned those of the circumcision. Epaphras was one of the Colossians, a Gentile, and then follow the names of Luke and Demas, both of them undoubtedly Gentiles. The reason that the Holy Spirit selected a Gentile to write the Gospel which pictures our Lord as the Man and the Saviour and the Book of Acts, is as obvious as it is interesting. Israel had rejected God's gift and the glad news of salvation is now to go to the Gentiles. The Gospel of Luke addressed by a Gentile to a Gentile (Theophilus) is the Gospel for the Gentiles and Luke the Gentile was chosen to give the history of the Gospel going forth from Jerusalem to the Gentiles.

There are numerous internal evidences which show likewise that the writer of the third Gospel is the instrument through whom the Book of Acts was given. For instance, there are about fifty peculiar phrases and words in both books which are rarely found elsewhere; they prove the same author for those two books.

Then we learn from the Book of Acts that Luke, the beloved physician, was an eyewitness of some of the events recorded by him in this book. He joined the Apostle during his second missionary journey at Troas (chapt. 14:10). This evidence is found in the little word *"we."* The writer was now in company of the Apostle, whose fellow laborer he was. He went with Paul to Macedonia and remained sometime in Philippi (see Fig. 24). He was Paul's fellow traveler to Asia and Jerusalem (ch. 21:17). He likewise was with him in his imprisonment in Caesarea and then on to Rome. There is no doubt that Luke had completely written and sent forth the Book of the Acts of the Apostles at the end of the two years mentioned in Acts 28:30, though the critics claim a much later period.

THE CONTENTS AND SCOPE OF THE BOOK.

The first verse gives us an important hint. The former treatise, the Gospel of Luke, tells "that Jesus **began** to do and teach." The Book of Acts contains therefore the continuation of the Lord's actions no longer on earth but from Glory. The actions of the risen and glorified Christ can easily be traced throughout the entire book. We give a few illustrations. In Chapter 1 he acts in the selection of the twelfth Apostle, who was to take the place of Judas. In Chapter 2 he himself poured forth the Holy Spirit, for Peter made the declaration: "Being therefore exalted at the right hand of God, and having received from the Father the promise of the Holy Spirit, *he* has poured out this that you yourselves are seeing and hearing" (Acts 2:33) And in the close of the second chapter we behold another action of the risen Lord: "And the Lord added to the church daily such as should be saved" (Acts 2:47) In the third chapter he manifested his power in the healing of the lame man. Throughout this book we behold him acting from the Glory, guiding, directing, comforting and encouraging his servants. These beautiful and manifold evidences of Himself being with his own and manifesting his power in their behalf we hope to trace in our exposition of the different chapters.

Then on the very threshold of the book we have the historical account of the coming of that other Comforter, whom the Lord had promised, the Holy Spirit. On the day of Pentecost the third Person of the Trinity, the Holy Spirit, came. His coming marks the empowerment of the Church. After that event we see him present with and in his people. In connection with the Lord's servants, in filling them, guiding them, fitting them, sustaining them in trials and persecutions as well as in the affairs of the church, we behold the actions of the Holy Spirit on earth. He is the great administrator in the church. Over fifty times we find him mentioned, so that some have called this book "the Acts of the Holy Spirit." While we have no doctrines about the Holy Spirit and his work in the Acts of the Apostles, we find here the practical illustrations of the doctrine found elsewhere in the New Testament.

In the third place another supernatural Being is seen acting in this book. It is the enemy, Satan, the hinderer and the accuser of the brethren. We behold him coming upon the scene and acting through his different instruments either as the roaring lion or as the cunning deceiver with his wiles. Wherever he can, he attempts to hinder the progress of the Gospel. This is a most important aspect of this book and indeed very instructive. Aside from the human instruments prominent in this Book of Acts, we behold three supernatural Beings acting. The risen, glorified Christ, the Holy Spirit and Satan.

Another hint about the contents of this book and its scope we find at the close of the Gospel of Luke. There the risen Christ said: "that repentance and forgiveness of sins should be proclaimed in his name to all nations, beginning from Jerusalem" (Luke 24:47). In the first chapter of Acts the Spirit of God reports the commission of the Lord, about to ascend, in full. "You will be my witnesses in Jerusalem and in all Judea and Samaria, and to the end of the earth" (Acts 1:8). The Book of Acts shows us how this mission beginning in Jerusalem was carried out. The witness begins in the city where our Lord was crucified. Once more an offer was made to the nation Israel. Then we behold the Gospel going forth from Jerusalem and all Judea to Samaria and after that to the Gentiles, and through the chosen Apostle of the Gentiles it is heralded in the different countries of the Roman empire. The parable of our Lord in Matthew 22:1–10 gives us prophetically the history of these events. First the guests were called to the wedding and they would not come. This was the invitation given by the Lord to his earthly people when he moved among them. They received him not. Then came a renewed offer with the assurance that all things are ready. This is exactly what we find in the beginning of the Book of Acts. Once more to Jerusalem and to the Jewish nation is offered the kingdom, and signs and miracles take place to show that Jesus is the Christ risen from the dead. In the above parable our Lord predicted what the people would do with the servants, who bring the second offer. They would ignore the message and treat the servants spitefully and kill them. This we find fulfilled in the persecution which broke out in Jerusalem, when Apostles were imprisoned and others were killed. The Lord also predicted in his parable the fate of the wicked city. It was to be burned. Thus it happened with Jerusalem. And after the second offer had been rejected the servants were to go to the highways to invite the guests. And this stands for the invitation to go out to the Gentiles.

Jerusalem is in the foreground of this book, for the beginning was to be in Jerusalem "to the Jew first." The end of the book takes us to Rome and we see the great Apostle a prisoner there, a most significant, prophetic circumstance.

THE DIVISION OF THE BOOK.

The division of the Book of the Acts is very simple. We divide it into three parts.

1. Chapters 1–7. These chapters give us the historical account of the beginning in Jerusalem, the renewed testimony to the nation concerning Jesus as the Christ and the Kingdom. The seventh chapter, the stoning of Stephen, closes that testimony.

The Acts of the Apostles

2. Chapters 8–12. These chapters mark a transition period. The Gospel goes forth to Samaria. Saul of Tarsus sees the Lord and is converted. Peter goes and preaches the Gospel to the Gentiles. Peter is cast into prison and miraculously delivered.

In these two parts Peter is in the foreground. He does most of the preaching and acting. He used the Keys of the Kingdom of Heaven in the second chapter by preaching to the Jews and in the tenth chapter by preaching to the Gentiles.

3. Chapters 13–18. These chapters contain the inspired accounts of the travels and labors of the Apostle Paul, the proclamation of the Gospel in the different lands and the events and circumstances connected with it. His journey to Rome and abode there closes the book.

Another division as given by Bengel in his *Gnomen* is also good.

1. Pentecost, with preceding events (Ch. 1, 2).
2. Acts in Jerusalem, and in all Judea and in Samaria among the circumcised (Ch. 3–9, 12).
3. Acts in Caesarea and admission of Gentiles (Ch. 10, 11).
4. First Journey among the Gentiles (Ch. 13, 14).
5. The deputation and council in Jerusalem (Ch. 15).
6. Second Journey of Paul (Ch. 16–19).
7. Journey to Jerusalem and Rome (Ch. 19:21–28).[2]

Graves suggests another outline divided between the Ministry of Peter (Ch. 1-12) and the Ministry of Paul (Ch. 13-28).

MINISTRY IN JERUSALEM (Ch. 1-8:3)

    Ministry of Peter (Ch. 1-5)

    Ministry of Stephen (Ch. 6-8:3)

MINISTRY IN JUDEA, GALILEE AND SAMARIA (Ch. 8:4-11:18)

    Ministry of Philip (Ch. 8)

    Ministry of Saul - Conversion (Ch. 9:1-31)

    Ministry of Peter (Ch. 9:32-11:18)

MINISTRY IN PHOENICIA, CYPRUS AND ANTIOCH (Ch. 9:32-12:25)

    Ministry of Peter (Ch. 9:32-11:18)

    Ministry of Barnabas (Ch. 11)

    Herod's Persecution and Death (Ch. 12)

MINISTRY IN PHRYGIA AND GALATIA (Ch. 13:1-15:35)

    First Missionary Journey (Ch. 13-14)

    Jerusalem Counsel (Ch. 15:1-35)

MINISTRY IN MACEDONIA (Ch. 15:36-21:14)

    Second Missionary Journey (Ch. 15:36-18:22)

    Third Missionary Journey (Ch. 18:23-21:14)

MINISTRY IN CAESAREA AND ROME (Ch. 21:15-28:29)

    Jerusalem Imprisonment (Ch. 21:17-23:35)

    Caesarea Imprisonment (Ch. 24-26)

    Trip to Rome (Ch. 27:1-28:15)

    Rome Imprisonment (Ch. 28:16-31)

In closing these brief introductory remarks to this great book we wish to say that the careful study of its contents is very needful at the present time. It will take us back to the beginning and show us the path which the Lord has marked out for his church on earth. In the light of this book we shall discover the dark picture of the present day confusion and departure from God and from his Word. There is much comfort and direction for the faithful remnant of God's

---

[2] Johann Albrecht Bengel, *Gnomon of the New Testament*, trans. Andrew Robert Faussett, 3rd ed., vol. 2 (Smith, English & Company, 1860).

people living in our days in this book. There is much earnest exhortation to greater faithfulness, to more holy boldness in preaching the Gospel and standing up for the faith, which comes to us from this book. Most blessed it is to follow the Holy Spirit in his work in, upon and with the believer. With the gracious help of our Lord and the help of his Spirit we hope to touch upon all these blessed phases, and we are confident that he will make the closer study of the Acts of the Apostles a blessing to our readers as well as to the writer.

Chapter One

The opening chapter of this book gives the events which preceded the great day of Pentecost. However, of the many things which must have transpired in Jerusalem during the fifty days between the resurrection day and the outpouring of the Holy Spirit not all are mentioned in this chapter. Here, as in the great historical books of the Old Testament and in the Gospels, only certain events are reported while others are passed over. Not man but God by his Spirit arranged the matter to give us more than a mere historical account of what took place. As the Book of Exodus in its history foreshadows spiritual and dispensational truths, so, as we shall find, does this New Testament Exodus book teach spiritual and dispensational lessons.

The events preceding Pentecost written in this first chapter are:

1. An account of events preceding the ascension of the Lord, the ascension itself and the message of his personal, visible and glorious return. vs. 1–11.
2. The waiting company in prayer. Matthias added to the Apostles in the place of Judas. vs. 12–26.

1. Events Preceding the Ascension and Return (vs. 1–11).

Introduction to Theophilus (vs. 1–3).

The first three verses of the chapter form the introduction.

> In the first book, O Theophilus, I have dealt with all that Jesus began to do and teach, until the day when he was taken up, after he had given commands through the Holy Spirit to the apostles whom he had chosen. He presented himself alive to them after his suffering by many proofs, appearing to them during forty days and speaking about the kingdom of God.

As shown in the introduction the first verse proves that Luke, the beloved physician, the writer of the Gospel of Luke, was the chosen instrument to write the Book of Acts. Theophilus (*Friend of God*) is as prominent in the beginning of the Acts as he is in the Gospel of Luke, where he is addressed as "most excellent." From a reliable source dating back to the second century we learn that he was an influential and wealthy man residing in the city of Antioch. He dedicated his magnificent palace, called a Basilica, to the preaching of the Gospel. Luke came most likely also from Antioch. He may have belonged to the household of Theophilus. It is not unlikely that Luke had received great kindness from Theophilus; some claim that he used to be a slave and became through Theophilus a free man. That both the *Gospel of Luke* and the *Book of Acts* are addressed to Theophilus does not mean that these discourses (the word meaning of treatise) were meant for Theophilus alone. Luke addressed Theophilus as a prominent man, a responsible person, whose name bespeaks close walk with God, and through him to that assembly to which Theophilus belonged, and in a larger sense to all the Gentile—Christian churches.

According to the address to Theophilus we have in the Gospel of Luke the beginning of what Christ did and taught and therefore in Acts a continuation of these. He began on earth and now the scene is changed. He is the Man in Glory and from there he continues his work.

It is beautiful to see how the Lord Jesus is brought to our view in these few sentences with which this book opens. How this manifests the One who guided the pen of the beloved physician, that is the Holy Spirit. Seven things are mentioned concerning our Lord.

1. His earthly life of doing and teaching.
2. He charged his Apostles by the Holy Spirit.
3. He was taken up.
4. He had suffered.
5. Presented Himself living with many proofs.
6. He was seen by them for forty days.
7. He spoke of the things which concern the Kingdom of God.

What an array of wonderful facts we find in these few sentences! The fact of his resurrection after his passion is the leading feature of the passage. It must be necessarily so for his resurrection is the great foundation upon which the Gospel and the Church rests. He presented Himself living with many proofs and was seen by them for forty days. It is only here in this passage that the period of time during which he manifested Himself is mentioned. And during that time the "many proofs" were given. He appeared in their midst; he walked with them, ate with them, they touched his body, his hands and feet, and they found he was not an apparition, but had a body of flesh and bones. Blessed fact, he presented Himself living, he is the living One! That he thus showed Himself with many proofs is beyond controversy. But these forty days are likewise shrouded in mystery. It is easy to make fanciful applications of these forty days and to teach unscriptural doctrines by such applications. For instance, a widespread evil system which denies some of the fundamentals of the faith, holds that the Lord is now present on the earth as he was present for forty days after his resurrection. According to this teaching (Russellism or Millennial Dawn), he came in a secret manner in 1874 and is to remain here for forty years, when he will reveal Himself. Such teaching, if it can be called that, lacks all scriptural support. During these forty days, a number which stands for testing, he not only showed Himself, but also spoke of the things which concern the Kingdom of God. The words he gave them at these occasions, the instructions they received from his lips are not reported to us.

Promise of the Holy Spirit (vs. 4–11).

The verses which follow describe the farewell meeting, his last words to his disciples, the ascension of the Lord, and the promise of his return to earth.

> And while stayinga with them he ordered them not to depart from Jerusalem, but to wait for the promise of the Father, which, he said, "you heard from me; for John baptized with water, but you will be baptized withb the Holy Spirit not many days from now."
>
> So when they had come together, they asked him, "Lord, will you at this time restore the kingdom to Israel?" He said to them, "It is not for you to know times or seasons that the Father has fixed by his own authority. But you will receive power when the Holy Spirit has come upon you, and you will be my witnesses in Jerusalem and in all Judea and Samaria, and to the end of the earth." And when he had said these things, as they were looking on, he was lifted up, and a cloud took him out of their sight. And while they were gazing into heaven as he went, behold, two men stood by them in white robes, and said, "Men of Galilee, why do you stand looking into heaven? This Jesus, who was taken up from you into heaven, will come in the same way as you saw him go into heaven." (vs. 4–11).

This occurred ten days before the day of Pentecost. Their place was to be in Jerusalem and to wait in that city for the promise of the Father, which they had heard from his lips. He had given them this promise, when he talked to them before his death, as written in the Gospel of John. The same command to remain in the city is found at the close of the Gospel of Luke as well as the fact that the promise of the Father was soon to be fulfilled. Then he refers to John and his baptism with water, that they were to be baptized with the Holy Spirit; the "fire" of which John spoke (Matt 3:12) the Lord does not mention, because the baptizing with fire does not refer to the day of Pentecost, but to the time when: "His winnowing fork is in his hand, and he will clear his threshing floor and gather his wheat into the barn, but the chaff he will burn with unquenchable fire;" (Matt 3:12) that is, his second coming. He announced once more the "other Comforter" who was to come to be with them and in them. All this we shall follow in detail when we come to the great second chapter in our study of the outpouring of the Holy Spirit. Here we only wish to add that the waiting of the disciples for the promise of the Father remaining in Jerusalem for ten days cannot be repeated now. Often people, well meaning and spiritually-minded, have appointed meetings for days of waiting and prayer that "the promise of the Father" might be given to them. Such expectations are out of order. The Father has kept his promise, the Holy Spirit has come. To ask the Father now to keep his promise amounts to the same thing as to ask God to make peace by the death of Christ. Peace has been made; the Holy Spirit has been given.

And now we hear the assembled disciples addressing the Lord. What blessed intercourse they had with Him! he spoke to them in all his former tenderness and sympathy and they could ask him their questions. And so he is still accessible for his Own who draw dear to Him. "Lord, will you at this time restore the kingdom to Israel?" (1:6). This was their question, and a very natural question it was for them to ask. They were still Jews and knew only the earthly kingdom as their hope. He had risen from the dead and to their minds this must be the time in which the kingdom is restored to Israel.

Frequently the inquiry of these men who had believed in Jesus and followed him is declared to have been prompted by ignorance and selfishness. They were, so it is said, still expecting an earthly kingdom, to be established in the land with Jerusalem as the center; they were not yet delivered from their Jewish ideas. Others tell us that at the time they asked this question, they were ignorant of the true meaning of the kingdom. According to these interpreters the kingdom is the New Testament Church; the Holy Spirit swept away these earthly kingdom expectations. Such and similar reasons have been given to explain the question of the disciples.

It has occurred to but a few that this question was perfectly in order for them as Jews, which they were still, and did not emanate from ignorance, but was asked by reason of their superior knowledge of God's purposes as revealed in the Old Testament, a knowledge which is so sadly lacking in the present-day professing church.

The Lord does not rebuke their supposed ignorance nor does he tell them that they were mistaken. "He said to them, "It is not for you to know times or seasons that the Father has fixed by his own authority" (1:7). This answer approves the subject of their question. The Kingdom is to be restored, the times and the seasons were not then to be revealed, for the Father hath put these in his own power.

And this answer is most instructive. In connection with the restoration of the kingdom to Israel, the establishment of the theocratic kingdom on earth, as promised by God's holy prophets, times and seasons are expressly stated, and the declaration was made that at the time of the end, preceding the coming of the kingdom, the wise should understand (Dan 12:10). But the Lord does not here, as he did in his Olivet discourse, direct their attention to Daniel. "It is not for you to know times or seasons." A better hope, a heavenly hope was to be theirs, and in connection with that blessed hope of the Coming of the Lord for his Saints to bring them not to Palestine and given them an earthly kingdom, but into the Father's House in Glory, there are no "times or seasons" revealed. For his Saints he may come at any time. These disciples were soon to be formed into the one body, the church, by the Baptism of the Holy Spirit. The Lord anticipating this gave them this answer. It pointed them away from the earthly Hope of the Kingdom. Others in the future, Jewish disciples once more, a faithful remnant of Israelites, called after the completed church has left this earthly scene, will surely know the times and the seasons which the Father has put in his own authority.

Once more he announces their great mission, and that before they could be such witnesses they were to receive power by the Coming of the Holy Spirit upon them. Such was the case on the day of Pentecost as we shall find when we reach the events of that day.

One verse only gives us the account of the ascension of our Lord, his Return to the Father. He was taken up, they beholding, and a cloud received him out of their sight. What a spectacle this must have been! he in whom they had believed, in whose company they had been, to whose loving, tender words they had listened, whom they had forsaken when the hour of his suffering had come; he who had died on a cross, reckoned among the evil-doers, who had rested in a tomb and was raised from the dead by the power of God; he who had been with them in a glorified human body and manifested Himself in his resurrection glory and power during the forty days was now taken up, "received into Glory." Gradually he must have been lifted out of their midst. Lovingly his eyes must have rested upon them while their eyes beheld only Him. Now he is lifted higher and still they behold him in human form. And then a cloud received him out of their sight. The Greek verb used is "to take in;" so that it reads literally, "And then a cloud took him in out of their sight." This cloud surrounded Him, and the last they saw of him was that he disappeared from their view in this human glorified body in a cloud.

And that cloud was not a cloud of vapor. It was the same cloud which had appeared on the Mount of Transfiguration, the Shekinah. It was the same cloud of glory which had filled Solomon's temple, It was the same cloud which so often in Israel's past history had appeared as the outward sign of the Lord's presence with his people. The Glory-cloud came to take him in, to bring him back to the Father from whence he had come. What human tongue or pen can picture what took place after he had disappeared from human vision! The Shekinah cloud had come to meet him and where that Glory began sight ceases and faith begins. What must it have been when he came into the presence of the Throne of his Father when he took his seat, greeted with the word of welcome: "You are a priest forever, after the order of Melchizedek (Heb 7:17). . . sit at my right hand, until I make your enemies your footstool" (Ps 110:1). What a glorious scene it must have been participated in by the angels in heaven! And now he is back with the Father. In his Name we can approach God; he is our Advocate, our Priest in the presence of God, appearing for his own. The evidence that he is thus with the Father is soon given by the answered prayer of the first chapter, and the greater evidence, the outpouring of the Holy Spirit, the Coming of the third person of the Trinity.

We must not overlook the teaching of one great truth assailed so much in our times by higher critics and infidels. The Lord Jesus Christ passed through the heavens with a real human glorified body, a body of flesh and bones and went with that body to a literal place, the throne of God, where he sat down and where he is now "the Man" in the Glory. The denial of this fact, so universal in our day, strikes at the very foundation of the Gospel, our salvation and our heavenly Hope. This great truth that the Lord left bodily his own and bodily returned to the Father is indisputably seen in this account of his ascension. May his person, his ascension and bodily presence in Glory be as real to our hearts, dear readers, as it must have been to the hearts of the eyewitnesses of this great event.

The cloud had taken him in and still they were gazing into heaven. It was because they had still a vision of that cloud; "as he was going." The verb indicates this. They could not take their eyes away from that bright spot where he was, their Saviour, their Lord, their Hope, their All in All. This upward look should have been the attitude of the church. Two heavenly visitors appear now upon the scene and they give utterance to that familiar promise of his Second Coming, which establishes that great event beyond the shadow of a doubt. "This Jesus, who was taken up from you into heaven, will come in the same way as you saw him go into heaven" (1:11). Could human language make it any plainer? It seems almost impossible that any intelligent human being could not grasp the simple fact of his return, personal, visible and glorious, as revealed in this angelic message. The same glory cloud will bring him back, yea even to the same place, for Zechariah tells us that "on that day his feet shall stand on

1. The Church of All Nations. It is located on the Mount of Olives outside Jerusalem. This mount is where Jesus ascended into heaven.

the Mount of Olives that lies before Jerusalem on the east" (Zech 14:4).

However, we must beware of confounding this event given here with that blessed Hope, which is the Hope of the church. The Coming of the Lord is his visible Coming as described in the prophetic books of the Old Testament; it is his coming to establish his rule upon the earth. It is the event spoken of in Daniel 7:14 and Revelation 1:7. When he comes in like manner as he went up, his Saints come with him (Col 3:4; 2 Thessalonians 1:10). The Hope of the church is to meet him in the air and not to see him coming in the clouds of heaven. The coming here "in like manner" is his Coming for Israel and the nations. The Coming of the Lord for his Church before his visible and glorious Manifestation, is revealed in 1 Thessalonians 4:16–18. It is well to keep these important truths in mind. Confusion between these is disastrous. He left them to enter into the Holy of Holies, to exercise the priesthood which Aaron exercised on the day of atonement, though our Lord is a priest after the order of Melchizedek. And when this promise of the two men in white garments is fulfilled, he will come forth to be a priest upon his throne.

2. MATTHIAS ADDED TO THE APOSTLES (VS. 12–26).

The waiting company in prayer (vs. 12–14).

> Then they returned to Jerusalem from the mount called Olivet, which is near Jerusalem, a Sabbath day's journey away. And when they had entered, they went up to the upper room, where they were staying, Peter and John and James and Andrew, Philip and Thomas, Bartholomew and Matthew, James the son of Alphaeus and Simon the Zealot and Judas the son of James. All these with one accord were devoting themselves to prayer, together with the women and Mary the mother of Jesus, and his brothers. (vs. 12–14).

With what emotions they must have left the blessed spot from which the Lord had visibly gone to the Father! And now we behold them in a waiting attitude. Obedient to the command of their Lord they tarry in Jerusalem and wait for the promise of the Father. Their waiting was unique as a company of disciples, believers in Jesus as the Christ. Ten days after, the promise of the Father came, the Holy Spirit was poured out. Ever since he is here. There is no need of waiting now for the promise of the Father. No company of believers in this age could ever be again in the position in which the disciples were before Pentecost. It is, therefore, incorrect and unscriptural to hold prayer meetings, as stated before, waiting for the outpouring of the Holy Spirit. Persons who expect a repetition of what took place on Pentecost, who pray for and expect another sending of the Holy Spirit are on unscriptural ground.

We see the disciples gathered in an upper chamber. This was not in the temple, but in a private house. Perhaps it was the same room, which is mentioned in the Gospel of John. Such rooms of good size were used by Hebrews for prayer and meditations. They do so still and have large assembly rooms for prayer (Beth Midrash) in private houses in different cities. The

2. Tradition locates the "upper room" in the Cenacle on Mount Zion.

expression "upper room" (see Fig. 2) is used often in Talmudical writings. Peter's name is put in the first place, as he appears in the foreground throughout the first part of this book. After the names of the disciples are given and that they gave themselves with one accord to continual prayer the fact is mentioned that the women were present likewise. These, no doubt, are the same mentioned in Luke 8:2–3. They are mentioned not by name. Last of all appears Mary the mother of Jesus and his brethren. That the Holy Spirit gives the name of Mary the mother of Jesus, is most significant. It reminds us of the whole story of the incarnation and the blessed life of Him, the Son of God, who came of a woman, Mary, the virgin of prophecy (Isa 7:14). But the significance is in the fact that she, who was chosen by God's grace to be the blessed vessel, through whom the Creator, the Son of God, entered in human form the world he had created, is mentioned here in company with the other waiting disciples. She has no place of superiority among them, but with the rest, waited for the promise of the Father; when the Holy Spirit was poured forth she too was baptized by the one Spirit into the one body of which through the Grace of God, she is a member like any other believer in the Lord Jesus Christ. She was fallible and sinful like every other person, and all which a corrupt form of Christianity has made of her is wicked teaching. Not once is she mentioned after this chapter in the Book of Acts. In vain do we look for her name in the Epistles, in which the Holy Spirit reveals Christian doctrine and privileges. Mary, the mother of Jesus, has absolutely no relation to the redemption work of the Son of God. Then the brethren of our Lord are mentioned, the same, who with Mary, their mother, attempted to interfere with the ministry of our Lord (Mark 3:21–31–35). Not one of these was an apostle. It is positively stated that up to a certain point his brethren did not believe in Him. "For not even his brothers believed in him" (John 7:5). How they believed later we do not know. Their presence in the waiting company shows that they had believed.

Peter argues to replace Judas (vs. 15–20)

> In those days Peter stood up among the brothers (the company of persons was in all about 120) and said, "Brothers, the Scripture had to be fulfilled, which the Holy Spirit spoke beforehand by the mouth of David concerning Judas, who became a guide to those who arrested Jesus. For he was numbered among us and was allotted his share in this ministry." (Now this man acquired a field with the reward of his wickedness, and falling headlongd he burst open in the middle and all his bowels gushed out. And it became known to all the inhabitants of Jerusalem, so that the field was called in their own language *Akeldama*, that is, Field of Blood). For it is written in the Book of Psalms, "May his camp become desolate, and let there be no one to dwell in it";[1] and "Let another take his office."[2] (vs. 15–20).

On a certain day, which is not mentioned, the number of the disciples present were one hundred and twenty. This however, was not by any means the whole number of believers before Pentecost. We read elsewhere that the risen Christ had appeared to about five hundred brethren at once (1 Cor 15:6). These no doubt belonged to Galilee. On that day before Pentecost, Peter arose in the midst of the one hundred and twenty and addressing them as brethren, laid before them the sad case of Judas, who had been numbered among the twelve apostles. The awful fate of Judas is mentioned once more. There is no discrepancy between Matthew's account and the words here. He committed suicide by hanging, and the rope broke, and the terrible thing happened, which is reported here. The Apostle Peter, in bringing the case before the disciples, quotes the Word of God in a most remarkable way, which shows its inspiration.

The question arises at once about the legitimacy of Peter's action. Was it right to act in this way? Was he authorized to address the assembled company and propose the addition of another apostle in the place of Judas? Or was his action another evidence of his impulsiveness, wholly wrong? We are aware that some good brethren, teachers of the Bible, declare that Peter made a mistake. They tell us that this action was not according to the mind of the Lord. They assert furthermore, that not Matthias, but Paul, should have been the Apostle in the place of Judas.

We do not agree at all with their teaching. Peter and the gathered company did not make a mistake. He acted by inspiration and what they did was not only according to the mind of the risen Christ, according to the Word of God, but it was a manifestation of Christ in their midst. It was the Lord who added Matthias to the twelve. To say that Paul was meant to be the twelfth apostle is a *great* blunder. Paul's apostleship is entirely different from that of the men, who were called to this office by our Lord, in connection with his earthly ministry. Paul is the apostle of the Gentiles and received from the risen and glorified

---

[1] Psalm 69:25
[2] Psalm 109:8

Christ the double ministry, that of the Gospel, which he called "my Gospel" and the ministry of the church. Not till Israel's failure had been fully demonstrated in the stoning of Stephen, was Saul of Tarsus called to his apostleship. Furthermore twelve apostles were necessary. Twelve is the number denoting earthly government. Inasmuch as there was to be given another witness to Jerusalem after the ascension of our Lord, a national witness, a second offer of the Kingdom (Acts 3:19, 20) twelve apostles were necessary as a body of witnesses to the nation. If only eleven apostles had stood up on the day of Pentecost, it would not have been in harmony with the divine plan and order. How strange it would have sounded if the record said "but Peter standing up with the *ten*" instead of "with the eleven" (ch. 2:14). Twelve had to stand up on Pentecost to bear witness to the resurrection of Jesus Christ, therefore another one had to be added *before* that day. Besides this, there is positive proof that the Holy Spirit endorsed the action of the disciples in the upper room. In 1 Corinthians 15:5 the Holy Spirit mentions the twelve, who saw the Lord, to whom he appeared. Paul then is mentioned apart from the twelve; he saw the Lord in glory as one born out of due season (v. 8).

A closer examination of the record of their action shows that the Lord guided them in this matter. Peter begins by quoting scripture. He does it in a way which clearly proves that he was guided by the Lord. "The Scriptures should be fulfilled" is what Peter said. How different from the Peter in Matthew 16 when he took the Lord aside and said after he had announced his coming death, "far be it from you, Lord." he had then no knowledge of the Scriptures. Repeatedly it is said that they knew not the Scriptures and that their eyes were holden. Here, however, he begins with the Scriptures. Surely this was the right starting

3. Dice made of bone found in Jerusalem during the Temple Mount Sifting Project and date to the early Roman period.

point, and thus ordered by the Lord. He quotes from the Psalms. Part of Psalm 69:25 and Psalm 109:8 are given by him as the foundation of the purposed action. These Psalms are prophetic of the events, which had taken place. The Lord Himself had opened his understanding as well as that of the other disciples. In Luke 24 we read that he spoke of what was written in the law of Moses and the Prophets and the Psalms. "Then he opened their minds to understand the Scriptures" (Luke 24:45). It was a gift of the risen Lord and here Peter guided by the Spirit of God uses the prophetic Word. All the company is one with him in the undertaking. It must be done. The Lord moved them in this matter.

Matthias replaces Judas (vs. 21–26)

"So one of the men who have accompanied us during all the time that the Lord Jesus went in and out among us, beginning from the baptism of John until the day when he was taken up from us—one of these men must become with us a witness to his resurrection." (vs. 21–22).

Here he defines the qualification of an apostle. He must be a witness of the resurrection of Christ as well as of what he said and did in his earthly ministry.

And they put forward two, Joseph called Barsabbas, who was also called Justus, and

> Matthias. And they prayed and said, "You, Lord, who know the hearts of all, show which one of these two you have chosen to take the place in this ministry and apostleship from which Judas turned aside to go to his own place." And they cast lots for them, and the lot fell on Matthias, and he was numbered with the eleven apostles. (vs. 23–26).

How simple it all is! How can anyone say that they erred in this action! Two are selected. Then they prayed; no doubt Peter led in audible prayer. And the prayer is a model of directness and simplicity. They address the Lord and believe that he had made a choice already. What they pray for is that the one chosen by him may now be made known by Himself. The lot was perfectly legitimate for them to use. The Scriptures speak of it. "The lot is cast into the lap, but its every decision is from the Lord" (Prov 16:33). As they were still on Old Testament ground, it was perfectly right for them to resort to the lot (see Fig. 3). It, however, would be wrong for us to do it now. We have his complete Word, and the Holy Spirit to reveal his will. The Lord selects Matthias. His name means "the gift of the Lord." Thus the Lord gave him his place. The Apostolate complete, all was in readiness for the great day of Pentecost.

CHAPTER TWO

A chapter of great importance is before us. Never was its closest and prayerful study so needed as in our days. Most of God's people are ignorant of that which God in his Grace did on the day of Pentecost; they know little of the exact meaning of the great event, which took place and their share and part in it as believers. This lack of knowledge is often responsible for all the fads and fanciful interpretations we meet about us.

We divide this chapter into five parts.

1. The Outpouring of the Holy Spirit (vs. 1–4).
2. The immediate effect of his Presence (vs. 5–15).
3. Peter's address (vs. 14–36).
4. The result of the delivered testimony (vs. 37–41).
5. The gathered company in fellowship (vs. 42–47).

Before we take up the first part and study the text, we desire to make a few general remarks on the great historical event, the gift of the Holy Spirit on the day of Pentecost. What took place on that memorable day and what was accomplished? First of all the promise of the Father as well as of the Son was accomplished. It is familiar to every reader of the New Testament that John the Baptist had witnessed concerning him who was to baptize them with the Holy Spirit (Matt 3). The Lord also had spoken repeatedly to his disciples about the gift of the Holy Spirit. In Luke 11 we read his words: "If you then, who are evil, know how to give good gifts to your children, how much more will the heavenly Father give the Holy Spirit to those who ask him!" (Luke 11:13; cf. Matt 7:11). This promise related to the future. In John 7:37–39 we read:

> On the last day of the feast, the great day, Jesus stood up and cried out, "If anyone thirsts, let him come to me and drink. Whoever believes in me, as[1] the Scripture has said, 'Out of his heart will flow rivers of living water.'" Now this he said about the Spirit, whom those who believed in him were to receive, for as yet the Spirit had not been given, because Jesus was not yet glorified.

The promised Spirit could therefore not come, the promise could not be fulfilled till the great work of redemption on the cross had been accomplished and the Lord Jesus Christ had risen from the dead and taken his place in Glory. In the subsequent promises in this Gospel, the Lord always spoke of the coming of the Comforter in connection with his own departure. He promised that the other Comforter, the Spirit of Truth, was to be in them; but none of these promises could be fulfilled before he Himself had been glorified. We have already seen how He, before his departure to be with the Father, had told them to tarry in Jerusalem, to await the promise of the Father, and how he had reminded them that: "for John baptized with water, but you will be baptized with[2] the Holy Spirit not many days from now" (1:5). On the day of

---

[1] Or *let him come to me, and let him who believes in me drink. As*

[2] Or *in*

Pentecost all these blessed promises were once and for all fulfilled. As all believers are sanctified through the offering of the body of Jesus Christ once for all (Heb 10) so all believers share in the accomplished promise of the Father and are in the possession of the Holy Spirit. But we must emphasize that he was not given by measure, but He, the person, came Himself. What a blessed work, a work we cannot fully estimate, the Lord Jesus Christ must have accomplished on the cross, that the third person of the Trinity came down from heaven and has made his abiding place in believing sinners! his presence therefore testifies not only to the fact that the promise of the Father has been accomplished, but also to the efficacy of the precious blood, and that Jesus is in glory at the right hand of the Majesty on high.

It is therefore incorrect to ask God for the gift of his Spirit, or to plead promises which he fulfilled on the day of Pentecost. It is not scriptural to pray for a greater baptism of the Spirit, as it is often done, or, to ask God to give more of the Spirit. He has given us his Spirit, he seals every believer and indwells every child of God. And what are the purposes of the gift of the Spirit on the day of Pentecost? Without giving a lengthy dissertation on the work of the Holy Spirit in this age we only point out that the purpose of his coming is revealed in the historical event reported to us in this chapter. Other purposes are indicated, and these are later fully revealed in the Pauline Epistles. The Book of Acts, as a purely historical book, does not contain a single doctrine of the Holy Spirit; it rather shows revealed doctrine in its practical side.

Two things are at once apparent. He came upon the assembled believers individually, and also did a work in a corporate way. Each believer on that day was filled with the Holy Spirit. He came as the indweller to each. But he also was present as the mighty rushing wind which filled all the house. He did not only come upon each, but all were baptized of the Holy Spirit, and he united them into a body. In 1 Corinthians 12:13 the more complete revelation is given concerning this fact. "For in one Spirit we were all baptized into one body—Jews or Greeks, slaves[3] or free—and all were made to drink of one Spirit." The One Spirit is the Holy Spirit as he came on the day of Pentecost, the One Body is the church. All believers were on that day united by the Spirit into the one body, and since then, whenever and wherever a sinner believes in the finished work of Christ, he shares in that baptism and is joined by the Spirit to that one body. He may be in dense ignorance about all this, as indeed, the great majority of believers are; but this does not alter the gracious fact of what God has done and is doing. The believing company was then formed on the day of Pentecost into one body. *It was the birthday of the church.*

There is an interesting correspondency between the second chapter of Luke and the second chapter of Acts, which we cannot pass by without mentioning. In the first chapter of Luke we have the announcement of the birth of the Saviour. The angel said to Mary, "the Holy Spirit will come upon you, and the power of the Most High will overshadow you; therefore the child to be born will be called holy—the Son of God" (Luke 1:35). In the second chapter of the Gospel of Luke, the same who penned the book of Acts, we read of the accomplishment of that promise given to the virgin. And so the second chapter of Acts contains the fulfillment of a similar promise. The Holy Spirit came and the church, the mystical body of Christ began.

We said that Pentecost marks the beginning of the church on earth. This is often doubted by Christian believers. Some

---

[3] Or *servants*; Gr. *bondservants*

claim that the church began in the Old Testament. The sixteenth chapter of the Gospel of Matthew answers this wrong statement and belief completely. Others teach that the church did not begin on Pentecost, but some time later, after the Apostle Paul had begun his activity. So far has this point been pressed that membership in the body of Christ has even been denied to the twelve apostles, that they were exclusively on kingdom ground. That such theories and views are not only fanciful but very confusing and harmful needs not to be demonstrated. It is quite true that the doctrine concerning the church as the body of Christ as well as the other relationships was not made known on the day when the Holy Spirit was poured out. In fact, any doctrine would be out of place in a book which gives a historical account. But this does not mean that the start was not made. The foundation of the building as described in Ephesians are the Apostles and Prophets (not Old Testament Prophets, but the New Testament Prophets). Later Gentiles were added to be joint heirs of the same body and joint partakers of the promises. Then through the chosen instrument, the Apostle Paul, the secret which was not made known in other ages was made known. The Apostles and the Prophets knew of it according to Ephesians 3:5, but only to the Apostle Paul was it given to reveal it.

That the church as the body of Christ existed before Paul ever revealed the mystery is clearly seen from the account of the conversion of Saul of Tarsus. The glorified Christ was seen by him on the road to Damascus. He heard him speak and these were his words: "Saul, Saul, why are you persecuting me?" (9:4 cf. 22:7) he was not persecuting Jesus Christ personally, but he was persecuting such who had believed in Christ. The Lord from the glory owns these as part of Himself. They were indeed members of his body.

We state it again, the Holy Spirit came to each believer on the day of Pentecost, they received Him, he filled them individually and corporately they were united into one body. And what was done then is done in the case of every believing one who rests on the finished work of Christ. As a believer each receives the Holy Spirit and becomes a member of the body of Christ.

> There may be a variety of forms and measures in which his power is displayed; there may be and are different degrees in which the joy of his presence is entered into; but the fact remains (and what can be more glorious and blessed than the fact) that, as to Himself he dwells equally in every believer who rests now on the finished redemption in Christ Jesus.[4]

Of many other things which might be mentioned by way of introduction we only mention two.

The testimony was given by the Spirit filled disciples and every man heard them speak in his own language; those who were present were "devout men from every nation under heaven" (2:5). They were all Jews not a single Gentile was present. However, the event shows that the good news was to go forth in the new age, to every nation under heaven.

Lastly we call attention to the fact that the events on the day of Pentecost have a special Jewish national significance. The resurrection of Jesus Christ is demonstrated. The signs are given to show to the people Israel that Jesus of Nazareth whom they rejected is the Christ and at the right hand of God. The day of Pentecost marks the beginning of a second offer of mercy to the nation. This fact will be carefully studied as we expound this chapter and the chapters which follow. And now we turn to the text itself.

---

[4] *Lectures on the doctrine of the Holy Spirit.*

1. The Outpouring of the Holy Spirit (vs. 1–4).

> When the day of Pentecost arrived, they were all together in one place. And suddenly there came from heaven a sound like a mighty rushing wind, and it filled the entire house where they were sitting. And divided tongues as of fire appeared to them and rested[5] on each one of them. And they were all filled with the Holy Spirit and began to speak in other tongues as the Spirit gave them utterance. (vs. 1–4).

Pentecost is a Jewish feast. This name was given to this feast by the Greek-speaking Jews, because it occurred 50 days after the offering of the barley sheaf during the Passover feast. In the Old Testament it has three names. *"Chag Ha Kasir"* Feast of Harvest, Exodus 23:16; *"Chag Shavuoth"* Exodus 34:22, Feast of Weeks and *"Yom ha-Bikkurim"* Numbers 28:26; Day of the First Fruits. The orthodox Jews call it simply *"Shavuoth."* It commemorates the wheat harvest. After the exile it became the traditional feast to remember the giving of the law, the birthday of the Torah (law). The orthodox Jews in keeping it at the present time, besides the prayers they offer, read publicly in their synagogues the account of the giving of the law as recorded in Exodus.

From the prophets they read the first chapter of the Prophet Ezekiel and the third chapter of Habakkuk. No doubt this was their custom at the time when the Holy Spirit was poured out. It is not unlikely that the Jews were occupied with the reading of these portions of God's Word, when suddenly there came the sound from heaven. It is certainly a significant fact that some of the outward signs which were present when the law was given, the "tempest," "fire" and "the voice of words" (Heb 12:18–19) were prominent on the day when the Holy Spirit came: A new dispensation was inaugurated with outward signs and wonders. But as the outward signs were not present at all times during the dispensation of the law, but simply in the beginning, so in this new dispensation these outward signs were only for the beginning.

The reading on the day of Pentecost of the first chapter of Ezekiel and the third of Habakkuk, especially the latter, is prophetic. It points towards that time when the Lord Jesus will be manifested in visible glory, and when all that will be fulfilled spoken concerning the nation Israel, which was not fulfilled on the day of Pentecost, nor ever after up to the present time.

Before we look at the details of the outpouring of the Holy Spirit we wish to mention the day of the week on which the event occurred. This is an interesting question. It was no doubt on the Lord's day. The best which has been written on this point is by Lightfoot. As his statements are not accessible to all we quote here from his *Horae Hebraeicae*:

> Let us inquire, therefore, whether the day of Pentecost fell on their sabbath day. I know, indeed, that the fifty days are reckoned by some from the resurrection of our Lord; and then Pentecost, or the fiftieth day, must fall on the fiftieth day of the week, that is our Lord's day; but if we number the days from the common epoch, that is from the time of offering the sheaf of firstfruits, which account doubtless Luke follows, then the day of Pentecost fell on the Jewish sabbath. And here, by the good leave of some learned men, it may be questioned, whether the Holy Spirit was poured out upon the disciples on the very day of Pentecost, or not. The reasons of this question may be these:
>
> 1. The ambiguity of the words themselves 'when the day of Pentecost was fully come.' In Italian they are translated *'E nel finire del giorno delta Pentecoste"* that is, when it was fully gone.' So that the phrase in the Greek leaves it undetermined, whether the day of Pentecost was fully come or fully gone, and what is there could be alleged

---

[5] Or "And tongues as of fire appeared to them, distributed among them, and rested."

against it, should we render it in the latter sense?⁶

2. It is worthy of our observation, that Christ the antitype, in answering some types that represented Him, did not tie Himself up to the very day of the type itself for the fulfilling of it, but put it off to the day following. So it was not upon the very day of Passover, but the day following, that Christ, our passover, was sacrificed for us; it was not on the very day that the sheaf of the firstfruits was offered, but the day following, that Christ became the firstfruits of them that slept. And so it was agreeable to reason and to the order wherein he disposed of things already mentioned, that he should give the day following, the day of his own resurrection from the grave; that the Spirit should not be poured out upon the same day wherein the giving of the law was commemorated, but upon a day that might keep up the commemoration of Himself forever.

3. We can hardly think of a more fit and proper reason why upon this day they should be gathered together in one place, than that they were so gathered together for the celebration of the Lord's day . . . On that day beyond all controversy, the Holy Spirit did come down amongst them.⁷

On the Lord's day they were all together. How large the number we do not know, yet it is more than probable that every believer in the Lord was present. Suddenly something happened. A sound was heard from heaven. The sound was more than a mighty wind; the literal rendering of the description is "as a violent, impetuous blowing." This mighty rushing, blowing wind filled the house where they were sitting. It all came to pass in the twinkling of an eye.

Before we continue our meditation on this event we call attention briefly to the mode and manner of the departure of the church from the earth. It will be "suddenly."

This is according to his own and last promise, "Behold, I am coming soon" (Rev 22:12; lit.: speedily). Some day he will come suddenly for his saints and take them to Glory into his own presence as revealed in 1 Thessalonians 4:13–18. The birth of the church was an instantaneous event as well as miraculous. The departure of the true church will be the matter of a moment and will be miraculous. But this is only a passing thought suggested by the word "suddenly."

The rushing wind, which filled the whole house, was the first sign of the advent of the Holy Spirit. As an outward sign it accompanied the descent of the divine Person who had come to dwell in these believers and to form and start the building, which is his habitation. In I Kings 8, verse 2 we read that the cloud, the sign of the Lord's presence, filled the whole house after the sacrifices had been brought. But here was a still greater event than that which took place at the dedication of the great Solomonic temple. The whole house was filled in which the believers were gathered to signify thereby that from now on there would be a nobler building on earth, the church, the habitation of God through the Spirit (Eph 2:22).

Besides this outward sign for the sense of hearing there was also a visible sign that the Holy Spirit had come. There appeared to them parted tongues as of fire, and it sat upon each one of them. While the filling of the house indicated the fact that his abode would be the church, the parted tongues as of fire sitting upon each, testified to the fact that every one of the company had received Him. There was no difference among them. Peter, John and James did not receive "more of Him" than the youngest and weakest of these believers. The person, not a power or influence: given by measure, had filled each and every believer. He came as the gift of God.

---

⁶ Rotherham translated it "when the day of Pentecost was being filled up." The language shows that the feast was in process.

⁷ John Lightfoot, *Horæ Hebraicæ et Talmudicæ*, trans. Robert Gandell (Oxford, U.K.: Oxford University Press, 1859), 4:25–26.

The parted tongues as of fire were the symbols of the diverse languages in which the testimony concerning Christ and the blessed Gospel was now to go forth. The fire was of course not literal fire. It is symbolical of the righteousness and holiness of God, as well as of judgment. Kelly states:

> The tongues were "as of fire," for the testimony of Grace was none the less founded on righteousness. The Gospel is intolerant of evil. This is the wonderful way in which God now speaks by the Holy Spirit. Whatever the mercy of God, whatever the proved weakness, need and guilt of man, there is not nor can be the least compromise of holiness. God can never sanction the evil of man. Hence the Spirit of God was thus pleased to mark the character of his presence, even though given of the grace of God, but founded on the righteousness of God. God could afford fully to bless. It was no derogation from his Glory; it was after all but his seal on the perfectness of the work of the Lord Jesus.[8]

And this great gift was not only given to that assembled company of believers, but everyone who is born again throughout this age in which the church is forming, shares in this gift and the Holy Spirit is through Grace the heavenly and abiding guest in the believer. There is no need for the believer to ask him to come, but the need is to realize in faith that we are the temples of the Holy Spirit and then live and act according to this great truth. But there was a third sign. They began to speak in other tongues as the Spirit gave them utterance. Thus we have three great signs: The mighty rushing winds, the parted tongues as of fire and the speaking in other tongues, the result of the Holy Spirit's inward presence.

Wind, fire and voices. As stated before the Law at Sinai was given under some of these accompanying signs. This is likewise true of some of the other Theophanies of the Old Testament, for instance in the history of Elijah, where the tempest, the fire and the still small voice are prominent. All this shows that a divine person, God the Holy Spirit, had come. A most interesting Talmudical tradition declares that when God gave the Law from Sinai the voice of God parted into seven voices; each of the seven voices again parted into different voices, so that God heralded the law in seventy different tongues heard by all the nations of the earth.

This is only a tradition and no doubt incorrect, but here on the day of Pentecost a miracle took place in that all who had received the Holy Spirit spoke in other tongues.

We give this part of the chapter the most careful attention. It is of great importance that we examine this miraculous evidence of the advent and presence of the Holy Spirit as thoroughly as we can. Of late a movement has sprung up, which appears in different sects and calls itself either the Apostolic Faith, or the Pentecost Movement, etc. These movements claim that the Holy Spirit is poured out again and that along with his coming there is the same miracle of the gift of tongues.

And now before we take up this subject in detail we read the contents of the next paragraph of this chapter.

2. THE IMMEDIATE EFFECT OF HIS PRESENCE (VS. 5–15).

> Now there were dwelling in Jerusalem Jews, devout men from every nation under heaven. And at this sound the multitude came together, and they were bewildered, because each one was hearing them speak in his own language. And they were amazed and astonished, saying, "Are not all these who are speaking Galileans? And how is it that we hear, each of us in his own native language? Parthians and Medes and Elamites and residents of Mesopotamia, Judea and Cappadocia, Pontus and Asia, Phrygia and Pamphylia, Egypt and the parts of Libya belonging to Cyrene, and

---

[8] William Kelly, *Lectures Introductory to the Study of the Acts, the Catholic Epistles, and the Revelation* (London, U.K.: W.H. Broom, 1870), 11.

visitors from Rome, both Jews and proselytes, Cretans and Arabians—we hear them telling in our own tongues the mighty works of God." And all were amazed and perplexed, saying to one another, "What does this mean?" But others mocking said, "They are filled with new wine."

But Peter, standing with the eleven, lifted up his voice and addressed them: "Men of Judea and all who dwell in Jerusalem, let this be known to you, and give ear to my words. For these people are not drunk, as you suppose, since it is only the third hour of the day.[9] (vs. 5–15).

It is clear from the inspired narrative that all the assembled believers spoke in other tongues, that is, in different languages, and that it was as the Holy Spirit gave them to speak forth. This third great sign which happened on the day of Pentecost has been differently interpreted, and by Some the miracle has been altogether denied. We mention very briefly some of these different views.

One prominent view which was already advanced by some of the so-called "church-fathers," and which has not a few modern followers, is that the miracle consisted in the way the multitude heard rather than in the speaking of the Spirit-filled disciples. According to this view the people heard in the different languages, while the company of the believers only spoke in their own tongue. This view hardly needs an answer, because it states something which is in direct opposition to the words of the record, "and began to speak in other tongues" (2:4).

Some of the critics claim that the speaking and hearing must have been the result of a "magnetic report" between the speakers and the hearers. Such a foolish view is easily answered by the fact that they first spake and there was none there to listen, some time later the multitude crowded in, attracted by the rumor. Others declared that the new or other tongues meant a new spiritual language, or that they spoke in an unusual, enthusiastic poetical phraseology, etc. All these versions as well as others are in such flagrant contradiction with the simple words here before us that it is unnecessary to follow them any further.

The speaking in other languages was a miracle produced by the Holy Spirit who had come upon them in mighty power. These Galileans spoke in different tongues, sixteen at least, if not more.

> By a sudden and powerful inspiration of the Holy Spirit, these disciples uttered, not of their own minds, but as mouthpieces of the Holy Spirit, the praises of God in various languages hitherto, and possibly at the time itself, unknown to them.[10]

The significance of this miracle speaking in other tongues is not hard to discover. It was the oral manifestation of the parted tongues of fire, which had come upon each. Besides this it proclaimed the great fact that the Holy Spirit had come to make known the blessed Gospel to all nations under heaven, and though no Gentiles were present when this took place, the languages of the Gentiles were heard, and that from Jewish lips, indicating that the Gospel should indeed go forth to the uttermost parts of the earth. For the unbelieving multitude it was a sign though we do not read anything in the record that they were converted by hearing their different languages spoken. They were amazed and in perplexity, while others mocked; upon those it made no impression at all. The great result on the day of Pentecost was by the preaching of the Gospel from Peter's lips.

This brings before us the question, What did they speak in these different tongues? Did they all proclaim in an orderly discourse the Gospel, or relate something

---

[9] That is, 9 a.m.

[10] Dean Alvord in *Greek New Testament*.

concerning the person of Christ, or were their utterances rather of an ecstatic nature, in the form of praising God, exalting his Name? We believe the latter was the case. It was rather an outburst of praise to God for the great things he had done, than the preaching of the Gospel. All was done, no doubt, in perfect order and not in confusion. The gift was bestowed just for this occasion and not for future use.

We look in vain through this Book to find that they continued in speaking in these different languages. It is a wrong conception to think that they exercised this gift ever after in preaching the Gospel. From the sixteenth chapter we learn that Paul and Barnabas did not understand the Lycaonian speech; the Greek language was universally used and made the use of the other languages almost unnecessary.

Twice more we find in this book the tongues mentioned in connection with the gift of the Holy Spirit in Acts 10:46 and chapter 19:6. In the first passage Cornelius and his household having believed the Gospel received the Holy Spirit and they spake with tongues. Not a word is said in this instance that other languages were used. There was no need for it. It was an ecstatic speech glorifying God. In chapter 19 after the Apostle Paul had laid hands upon the disciples of John whom he had found in Ephesus (a thing which Peter did not do with Cornelius) the Holy Spirit came upon them and they spoke with tongues and prophesied. Here again not a word is said about anyone hearing a strange language. The speaking in tongues is here paired with prophesying. These are the three instances in the Book of Acts where speaking in tongues is mentioned. On the day of Pentecost; Cornelius and his house and the Jewish disciples found in the dispersion, waiting for the Hope of Israel. In each case it was for a sign and for a specific purpose, but only in the first instance are different dialects and languages mentioned. On the day of Pentecost the gift was for a sign to the multitude; In chapter 10 the evidence to Peter and the Apostles that the Gentiles had received the same gift (11:15) and In chapter 19 the outward evidence that the Jewish disciples of John had also received the Holy Spirit and shared in the same gift.

We read not a word about this gift in connection with the other places visited by the apostles, not a word is said about speaking in tongues in the ministry of Philip in Samaria, nor during the great journeys of the Apostle Paul, with the exception of the case mentioned above. It is therefore clear that the speaking in tongues was neither a universal nor a permanent gift, and that it appeared only in these three cases for a sign.

We emphasize these facts on account of these spurious movements which claim that a greater outpouring of the Holy Spirit is now in progress, that each believer must seek "his Pentecost" and that the true evidence of being filled with the Holy Spirit is the speaking in an unknown tongue. Such claims are unscriptural and cannot at all be confirmed by the historical account of this book for thousands and tens of thousands were saved and baptized by the one Spirit into the one body, the Holy Spirit filling them, without ever speaking in an unknown tongue. Stephen was a believer who was indeed full of the Holy Spirit. Nowhere do we read that he had the gift of tongues.

However in the first Epistle of Paul to the Corinthians we find a long chapter in which "speaking in unknown tongues" is largely entered into. From this chapter we learn that that gift was prevalent in the Corinthian assembly (2:14). In the twelfth chapter where the different gifts of the Spirit are enumerated we find the speaking in tongues and the interpretation of these tongues mentioned. They stand last in the list, showing thereby their inferior place. In the Epistle to the Ephesians, addressed to that assembly of believers who enjoyed the best gifts of the Holy Spirit, the Word of Wisdom and the Word of Knowledge, no mention whatever is made of the speaking in tongues. What the spiritual condition of the assembly in Corinth was we learn from this entire epistle.

Their walk was carnal, all kinds of wicked things had been tolerated in their midst; sectarianism and vain-glory held sway. Their spiritual knowledge was very low indeed, and the Holy Spirit could not flash forth the great truths, which he so fully reveals in the Epistle to the Ephesians. Paul had to take up a good part of the Epistle with correcting their evil habits and walk. That the gift of tongues was sought for by these Corinthians can be learned from the chapter in which the Holy Spirit through Paul enlarges upon this gift. May they not have sought it for the sake of display rather than to glorify God with it? Then no doubt women were in the foreground, and they are especially cautioned.

> The women should keep silent in the churches. For they are not permitted to speak, but should be in submission, as the Law also says. If there is anything they desire to learn, let them ask their husbands at home. For it is shameful for a woman to speak in church. (1 Cor 14:34–35).

In this modern movement women seem to be very much in the foreground, acting in many instances as preachers and leaders, and therefore in direct disobedience to the Word of God. Eyewitnesses have told us that they were in such "gift of tongue meetings" where women became hysterical, rolled on the floor, uttered all kinds of queer noises, screeched like the former prophets of Baal "Oh God, send the power!" One friend said he felt he was among demons. Convulsions, rigor and foaming at the mouth like madmen were also noticed. Some such things may have also happened in Corinth for we read several exhortations in this chapter which point in this direction. "For God is not a God of confusion (lit.: tumult)" (1 Cor 14:33). "But all things should be done decently and in order" (v. 40).

We quote here from a pamphlet by Dr. Arthur T. Pierson, on 1 Corinthians 14.

> (1) Speaking in an unknown tongue is *unintelligible to the hearer.* If it be genuine, it is only known as such to God, so that even when one so speaks in the Spirit he speaks mysteries to all others-which we take to be the true reading here.
>
> (2) Speaking with tongues, therefore, is not in and by itself *edifying* to men. While prophesying is profitable for "edification, exhortation and comfort," the gift of tongues in itself can do no more than cause the hearer to wonder and be in awe at what he understands not.
>
> (3) Speaking with tongues, therefore, is comparatively *undesirable* and *unserviceable.* It ranks last among all the Spirit-gifts and manifestations, and is mentioned among the last in the enumeration in chapter 12:7–10, where seven other gifts out-rank it.
>
> (4) Speaking with tongues is *dependent for all real value* upon the companion gift of *interpretation* of tongues, and hence is coupled with it in the previous category of gifts (12:10). In fact, only such interpretation of what is uttered can lift it to the level of "that which is good to the use of edifying, that it may minister grace to the hearers" (Eph 4:29). There is no speaking with tongues apart from such interpretation, no profit, for it brings no "revelation," "knowledge," "prophesying," or "doctrine" (v. 6).
>
> (5) More even than this: speaking with tongues may degenerate into an *empty display of the mysterious* a mere babble, if not Babel, of confusion, like many "sounds" (or "tunes" margin), in which no one can tell what is sense and what is nonsense, what is spurious and what is genuine.
>
> (6) Speaking with tongues is rather a means of *dispersion than of closer association.* Its tendencies are divergent, not convergent. As at Babel, when they could not understand one another's speech they separated and scattered, so, if the hearer "know not the meaning of the voice," the speaker will 'be to him a barbarian" i.e., a foreigner, and conversely.
>
> (7) Such a gift, therefore, acts rather as a *hindrance* than a *help to common joint worship.* Part of the power and acceptableness of all worship and

service in the assembly depends on the *responsiveness of the worshipper to the leader*. Whether it be the service of song, praise, or prayer, or hearing of the Word, what is in a dead language cannot evoke the hearer's "Amen." How can the heart intelligently answer to what is not understood by the "unlearned?" However well the speaker does, the hearer cannot enter into the sentiment of what is spoken, and *joint* worship or communion is impossible.

(8) The Apostle hints further that speaking with tongues alone independent of interpretation may even *work damage*. He pictures an assembly, where all speak with tongues, as impressing an unbelieving outsider so unfavorably that he declares them "*mad*" (v. 23). In such a jargon of confused sounds, he thinks himself in a mad house.

(9) Paul goes even further, and by the Spirit enjoins that, when such gift actually is bestowed, *its exercise shall be carefully regulated*. And for such regulation he gives two distinct laws: (a) The law of *precedence*; (b) the law of *silence*. "If any man speak in an unknown tongue, let it be by two, or at the most by three at a time, and these in succession, not all at once; and let the interpretation accompany each utterance. And, secondly, if there be no *interpreter*, let the speaking with tongues be *suppressed altogether*- let him who has the gift keep *silence* toward man, and use his gift towad *God*, who can understand him."

(10) his final argument is that what produces *confusion and not order* cannot be of God, for he is not the author of disorder, but of decent conformity to law and order, and "peace." While, therefore, speaking with tongues is not to be *forbidden*, it is not to be *coveted*, but rather the edifying, instructive, intelligible utterances of inspired *teaching*.

(11) It is more than hinted here also that speaking with tongues is peculiarly open to *spurious imitation*. The Devil, who is the master counterfeiter, is always with peculiar subtlety *imitating* the manifestations of the Spirit. When God is mightily working, so is he; and no one gift of the Spirit is so easily "aped" as this. So long as there be no interpretation to make the language intelligible, who shall tell whether it be blessing or cursing, reverent or profane! Not only can interpretation alone make speaking with tongues edifying, but this alone can attest it as genuine.

(12) Some think that the injunction here, bidding the Corinthian "*women* keep silence in the churches," has special reference to this speaking with tongues. Women in the Orient were then, as now, especially excitable and prone to excess. When once emerging from seclusion and privacy of their home life, and introduced into the new freedom of the Christian brotherhood, they often ran into the wildest fanaticism, and might easily have mistaken an hysterical mania, with its incoherent mutterings, for a gift of supernatural utterance.

Another recent writer on the glossolaly or gift of tongues states the matter still more briefly.

"We notice that, though Paul spoke with tongues more than all the Corinthians, he does not set a high value on the gift of glossolaly. He ranks it last of the gifts and apparently among childish things (1 Cor 14:18–20). For (1) it did not edify others. Rather (2) it tended to cause disorder in the church. (3) The fact that the speaking in tongues lay in the spiritual and not in the rational sphere opened the door to dangerous confusion. Its phenomena might be counterfeited either by evil spirits, or by religious impostors and charlatans of which the world was then full. Again it might be hard at times to distinguish them from similar symptoms due to physical causes, etc."

This warning is well founded indeed. It is a territory on which Satan appears as an angel of light and it is to be expected that he will develop an increasing energy in this direction as the coming of our Lord draws nigh. In an address on the characteristics of the age, Mr. Philip Mauro spoke a timely word on this matter which bears repeating:

The wicked spirits, or demons, who form part of this spiritual host, display abnormal activity at the time of our Lord's first coming; and now again, as his second coming approaches, they are aroused to a state of great activity. Spirit 'control' and 'possession,' accompanied by unusual physical demonstrations, rigor, protracted unconsciousness, convulsions, hysterics, spasmodic movements, strange noises, which may or may not be articulate speech of some sort (and hence easily confounded with the Holy Spirit's gift of tongues) are now quite common and becoming more so. These abnormal manifestations are no longer confined to circles where Spiritism, hypnotism and the like are openly cultivated, but are now breaking out among groups of God's people who have been induced to stray away from scriptural ground, and to seek for excitements and 'experiences,' who are urged by misguided teachers to yield themselves, to come under 'control,' to seek 'power' instead of weakness, and otherwise to disregard the plain injunctions of Scripture.[11]

Now while it is true that there was such a gift as speaking in an unknown tongue in the apostolic age, and no Christian believer would doubt the power of God to impart to a person the gift to preach the Gospel in a foreign tongue, we do not believe that this gift of speaking in an unknown tongue was to abide in the church. Repeatedly claims were made in years gone by that it had been restored (for instance during the Irvingite delusion in England), but in every case it was found to be spurious or emanating from the enemy. The present day "apostolic or Pentecostal movement" with its high pretensions and false doctrines, lacking true scriptural knowledge and wisdom, creating new schisms in the body, with its women leaders and teachers, has all the marks of the same great counterfeiter upon it.

The Epistle to the Ephesians, that highest revelation of God, speaks of the gifts which are to abide. Apostles, prophets, evangelists, pastors and teachers; we still have them. The apostles are of course the men of God, the great gifts through whom the Holy Spirit revealed the great doctrines and truths of the New Testament, Peter, John, James, Paul as well as those who were not apostles, but the prophets, the mouthpieces of the Holy Spirit. Evangelists preach the Gospel so that the body of Christ may become complete as to numbers; these will ever remain till the last member is added to the body. Then pastors and teachers to shepherd the flock of God, for the perfecting of the Saint. These gifts of our risen Head will abide. But there is not a word said about miraculous sign-gifts in this great Epistle.

But some have suggested that when the age draws to its close the Holy Spirit will once more unfold special energies to give a last witness, and that in the closing of the age the Gospel of the kingdom will be heralded with accompanying signs and miracles among all the nations. This is partially founded on truth. The Gospel of the kingdom is to be preached and most likely special signs may accompany that preaching during that period known as "the great tribulation." However, the preachers of that last witness are not Christian believers, members of the one body, but the Jewish remnant will do this great work.

On the other hand, everything in the New Testament Epistles as well as in the Book of Revelation, shows that decline, ruin and apostasy and not restoration of apostolic gifts and power mark the close of this Christian age. To demonstrate this fully would be quite impossible in this connection.

Before we follow Peter's great address to the assembled multitude, a brief word on the peoples, which are mentioned as composing the amazed company, may be in order. When it says "every nation under heaven," it does not mean that representatives of all the Gentile nations were there. The phrase has reference to the Jews and proselytes living then in dispersion outside of the land. All the countries into which they had wandered were represented in the multitude. Gentiles as such were not present. Nor were those present only from the house of Judah. The ten tribes were most likely also represented. This may be learned from Peter's address. He first addresses the men of Judah and all that dwell at Jerusalem; then he addresses them as men of Israel. So that in all probability

---

[11] Published in pamphlet form by "Our Hope."

Judah and Israel, the two houses into which the people of God had been divided, were represented. These may have dwelt in Parthia, Media, Elam and Mesopotamia. That the ten tribes were known in apostolic times is also seen by the fact that James addressed his Epistle to "the twelve tribes which are scattered abroad [in the dispersion]." We mention this because occasionally someone inquires about that fanciful theory called "Anglo-Israel," which claims that the Anglo-Saxon race is composed of the lost tribes.

Representatives of "all Israel" were present when the Holy Spirit was poured out in Jerusalem upon the believing Jews and when Peter arose to address them.

3. Peter's Address (vs 14–36).

> But this is what was uttered through the prophet Joel:
>> "And in the last days it shall be, God declares, that I will pour out my Spirit on all flesh, and your sons and your daughters shall prophesy, and your young men shall see visions, and your old men shall dream dreams; even on my male servants[12] and female servants in those days I will pour out my Spirit, and they shall prophesy. And I will show wonders in the heavens above and signs on the earth below, blood, and fire, and vapor of smoke; the sun shall be turned to darkness and the moon to blood, before the day of the Lord comes, the great and magnificent day. And it shall come to pass that everyone who calls upon the name of the Lord shall be saved."[13] (vs. 14–21).

What an impressive scene it must have been when, in the midst of the tumult the outbursts of praise and adoration, the ever-increasing multitude, Peter and the eleven with him arose. Twelve divinely appointed men, the twelve apostles, faced the representatives of the twelve tribes of Israel. Peter is the spokesman. What boldness, courage and directness characterizes now the man and his speech! What a change from the Peter before Pentecost! It was all the result of the coming of the Holy Spirit. Such boldness and courage to witness for the absent Lord is our blessed privilege likewise, for we have received the same Spirit.

Peter's address deals with the great historical facts of the gospel; the heart and center of it is the resurrection and exaltation of the Lord Jesus. In its scope and pointedness it is a most wonderful production. It is in itself an evidence that the Holy Spirit had come and that he witnessed through Peter.

The main part of the address has three divisions. Each begins with a personal address to the hearers, states a great vital fact in terse language and closes with a passage from the Scriptures.

1. vs. 14–22. In the opening of his address he speaks to them as "Men of Judea and all who dwell in Jerusalem." Then, after briefly refuting the charge of drunkenness, he quotes from the book of Joel. With this Scripture quotation the first part of the address closes.

2. vs. 22–28. Now he addresses them as "men of Israel." Here we find a brief witness of the life, the crucifixion and resurrection of Jesus the Nazarene. Then he quotes, from the Book of Psalms, the sixteenth Psalm.

3. vs. 29–36. The last part he begins with "Brethren"; in it he speaks of the coming of the Holy Spirit as the result of the resurrection and exaltation of the Lord Jesus Christ. The briefest but deepest of all the Messianic Psalms is quoted, the one hundred and tenth. The chief part of his address closes with the following words: "Let all the house of Israel therefore know for certain that God has made him both Lord and Christ, this Jesus whom you crucified" (2:36). After the interruption

---

[12] Greek *bondservants*; twice in this verse
[13] Joel 2:28-32

which followed, addressed to the twelve, "Brothers, what shall we do?" (2:37). Peter spoke again, and not all his words are reported. "And with many other words he bore witness and continued to exhort them, saying, 'Save yourselves from this crooked generation' " (2:40).

What a great model this first sermon after the gift of the Holy Spirit ought to be for all who preach the Word. The Holy Word of God has the leading part in it to witness to the person of Christ. The difference between Peter's preaching and much of the modern day preaching is indeed appalling.[14]

But briefly we shall now meditate on these different parts of Peter's address. Its aim as already stated, was to prove to the house of Israel that the crucified Jesus is raised from the dead and that God made him Lord and Christ, witnessed to by the presence of the Holy Spirit.

The accusation had been, "they are filled with new wine" (2:13). To answer this false charge was the first necessary step. Peter lifted up his voice, which means that he spoke in loud tones, which was no doubt needed on account of the confusion which must have prevailed. He declared that it was but the third hour of the day and for this reason it would be next to impossible that the Spirit-filled disciples were drunk with new wine. The third hour corresponds to our ninth hour of the morning. On the Sabbath or other feast days no Jew would eat or drink before that hour; this custom was universally observed at that time, and it is still so with the so-called "Chasidim," the most orthodox Jews. Nothing is tasted before the prayers of the synagogue are ended; these are sometimes prolonged till noon. This fact, apparent to all and not controvertible, disposed at once of the false charge. And now Peter states what it is they were witnessing. He quotes from one of the great Old Testament prophecies in the book of Joel.[15] That Peter quotes Joel in connection with his address to the men of Judah and the inhabitants of Jerusalem shows the accuracy of the Scriptures, for Joel's prophecy was addressed to Judah and Jerusalem. In the next place we notice the language Peter uses in quoting Joel: "But this is what was uttered through the prophet Joel" (2:16); careless and superficial expositors have often stated that Peter said that all this happened in fulfillment of what was spoken by Joel. He did not use the word fulfilled at all. Had he spoken of a fulfillment then of Joel's prophecy, he would have uttered something which was not true, for the great prophecy of Joel was not fulfilled on that day. Nor has this prophecy been fulfilled since Pentecost, nor will it be fulfilled during this present Gospel age. This great prophecy which Peter quotes in part will be accomplished at the end of the Jewish age, that end which has not yet come and which cannot come as long as the church is on the earth.[16] Joel's prophecy will be fulfilled in connection with the coming of the Lord. Before that day comes there will be visible signs of which the prophet speaks. All this is still in the future. Before it can all be fulfilled, the events spoken of by Joel as preceding this prophecy must be accomplished, and, besides this, the church

---

[14] The continual use of anecdotes, pleasant little stories, which make old people smile and send the young folks a-giggling is especially to be condemned in Gospel preaching. The Gospel is too solemn a thing to be mixed with hilarity.

[15] Arno Clemens Gaebelein, *The Prophet Joel, an Exposition* (New York, N.Y.: Our Hope, 1909).

[16] There remains one week (seven years) of Daniel's seventy-week prophecy to be fulfilled. That last week comes in after the church is completed and these seven years constitute the end of the Jewish age, interrupted by this present church age.

must be removed from the earth in the way as revealed in the Word (1 Thess 4:15–18).

Comparing Peter's words here with Joel's words we find that Peter uses instead of the phrase found in Joel, "it shall come to pass afterward," (Joel 2:28) the expression, "And in the last days it shall be" (2:17).[17] The prophecy relates, therefore, to the last days. This phrase, found in the Old Testament, has reference to the coming days of the Messiah, when he shall come as King and establish his Kingdom in the midst of his earthly people. See Isaiah 2:2–4; Micah 4:1; Jeremiah 23:20; Hosea 3:4–5, etc. In this sense Peter uses the phrase here and not as applying to this present age at all. He tells the assembled multitude that something similar to that which they now were witnessing God had promised in connection with the days of Messiah. With his coming as King, the Spirit was to be poured out upon all flesh. That which they saw and heard was indeed the outpouring of the Holy Spirit, but not in the full sense as given in the prophecy of Joel. What took place was an evidence that, Jesus, whom they had crucified, is the true Messiah and that what had taken place is a pledge that in due time all of the prophecy contained in the book of Joel would be fulfilled. What had really taken place was not known to Peter and to the eleven at that time. It was only subsequently revealed that by the one Spirit all were baptized into one body; the great purpose of the gift of the Holy Spirit for this present age was not revealed or stated on the day of Pentecost. It was the fact only which Peter speaks of, that God had promised the gift of the Spirit in connection with the coming of the Messiah.

In regard to the fulfillment of Joel's prophecy we say once more than it cannot fall into the present age. Nor will it be fulfilled as long as the church is not removed from the earth. It comes with the second visible coming of the Lord Jesus Christ, preceding the establishment of his Kingdom. Pentecost was only the earnest of what is yet to take place in Jerusalem.

> "Men of Israel, hear these words: Jesus of Nazareth, a man attested to you by God with mighty works and wonders and signs that God did through him in your midst, as you yourselves know—this Jesus,[18] delivered up according to the definite plan and foreknowledge of God, you crucified and killed by the hands of lawless men. God raised him up, loosing the pangs of death, because it was not possible for him to be held by it. For David says concerning him,
>
> 'I saw the Lord always before me, for he is at my right hand that I may not be shaken; therefore my heart was glad, and my tongue rejoiced; my flesh also will dwell in hope. For you will not abandon my soul to Hades, or let your Holy One see corruption. You have made known to me the paths of life; you will make me full of gladness with your presence.'"[19] (vs. 22–28).

Peter now puts before them in the second part of his address the whole story of the Messiah, whom they had rejected. He could therefore use, not the name as he had confessed him at Caesarea Philippi, but he speaks of him as "Jesus of Nazareth." By that name, the Nazarene, the lowly, blessed One had been known to them. That name, too, was written above his Cross; it was the name which was an offence to them. Inasmuch as it was the aim of the Holy Spirit to show the guilt of the nation, to demonstrate the humiliation and rejection of Christ and to declare his resurrection, no other name could be used. For us it would be improper to speak of him as "Jesus of Nazareth"; we call him by his name as he is

---

[17] David Kimchi, who lived from 1160–1234 AD.

[18] Greek *this one*.

[19] Psalm 16:8–11.

revealed in resurrection, "The Lord Jesus Christ."

Briefly Peter traces the events during the past three years. These events were familiar to them. This Jesus the Nazarene was a man witnessed to by God by works of power and wonders and signs, which God had wrought. Many of his hearers had been, no doubt, eye-witnesses of the power of God and the wonders done. They were fully convinced, like Nicodemus, that no one could do these signs unless God was with him (John 3:2). This same argument that his works prove him to be that which he claimed to be was used by Himself. "The works that the Father has given me to accomplish, the very works that I am doing, bear witness about me that the Father has sent me" (John 5:36). But the stumbling block was that he had been crucified. Could he be truly the Messiah, who was spit upon, mocked, crowned with thorns, nailed to a cross? Was such an end in a shameful crucifixion not a sure evidence that he was not the One who was to possess glory and honor? The cross of Christ was the stumbling-block. But the Holy Spirit removes this and gives his answer.

The death of Jesus of Nazareth was by the determinate counsel and foreknowledge of God. The sufferings of the Messiah had been fully revealed in the Old Testament; he must suffer these things and so enter into glory. All had come to pass according to the foreknowledge of God. Eternally, from before the foundation of the world, God had made his plan and arranged all in his counsel. But Peter also shows that they were the guilty instruments. They by lawless men that is, the Gentiles, into whose hands they had delivered Jesus had crucified and slain Him. They were responsible for what had taken place. Thus the death of Christ is described.

But next follows the great climax, the resurrection of the One who had been slain.

God raised him up from the dead. By resurrection through God's power the final proof is given, yea, the highest proof, that Jesus of Nazareth is the Christ. It was impossible that he could be held by the power of death. In being raised from the dead the "pains of death" were loosed. He came forth as the Firstfruits, victor over death and the grave. His redeemed people can now shout: "O death, where is your victory? O death, where is your sting?" (1 Cor 15:55). The deliverance for them who through fear of death were all their lifetime subject to bondage (Heb 2:15) had come. Three great evidences are therefore given by Peter that Jesus of Nazareth is the Messiah: his life, his death, fulfilling what had been in the counsel and foreknowledge of God, his resurrection.

The quotation from the sixteenth Psalm follows. What mind of man could ever have discovered in that Psalm a prophecy about Christ? The Holy Spirit throws his light upon the Psalm. The Spirit who spoke through David had Christ in view. What David uttered he said *concerning Him.*" This ought to silence every "higher critic." All this needs no further explanation.

In this portion of his address Peter shows the path of Christ from humiliation to the death of the cross and his resurrection and all God's doings. In the next paragraph, the last part of the address of Peter, we behold him by God made Lord and Christ.

> The Man Jesus of Nazareth was by God demonstrated, *by God* wrought in among them, *by God's* counsel delivered to death, *by God* raised up, and finally *by God* made Lord and Christ.[20]
>
> "Brothers, I may say to you with confidence about the patriarch David that he both died and was buried, and his tomb is with us to this day. Being therefore a prophet, and knowing that

---

[20] Henry Alford, *The New Testament for English Readers* (London, U.K.: Rivingtons, 1863), 1:660.

God had sworn with an oath to him that he would set one of his descendants on his throne, he foresaw and spoke about the resurrection of the Christ, that he was not abandoned to Hades, nor did his flesh see corruption. This Jesus God raised up, and of that we all are witnesses. Being therefore exalted at the right hand of God, and having received from the Father the promise of the Holy Spirit, he has poured out this that you yourselves are seeing and hearing. For David did not ascend into the heavens, but he himself says,

"'The Lord said to my Lord, "Sit at my right hand, until I make your enemies your footstool."'"[21]

Let all the house of Israel therefore know for certain that God has made him both Lord and Christ, this Jesus whom you crucified." (vs. 29–36).

With these words Peter has reached the climax of his address. "Brothers," a Hebraism meaning simply "Brother and sisters," the same phrase he had used in addressing the waiting company before Pentecost, is how he addresses the gathered people. This loving expression shows how the Holy Spirit had filled him with love and how his heart was full of affection for his brothers according to the flesh. But he also is made very bold by the Spirit. His boldness, however, is not harshness, but characterized by tenderness; what he says is couched in humble and polite language. "Brothers, I may say to you with confidence" he addresses them on the matter of the prophecy already quoted from the sixteenth Psalm concerning "the patriarch David." Here alone David is called a patriarch because he is the progenitor of the kingly race. There was a reason for enlarging upon that prophecy, which becomes the foundation of his appeal. None of the rabbis ever thought of applying the Psalm to the promised Messiah. There is, however, an old tradition, which no doubt was known and believed in that day, which applied the Psalm literally to David. This application was as follows: "Those words, "my flesh also will dwell in hope," teach us that neither worm nor insect had any power over David." Peter shows that such a traditional belief that the words referred to David himself were incorrect. They could not mean King David. David had died and been buried (1 Kgs 2:10). Moses' burial place was not known, but the tomb (literally monument) of David was known amongst them in that day (Neh 3:16). David saw corruption. It was, therefore, impossible that the prophecy could mean him. But David was a prophet and as such he spoke, not of himself, but of the promised descendant, who was to come out of his loins to occupy his throne. The promised son of David was none other than the Christ. So, "seeing this before" by the Word of God (see the similar expression in Gal 3:8), he spoke concerning the resurrection of the Christ; in him alone were these words fulfilled.

And now comes Peter's witness and that of the eleven as well as the other assembled believers. "This Jesus God raised up, and of that we all are witnesses" (2:32). They had talked with Him, seen his body, knew that it was a real body of flesh and bones.[22] But Peter does not stop here with the fact of his resurrection. The Holy Spirit bears witness to an exaltation which human eyes had not beheld at that time. Stephen, Saul of Tarsus and the Apostle John were later privileged to behold the Christ in Glory. Here it is the direct witness of the Holy Spirit. This Jesus has been exalted by the right hand of God. The presence of the

---

[21] Psalm 110:1

[22] The perniciousness of the denial of the physical resurrection of our blessed Lord as taught in different evil "isms" (Millennial Dawn also called "International Bible Student Association") of the present day is fully laid bare in meditating on these words.

Holy Spirit, who had been poured forth, as they beheld and heard, was the evidence that Jesus was with the Father at the right hand of the Majesty on high.

Again the Holy Spirit turns to the Scriptures. How clearly he proves Himself on the day of his advent that he testifies in the Word and through the Word! he quotes now another Psalm, which was known among the Jews as prophesying about the Messiah. "For David did not ascend into the heavens, but he himself says, The Lord says to my Lord: Sit at my right hand, until I make your enemies your footstool" (Ps 110:1). This is the beginning of that sublime 110th Psalm. This Psalm our Lord had used to silence his enemies. His own testimony had brought out four indisputable facts about that Psalm.

1. That David wrote the Psalm.
2. That he wrote it by the Spirit.
3. That the Psalm spoke of Himself.
4. That it revealed Himself as both David's son and David's Lord (cf. Matt 22:41–46).

And now the Holy Spirit uses this Psalm likewise to show that the Christ had to ascend into heaven and take his place at the right hand of God till the time should come when his enemies are made his footstool. This exalted place Jesus the Nazarene had now taken; that he was really there was fully demonstrated by the outpouring of the Holy Spirit. But we must not overlook something else which this prophecy teaches. These Jews might have said, If Jesus of Nazareth is the Messiah, why does he not take the throne of his father David and begin his Kingdom reign? The 110th Psalm gives the answer. He was to go to heaven first and sit upon his Father's throne. He was to wait there for the promised Kingdom while his enemies are in opposition to Him. How perfect the Word of God is!

Here, then, was perfect proof, perfect evidence of the rejected One being the promised Messiah, raised from the dead, seated in Glory, waiting for the Kingdom, the throne of his father David. The Holy Spirit witnessed to all this.

Solemnly brief is the summing up and the appeal. "Let all the house of Israel therefore know for certain that God has made him both Lord and Christ, this Jesus whom you crucified" (2:36). The crucified One is Lord and Christ. This was the great theme of Peter's address on the day of Pentecost. And this is still the great and blessed theme of the Gospel, which, whenever it is preached, has the power of God with it: Christ died Christ arose Christ is Lord Christ is in Glory Christ is coming again.

4. THE RESULTS OF THE DELIVERED TESTIMONY (VS. 37–41).

> Now when they heard this they were cut to the heart, and said to Peter and the rest of the apostles, "Brothers, what shall we do?" And Peter said to them, "Repent and be baptized every one of you in the name of Jesus Christ for the forgiveness of your sins, and you will receive the gift of the Holy Spirit. For the promise is for you and for your children and for all who are far off, everyone whom the Lord our God calls to himself." And with many other words he bore witness and continued to exhort them, saying, "Save yourselves from this crooked generation." So those who received his word were baptized, and there were added that day about three thousand souls. (vs. 37–41).

Such were the wonderful results. It could not be otherwise. The Word had been preached. The Holy Spirit carried it home with convicting power to the hearts of the hearers. Before his ascension the Lord had left the promise to his disciples that they were to receive power with the gift of the Spirit. This power to witness had been bestowed upon the disciples and was fully manifested in Peter's bold testimony. The Holy Spirit backed it with his mighty power and the hearts and consciences of the hearers were pierced. They were convicted, after hearing all these words, of the great sin which had been committed by them in the rejection of Jesus. The guilt had been fully demonstrated, and now they cried out in terror: "Brothers, what shall we do?"

There is not a moment's delay in answering the great question. The divinely given instruction comes at once from Peter's lips. Repentance and baptism stand out very prominently in this answer to the conscience-stricken Jews, and attached to it is the promise of the remission of sins and the gift of the Holy Spirit. These words not being correctly understood, have led to much confusion. Upon these words doctrines, especially concerning water baptism, have been built, which are not alone nowhere else taught in the Bible, but which are opposed to the Gospel. The words of Peter to his Jewish brethren have been used to make water-baptism a saving ordinance, that only by submission to water-baptism, with repentance and faith in the Lord Jesus, can remission of sins and the gift of the Holy Spirit be obtained. We do not enlarge upon these unscriptural conceptions nor controvert the utterly false doctrine of "baptismal regeneration," but rather, point out briefly what these words of Peter mean. We must bear in mind that Peter addressed those who had *openly* rejected Jesus. They had, therefore, also openly to acknowledge their wrong and thus openly own him as Messiah, whom they had disowned by delivering him into the hands of lawless men. Repentance meant for them to own their guilt in having opposed and rejected Jesus. Baptism in the name of Jesus Christ (in which it differs from the baptism of John) was the outward expression of that repentance. It was for these Jews, therefore, a preliminary necessity. And here we must not forget that Peter's preaching on the day of Pentecost had it still to do with the kingdom, as we shall more fully learn from his second address in the third chapter. Another offer of the kingdom was made to the nation. The great fact that the Holy Spirit had begun to form the body of Christ, the church, as stated before, was not revealed then. In this national testimony the word "repent" stands in the foreground, and their baptism in the name of him whom they had crucified was a witness that they owned him now and believed on Him. As soon as we leave the first part of this book in which Peter's preaching to the Jews is prominent, we find the word repentance no longer in the foreground; all the emphasis is upon "believe." [23] The Gospel in all its blessed fullness as revealed to the great apostle to the Gentiles, Paul, which he called "my Gospel," and as preached by him, makes "faith" "believe" as prominent as Peter's preaching "repent."

Remission of sins and the gift of the Holy Spirit comes by faith in the Lord Jesus Christ. In connection with the Jews, baptism was a condition. There is no such condition for Gentiles. The case of Cornelius and those who were assembled in his house to whom Peter preached the Gospel, illustrates this fully. He had not mentioned a word about baptism for the remission of sins and the gift of the Holy Spirit. When he had declared that through "his Name" whosoever believeth in him shall receive remission of sins, his address was cut short: "the Holy Spirit fell on all who heard the word" (10:44). This clearly proves that baptism in water has nothing to do with the gift of the Holy Spirit to these believing Gentiles. Water baptism followed in their case. He commanded them to be baptized in the name of the Lord. "For the Jews who had openly rejected the Lord,

---

[23] Of course faith and repentance are inseparably connected.

4. Pool of Siloam (John 9:11), discovered in 2004. Currently over 20 steps have been excavated leading down into the Pool. Some scholars believe that this was used as a *mikvah* (ritual purity bath). This was one location where 3,000 people could easily be baptized on the day of Pentecost.

baptism is always pre-requisite; they must openly Own him whom they had disowned." The entire setting aside of ordinances in the case of the Gentiles at once destroys the ritualistic teaching as to baptism. According to this ritualistic teaching Cornelius must have received the Spirit while in an unregenerate condition, for he had not yet received "the sacrament of regeneration!"[24]

Peter told his hearers that the promise (remission of sins and the gift of the Spirit) is for them and their children. Blessed assurance to them and their offspring! Theirs are still the promises (Rom 9:1–5). In a future day the Spirit will be poured out upon them, after their great national repentance, when they will mourn for him (Zech 12:9–14; Ezekiel 39:29). But the promise is also to them who are afar off, as many as the Lord Our God shall call. Those afar off are the Gentiles. Peter, no doubt, could not fully realize the far-reaching meaning of this utterance. The Holy Spirit put these words into his mouth, but Peter did not understand then that the far-off Gentiles were to participate in the gift of the Spirit and become fellow heirs. To make it possible for him to go to the Gentiles the Lord had to give him a special vision. But the statement that the promise is to those who are far off, to as many as the Lord shall call, is otherwise significant. It shows that not all the Gentiles are to be brought into the one body, that not all the Gentiles will accept God's gracious offer during the age which began with Pentecost. Those who received the word were baptized and in that day about three thousand were added (see Fig. 4).

It is not correct to speak of this as a fulfillment of the prediction in Psalm 110, as it has been done repeatedly. There it says: "Your people will offer themselves freely on the day of your power" (Ps 110:3). The day of Pentecost was not that promised "day of . . . power." Nor is this age the age when he manifests his power. When he returns in power and in glory, the day of his power begins and then his earthly people will be a willing people. What took place on Pentecost was only the earnest of what shall yet take place amongst that nation.

5. THE GATHERED COMPANY IN FELLOWSHIP (VS. 42–47).

And they devoted themselves to the apostles' teaching and the fellowship, to the breaking of bread and the prayers. And awe [25] came upon every soul, and many wonders and signs were

---

[24] Frederick W. Grant, *The Numerical Bible: Acts to 2 Corinthians* (New York, N.Y.: Loizeaux Brothers, 1978), 2:24.

---

[25] Or *fear*

being done through the apostles. And all who believed were together and had all things in common. And they were selling their possessions and belongings and distributing the proceeds to all, as any had need. And day by day, attending the temple together and breaking bread in their homes, they received their food with glad and generous hearts, praising God and having favor with all the people. And the Lord added to their number day by day those who were being saved. (vs. 42–47).

About three thousand had been added. We ask, added to what? Certainly to the company of the believers, which by the baptism of the Holy Spirit had been formed into one body. And now we learn at the close of this great chapter, that the church, or assembly, yet unrevealed, was indeed in existence. It is a most precious scene which is pictured to us in the above words. It shows the energy of the Holy Spirit in uniting these believers into one body, gathered together around the blessed person of the Lord. While Peter gave that great testimony to the people, concerning the rejected, crucified and risen Jesus, that he is Lord and Christ, those who repented, having believed the message, were added by the Spirit to the body.

In the foreground of the description of this happy, gathered company stands the fact that they "devoted themselves to the apostles' teaching." There was need of instruction and the Lord had given command that the apostles were to teach (Matt 28:20). The teaching of the apostles must, of course, have been concerning the Lord Jesus Christ. They were, as revealed later, the foundation of the great spiritual building (Eph 2:20). That teaching is placed in the first place shows its great importance. True fellowship and prayer as well as right living, is only possible in the truth. Throughout the Epistles, which concern the church, doctrine is always the first thing. One of the last exhortations the Holy Spirit gave through Paul, is an exhortation to be true to right teaching. "Follow the pattern of the sound words that you have heard from me, in the faith and love that are in Christ Jesus" (2 Tim 1:13). Almost one of the last words in this Epistle Paul wrote from the Roman prison predicts the departure from the doctrine of Christ.

> For the time is coming when people will not endure sound teaching, but having itching ears they will accumulate for themselves teachers to suit their own passions, and will turn away from listening to the truth and wander off into myths (2 Tim 4:3–4).

This is exactly what we see about us in the present day. An unrecoverable apostasy has set in and the true doctrine, the faith delivered to the saints, has been given up. In accepting the teaching of the apostles they were in fellowship together. But the fellowship which they possessed and enjoyed was expressed in a special way. It was expressed "in the breaking of bread." Some expositors of this book make this "breaking of bread" a common meal.

A learned expositor, after a lengthy discussion on the phrase "breaking of bread," as used by the Jews, concludes by saying,

> "The breaking of bread must not be understood by their eating together, but of the Eucharist (the Lord's Supper); which the Syriac interpreter does render so in express terms; a parallel to which we have in 1 Corinthians 10:16 and Acts 20:7."

It was the carrying out of the request which the blessed Lord had uttered during that memorable night in the presence of his disciples, "Do this in remembrance of Me." It is significant that we find this mentioned at once in this great historical book. The Holy Spirit having come to glorify Christ, did exactly what the Lord had foretold.

> But the Helper, the Holy Spirit, whom the Father will send in my name, he will teach you all things and bring to your remembrance all that I have said to you (John 14:26).

One of the first things he brought to the remembrance of the disciples was the loving, tender request the Lord had made when he had broken the bread, foretelling the giving of his holy body, and handed them the cup filled with wine, the emblem of the precious blood to be shed. At that time they knew not what it all meant. But now the sufferings were ended; Christ had risen from the dead and returned to the Father. The Holy Spirit had come and opened their understanding. United by him they met, as it seems for a time at least, daily, to break the bread and to pass the cup in remembrance of the Lord Jesus Christ. Inasmuch as the Holy Spirit led to this at once he signified by it how pleasing it is to him to remember the dying love of the Son of God.

And if we had been there we would have beheld a simple gathering. No long robed priests officiating, no preparatory service, no ritual; nothing of the other things which tradition has connected with communion and by which the request of the Lord has been so completely obscured. They were just together praising God; exercising their holy priesthood by giving thanks in his Name. Then someone, moved by the Holy Spirit would arise and give thanks and break the bread, of which all partook, and the same was done with the cup, which passed from hand to hand.

It must have been this breaking of bread which kept them close to the Lord and which kept his Person and his great love ever fresh before their hearts. There is no command given anywhere how often the Lord's supper is to be observed. Elsewhere we find that they came together on the first day of the week to break bread (20:7). No doubt that was the custom in the assemblies at that time. Is it too much to carry out his loving request every Lord's Day, the day on which he left the grave? It is a sad evidence of the spiritual condition of Christendom, the way the request of the Lord is ignored. How grieving this must be to the Spirit of God. And what shall one say of such, who had the knowledge of the preciousness and simplicity of all this and who have given up the Lord's Supper altogether because they believe it is *an ordinance of the Kingdom.*

Then prayer is mentioned. They had their prayer meetings in which they prayed to God in the name of the Lord Jesus Christ. "And fear came upon every soul." The power of God was manifested in the gathered company; besides this many signs and wonders were wrought through the Apostles.

Then we find something additional. They had all things common and sold their possessions and goods. This was peculiar to Jerusalem and was an additional testimony to the existence of the one body, that they were members one of another. It was like a great happy family, which in reality they were through the Grace of God. It has often been attempted to reproduce these conditions, which has invariably led to great failure and dishonor to the Lord and the cause of Christ. All this was perfectly in order in the beginning in Jerusalem. We believe it was arranged just in that way to give at once the strongest possible picture of that into which the united gathered company had been formed one body.

They also went to the temple with one accord. In this they fulfilled but their great mission of being a testimony to the nation. The breaking of bread, however, was carried on from house to house; in this respect they were outside of the camp.

And how happy they were! They had Christ, and that was enough. No system of theology, creeds, set of forms or any such thing, with which historical Christianity abounds "Nothing but Christ." They received their food with gladness and singleness of heart, praising God and having favor with all the people. Joy and singleness of heart are the two great characteristics of the true believer.

The good work went on. Many more were added to the assembly. They were added not by the efforts of themselves, by all kinds of methods, as it is done in our days to increase "church membership," but the Lord added to the assembly. He alone can add to that body of which he Himself is the head. Some have translated "Added daily those being saved." There is no need of doing this. It is correct "added to their number day by day those who were being saved." All those who were added by the Lord daily were true believers and as such they were saved. And yet they also were to be saved. The clouds of judgment were fast gathering over Jerusalem and over the nation; all who were added to the assembly were to be saved out of the judgment soon to fall upon that nation.

Thus ends the great and blessed chapter, the historical record of the advent of the Holy Spirit and the empowerment of the church.

CHAPTER THREE

After the outpouring of the Holy Spirit upon the church on earth we find in this book the record of a second address given by the Apostle Peter. This utterance is Jewish and national, that is, an appeal to the nation to repent and to accept the rejected Jesus as the Christ. Connected with this solemn appeal is the promise of national blessing. Peter promises by the Spirit of God "times of refreshing" and "the restitution of all things," two expressions, which describe the kingdom as promised to Israel in the Old Testament. The condition upon which this promise of baptismal blessing is made by Peter is the repentance and conversion of the nation. The second coming of the Lord Jesus is likewise mentioned by the Apostle. His second coming will result in the times of refreshing, and the restitution of all things. This other testimony was occasioned by the healing of the lame man. But we must look at all this more closely.

The chapter is clearly divided into two parts: The healing of the lame man The address of Peter. The first verses of the fourth chapter belong to the third chapter. We make therefore the following division:

1. The healing of the lame man (Ch. 3:1–10).
2. Peter's address and appeal (vs. 11–26).
3. Their arrest (ch. 4:1–3).
4. The blessed results of the given testimony (ch. 4:4).

We take up each of these sections separately to point out some of the leading features.

1. THE HEALING OF THE LAME MAN (VS. 1–10).

> Now Peter and John were going up to the temple at the hour of prayer, the ninth hour.[1] And a man lame from birth was being carried, whom they laid daily at the gate of the temple that is called the Beautiful Gate to ask alms of those entering the temple. Seeing Peter and John about to go into the temple, he asked to receive alms. (vs. 1–3).

It is not stated when this occurred. It could have been hardly on the same day on which the Holy Spirit came; it must have been a short time afterwards. Peter appears again upon the foreground as the leader. Though John was with him, there is no record of a single word which he spoke. Later we read once more of John when he went with Peter to Samaria. If a human pen had written the Acts of the Apostles, John, no doubt, would have been more frequently mentioned.[2]

Peter was the chosen instrument to preach the Gospel to the circumcision and deliver to the nation this new message of repentance. He is the leading figure throughout the first part of the Book of Acts. Both Peter and John went together into the temple. Though the Holy Spirit had come and filled them and separated them from the nation as such, giving them a new

---

[1] That is, 3 p.m.

[2] This is the case in "The Mythological Acts of the Apostles," as old work composed of traditions concerning the Apostles.

The Acts of the Apostles

5. A reconstruction of the gate from a model of the temple in Jerusalem. The Golden Gate (the beautiful Gate) is indicated as the entrance to the outer court.

position, yet they still continued in their Jewish customs and observances. All this was for a purpose as long as God's mercy lingered over Jerusalem. The hour when they went up was the ninth hour, three in the afternoon, the usual hour for sacrifice and prayer. The people assembled for this purpose in the part of the temple called "the Court of the Women," because women were only permitted to go so far and were never allowed to go beyond. This court, 135 cubits square, was generally thronged with people at the ninth hour. The entrance to it was through a magnificent gate covered with bronze. To this place the Apostles went.

At the same time a lame man, who had been in this condition from his birth, was being carried towards that beautiful gate. There they laid him down in his helpless condition that he might beg from those who entered in. Daily he was to be seen; most likely for many years had he been there. Then he must have seen the Lord as he went to the temple and the miracles he did; yet this helpless beggar had not been healed. He reminds us vividly of that other lame man, who laid in the five porches and whom the Lord healed (John 5). From the chapter which follows we learn that this lame man at the temple gate was forty years old. His condition and position is typical of the moral condition of the nation. Like this man, Israel was helpless with all its beautiful religious ceremonies, laying outside, with no strength to enter in. The age of the lame man finds a similar application; forty is the number of testing. The nation's condition as helpless, unable to walk in the statutes and laws of God, without strength, outside, and a beggar, is therefore fully picture in this lame man.

And Peter directed his gaze at him, as did John, and said, "Look at us." And he fixed his attention on them, expecting to receive something from them. But Peter said, "I have no silver and gold, but what I do have I give to you. In the name of Jesus Christ of Nazareth, rise up and walk!" And he took him by the right hand and raised him up, and immediately his feet and ankles were made strong. And leaping up he stood and began to walk, and entered the temple with them, walking and leaping and praising God. And all the people saw him walking and praising God, and recognized him as the one who sat at the Beautiful Gate of the temple, asking for alms. And they were filled with wonder and amazement at what had happened to him. (vs. 4–10).

The beggar had stretched out his hands to receive something from the two apostles. What prompted Peter and John to notice this lame man among the many others, who were there begging as he did, is not mentioned. Some have suggested that there was a special look and appeal in his eyes which attracted the two servants of the Lord. Did perhaps the lame man recognize them from former visits to the temple when they came as the followers of Jesus of Nazareth? We believe it was the Holy Spirit who directed Peter and John to look steadfastly upon him. The glorified Christ was about to act in his gracious power; the two apostles filled with his Spirit were his chosen and willing instruments.

Peter's word had been, "look at us." Obediently, the eyes of the lame man rest upon them. His expectation up to this point was to receive some help from their hands. He was indeed to receive something, but a far greater gift than he could have imagined. Silver and gold Peter declared he had not, but he had something else in store for him. He now speaks in that blessed Name, which is above every other Name, in the Name of Jesus Christ, the Nazarene, to rise up and to walk. It was then that faith was exercised by the lame man in that Name. The power of God is at once manifested. Peter takes hold of him and raised him up and immediately, not gradually, but without a moment's delay, his feet and ankle bones were made strong. The power of God in answer to that precious Name had come upon the lame man and he was instantly healed. He then walked and leaped and entered through the beautiful gate as a worshipper into the temple to praise God. What a sight it must have been!

But why was this miracle wrought at this time? It was wrought as another evidence for the unbelieving people that Jesus of Nazareth, whom they had rejected and delivered into the hands of the Gentiles, is the Messiah and their King. It was an evidence that he who hung on the cross and had been laid into the tomb is living in heaven and that God's omnipotent power was revealed in answer to that Name whom they had hated without a cause. God had promised to Israel his people a Kingdom, the blessings and glories of which prophet after prophet had announced. It was not to be a spiritual Kingdom, but a literal one, with the King of Righteousness ruling in the midst of them. One great Kingdom prophecy in the Old Testament mentions the lame man, too. "Then shall the lame man leap like a deer" (Isa 35:6). When the King, the Son of David, the Immanuel, had appeared in their midst, preaching the nearness of that kingdom, he manifested his kingly divine power, and the blind saw, the deaf heard and the lame walked. The people rejected Him. And now once more an offer of that Kingdom is to be made to the people. But before the Apostle Peter gives the message he received from the Lord, the rejected One, who had taken his place upon his Father's throne manifests his power once more in the healing of the lame man.

6. Solomon's Colonnade (Also called a Protico or Porch) was a covered hallway that ran along the inner side of the Court of the Gentiles outside the Temple. It had 27 foot-high columns with the roof made of cedar.

And as this lame man had been perfectly healed, that he not alone walked, but leaped, with songs of praises on his lips, entering the temple, so the Lord was ready and willing to heal his people. The lame man so wonderfully healed, leaping and praising God, is a picture of what the whole nation will be in a future day, when they will look upon him whom they have pierced (Zech 12:10). God's promise to them, still unfulfilled, is: "And I will put my Spirit within you, and cause you to walk in my statutes and be careful to obey my rules[3]" (Ezek 36:27). Then will the remnant of his people break forth in singing.

> You[4] will say in that day: "I will give thanks to you, O Lord, for though you were angry with me, your anger turned away, that you might comfort me. "Behold, God is my salvation; I will trust, and will not be afraid; for the Lord God[5] is my strength and my song, and he has become my salvation (Isa 12:1-2)... And the ransomed of the Lord shall return and come to Zion with singing; everlasting joy shall be upon their heads; they shall obtain gladness and joy, and sorrow and sighing shall flee away (Isa 35:10).

The commotion in the temple was great after this miracle had taken place. There could be no mistake about it. The man who had been healed was too well known by the multitude. They recognized him at once. It was the same familiar face, which they had seen again and again at the temple gate. What a change had taken place! his helplessness was completely removed and he leaped along. Instead of the miserable cry of the mendicant, his lips shouted the praises of God. A large multitude came together, greatly wondering. And now Peter opens his lips to speak to the people.

2. PETER'S SECOND ADDRESS (VS. 11–16).

> While he clung to Peter and John, all the people, utterly astounded, ran together to them in the portico called Solomon's. And when Peter saw it he addressed the people: "Men of Israel, why do you wonder at this, or why do you stare at us, as though by our own power or piety we have made him walk? The God of Abraham, the God of Isaac, and the God of Jacob, the God of our fathers, glorified his servant[6] Jesus, whom you delivered over and denied in the presence of Pilate, when he had decided to release him. But you denied the Holy and Righteous One, and asked for a murderer to be granted to you, and you killed the Author of life, whom God raised from the dead. To this we are witnesses. And his name—by faith in his name—has made this man strong whom you see and know, and the faith that is through Jesus[7] has given the man this perfect health in the presence of you all. (vs. 11–16).

This second address of Peter is characterized by a great calmness. He was not carried away by the great excitement of the astonished multitude. He does not see why they should be astonished at what had happened to the lame man. For some time greater miracles than the healing of the blind man had been wrought in the midst of them. One had walked among them who had rebuked the demons, opened the eyes

---

[3] Or *my just decrees*
[4] The Hebrew for *you* is singular in verse 1.
[5] Hebrew for *Yah*, the Lord

[6] Or *child*; also verse 26
[7] Greek *him*

of the blind, healed all manners of diseases and raised the dead. Why should they be so astonished at the healing of the lame man?

But they not only gazed with astonishment upon the healed beggar, they also looked with wondering eyes upon the apostles themselves, as if they themselves by their own power or worth performed the healing. This, Peter disclaims. It was God Himself, who had glorified his servant Jesus in the healing of this man. Every word Peter utters, inbreathed by the Holy Spirit, shows the national Jewish character of the address. The Apostle does not speak of God as the Father of the Lord Jesus Christ, but as the God of Abraham, and of Isaac and Jacob. This is God's Name in connection with his covenant people. In vain do we look for this name of God in the rest of the New Testament. For us, as believers, God's Name is revealed as "Our God and our Father, the God and Father of our Lord Jesus Christ." Then of the Lord, Peter speaks as "his Son Jesus." Peter, indeed, knew the Lord as the Son of the living God, for he had confessed him thus at Caesarea Philippi. It was reserved for another Apostle to make known the full Glory and Sonship, both eternal and by resurrection from the dead, that is, through the Apostle Paul. The first time we find the Lord Jesus Christ preached as Son of God is in Acts 9:20, and the converted Saul of Tarsus is the preacher. In connection with the earth and his people Israel, the Lord is the servant of God. As such he Was predicted and described by Isaiah (ch. 53) and other prophets. That servant had been in the midst of his people and Jesus, the Nazarene, was that servant. The God of their Fathers had witnessed to it by healing the lame man; in it God had glorified his servant Jesus. But what had they done to that Servant of the Lord? All their guilt is flashed forth once more. They had delivered Him, and though a Gentile, convinced of his innocence, wanted to let him go, they had denied Him. That Servant of God was more than innocent, the Holy One and the Righteous One he was and they had denied such a one and chosen a murderer in his place; the Author of Life (Greek: the originator of life; what a title of our blessed Lord!) they had slain. The entire story of their wickedness and guilt is briefly rehearsed and pressed home to their hearts by the Holy Spirit. Could anyone of them deny these historical facts?

It is a significant fact that at this time many attempts are being made by the Jews to shift the responsibility of the crucifixion of the Lord Jesus Christ upon someone else. The strange thing is that rabbis who attempt to disprove the New Testament record of the part the Jewish people played in the death of the Lord are sometimes admitted into evangelical churches to lay their arguments before Christian people. Recently we received a pamphlet from a rabbi, in which an attempt is made to show that the Jewish people at that time had no share in the death of Christ. Instead of confessing the sin of the nation and the sin of the rejection of the Holy One they try to justify themselves. But the day will come when they will truly mourn for him as one mourneth for an only son (Zech 12:11–13).

Peter likewise refers to the resurrection. God had raised him from the dead and they were the witnesses of his resurrection. Then we hear of his Name as the power which had made the man strong and gave to him this complete soundness. The power of God had therefore been witnessed by them.

Here we mention briefly the fact that healing of this kind was perfectly in order in connection with the preaching we have here. Nowhere do we read that in connection with the church the gift of healing should be continued. That the Lord has the same power to heal, that his Name is as powerful as ever, none can doubt.

> And now, brothers, I know that you acted in ignorance, as did also your rulers. But what God foretold by the mouth of all the prophets, that his Christ would suffer, he thus fulfilled. (vs. 17–18).

What tenderness and mercy breathe in these words! he addresses them as brethren, but in a different sense as the word brethren is used in the church Epistles. As a member of the same nation Peter addressed them thus and offers them mercy. Their guilt could not be denied. All was true what Peter had just uttered; but God in his great mercy is ready to treat their great sin as a sin of ignorance. The Lord had prayed on the cross, "Father, forgive them, for they know not what they do." And God was now ready to answer this prayer. The application of the Cities of Refuge, to which one who had slain a man unwittingly could flee, can easily be made (Joshua 20). Though they had cried: "his blood be upon us and our children," God, in his mercy, delayed the carrying out of this awful wish, uttered by them in their blindness. If they accepted this offered mercy, all their guilt would have been wiped out, but if they rejected and did not repent of what they had done, they set themselves willfully against God and him whom he had sent. And Peter now makes his appeal and gives them the promise of God's mercy.

> Repent therefore, and turn back, that your sins may be blotted out, that times of refreshing may come from the presence of the Lord, and that he may send the Christ appointed for you, Jesus, whom heaven must receive until the time for restoring all the things about which God spoke by the mouth of his holy prophets long ago (vs. 19–21).

These are very interesting words and of great importance. They can only be understood in the right way if we do not lose sight of the fact to whom they were addressed, that is to Jews, and not to Gentiles. They are the heart of this discourse, and as such a God-given appeal and promise to the nation. If this is lost sight of, the words must lose their right meaning. The repentance which is demanded of them is an acknowledgment of the wrong they had done in denying the Holy and righteous One, a confession of their blood-guiltiness in having slain the author of life. This, of course, would result in their conversion and the blotting out of their sins as a nation. This God had promised before to the nation. "I, I am he who blots out your transgressions for my own sake, and I will not remember your sins" (Isa 43:25). Anticipating that glorious day in which this shall be accomplished, a day still to come, the prophet spoke the following glorious words:

> I have blotted out your transgressions like a cloud and your sins like mist; return to me, for I have redeemed you. Sing, O heavens, for the Lord has done it; shout, O depths of the earth; break forth into singing, O mountains, O forest, and every tree in it! For the Lord has redeemed Jacob, and will be glorified[8] in Israel (Isa 44:22–23).

It is significant that in his second address Peter has nothing more to say about the gift of the Holy Spirit. This is in perfect keeping with the scope of his address. It being national, the blotting out of the sins of that people is mentioned first, and in the next place, the times of refreshing and the second coming of the same Jesus who had been received into heaven. The Holy Spirit had been given and that for the empowerment of the church, the body of Christ. The present address of Peter has it to do exclusively with the nation and their future, therefore the Holy Spirit, as he came on the day of Pentecost, is not mentioned. However, the promise of the Spirit in a future outpouring upon that nation is included in the promise, "the times of refreshing" (3:19 KJV).

This term means a future time of blessing which is in store for God's earthly people. The other expression used, "the

---

[8] Or *will display his beauty*

time for restoring all the things" (3:21) means practically the same as the times of refreshing. In these two expressions the Holy Spirit gathers together the hundreds of promises he gave through the different prophets of God, concerning a time of great blessing for his people and through them for the nations of the world. It would be impossible to mention all these promises and in what the times of refreshing and restoration of all things consist. These days of a coming age, the kingdom age, or as we call it, because its duration will be a thousand years, the Millennium, are fully described on the pages of Old Testament prophecy. Not alone will the nation be blessed, but Jerusalem will be a great city, the land will be restored and become the great center for blessing; the nations of the earth will receive blessing and groaning creation will be delivered from its groaning, and the curse which rests upon it. If we interpret the Word of Prophecy literally and cease spiritualizing it, we shall have no difficulty to behold the full meaning of the times of refreshing and the restitution of all things. The latter word does not include a restoration of the wicked dead, a second chance for those who passed out of this life in an unsaved condition. A false teaching refers to this passage as one of the arguments for the restoration of the wicked dead, including even Sodom and Gomorrah. But when did ever a prophet of God teach the restitution of the wicked dead? The prophets predicted the restoration of all things, but that restoration is clearly defined as concerning the things on the earth and not the beings which have passed out of this life.

Not only in the Old Testament do we find a description of what is to come for Israel, the nations and creation, but elsewhere in the New Testament these times of refreshing and restoration of all things are clearly indicated. See Matthew 19:28; Romans 8:19–23; Ephesians 1:10, etc. But between these two words of promise of what shall be Israel's portion if they repent, stands another fact: It is the second coming of Jesus Christ. This is a great fundamental passage of that great doctrine, the second coming of Christ. Peter declares that God is going to send Jesus Christ. This must mean a second coming. To teach this in the clearest manner, he adds that the heavens received Him, but they will not retain him forever. He has gone into the heavens *till* the true restoration of all things comes. The second coming of Christ will result in the times of refreshing and restoration of all things. This event is, of course, his visible and glorious coming back to earth again, to the Mount of Olives (see Fig. 1) from where he ascended, and for the deliverance and blessing of his earthly people. The coming of the Lord for his church as revealed through the Apostle Paul in 1 Thessalonians 4:13–18 must be distinguished from this visible return to the earth. The resurrected and living saints will be caught up together in clouds to meet the Lord in the air, into which the Lord descends when he redeems his promise to his own: "I will come again and will take you to myself" (John 14:3). Of this Peter had no knowledge at all when he delivered this testimony to the nation. What he speaks of is the coming of Christ in power and glory to establish his Kingdom in the midst of his people to extend over the entire earth, so that the knowledge of the glory of the Lord shall cover the earth as the waters the deep. Of that coming prophets had spoken again and again. Indeed, it is impossible to separate in the prophetic Word the blessings promised for Israel, the nations and creation and the coming of Christ in glory as the King of kings.

All this is so plain that it seems almost impossible for any man not to see the teaching of the premillennial coming of Christ, that there can be no age of blessing, no millennium, before Christ has returned. And yet one of the most learned men and Bible expositor, Dr. John Lightfoot, labors hard to explain away the literal coming of Christ, whom the heavens received. The words of this learned man are the weakest we have ever seen. He says in his *Horae Hebraeicae* on this passage the following:

> "Was that Jesus, whom we have crucified, the true Christ? (The Jews would ask after hearing Peter). Then is all our hope for refreshing by the Messiah vanished, because he Himself is vanished and gone. Then our expectation as to the consolation of Israel is at an end, because he who should be our consolation is perished. Not so (says Peter) but the Messiah, and the refreshing by Him, shall be restored to you if you will repent; yet so that he Himself shall continue in heaven. He shall be sent to you in his refreshing and consolatory Word, and in his benefits if you repent."

This great scholar allowed himself a great liberty with the Word of God and teaches the very opposite which Peter spoke to the nation.

The offer of God through Peter and his message to the nation contains the great revealed purposes of God, as spoken by the mouth of his prophets since time began. Sometimes it is asked, What would have happened if the nation had then repented? Undoubtedly all would then have come to pass. In rapid succession all the events preceding the return of the Lord as recorded in the prophets Would have come to pass and then he would have come and brought the restoration of all things. This, however, was not in the purpose of God. He knew that Israel would reject this offer. The Lord had predicted it likewise. The prophets spoke of the dispersion of the nation and a long period of judgment for them.

This period is the present age, during which Israel is set aside nationally, and at the same time God calls out a people for his Name from the Gentiles, that is the church. This may end at any time. We are living in significant days, surrounded by signs which herald the speedy ending of this present age. Then, once more, after the completion and removal of the church from earth, will Israel hear the message concerning the Kingdom. There will then be the repentance of a national remnant, the return of the Lord Jesus Christ and the times of refreshing and restoration of all things as the result of his coming.

> Moses said, "The Lord God will raise up for you a prophet like me from your brothers. You shall listen to him in whatever he tells you. And it shall be that every soul who does not listen to that prophet shall be destroyed from the people."[9] And all the prophets who have spoken, from Samuel and those who came after him, also proclaimed these days. You are the sons of the prophets and of the covenant that God made with your fathers, saying to Abraham, "And in your offspring shall all the families of the earth be blessed."[10] God, having raised up his servant, sent him to you first, to bless you by turning every one of you from your wickedness. (vs. 22–26).

Next Peter mentions Moses, whom the nation held in such great reverence that they called him, and still do so, "Moses our teacher." Moses had spoken in Deuteronomy of another prophet whom the Lord would raise up. God promised that he would put his words into the mouth of the prophet. "And whoever will not listen to my words that he shall speak in my name, I myself will require it of him" (Deut 18:19). The one of whom Moses spoke, one greater than himself, was none other than Christ. That prophet had spoken and they had not heard. The threatening Word of the Lord was over them as a nation.

Then he reminds them of the testimonies of the prophets beginning with Samuel, who all had announced these days. He closes with an appeal, telling them that they are the sons of the prophets and of the

---

[9] Deut 18:15, 18, 19.
[10] Gen 22:18; 26:4.

covenant and that it is first to them that God had raised his servant up. He was ready to bless them and turn every one from their iniquity.

This second address of Peter is much shorter than the one delivered by him on the day of Pentecost and yet the brief words, which took a few minutes to deliver, contain the greatest truths. The Name of the Lord is mentioned by Peter in seven different forms: As the Son of God, The Holy One, The Righteous One, The Author of Life, The Christ of God, The Prophet and The Seed of Abraham. Repentance, Conversion, the Blotting out of sins, the second coming of Christ, the coming age and its blessing, besides the suffering, death and resurrection of the Lord Jesus Christ are stated.

But would they heed these solemn words? Do we hear the multitude crying out, "What shall we do?" Do they bow in true repentance? The address of Peter and the words of John, which the Holy Spirit has not put on record, were not finished, when an interruption took place. While they were yet speaking something happened. This we read in the next paragraph, with which the fourth chapter begins.

3. THEIR ARREST (4:1–3).

> And as they were speaking to the people, the priests and the captain of the temple and the Sadducees came upon them, greatly annoyed because they were teaching the people and proclaiming in Jesus the resurrection from the dead. And they arrested them and put them in custody until the next day, for it was already evening (ch. 4:1–3).

The large number of people, the news of the healing of the lame man and that the two men were addressing the people in Solomon's porch, attracted the attention of the priests and the captain of the temple. The latter was a leading figure in the temple with much authority; it is probable that he had a rank next to the high priest. The enemy begins now his acts and the first indication is given that the offer God's mercy was making to the nation would not be accepted. The Holy Spirit was acting mightily through the spoken Word, but these ecclesiastical leaders were hardening their hearts against the Word and the Spirit of God. The hate against that blessed Name broke out anew under the satanic power to which they had yielded. Soon it became evident that blindness is to become their portion. And the Sadducees came too. Though not much has been said on the resurrection, yet these rationalists, or as we would call them today, "higher critics," were much distressed because they preached Jesus and the resurrection. The next step is the arrest and imprisonment of the two apostles. Rough hands seize them. Persecution began. Of the Apostles we read nothing else. They submitted. The power of the Holy Spirit now manifested itself in a new way with them. They could suffer and perhaps with great joy, in perfect peace, they allowed themselves to be taken away.

4. THE RESULT OF THE TESTIMONY (4:4).

> But many of those who had heard the word believed, and the number of the men came to about five thousand (v. 4).

Their labor had not been in vain. God's power had accompanied the Word; a remnant heard and believed. The men are numbered and that is specifically a Jewish thing and a feature of the Kingdom. This is the last time that the converts are numbered. There can be no numbering in this church age; no one knows the number of the members of the body of Christ, but God only. The numbering is only on Kingdom ground.

Chapter Four

The first few verses of this chapter giving the record of the arrest of the Apostles we expounded in connection with the third chapter to which they properly belong. What became of Peter and John, their appearing before the ecclesiastical authorities and final release, their return to their own company is given in the rest of this chapter. We meditate on it briefly, dividing the chapter into five parts.

1. Peter and John before the rulers, elders, scribes and high-priestly family (vs. 5–7).

2. Peter's bold witness (vs. 8–12).

3. The astonishment of the Sanhedrin, the release of the Apostles (vs. 13–22).

4. With their own company, their praise and prayer (vs. 23–31).

5. The saved multitude one heart and one soul (vs. 32–37).

1. Peter and John before the Rulers (vs. 5–7).

> On the next day their rulers and elders and scribes gathered together in Jerusalem, with Annas the high priest and Caiaphas and John and Alexander, and all who were of the high-priestly family. And when they had set them in the midst, they inquired, "By what power or by what name did you do this?" (vs. 5–7).

The company before whom they were to appear was the Sanhedrin, the same before which the Lord had also appeared. They were gathered in Jerusalem; perhaps the different members which were some distance from the city were summoned to meet in the city. Besides Annas and Caiaphas, John and Alexander are mentioned. Nothing definite is known about these two persons. They were most likely relations of the high priest. Another view is that the John mentioned is a priest who was famous at that time, Rabban Jochanan Ben Zaccai. He lived to a very old age, and it is said of him that forty years before the destruction of Jerusalem, when the gates of the temple flew open of their own accord, he predicted that the temple was to be destroyed by fire. Before this company, who no doubt had all gazed in the face of the Lord when he stood before them, the two Apostles had to appear.

We have here the first fulfillment of the many predictions given by our Lord that his beloved disciples were to suffer persecutions.

> Remember the word that I said to you: "A servant is not greater than his master." If they persecuted me, they will also persecute you. If they kept my word, they will also keep yours. (John 15:20). . . Behold, I am sending you out as sheep in the midst of wolves, so be wise as serpents and innocent as doves. Beware of men, for they will deliver you over to courts and flog you in their synagogues (Matt 10:16-17). . . But be on your guard. For they will deliver you over to councils, and you will be beaten in synagogues, and you will stand before governors and kings for my sake, to bear witness before them (Mark 13:9).

They had to appear before the council in fulfillment of these predictions. Beaten they were later. In the fifth chapter we read how all the twelve were brought before them, then they were beaten (v. 40), and later other deeds of violence were committed against them. But while these predictions of our Lord were fulfilled then and throughout this entire age, a special end fulfillment is yet to come as it will be seen from the context in Matthew 10 and Mark 13. During the great tribulation with which this age closes Jewish disciples will witness as they did in the beginning and then they will suffer once more as did the Apostles and the Jewish Christians.

Peter and John must have remembered all these words spoken by their departed Lord. The Holy Spirit brought them to their remembrance and filled them with joy and peace. What a privilege theirs was to appear before this ecclesiastical court before which the Lord had appeared! Then, too, the same question which the chief priests and elders had asked the Lord (Luke 20:1–2) was now put to them by the same men.

2. PETER'S BOLD WITNESS (VS. 8–12).

> Then Peter, filled with the Holy Spirit, said to them, "Rulers of the people and elders, if we are being examined today concerning a good deed done to a crippled man, by what means this man has been healed, let it be known to all of you and to all the people of Israel that by the name of Jesus Christ of Nazareth, whom you crucified, whom God raised from the dead—by him this man is standing before you well. This Jesus[1] is the stone that was rejected by you, the builders, which has become the cornerstone. [2] And there is salvation in no one else, for there is no other name under heaven given among men[3] by which we must be saved." (vs. 8–12).

Here we have another accomplishment of what the Lord had said.

> And when they bring you to trial and deliver you over, do not be anxious beforehand what you are to say, but say whatever is given you in that hour, for it is not you who speak, but the Holy Spirit (Mark 13:11).

Even so it was here. Peter was filled with the Holy Spirit as he arose to answer. The Holy Spirit then filled him and spoke through him. This third address of Peter reported in this book is as bold and clear as the previous addresses. How else could it be for he was but the mouthpiece of the third person of the Godhead, God the Holy Spirit. It is the briefest address and contains in the only ninety-two words in the Greek. It took only a few minutes to deliver, and yet how comprehensive it is. We notice seven things:

1. Peter brings at once forward the deed which had been done, the healing of the infirm man. This was the cause of their arrest and he is now to make known how this man was made whole. He calls the deed a "good deed." They had done nothing evil; there was no occasion whatever for their arrest.

2. The name of the Lord is next mentioned by him. He does not speak of him as the Son of God but as Jesus Christ the Nazarene; the significance of these three words is as simple as it is interesting. Jesus that was his name as he walked amongst them; Christ such he was and is now exalted to the right hand of God; The Nazarene his name as the rejected One by his own, a rejection which rested upon these rulers of the nation. And now Peter with a holy boldness accuses the assembled Sanhedrin[4] that they crucified the Lord Jesus Christ: "whom you crucified." This was the truth for the Sanhedrin had condemned the Lord. What a change had taken place with Peter. A short time ago he faced a female servant of the high priest, and when that girl accused him of being a follower of the Lord

---

[1] Greek *This one*

[2] Greek *the head of the corner*

[3] The Greek word *anthropoi* refers here to both men and women

[4] Craig A. Evans, "Sanhedrin," in *The Eerdmans Dictionary of Early Judaism*, ed. John J. Collins and Daniel C. Harlow (Grand Rapids, Mich.: Eerdmans, 2010), 1193–94; T. Alec Burkill, "The Competence of the Sanhedrim," *Vigiliae Christianae* 10 (1956): 80–96.

Jesus Christ, he denied Him. And now filled with the Holy Spirit he accuses the Sanhedrin in presence of the high priest that, they crucified Jesus. What a contrast with the Peter who had feared that servant.

3. Again the resurrection of the Lord Jesus Christ is mentioned in this witness. This was the great object of apostolic preaching: him "God raised from the dead."

4. The infirm man had been made sound in his body through the name of Jesus Christ whom they had crucified. The healing of the lame man was an evidence that the crucified One lives and that he is the Christ. The lame man stood there with the Apostles. This shows that when they were arrested, the healed one was likewise put into prison with them, for he stood up with Peter and John before the Sanhedrin.

5. In the next place Peter quotes the Word of God. The Holy Spirit puts the same Scripture before these rulers, elders and the chief priests, which the Lord had mentioned in their presence. "By what authority are you doing these things" the same men had asked Him, who now asked his disciples. And the Lord had answered them in parables (Matt 21:23–41). At the close of his second parable, the Gospel of Matthew tells us, the Lord quoted the words to them which Peter now uses in their presence:

> Jesus said to them, "Have you never read in the Scriptures: "'The stone that the builders rejected has become the cornerstone; this was the Lord's doing, and it is marvelous in our eyes'? Therefore I tell you, the kingdom of God will be taken away from you and given to a people producing its fruits. And the one who falls on this stone will be broken to pieces; and when it falls on anyone, it will crush him. When the chief priests and the Pharisees heard his parables, they perceived that he was speaking about them (Matt 21:42–45).

The One Hundred and Eighteenth Psalm from which the verse of the rejected stone is taken, belongs to the hymn mentioned in Matthew 26:30. It belongs to the Jewish ritual, known by the name of "the great Hallel," still used by the Jews during the Passover celebrations. But neither the modern nor the older Jewish expositors apply the words about the rejected stone to the Christ, their promised Messiah. Some say it refers to David himself, that he was the rejected stone and others apply it to the nation, rejected now but destined to be the corner stone of the nations. But the Lord had told them that he was the rejected stone mentioned in that Psalm, and here the Holy Spirit presses the same truth home to their hearts. They knew that the Lord meant them when he quoted that verse, that they were the builders, who were to reject Him. They had done so in fulfillment of that prophecy. Peter's words are directed straight at them, "This Jesus is the stone that was rejected by you, the builders, which has become the cornerstone" (4:11).

6. The rejected stone had become the corner stone. The One whom they had delivered up and cast out had been given the prominent place of the corner stone upon whom as the foundation stone everything rests and who unites the building. The truth concerning him as the corner stone is fully revealed in Ephesians, where we read:

> Built on the foundation of the apostles and prophets, Christ Jesus himself being the cornerstone, in whom the whole structure, being joined together, grows into a holy temple in the Lord. In him you also are being built together into a dwelling place for God by[5] the Spirit (Eph 2:20–22).

The Holy Spirit aimed at their conscience. Will they hear and acknowledge their awful mistake in having rejected the Holy One? Will this striking incident of the healing of the lame man convince them that the rejected stone is the corner stone now?

---

[5] Or *in*

7. Peter closes with the statement that salvation is only in him whom they had set at naught. There is no other Name given to men by which man can be saved, and that is the Name of him who had made this lame man whole. Salvation they all needed. They, too, rulers, elders, chief priests must be saved. But only in him God had procured salvation free and complete for all, who will have it by believing on Him. This salvation was offered to these rulers, the builders who had rejected the Lord.

3. THE ASTONISHMENT OF THE SANHEDRIN. AND THE RELEASE OF THE APOSTLES (VS. 13–22).

> Now when they saw the boldness of Peter and John, and perceived that they were uneducated, common men, they were astonished. And they recognized that they had been with Jesus. But seeing the man who was healed standing beside them, they had nothing to say in opposition. But when they had commanded them to leave the council, they conferred with one another, saying, "What shall we do with these men? For that a notable sign has been performed through them is evident to all the inhabitants of Jerusalem, and we cannot deny it. But in order that it may spread no further among the people, let us warn them to speak no more to anyone in this name." So they called them and charged them not to speak or teach at all in the name of Jesus. But Peter and John answered them, "Whether it is right in the sight of God to listen to you rather than to God, you must judge, for we cannot but speak of what we have seen and heard." And when they had further threatened them, they let them go, finding no way to punish them, because of the people, for all were praising God for what had happened. For the man on whom this sign of healing was performed was more than forty years old. (vs. 13–22).

The rulers, elders, scribes and the high priest were astonished. But they were not astonished at what they had heard; they did not wonder at the divine voice which had spoken to them through an humble Galilean. The whole account shows how these ecclesiastical leaders had hardened their hearts, how they despised that blessed Name which is above every other name. Their astonishment was on account of Peter's and John's boldness. In the presence of this great council, so revered by the whole nation, these two men had uttered a great accusation. They had accused them of having crucified one who not alone was innocent, but who was the long promised Messiah. Then they were astonished on account of the language and Scripture quotation used. They knew they were illiterate and uninstructed (Gr. *idiots*). How then could a man like Peter speak such wonderful words in so brief a period? Then they recognized them as having been with Jesus, which does not mean, as it is so often said, that they were known by their meek manner or spirituality, that they were in fellowship with the Lord, but they recognized them as having been with the Lord Jesus during the last week in Jerusalem before he suffered and died. But their dilemma is still greater. The healed man, who was above forty years old, stood there. It was impossible to deny that the miracle was not genuine. They had nothing to reply. When they find words it is to request them to go outside so that they might speak together on their case and about the situation. There was no repentance, no willingness to accept what had been so powerfully presented to them. Faster and faster these men were rushing into the outer darkness. Peter, John and the healed man went outside under guard, while inside they discussed their case. But who knew what they said? How did it become known? This is one of the many incidents in the Word of God illustrating what inspiration is. No one reported to Luke what took place in that council chamber nor the other secret things reported in this book. But One saw and heard, and he the Holy Spirit, revealed these secret things to his chosen instrument, the beloved physician, Luke. We learn what happened. They could not deny the miracle. A miracle had taken place. They could not deny it. If there had been a way to deny the healing of that man, they would have done so. Furthermore, we see their wicked impenitent state. Not a word is said by them about the person of Christ. Not one voice is heard to consider the strong witness they had heard. When they mention the Lord's name it is only in connection with forbidding the disciples to use the Name in speaking and teaching. They charged them never to mention that Name again.

The courageous words of the two Apostles need no further comment. In all boldness they declared that they would obey God more than man's word. This holy courage was the product of the indwelling Spirit. And we, too, beloved readers, need such courage as witnesses for our absent Lord. But few of God's people have it and often they fear men and bow to ecclesiastical institutions and leaders, which deny the Holy One of God as much as these rulers and scribes did. The Holy Spirit grant us a greater boldness in these last and evil days, when God calls to contend earnestly for the faith.

The only answer the learned rulers and scribes could give was a renewed threat. They were sorry that they could not punish them. They did not dare to lay hands on them on account of the people. Too many knew what had taken place, and God was glorified by those who had been witnesses of the healing of the lame man. The great ecclesiastical council was the coward.

4. WITH THEIR OWN COMPANY; THEIR PRAISE AND PRAYER (VS. 23–31).

> When they were released, they went to their friends and reported what the chief priests and the elders had said to them. And when they heard it, they lifted their voices together to God and said, "Sovereign Lord, who made the heaven and the earth and the sea and everything in them, who through the mouth of our father David, your servant,[6] said by the Holy Spirit,
>
> > "Why did the Gentiles rage, and the peoples plot in vain? The kings of the earth set themselves, and the rulers were gathered together, against the Lord and against his Anointed?"—[8]
>
> for truly in this city there were gathered together against your holy servant Jesus, whom you anointed, both Herod and Pontius Pilate, along with the Gentiles and the peoples of Israel, to do whatever your hand and your plan had predestined to take place. And now, Lord, look upon their threats and grant to your servants[9] to continue to speak your word with all boldness, 30while you stretch out your hand to heal, and signs and wonders are performed through the name of your holy servant Jesus." And when they had prayed, the place in which they were gathered together was shaken, and they were all filled with the Holy Spirit and continued to speak the word of God with boldness (vs. 23–31).

With great joy they must have turned towards the place where their own company assembled. We do not understand by this expression only the Apostles, but it was a much larger gathering. The news of the arrest of Peter and John must have reached them soon after it took place. And as the assembly made increasing prayer for Peter, when Herod had cast him into prison (12:5) so in all probability were they continuing in prayer for the two Apostles, who were later called "pillars of the church" (Gal 2). There must have been great joy when they appeared again with them. A report is given of what had taken place and what the chief priests and elders had demanded of them. No idle discussion follows; no schemes or plans are made how to act with this injunction against their speaking in his Name. They did something far better and grander. Hezekiah, the good king, when he had received the threatening words of

---

[6] Or *child*; also verses 27, 30
[7] Or *Christ*
[8] Psalm 2:1–2
[9] Greek *bondservants*

Rabshakeh, the mouthpiece of Sennacherib, the Assyrian king (2 Kgs 19), laid the whole matter before the Lord. So this company in their perplexity turns to the Lord in prayer. It concerned God and his Christ, his holy servant Jesus; him they are willing to glorify by serving or suffering. While they had made the positive declaration to the assembled rulers that they could not and would not keep silence, they now ask counsel of the Lord. The precious lessons and instructions we receive from this fact are not difficult to discover. The Holy Spirit leads to prayer, and prayer is the expression of dependence on the Lord.

With one accord they lift up their voice to God. This does not mean that they all prayed at once. That would have been confusion. Disorder in meetings, a number of people talking at the same time in a boisterous way with outward demonstrations, is an evidence that the Holy Spirit is not leading, for God is not a God of disorder, but of peace (1 Cor 14:33). Most likely Peter uttered the words of prayer and the rest followed in their hearts with one accord. God is addressed as the Lord (Master) and God who made the heaven and the earth and the sea and all that is in them. Later after the complete revelation of the Gospel of the Son of God, prayer is addressed to the God and Father of our Lord Jesus Christ, which is the proper way now to address God. Nowhere in this book is a prayer addressed to the Holy Spirit. Nowhere in the Epistles do we find a prayer addressed to the third person in the Godhead or an exhortation to pray for his coming. Prayer to the Holy Spirit or for him by those who are indwelt by him (as every true Christian is) is not scriptural. We also do not find anywhere in this Book of the Acts that the Apostles or the other disciples ever prayed the so-called "Lord's prayer;" that is the "Our Father." That form of prayer had been given to the disciples for a certain time only. Before he left them he had, so to speak, cancelled that form of prayer. "Until now you have asked nothing in my name. Ask, and you will receive, that your joy may be full" (John 16:24). Prayer is to be made in his Name in the power of his Spirit.

The foundation of this first recorded prayer in the Acts is the Word of God. The Holy Spirit brings the Word to their minds and with that Word before their hearts they utter their petition. This is the true way of prayer. Daniel prayed in this way as well as others. The Scripture which is mentioned is the Second Psalm. Throughout the New Testament the prophetic importance of that great collection of inspired prayers and songs of praise, the Book of Psalms, is seen. The Second Psalm is a great prophecy. The Psalm itself bears no title nor the name of the instrument through whom it was given. Here in this prayer we learn that David by the Holy Spirit is the author of this Psalm. The Psalm begins with a prediction that the Gentiles were to oppose the Lord and his anointed, that is Christ. And here we lee a *partial* fulfilment of this prophecy. Herod, Pontius Pilate, the Gentiles and the peoples of Israel had indeed gathered together in that city to do what the hand and the counsel of the Lord had determined before should come to pass. The Anointed of the Lord had been rejected and refused. The Gentiles had an equal share in it. The rulers of the peoples of Israel had given command that his blessed Name should no more be mentioned. All was pre-determined by God, which, of course, did not clear them from responsibility and guilt. It is an interesting fact that the text of the Second Psalm does not show that his own people Israel were to have part in that rejection. But this does not exhaust the prophetic meaning of the Second Psalm. The rejection of the Christ of God by the Gentiles and the peoples of Israel in the beginning of this age is only the prelude to the greater rejection of the Lord at the end of the age. Then the kings of the earth will form a great confederacy and say: "Let us burst their bonds apart and cast away their cords from us" (Ps 2:3). This will be followed by the great event which is so clearly revealed in the Second Psalm, the Coming of the King to rule over these nations and to break them with a rod of iron. The rejected Christ will be enthroned as King upon the holy hill of Zion. Of him the Lord will declare: "You are my Son; today I have begotten you" (Ps 2:7). (In resurrection from the dead). Only then will the Second Psalm be fulfilled.

With such a word before their hearts opened to their vision by the Holy Spirit while they were praying, they can come boldly to the Lord. They implore him to look upon their threatenings. He knew all. But their prayer was not that their enemies might be destroyed nor that they might be delivered from further attacks. Their prayer was for boldness to speak the Word. They cast themselves upon the Lord for Grace and help. They also ask, which was perfectly in order on the ground they occupied, that his hand might be outstretched to heal and that signs and wonders take place through the name of his holy servant Jesus. Such a prayer which concerned only the Lord and his Glory could not remain unanswered. The answer came at once. The place was shaken; they were filled with the Holy Spirit and spoke the Word of God with boldness. The outward sign was that the place in which they assembled was shaken. The Lord and God, the Creator, manifested his power. It was no doubt a shaking of the earth, and in connection with the prediction of the Second Psalm, this is likewise significant. As that place was shaken, so, in the future, when the kings and the nations of the earth are in complete opposition to God and his Christ, heaven and earth will be shaken, when the King of king returns.[10]

The filling with the Holy Spirit was not another outpouring or Baptism. He filled them anew. "Be filled with the Spirit" (Eph 5:18) is the word to us, and he will fill us if our constant aim is in word and deed to glorify the Lord Jesus Christ. The filling with the Holy Spirit manifested itself by their boldness in speaking the Word of God. They had great courage and liberty preaching the good news in the blessed Name of the Lord.

5. THE SAVED MULTITUDE ONE HEART AND ONE SOUL (VS. 32–37).

> Now the full number of those who believed were of one heart and soul, and no one said that any of the things that belonged to him was his own, but they had everything in common. And with great power the apostles were giving their testimony to the resurrection of the Lord Jesus, and great grace was upon them all. There was not a needy person among them, for as many as were owners of lands or houses sold them and brought the proceeds of what was sold and laid it at the apostles' feet, and it was distributed to each as any had need. Thus Joseph, who was also called by the apostles Barnabas (which means son of encouragement), a Levite, a native of Cyprus, sold a field that belonged to him and brought the money and laid it at the apostles' feet. (vs. 32–37).

A fresh glimpse is given to us of the assembly in Jerusalem. The first description we had at the close of the second chapter. After the great events recorded in the third and fourth chapters we behold again the happy condition of the multitude who had believed. This is a precious picture once more. There was a divine oneness among them. While in the second chapter we are

---

[10] Compare the outward signs on the day of Pentecost and the shaking of the place with I Kings 19:11, 12. Four outward signs were present when the Lord passed by Elijah: Wind, earthquake, fire and the still small voice. So at Sinai.

told that they sold their substance and possessions, here we read that not one said that anything of what he possessed was his own. They realized that their real possessions were now in a better place, no longer on earth, but in heaven. A marvellous change had taken place from the earthly calling and hope of the Jew, to the heavenly calling and heavenly hope. It is true the full revelation of the heavenly had not yet been given, but what they knew of Christ, his resurrection and his place at the right hand of God was sufficient to detach them from earthly things. It was the Holy Spirit who made this so real to them, and through his power they were enabled to bear such a witness to the truth. That the resurrection of the Lord Jesus is again mentioned in these verses shows the prominence this great event held in their hearts. It was this which separated them and on account of which great grace was upon them all. Well may we remember here the words of the Apostle with which he begins the practical part of that Epistle, which reveals the glory of our risen and exalted Lord:

> If then you have been raised with Christ, seek the things that are above, where Christ is, seated at the right hand of God. Set your minds on things that are above, not on things that are on earth. For you have died, and your life is hidden with Christ in God (Col 3:1–3).

The great truth of the resurrection and exaltation of Christ and that we are raised with him and belong there where he is can do only one thing and that is, wean us away from the things on earth. How much this ought to be the case in these last days when the Lord's Coming is so near.

In consequence of having all things in common, want and poverty were unknown amongst them. The need of all was supplied. All this was for a purpose. It was a great testimony to the nation. It lasted for but a brief period. We do not find it again. The next chapter begins with a "but" and shows how the sweet picture was marred by the sin of Ananias and Sapphira. In the sixth chapter we have the record of the murmuring one against the other. Thus failure soon came in. On Gentile ground we find nowhere these conditions as given in these verses.

One is mentioned especially, Joses Barnabas, as he had been named by the Apostles, the Son of Consolation. He was a Levite, born in the island of Cyprus (see Fig. 14). He was a well-to-do man, and had relations in Jerusalem, for John Mark was his cousin. The Grace of God enabled him to sell the land he possessed. How richly he was blessed and how the Lord chose him for an instrument we shall find later.

Chapter Five

The contents of this chapter are as follows:

1. The manifestation of evil in the church; Ananias and Sapphira (vs. 1–11).
2. Signs and wonders by the hands of the Apostles (vs. 12–16).
3. The second arrest of the Apostles and their miraculous deliverance (vs. 17–25).
4. Before the council; the defense of the Apostles, Peter's renewed witness (vs. 25–34).
5. Gamaliel's advice (vs. 34–39).
6. The Apostles beaten, dismissed from the council but continuing teaching and preaching the glad tidings (vs. 40–42).

1. The Manifestation of evil in the church; Ananias and Sapphira (vs. 1–11).

But a man named Ananias, with his wife Sapphira, sold a piece of property, and with his wife's knowledge he kept back for himself some of the proceeds and brought only a part of it and laid it at the apostles' feet. But Peter said, "Ananias, why has Satan filled your heart to lie to the Holy Spirit and to keep back for yourself part of the proceeds of the land? While it remained unsold, did it not remain your own? And after it was sold, was it not at your disposal? Why is it that you have contrived this deed in your heart? You have not lied to man but to God." When Ananias heard these words, he fell down and breathed his last. And great fear came upon all who heard of it. The young men rose and wrapped him up and carried him out and buried him.

After an interval of about three hours his wife came in, not knowing what had happened. And Peter said to her, "Tell me whether youa sold the land for so much." And she said, "Yes, for so much." But Peter said to her, "How is it that you have agreed together to test the Spirit of the Lord? Behold, the feet of those who have buried your husband are at the door, and they will carry you out." Immediately she fell down at his feet and breathed her last. When the young men came in they found her dead, and they carried her out and buried her beside her husband. And great fear came upon the whole church and upon all who heard of these things (vs. 1–11).

Up to this chapter we have beheld a beautiful picture of the work of the Holy Spirit in the gathering of those who had believed and their fellowship, as well as in the bold testimony of the Apostles. The acts of the Holy Spirit in his mighty power are fully demonstrated in the second, third and fourth chapters of this book of Exodus of the New Testament. Then we likewise saw how the enemy began to act in the arrest of Peter and John.

With this chapter the scene changes. Beautiful is the ending of the previous chapter, Barnabas having sold his land, laid the money at the feet of the Apostles. He gave by it a striking testimony how he realized as a believing Jew his heavenly portion, by giving up that which is promised to the Jew, earthly possessions.

Our chapter begins with the significant word "But." It is the word of failure and decline. All was evidently perfect; nothing marred the precious scenes of fellowship "but" and with this little word the story of evil begins. The enemy seeing himself so completely defeated by his attacks from the outside now enters among the flock and begins his work within.

The instruments were Ananias and Sapphira, man and wife. They too had an estate, which they sold. They had beforehand agreed to surrender only a part of the money they received from the sale, the balance they were keeping back for themselves. It was deception they had deliberately planned. Behind it stood unbelief; they did not realize in faith that God Himself in the person of his Spirit had made his abode in the assembly of which they were a part. They did not consider this stupendous fact that the Holy Spirit had come and was present in the gathered company. But what was the motive? The surrender of possessions as done by Barnabas was entirely voluntary. No one had asked Ananias and Sapphira to do the same thing. The motive was selfishness. Barnabas had done a good deed in obeying the Holy Spirit and no doubt he received praise and blessing for it. This moved Ananias and Sapphira to jealousy and they desired to have the same reputation. But their hearts were covetous; they loved the earthly things and they did not want to part with all the purchase money. Human glory and money were the downfall of Ananias and his wife. They were double-minded. The Spirit of God was working in great power, but what they manifested was an imitation, hypocrisy, a lie.[1] Satan himself had filled the heart of Ananias using his flesh to commit this sin of lying to the Holy Spirit. Satan had begun his work in the midst of the gathered company and he worked through the flesh of those who had believed on the Lord. Swift judgment followed as to their earthly existence. They were cut off by death. The sin they had done was "a sin to death" and the sentence, physical death, was immediately carried out. Peter is still in the foreground. We must remember here the words of the Lord which he spake to Peter, after this disciple had confessed him as Son of God.

> I will give you the keys of the kingdom of heaven, and whatever you bind on earth shall be bound in heaven, and whatever you loose on earth shall be loosed[2] in heaven (Matt 16:19).

The same words concerning binding and loosing the Lord addressed to all the disciples (Matt 18:18). The binding and loosing refers to discipline on earth. It has nothing whatever to do with forgiveness of sins or eternal salvation. Peter here exercises this authority, it was the first discipline. We must likewise remember that these events happened on Jewish, on kingdom ground. The witness was still to the nation. The sudden judgment which came upon Ananias and Sapphira was a strong witness to the nation that the Holy One of Israel, the Lord, dwelt in the midst of this remnant, who believed in the One whom the nation had rejected. When the kingdom is established on earth and the Lord Jesus Christ rules in righteousness, then, no doubt every sin will be swiftly judged by death. If it is asked why such judgments do no longer occur, we answer that the Holy Spirit then was ungrieved; now the Spirit is grieved on account of unfaithfulness and God no longer acts in this way to bear testimony to his presence in the church. Besides this it is nowhere stated that such manifestations of his presence were to continue. If God would thus act in judgment in every case of double-mindedness, unfaithfulness and sinning against the Holy Spirit, it would be contrary to one great characteristic of this present age. That is "the silent heavens." The many misguided people, who think they have gone back to Pentecost, have received

---

[1] There is an interesting correspondency between the sin of Achan, the first failure reported after Israel entered the land, and the sin of Ananias and Sapphira.

[2] Or *shall have been bound… shall have been loosed*

their Pentecost, speak with new tongues, that the gift of tongues and of doing miracles is restored to them and that they are now once more in "apostolic times," should also expect such judgments in their midst.

There are some important lessons to be gathered from this solemn event which we cannot pass by.

(1) The fact of the presence of the flesh in the believer. Ananias and Sapphira were believers. They gave way to follow the flesh, and Satan came in with his power and tempted them. The doctrine of the eradication of the old nature by having received "the baptism with the Holy Spirit" is unscriptural.

In this case of Ananias and Sapphira it is fully demonstrated what is written in the Epistle to the Galatians

> For the desires of the flesh are against the Spirit, and the desires of the Spirit are against the flesh, for these are opposed to each other, to keep you from doing the things you want to do (Gal 5:17).

(2) The power of Satan is revealed in the event. What Ananias and Sapphira did was suggested to them by Satan. Vainglory was in their hearts; they followed pride to win fame and get the praise from man. They had the root of all evil "the love of money" in their hearts and yielded to it. Acting thus in the flesh Satan came and suggested the lie to them. Their eyes were then blinded and they lost sight of the great truth so well known to them that he who is "perfect in knowledge" dwelt in them and in the midst of the congregation as the Lord had dwelt in the midst of Israel.

(3) The event bears witness to the fact that the Holy Spirit is not an influence but a divine person, he is God. Ananias had lied to the Holy Spirit. Peter tells him "You have not lied to man but to God" (5:4). To tempt the Holy Spirit is to tempt God and to lie to the Spirit is a lie to God.

(4) All sin of the Christian believer is now against the Holy Spirit. The Holy Spirit indwells the believer and whenever the believer walks not in the Spirit but in flesh, when he is carnally minded, the believer sins against the Holy Spirit. Satan has then an advantage over him. But thanks be to God for his gracious provision! We can judge ourselves and confess our sins (not to the Holy Spirit but to God), and he is faithful and just to forgive and cleanse us.

(5) The presence of the Holy Spirit demands separation from evil. If believers would recognize the great truth, believe it fully that the Holy Spirit dwells in them, they would walk in the Spirit and be separated from evil. With all the singing about the Holy Spirit, the teaching and the great amount of scriptural literature on the doctrine of the Holy Spirit, but few believers enjoy the reality of the presence of the Spirit of God and are governed by it. Those who are the Lord's must be separated from evil of every form. One has well said: "In the first days of the Holy Spirit he took out what dishonored Him. In later days he called upon the assembly to act, to purge out the leaven, to 'put away' that wicked person" (1 Cor 5). In these last days, when the whole has become leavened with legality, worldliness, hypocrisy, sensuality, ritualism and rationalism, the faithful are to come out from among them and be separate, to follow righteousness, faith, love, and peace with those who call upon the Lord out of a pure heart (that is unmixed with any evil). In Israel the Lord judged in the beginning, at once and severely, for "holiness befits your house, O LORD, forevermore" (Ps 93:5). But in later days, when all had gone aside, and they who regarded him were but few they were told to stand apart from the whole. The condition of the professing company may change, but the grand principle remains. The holiness of

his presence excluding and separating us from evil.

Oh that God's people in these solemn days, when judgment is so near, may hear the call of the Holy Spirit in the last Pauline Epistle, the Epistle which so clearly describes the present apostasy, Second Timothy. It is his call to separation from evil (2 Tim 2:20, 21; 3:5).

2. THE SIGNS AND WONDERS DONE BY THE HANDS OF THE APOSTLES (VS. 12–16).

> Now many signs and wonders were regularly done among the people by the hands of the apostles. And they were all together in Solomon's Portico. None of the rest dared join them, but the people held them in high esteem. And more than ever believers were added to the Lord, multitudes of both men and women, so that they even carried out the sick into the streets and laid them on cots and mats, that as Peter came by at least his shadow might fall on some of them. The people also gathered from the towns around Jerusalem, bringing the sick and those afflicted with unclean spirits, and they were all healed. (vs. 12– 16).

Signs and wonders were done by the Apostles. Their habitual place seems to have been in Solomon's porch. No one dared to join them. They held the position of authority. Though they had been forbidden the public ministry they are back in a prominent place. The people magnified them, too. Then another result was that more believers were added. Added to what? The First Hebrew Christian Church of Jerusalem? The First Jewish Christian Society? No. They were added to the Lord. The sinner believing is saved, receives the Holy Spirit, is joined to the Lord, becomes one spirit with the Lord, a member of the body of which he is the Head. Signs and wonders were done by the Apostles. The sick were healed, unclean spirits were driven out. Multitudes of people from the surrounding country flocked to Jerusalem, bringing their sick, and they were all healed. The streets presented another strange picture. Everywhere one could see the sick on beds and couches. They waited for the time when Peter walked through these streets so that his shadow might fall on some of them. These were great manifestations of the power of God. The words spoken by the Lord were then fulfilled. They did the works he did. These signs and wonders, however, are nowhere mentioned as to their permanency throughout this age. They were only for the beginning of this age; after the Gospel of Grace and the mystery hidden in former ages had been fully made known they disappeared. It has been said of late that "God's gifts and calling are without repentance" and that therefore God has not taken back the sign gifts and the extraordinary powers as manifested here in this chapter in connection with the testimony to Israel. The reader must remember that the verse concerning the gifts and calling of God is written in Romans 11 and has no application in connection with this age but refers us to Israel's calling.

Nor has God promised for the end of this age a restoration of these gifts. When certain men, claiming to be great teachers of the Word, speak of "the latter rain," great spiritual blessings coming in the end of this age, they but reveal their ignorance. Nowhere is there found such a promise. The testimony of the Holy Spirit in the New Testament holds out no hope for a restoration of gifts, but his testimony tells us of apostasy, departure from the faith, and delusions. There will be "signs and wonders" in the end of the age. But these signs and wonders will be the most awful imitations of the power of the Holy Spirit: signs and lying wonders are predicted through the working of Satan. These have already commenced, but the real working of Satan will begin after the true church is removed from the earth (2 Thess 2).

3. The Second Arrest of the Apostles and Their Miraculous Deliverance (vs. 17–25).

> But the high priest rose up, and all who were with him (that is, the party of the Sadducees), and filled with jealousy they arrested the apostles and put them in the public prison. But during the night an angel of the Lord opened the prison doors and brought them out, and said, "Go and stand in the temple and speak to the people all the words of this Life." And when they heard this, they entered the temple at daybreak and began to teach.
>
> Now when the high priest came, and those who were with him, they called together the council, all the senate of the people of Israel, and sent to the prison to have them brought. But when the officers came, they did not find them in the prison, so they returned and reported, "We found the prison securely locked and the guards standing at the doors, but when we opened them we found no one inside." Now when the captain of the temple and the chief priests heard these words, they were greatly perplexed about them, wondering what this would come to. And someone came and told them, "Look! The men whom you put in prison are standing in the temple and teaching the people." (vs. 17–25).

The startling manifestations of the Holy Spirit in signs and miracles brought forth another and more severe action of the enemy. The second arrest of the bold witnesses is marked by greater hatred and violence than the first arrest. The Apostles were treated like common criminals and were put into the public prison. The Sadducees, the deniers of the resurrection and the miraculous, are mostly concerned in this second arrest. Their miserable unbelief had been endangered by the supernatural manifestations and these again fully demonstrated the great truth they were denying, the resurrection of the Lord Jesus. They were filled with jealousy (the word used in the Greek). But there was another manifestation of the power of God. During the night an angel of the Lord opened the doors of the prison and led them out. They were delivered by divine interference through the power of God by a heavenly messenger. Critics have denied this. One recently has made the statement that the phrase "angel of the Lord" must be understood, "as a Hebraic expression for some divine intervention, the manner of which is not defined. It may have been connivance on the part of an officer, or the help of a friend." Such weak statements need no answer. We shall find the appearance of heavenly messengers again. It was an angel of the Lord who guided Philip, who liberated Peter out of prison, and who smote Herod when he blasphemed (Acts 12). In the Old Testament we find "the angel of the Lord" (*Malach Jehovah*) and he is an uncreated angel, the Lord Himself. But here it is a heavenly messenger. He appeared, no doubt, in the form of man, like the two at the ascension of the Lord. Such a manifestation of angels was perfectly in order at that time, and fully corresponds with the other kingdom characteristics in the beginning of the Book of Acts. But the supernatural manifestations soon ceased. Hundreds and thousands of others throughout this present age were put into prison, they remained in dungeons, were slowly tormented, walled up to die a slow death, eaten by vermin, all for righteousness sake, and yet no angels came to open their doors and lead them forth. With this we do not say that the angels have no ministry now toward us. This would be contrary to Scripture (Heb 1:14). But visible manifestations of heavenly messengers have ceased like the miraculous sign gifts. It will not always be so. The heavens will speak again and there will be startling manifestations on judgment through angels and with the beginning of the coming age, angels will be manifested once more, and God's power and glory will be visibly displayed.

The delivering angel had also commissioned the Apostles to speak the words of life to all the people. This they did at once with the early morning. The assembled council is in great perplexity when the prison is found empty and the report reaches them, that the men are again standing in the temple teaching the people. Yet this evident miracle does not bring them to their knees to acknowledge the power of God.

4. Their Trial and Witness before the Council (vs. 26–32).

> Then the captain with the officers went and brought them, but not by force, for they were afraid of being stoned by the people.
>
> And when they had brought them, they set them before the council. And the high priest questioned them, saying, "We strictly charged you not to teach in this name, yet here you have filled Jerusalem with your teaching, and you intend to bring this man's blood upon us." But Peter and the apostles answered, "We must obey God rather than men. The God of our fathers raised Jesus, whom you killed by hanging him on a tree. God exalted him at his right hand as Leader and Savior, to give repentance to Israel and forgiveness of sins. And we are witnesses to these things, and so is the Holy Spirit, whom God has given to those who obey him." (vs. 26–32).

With cowardly fear they led them into the presence of the council. They did not dare to use violence as this might have resulted in an open outbreak from the side of the people, who heard the Apostles gladly. Two charges are brought now against them. They had broken the command of the council. They had been forbidden to speak in this Name and they had continued to do so, utterly disregarding the injunction. This was the first charge and it was true enough. The second charge was but the working of their guilty conscience. They accused them that they purposed to bring this man's blood upon them. They feared that the people stirred up by their teaching, might take them to task for having condemned Jesus of Nazareth. But another fact stands behind this fear. The people had cried "His blood be on us and on our children!" (Matt 27:25).

The leaders of the people were responsible for this awful word. They must have remembered it and they feared that this might soon be true in open vengeance from the side of the people against them. It is also a remarkable fact that they themselves do not speak the name of the Lord. They speak of him as "this man" and "this name."

Once more we find the record of the apostolic testimony. It does not differ from the previous bold and powerful witnesses given. After the statement that God must be obeyed rather than man, we find three great facts mentioned by Peter:

1. The Jesus, whose Name they were loath to pronounce, whom God had raised up, they had slain and hanged on a cross. This fully establishes their guilt. Once more the blood guiltiness is brought home to their consciences.

2. The exaltation of Jesus is mentioned next. Raised from the dead, exalted by the right hand of God, he is a Prince and Saviour. In his Name repentance is offered to Israel and forgiveness of sins.

3. The third part of this brief and logical defense concerns the Holy Spirit, the third person of the Godhead. They were witnesses of these things, and also the Holy Spirit. This Holy Spirit is now bestowed upon them that obey Him, that is, who believe God. The Holy Spirit was upon them and in them, and with them as a believing company. The witness concerned the three great facts so prominent in the beginning of this book, the death of Jesus, the resurrection of Jesus, and the presence of the Holy Spirit, because the Lord Jesus Christ is glorified, highly exalted. The Father, the Son and the Holy Spirit, are thus mentioned. The Gospel is mentioned. Forgiveness of sins, the gift of the Holy Spirit is for them that obey, believe in Him, whom God exalted as Prince and Saviour. Surely this is a fulfillment of that

The Acts of the Apostles

word the Lord spoke to his disciples, when he predicted future events.

> When they deliver you over, do not be anxious how you are to speak or what you are to say, for what you are to say will be given to you in that hour (Matt 10:19).

But what was the result of this other powerful witness of the Apostles by the power of the Holy Spirit? Are they humbling themselves? Does perhaps this stirring testimony backed up by divine interference in the release of the Apostles from the prison make them thoughtful? No. The witness went to the heart; it struck home. But instead of repenting they took counsel to kill them. The story of their Lord is repeated, for they also took counsel to kill them, in order to silence his testimony. Under the control of him, who is a murderer from the beginning they are ready to shed more blood. What might have happened if Gamaliel had not stood up, none can tell. Perhaps they were ready then to rush upon them as later they rushed upon Stephen to murder him.

5. The Advice of Gamaliel (vs. 33–39).

> When they heard this, they were enraged and wanted to kill them. But a Pharisee in the council named Gamaliel, a teacher of the law held in honor by all the people, stood up and gave orders to put the men outside for a little while. And he said to them, "Men of Israel, take care what you are about to do with these men. For before these days Theudas rose up, claiming to be somebody, and a number of men, about four hundred, joined him. He was killed, and all who followed him were dispersed and came to nothing. After him Judas the Galilean rose up in the days of the census and drew away some of the people after him. He too perished, and all who followed him were scattered. So in the present case I tell you, keep away from these men and let them alone, for if this plan or this undertaking is of man, it will fail; but if it is of God, you will not be able to overthrow them. You might even be found opposing God!" (vs. 33–39).

Gamaliel was undoubtedly an instrument of God to restrain the wicked devices of the

7. West gate at Masada, Herod's plateau fortress. Jewish Zealots occupied the site in AD 66, but the Romans attacked it in AD 73. Upon breaching the wall, Eleazer, the Zealot leader, convinced 960 Jews to commit suicide rather than face Roman slavery. Gamaliel's advice in Acts 5 proved true in the case of Masada. The Zealots failed in their plans to resist the Romans, as they were of human origin and not from God.

council. But who was Gamaliel? The text itself gives the answer, a great man and teacher of the law. He is called in Hebrew writings Rabban Gamaliel the Old. His name means "bestowed of God." he was president of the council after his own father, Rabban Simeon, who was the son of Hillel. He is the great teacher at whose feet Saul of Tarsus sat. He died eighteen years before the destruction of Jerusalem, and died a Pharisee. If his advice here seems that he favored the Apostles, his subsequent career shows that he followed the wicked devices of his contemporaries. A prayer against the heretics (the believers in the Lord) was later formulated to be read in the synagogues, and he fully approved of it and recommended its use.

8. The "Seat of Moses" carved from a block of basalt and discovered in 1926 in the Synagoguge at Chorazin (Matt 11:21; Luke 10:13). According to Matthew the "Seat of Moses" was where the reader of the Torah sat (23:1-3).

The advice he gave is so well known and the words so simple that they need no further comment. His advice is, leave them alone. Wait for the issue. If it is of God, you then fight against God. If it is of man, like similar movements before, it will come to nought. God will take care of his own honor; there would be no need of their interfering. God rules supreme. But this advice has also another side. It was after all nothing but a cowardly way to dodge the issue by waiting for light by the issue itself. Ever since up to the present time men have hidden themselves behind the wisdom of Gamaliel. If certain movements spring up which are doubtful and contain erroneous teachings contradicting the revelation of God, we hear people say that they are content to wait for the issue. If the movement is of God it will stand, if it is of man it will come to nought. But what in the meantime? If it does not become apparent at once whether it is of God or of the enemy? There is no need to follow this clever advice of the great Jewish teacher. We are in possession of the completed Word of God and must test everything by it. There is no need to halt between two opinions. Evil can be detected and must be judged. But that the council acted upon this in hypocrisy is seen by what follows. And yet we must not lose sight of the fact that God used this politic advice of Gamaliel to keep his disciples in that hour of grave peril.

6. THE RELEASE OF THE APOSTLES. THEIR CONTINUED TESTIMONY (VS. 40–42).

> So they took his advice, and when they had called in the apostles, they beat them and charged them not to speak in the name of Jesus, and let them go. Then they left the presence of the council, rejoicing that they were counted worthy to suffer dishonor for the name. And every day, in the temple and from house to house, they did not cease teaching and preaching that the Christ is Jesus. (vs. 40–42).

Nothing of all this was known to the Apostles for they had been outside while Gamaliel delivered his address. The Holy Spirit through Luke gives the full account of what had been done under cover. The council agreed. But if they agreed, why did they beat the Apostles? It surely was contrary to the agreement. They should have let them go without laying their hands on them, but wait for the issue. If these men were right, then according to Gamaliel's word they were fighting against God. This was, of course, the case. The beating was according to Deuteronomy 25:2, 3. They were treated as wicked men and received the allotted number of stripes, forty save one. Physical suffering and shame was connected with this mode of punishment. This was the first actual suffering of the Apostles for the Name, which is above every other name. Then we see them departing. It was a departure in triumph; they were more than conquerors. If we could have seen them with their bleeding backs, we would not have beheld faces full of rebellion and pain, but we would have seen joyous countenances and heard words of praise from their lips, as later Paul and Silas sang and praised in prison. It was the Holy Spirit who filled them and made them rejoice that "they were counted worthy to suffer dishonor for the name" (5:41). Later the Holy Spirit speaks of suffering for Christ through Peter in a way which is so refreshing.

> But rejoice insofar as you share Christ's sufferings, that you may also rejoice and be glad when his glory is revealed. If you are insulted for the name of Christ, you are blessed, because the Spirit of glory[3] and of God rests upon you. (1 Pet 4:13, 14).

Thus his Spirit rested upon them and they rejoiced. How little we know of such experiences in our own days!

And then they continued. Nothing could hinder them. What a divine steadfastness was theirs. It was the result of the presence of the Holy Spirit in them. He was ungrieved because they exalted Christ and magnified Him. A wonderful activity they unfolded. It was indeed true what the council had said. All Jerusalem was filled by their doctrine. The work they did continually was not the working of miracles, or speaking in strange tongues. Some deluded Christians of our times seem to think that these outward signs were the chief things in the beginning of the age. They were not. Greater than doing miracles and speaking in other tongues is that, through which the body of Christ is gathered and edified. This is the preaching of the Gospel and the teaching of the Word. This they did. They did not cease teaching and preaching the glad tidings (the Gospel), that Jesus is Christ.

---

[3] Some manuscripts insert *and of power*

Chapter Six

This chapter has two parts. In the first part (vs. 1–7) we find the record of the murmuring of the Grecians against the Hebrews, and how this difficulty was overcome. In the second part (vs. 8–15) Stephen, one of the seven chosen, is in the foreground. This part properly belongs to the chapter which follows, in which Stephen's great address before the council and his glorious martyrdom is revealed.

1. The Murmuring of the Grecians against the Hebrews (vs. 1–7).

> Now in these days when the disciples were increasing in number, a complaint by the Hellenists [1] arose against the Hebrews because their widows were being neglected in the daily distribution. And the twelve summoned the full number of the disciples and said, "It is not right that we should give up preaching the word of God to serve tables. Therefore, brothers,[2] pick out from among you seven men of good repute, full of the Spirit and of wisdom, whom we will appoint to this duty. But we will devote ourselves to prayer and to the ministry of the word." And what they said pleased the whole gathering, and they chose Stephen, a man full of faith and of the Holy Spirit, and Philip, and Prochorus, and Nicanor, and Timon, and Parmenas, and Nicolaus, a proselyte of Antioch. These they set before the apostles, and they prayed and laid their hands on them.
>
> And the word of God continued to increase, and the number of the disciples multiplied greatly in Jerusalem, and a great many of the priests became obedient to the faith (vs. 1–7).

Another failure is brought before us. The enemy acts again. From without and from within Satan pressed upon that which was of God. While the Lord Jesus Christ and the Holy Spirit acted in Grace and power, the enemy came in to disturb. It is still so. Whenever there is a door opened there are also many adversaries (1 Cor 16:9).

The flesh manifested itself in murmuring. The assembly took care of the poor; widows being specially helpless, were the objects of daily ministrations. The Jews themselves in connection with the synagogue had special funds for them. They must have also formed a recognized group in the early church (1 Tim 5:9, 10). The ministration is the distribution mentioned in Chapter 4:35, and as the multitude was very great, including, perhaps, hundreds of widows, this work was quite a task. Murmurings arose and these were born of jealousy, the result of unbelief. It is the first indication of weakness and failure. This reminds us of the murmurings of Israel as recorded in the book of Exodus. The same old thing, the changeless flesh, shows itself among the saved and united company of believers, indwelt by the Holy Spirit. The murmurings were on the side of the Grecians. Their complaint was against the Hebrews that the Grecian widows were being overlooked. The Grecians were not, as some teach, Gentiles, but they were Greek-speaking Jews, born in countries outside of Palestine, and therefore called Hellenists, or Grecians. Between these two classes, the native and foreign-born Jews, there existed considerable jealousy. This rivalry was introduced in the assembly. The

---

[1] That is, Greek-speaking Jews
[2] Or *brothers and sisters*

Hebrew distributors were accused of overlooking the Grecians.

But the murmuring was arrested at once. A divine Person was present, the One perfect in wisdom, the Holy Spirit. As he was ungrieved in their midst, he at once meets the need of the assembly. The murmuring could not advance nor do its pernicious work in dividing the people. Later the Holy Spirit especially warns against murmuring. "Do all things without grumbling or disputing" (Phil 2:14). Murmurings belong to the works of the flesh and will lead to the things mentioned in Galatians: "enmity, strife, jealousy, fits of anger, rivalries, dissensions, divisions" (Gal 5:20). Alas! how sad is the condition of Christian churches at the present time in this respect. If believers walk in humility, in self-judgment, esteeming the other higher than themselves, and are controlled by the mind which was in Christ Jesus, all those things would not be. Any murmuring, if it arises through the weakness of the flesh, would at once be cut short by the Holy Spirit.

The Spirit of God, who had, as reported in the previous chapter, acted in judgment by removing the two transgressors, now acts in divine grace.

The twelve called the assembly together. As the murmuring of Israel in the wilderness was mostly directed against Moses and Aaron, their divinely-appointed leaders, so the murmuring here was in a certain measure against the Apostles, at whose feet was laid the price of what had been sold. There is no word of rebuke from the side of the Apostles. Neither do we read of any arguments they used. They act as guided by the Holy Spirit. Their great calling and gift was the ministry of the Word; they had been obliged to serve tables more or less. They discerned at once that the Lord had not called them to this double service. Here is another evidence of the existence of the church. The Holy Spirit who had united them at the day of Pentecost into one body, now begins to point out the order in that body. All of this, concerning the different gifts to the members of the body, is not revealed here, but is found in the doctrinal Epistles of the Apostle to the Gentiles, to whom the ministry of the church was committed.

Seven men, the Holy Spirit directs through the Apostles, are to be selected from among the assembly. Three conditions are mentioned.

1. They must be men of good report,
2. They must be esteemed by all on account of their character,
3. They must be full of the Spirit, and possess wisdom.

The Apostles themselves declared: "But we will devote ourselves to prayer and to the ministry of the word" (6:4). The Holy Spirit thus separated the gifts called to minister in spiritual things, from the ministry of temporal matters. What confusion there exists in this respect at the present time in the professing church, needs hardly to be pointed out.

In this word of the Apostles, there is an important statement concerning prayer and the ministry of the Word. It is not the ministry of the Word, teaching and preaching, first, but they put prayer into the first place. There can be no effectual ministry, no effectual preaching of the Gospel and Bible teaching unless it is preceded by prayer. Prayer is the expression of dependence upon God. Ministry of the Word must be in utter dependence on the Lord and therefore prayer is the right preparation for it.

Then the multitude, that is the entire assembly, chose the seven men, while the Apostles sanctioned their choice. Stephen is mentioned first, and described as a man full of faith and the Holy Spirit. Then follow the names of the others, Philip, Prochorus, Nicanor, Timon, Parmenas and Nicolas. The latter was a proselyte,[3] that is, one who had adopted Judaism by circumcision; he was from Antioch. There is absolutely no historical proof that this Nicolas formed later a special sect and that he taught wicked doctrines. His name can in no wise be connected with the Nicolaitanes in Revelation 2:6 and 15.

While we know little of these men and the service they rendered, with the exception of Stephen and Philip, it is an interesting fact that their names are all Greek. In this the grace of God is beautifully exhibited. The Grecians were the murmurers, and no doubt they were fewer in number than the Hebrews. A modern day church meeting would have proposed to elect a committee composed of equal numbers of the two parties. But not so here.

Grace and wisdom from above are manifested in this action. The entire seven were chosen from those who had complained. This was the blessed rebuke of Grace. The weakness and failure is made an occasion to bring out such graciousness. Into the hands of those who had murmured is given the distribution of the funds. This silenced the murmurings at once.

The seven were then set before the Apostles and when they had prayed, they laid their hands on them. This is the first time we find the laying on of hands in the Book of Acts. As this "laying on of hands" is so much misunderstood, and has been made an act by which authority, power and blessing is claimed to be conferred, we must say a brief word on it. It is always proper in reading and interpreting the Word of God, to see if not elsewhere in the Bible the terms or things to be interpreted are used, so that through them the right meaning can be ascertained. The laying on of hands is first mentioned in the Book of Leviticus. In the opening chapters of that book we read how the offerer was to lay his hand upon the head of the offering. Thus we read of the Peace offering: "he shall lay his hand on the head of his offering" (Lev 3:2). This meant the identification of the Israelite with the offering itself. And this is the only meaning of the laying on of hands from the side of the Apostles. They identified themselves and the assembly with them in their work for which they had been chosen. It was a very simple and appropriate act to show their fellowship with them. All else which has been made of the laying on of hands is an invention. There is no Scripture for the present day usage in Christendom, that a man in order to preach the Gospel or teach the Word of God must be "ordained." We shall return to this when we reach other parts of this book.

The Word of God increased. The Holy Spirit gave it power, and after this victory when the enemy attempted to disturb the assembly by the murmuring, he unfolded great energy. The number of disciples increased greatly and especially is it mentioned that a great company of the priests were obedient to the faith. The latter was apparently a new thing. No priests were mentioned before. May not the rent veil have had something to do with this great company of priests believing in the Lord Jesus Christ? They had found the new and living way into the Holiest by the blood of Jesus.

The office of the seven, we may add, was only of a short duration, for soon

---

[3] Gary G. Porton, *The Stranger within Your Gates*, Chicago Studies in the History of Judaism (Chicago, Ill.: The University of Chicago Press, 1994); S. J. F. Cohen, "Crossing the Boundary and Becoming a Jew," *Harvard Theological Review* 82 (1989): 13–33; N. Levison, "The Proselyte in Biblical and Early Post-Biblical Times," *Scottish Journal of Theology* 10 (1957): 45–56.

persecution of the worst type set in and the disciples were scattered.

2. STEPHEN, HIS MINISTRY AND ARREST (VS. 8–15).

> And Stephen, full of grace and power, was doing great wonders and signs among the people. Then some of those who belonged to the synagogue of the Freedmen (as it was called), and of the Cyrenians, and of the Alexandrians, and of those from Cilicia and Asia, rose up and disputed with Stephen. But they could not withstand the wisdom and the Spirit with which he was speaking. Then they secretly instigated men who said, "We have heard him speak blasphemous words against Moses and God." And they stirred up the people and the elders and the scribes, and they came upon him and seized him and brought him before the council, and they set up false witnesses who said, "This man never ceases to speak words against this holy place and the law, for we have heard him say that this Jesus of Nazareth will destroy this place and will change the customs that Moses delivered to us." And gazing at him, all who sat in the council saw that his face was like the face of an angel. (vs. 8–15).

With Stephen we reach an important stage in this book. The testimony, as given to Israel, is now soon to be closed and Stephen is the instrument chosen to deliver the most striking testimony to the representatives of the nation. Of the history of this remarkable man we know but little. As already seen, his name indicates that he was a Hellenist; Stephen means "crown." And he is indeed to have a great crown in the day when the Lord will take the award seat and his saints will appear before Him. We learned before that he was full of faith and of the Holy Spirit. He is, so to speak, the link between Peter and Paul; most significantly, at the close of Stephen's great witness and after his vision of the Glory of God and Jesus standing on the right hand of God, there is mentioned a young man named Saul, "approved of his execution" (8:1).

Here in the sixth chapter we read that Stephen was "full of grace and power," (6:8) the effect of faith, and filled with the Spirit. He is the first disciple mentioned who is not an apostle, who did great wonders and miracles among the people. Then we see those of the synagogues of the Libertines, and Cyrenians, and Alexandrians, disputing with him. These were also Hellenists, Jews brought up in foreign countries, and of much learning. There were many synagogues at that time in Jerusalem, and as it is the custom still among the orthodox Jews, the synagogues were called by the names of the places from which its adherents came. This synagogue then was composed of Libertines, that is, Jews from Rome,[4] for they were known by that name, Jews of Cyrene and Alexandria. To this synagogue Stephen may have belonged, and if this was the case, his presence with them is easily explained. The fullness of Grace in his heart reached out after them. These Jews disputed with Stephen and he with them; but also those of Cilicia and Asia are mentioned. May not this young man, Saul of Tarsus, the Pharisee of the Pharisees, hailing from Cilicia, been among these disputers? *It is more than likely.* All their great learning was of no avail in the presence of such a powerful witness. The Holy Spirit bore witness and they were not able to resist the wisdom and the Spirit in which he spoke. They would not accept the testimony of this gracious and powerful witness and therefore only another way was left to them. They are filled with satanic hatred against him, and as the chief priests did with the Lord, did these here suborn men who accused Stephen of blasphemy. The charge is "blasphemous words against Moses and God" (6:11). They succeeded in their satanic work by stirring

---

[4] It is wrong to call these "Libertines" free thinkers. Jews had been taken to Rome as slaves. Their descendants who had been liberated were called Libertines, that is freedmen. They were known as such in Jerusalem and hence the name "synagogue of the Libertines."

up the people, the elders and the scribes. Stephen is arrested and brought before the council. There the charge is repeated. Three things are mentioned by them. He ceaseth not to speak words against this holy place; against the law and that he should have said: "This Jesus of Nazareth will destroy this place and will change the customs that Moses delivered to us" (6:14). And then they looked upon him and behold his face was like the face of an angel. All eyes were attracted to this wonderful sight. Steadfastly they looked upon a face of Glory; a face reflecting heaven's light, heaven's Glory; a face reflecting the Glory of him into whose presence he soon would be called. And may not that young man named Saul also have been there and seen that face? And that dark countenance of that young Pharisee of Tarsus was soon to behold that same Glory-light and then tell the world of the Gospel of the Glory and that

> We all, with unveiled face, beholding the glory of the Lord, are being transformed into the same image from one degree of glory to another. For this comes from the Lord who is the Spirit (2 Cor 3:18).

Chapter Seven

The seventh chapter is the longest in the entire book and one of the most interesting and important. The whole council looked steadfastly upon that shining face, as if it had been the face of an angel. Thus we read in the closing verse of the previous chapter. How long they looked upon Stephen as he stood there we do not know. Perhaps after a few minutes of silence, an ominous silence, like the calm before a storm, the voice of the high priest is heard "Are these things so?" (v. 1)

Stephen then begins his great, God-given testimony. He is not permitted to finish it. They ran upon him with one accord and cast him out of the city and stoned him. The chapter is therefore divided into two parts.

1. The address of Stephen (vs. 2–53).

2. The martyrdom of Stephen (vs. 54–60).

1. The address of Stephen (vs. 2–53).

We request our readers to read his words carefully.[1]

We notice at once a marked difference between the previous preaching by the Apostle Peter and the address of Stephen. The testimony of Peter was marked on the day of Pentecost and at the other occasions by great brevity. Stephen's address is the longest discourse reported in the New Testament. The name of Jesus is prominent in all the addresses of Peter. The fact that he was rejected by the people, crucified and that he rose from the dead and the call to repentance, were the leading features of Peter's preaching. Stephen does not mention the name of Jesus at all,[2] though he has the person of Christ and his rejection as the theme of his testimony. At the close of his address he speaks of the Just One of whom they had become betrayers and murderers.

Stephen had been accused of speaking against Moses and against God, also against the temple and the law. These accusations he is asked to answer. What he declared before the council shows plainly that the accusations are utterly false. His speech is partly apologetic; but it is also teaching in that it shows certain truths from the historic

---

[1] Brian Peterson, "Stephen's Speech as a Modified Prophetic Rib Formula," *Journal of Evangelical Theological Society* 57, no. 2 (2014): 351–69; Martin Hengel, "Between Jesus and Paul: The 'Hellenists,' the 'Seven' and Stephen (Acts 6:1–15; 7:54–8:3)," in *Between Jesus and Paul: Studies in the Earliest History of Christianity* (Eugene, Ore.: Wipf & Stock, 2003), 1–29; Alan Watson, *The Trial of Stephen: The First Christian Martyr* (Athens, Ga.: University of Georgia Press, 1996); Dennis D. Sylva, "The Meaning and Function of Acts 7:56–60," *Journal of Biblical Literature* 106 (1987): 261–75; Charles H. H. Scobie, "The Use of Source Material in the Speeches of Acts 3 and 7," *New Testament Studies* 25 (1979): 399–421; John Kilgallen, *The Stephen Speech: A Literary and Redactional Study of Acts 7: 2-53*, AnBib 67 (Rome: Pontifical Biblical Institute, 1976).

[2] The name *Jesus* occurs in verse 45; and as does Hebrews 4:8, refers to *Joshua*.

events he cites. And before he finishes his testimony the accused becomes the accuser of the nation; the one to be judged becomes the judge. Indeed his whole testimony as he rapidly speaks of past history in his great and divinely arranged retrospect, is a most powerful testimony to the nation as well as against the nation.

Another striking fact is that he puts two persons into the foreground. These are Joseph and Moses. Why they occupy such a prominent place in Stephen's address we shall see later.

Another matter we have to mention briefly before we touch upon some of the special features of the address. A careful reading of the statements made by Stephen and comparison with the Old Testament records show that there are certain things added by Stephen of which we do not read in the previous records; there are also other variations. These are often called discrepancies and are used as evidences against the inspirations of the Scriptures. However, they are far from being that. The Holy Spirit through Stephen adds some details to the already existing records. Stephen who was a Hellenist, a Greek speaking Jew, spoke most likely in the Greek language and then used the text of the Greek translation of the Old Testament (the Septuagint, LXX), which explains some of these alleged discrepancies. We shall not attempt to explain any of the others as that would lead us too far. We turn now to the address of Stephen to examine its different parts.

Abraham's History (vs. 2–8).

And Stephen said:

"Brothers and fathers, hear me. The God of glory appeared to our father Abraham when he was in Mesopotamia, before he lived in Haran, and said to him, 'Go out from your land and from your kindred and go into the land that I will show you.' Then he went out from the land of the Chaldeans and lived in Haran. And after his father died, God removed him from there into this land in which you are now living. Yet he gave him no inheritance in it, not even a foot's length, but promised to give it to him as a possession and to his offspring after him, though he had no child. And God spoke to this effect—that his offspring would be sojourners in a land belonging to others, who would enslave them and afflict them four hundred years. 'But I will judge the nation that they serve,' said God, 'and after that they shall come out and worship me in this place.' And he gave him the covenant of circumcision. And so Abraham became the father of Isaac, and circumcised him on the eighth day, and Isaac became the father of Jacob, and Jacob of the twelve patriarchs (vs. 2–8).

He begins with the great father of the nation, Abraham. Very significant is the beginning of the address. "The God of glory appeared to our father Abraham when he was in Mesopotamia, before he lived in Haran" (7:2). The same expression is used in Psalm 29:3, "the God of glory thunders." In Ephesians 1:17 "The Father of Glory." In 1 Corinthians 2:8, where our Lord is called by the same title, "The Lord of Glory" and in 1 Peter 4:14, "the Spirit of Glory." With this beautiful phrase Stephen begins and when his testimony is finished he beheld this very Glory of the Lord and he saw him of whom he had borne witness, the One who had appeared to Abraham and to Moses in the burning bush. This beginning is significant for the greater Glory of the Lord and the light of the knowledge of the Glory of God in the face of Jesus Christ is now soon to be made known through that chosen instrument to whom was committed the Gospel of the Glory of God, the Apostle Paul.

From Joshua 24:2 we find that the God of Glory had appeared to Abraham when he was in the country of idolatry, himself an idolater. God had graciously called him out of it and Abraham had gone forth in faith, not knowing where he Went; God brought him to the land of Canaan. Concerning the promise Stephen said,

Yet he gave him no inheritance in it, not even a foot's length, but promised to give it to him as a possession and to his offspring after him, though he had no child (7:5).

Abraham believed the promise and was justified by faith. All this manifested the grace of God. It was unmerited favour. Abraham did nothing nor could do anything to earn all this. There was no temple then to boast of and no law to keep. The promise and the covenant were before the law. But they boasted in the law, which they did not keep and in the temple. It was true of the council then as Paul wrote later

> For, being ignorant of the righteousness of God, and seeking to establish their own, they did not submit to God's righteousness. For Christ is the end of the law for righteousness to everyone who believes[3] (Rom 10:3–4).

They had this righteousness and grace offered to them and they were rejecting it. The argument advanced here is similar to the one which Paul brings forth in Galatians 3. If the young Pharisee Saul of Tarsus heard Stephen, he heard for the first time, though still blinded, the great truth the Spirit of God unfolded through him after his conversion.

But Stephen also speaks of Israel's sojourn in a strange land as revealed to Abraham. For four hundred years they were entreated evil (vs. 6–7). This tells of the suffering of Israel before they came into the possession of the land, a hint, no doubt, of the great truth so clearly revealed in Israel's history of the suffering of Christ and the Glory that should follow. Here the Spirit of God once more came to their consciences in this historical outline of their father Abraham. Alas! their hearts were closed.

Joseph and his brethren (vs. 9–16).

And the patriarchs, jealous of Joseph, sold him into Egypt; but God was with him and rescued him out of all his afflictions and gave him favor and wisdom before Pharaoh, king of Egypt, who made him ruler over Egypt and over all his household. Now there came a famine throughout all Egypt and Canaan, and great affliction, and our fathers could find no food. But when Jacob heard that there was grain in Egypt, he sent out our fathers on their first visit. And on the second visit Joseph made himself known to his brothers, and Joseph's family became known to Pharaoh. And Joseph sent and summoned Jacob his father and all his kindred, seventy-five persons in all. And Jacob went down into Egypt, and he died, he and our fathers, and they were carried back to Shechem and laid in the tomb that Abraham had bought for a sum of silver from the sons of Hamor in Shechem (vs. 9–16).

Stephen in his inspired testimony passes over the entire history of Isaac and Jacob, and Joseph instead is prominently mentioned. The way the story of Joseph is given, the comprehensive style is really marvelous. The complete history of the suffering and glory, the humiliation and exaltation of Joseph, is pictured in a few sentences and that in a manner which greatly illuminates this interesting portion of God's Word. In bringing Joseph at once before their hearts, what was done to him and to what place God exalted him, the Holy Spirit reveals one of the finest and most perfect types of Christ contained in the Word of God. The main issue of Stephen's testimony is before us with Joseph's history. "The patriarchs, jealous of Joseph, sold him into Egypt" (7:9). Their own brother, because they hated him without a cause, was sold by them into the hands of the Gentiles. The price was twenty pieces of silver. The meaning of this was so clear that the assembled council must have fully understood the application. The chief priests and elders had hated another one, who was, according to the flesh, their brother. And their hatred against him was on account of envy. Pilate even knew this. "For he perceived that it was out of envy

---

[3] Or *end of the law, that everyone who believes may be justified*

that the chief priests had delivered him up" (Mark 15:10). This Jesus of Nazareth, the name they hated so much, had been sold for thirty pieces of silver. His Own had delivered him into the hands of the Gentiles, as Joseph had been sold into Egypt. Then we read the brief sentence, "but God was with him." The same phrase is used by Peter in reference to Jesus in preaching to the household of Cornelius (Acts 10:38). The council knew perfectly that God was with the One, whom they had condemned. One of their own number, Nicodemus, had even came to the One, they despised and envied, with the declaration Upon his lips "Rabbi, we know that you are a teacher come from God, for no one can do these signs that you do unless God is with him" (John 3:2).

A description of Joseph's exaltation follows. "And rescued him out of all his afflictions and gave him favor and wisdom before Pharaoh, king of Egypt, who made him ruler over Egypt and over all his household" (7:10). Then comes a brief account of the famine, which troubled the brethren of Joseph. They had to go and get bread from the brother they had rejected. The second time Joseph was made known to his brethren.

The typical meaning is obvious. God had also delivered Him, whom they had rejected and crucified. He had raised him from the dead and made Him, as Peter preached, both Lord and Christ. Then there is a great dispensational foreshadowing. The rejected One, like Joseph, is received by the Gentiles. Famine and tribulation awaits the nation who rejected him who came to his own, they must suffer as Joseph's brethren suffered. "the second visit Joseph made himself known to his brothers" (7:13), refers to the second coming of the Lord. Joseph was the salvation of his brethren.

Moses as Deliverer rejected (vs. 17–38).

The rejected One a Ruler and Deliverer.

But as the time of the promise drew near, which God had granted to Abraham, the people increased and multiplied in Egypt until there arose over Egypt another king who did not know Joseph. He dealt shrewdly with our race and forced our fathers to expose their infants, so that they would not be kept alive. At this time Moses was born; and he was beautiful in God's sight. And he was brought up for three months in his father's house, and when he was exposed, Pharaoh's daughter adopted him and brought him up as her own son. And Moses was instructed in all the wisdom of the Egyptians, and he was mighty in his words and deeds.

When he was forty years old, it came into his heart to visit his brothers, the children of Israel. And seeing one of them being wronged, he defended the oppressed man and avenged him by striking down the Egyptian. He supposed that his brothers would understand that God was giving them salvation by his hand, but they did not understand. And on the following day he appeared to them as they were quarreling and tried to reconcile them, saying, 'Men, you are brothers. Why do you wrong each other?' But the man who was wronging his neighbor thrust him aside, saying, 'Who made you a ruler and a judge over us? Do you want to kill me as you killed the Egyptian yesterday?' At this retort Moses fled and became an exile in the land of Midian, where he became the father of two sons.

Now when forty years had passed, an angel appeared to him in the wilderness of Mount Sinai, in a flame of fire in a bush. When Moses saw it, he was amazed at the sight, and as he drew near to look, there came the voice of the Lord: 'I am the God of your fathers, the God of Abraham and of Isaac and of Jacob.' And Moses trembled and did not dare to look. Then the Lord said to him, 'Take off the sandals from your feet, for the place where you are standing is holy ground. I have surely seen the affliction of my people who are in Egypt, and have heard their groaning, and I have come down to deliver them. And now come, I will send you to Egypt.'

This Moses, whom they rejected, saying, 'Who made you a ruler and a judge?'—this man God sent as both ruler and redeemer by the hand of the angel who appeared to him in the bush. This man led them out, performing wonders and signs in Egypt and at the Red Sea and in the wilderness for forty years. This is the Moses who said to the Israelites, 'God will raise up for you a prophet like me from your brothers.' This is the one who was in the congregation in the wilderness with the angel who spoke to him at Mount Sinai, and with our fathers. He received living oracles to give to us (vs. 17–38).

This is the largest section of Stephen's address.

In Moses they boasted continually. They were proud of him as their law-giver, the mighty man who had led their fathers forth from the house of bondage, through whom the God of the Glory had performed his great miracles. They called him, and orthodox Jews do so still, "Moses, our teacher." What was his experience? Was he at once received by their forefathers? Did they accept him when he came to deliver them? How was he treated? The Divine record is unrolled before their hearts and the history, so familiar to the council, speaks once more. Moses foreshadows likewise Christ. His experience outlines the experience of Him, who is counted worthy of more glory than Moses (Heb 3:3–5).

Stephen says "the time of the promise drew near, which God had granted to Abraham" (8:17). God remembered his Word. The people were in bondage in Egypt and needed a deliverer. God provided the deliverer through whom the promise, because the time of the promise drew nigh, should be accomplished. All is pregnant with meaning. The time of the promise of the coming of the Redeemer had indeed drawn nigh. He had appeared, whom God had sent to deliver his people. Had he been received? The story of Moses' rejection was repeated on a larger scale in the story of Jesus of Nazareth.

First we find a description of Moses. He was born just in the time when the oppression was great; "At this time Moses was born" (8:20). Even so, "when the fullness of time had come, God sent forth his Son, born of woman, born under the law" (Gal 4:4). Moses was "was beautiful in God's sight" (7:20). That is he was exceedingly lovely. But how much more was He, who came from the Glory, the only begotten of the Father. Moses was learned in all the wisdom of the Egyptians (v. 22); Christ is the Wisdom. Moses was mighty in works and in deeds, but Christ was far more than that and manifested his divine power and grace in the midst of his people. The next thing said of Moses is that "he was cast out." The application of this to Christ we need not to follow in detail. When Moses was full grown, forty years, it came into his heart to visit his brethren the children of Israel. He appeared for them as a deliverer out of the bondage and it is written

> He supposed that his brothers would understand that God was giving them salvation by his hand, but they did not understand (7:25).

He was rejected by those he had come to deliver. "Who made you a ruler and a judge over us?" (7:27), was the sneering word cast at him. Moses had to flee into a strange land and be among strangers for forty years. And something similar had but recently been repeated in the very midst of the people. The deliverer had appeared. He had visited his people and made Himself known to them; "God was giving them salvation by his hand" (7:25). But his own had not received Him. They understood not; they cast him out and denied Him. Like Joseph, Moses went to the Gentiles, rejected by his people. The application to Christ is easily made and we do not follow it in its particulars.

But Moses returned and the once rejected deliverer whom they knew not was after all the one who delivered them and brought them forth.

> This Moses, whom they rejected, saying, "Who made you a ruler and a judge?"—this man God sent as both ruler and redeemer by the hand of the angel who appeared to him in the bush. This man led them out, performing wonders and signs

in Egypt and at the Red Sea and in the wilderness for forty years (7:35–36).

The Holy Spirit pressed home these great foreshadowings. Must they not have been reminded of the words spoken before by Peter?

> The God of our fathers raised Jesus, whom you killed by hanging him on a tree. God exalted him at his right hand as Leader and Savior (5:30–31). . . . This Jesus is the stone that was rejected by you, the builders, which has become the cornerstone (4:11).

These were familiar words to them carried to their consciences by the Holy Spirit and now through the historical record of Moses, the Moses of whom they boasted, the same truth is flashed before them once more. "This Moses" the one who was rejected "this man God sent" meant "Jesus, whom you killed by hanging him on a tree. God exalted him at his right hand as Leader and Savior" (5:31).

Significant too is the event of the burning bush, the angel of the Lord had appeared there in his Glory to Moses and it was by the hand of that angel that Moses became the ruler and deliverer (v. 35). Wonders and signs were then accomplished through him. Of this uncreated angel the council believed that he was the Lord Himself, while their traditions well known and received at that time, spoke of him as the Messiah. This same Lord had been in their midst and manifested his presence by wonders and signs.

The Holy Spirit witnesses also in this to the truth, so often revealed, that in the future, at the second Coming of Christ (corresponding to the second time in the history of Joseph), the nation will know and accept Him, whom they rejected before.

The history of Moses is the foreshadowing of the history of Christ. In Moses they believed and boasted. The accusation was that Stephen spoke against Moses. His testimony proves that he believes in Moses. But did the council really believe in Moses? The accused becomes the accuser. They did not believe in Moses and in his words. "The LORD your God will raise up for you a prophet like me from among you, from your brothers—it is to him you shall listen" (Deut 18:15). If they believed in this prediction as given by Moses they would have looked for that prophet, whose coming was promised by Moses. That it was fulfilled in the person of the Lord Jesus Christ, Peter had stated in his second address (Acts 3:22–23). But they were unbelieving.

The Story of their Apostasy and Shame (vs. 39–53).

> Our fathers refused to obey him, but thrust him aside, and in their hearts they turned to Egypt, saying to Aaron, 'Make for us gods who will go before us. As for this Moses who led us out from the land of Egypt, we do not know what has become of him.' And they made a calf in those days, and offered a sacrifice to the idol and were rejoicing in the works of their hands. But God turned away and gave them over to worship the host of heaven, as it is written in the book of the prophets:
>
> "'Did you bring to me slain beasts and sacrifices, during the forty years in the wilderness, O house of Israel? You took up the tent of Moloch and the star of your god Rephan, the images that you made to worship; and I will send you into exile beyond Babylon.'
>
> "Our fathers had the tent of witness in the wilderness, just as he who spoke to Moses directed him to make it, according to the pattern that he had seen. Our fathers in turn brought it in with Joshua when they dispossessed the nations that God drove out before our fathers. So it was until the days of David, who found favor in the sight of God and asked to find a dwelling place for the God of Jacob.[4] But it was Solomon who built a house for him. Yet the Most High does not dwell in houses made by hands, as the prophet says,

---

[4] Some manuscripts *for the house of Jacob*.

> "'Heaven is my throne, and the earth is my footstool. What kind of house will you build for me, says the Lord, or what is the place of my rest? Did not my hand make all these things?'
>
> "You stiff-necked people, uncircumcised in heart and ears, you always resist the Holy Spirit. As your fathers did, so do you. Which of the prophets did your fathers not persecute? And they killed those who announced beforehand the coming of the Righteous One, whom you have now betrayed and murdered, you who received the law as delivered by angels and did not keep it." (39–53).

Even after the departure from Egypt and after witnessing the signs and wonders wrought, they did not obey Moses, they thrust him from them and their hearts turned back again to Egypt. So they had not obeyed Christ and had also thrust him from them. This is followed by a brief rehearsal of their shameful history. They rushed into idolatry. They worshipped the host of heaven and during the wilderness journey they brought sacrifices to Moloch and Remphan (Amos 5:25–27). Then their coming captivity had been announced. On account of the rejection of the One, who is greater than Moses, whose coming Moses had announced, greater apostasy and dispersion must follow.

Then he speaks of the tabernacle of witness in the wilderness, made according to the fashion as seen by Moses and how they came under Joshua in possession of the Gentiles, who were driven out of the land (vs. 44–45). David is briefly mentioned. He found favour before God and desired to build a tabernacle for the God of Jacob. But Solomon built him a house. But the most High dwells not in places made with hands. Solomon himself had made this declaration (1 Kgs 8:27) and the Prophet Isaiah had expressed the same truth (Isa 66:1–2). Furthermore, the Glory and the Lord of the Glory, who dwelt once in the temple had departed; *Ichabod* (the Glory is departed) was written there. But more than that the Lord who was present in the tabernacle and whose Glory had filled the house once had appeared in their midst and they had cast him out and slain the Prince of Glory. Could then that temple be called any longer "a holy place" as they said in their accusation? The tale of the apostasy of the nation was thus told out from the records of the nation.

But now the summing up comes. Perhaps throughout the discourse evidences of displeasure from the sides of the council must have been in evidence. If it had been in their power they would have stopped him before. They were, however, constrained to listen. Another power compelled them to hear the arraignment of themselves and of the nation. The climax is reached. Most likely they began to grind their teeth already. Their dark sinister countenances showed the wrath and bitterness of Satan. They are cut in their consciences. Perhaps some arose and disorder was about to issue.

Stephen ceases his retrospect. The Holy Spirit now addresses them directly. The accused Stephen becomes the mouthpiece of the Judge who pronounces the sentence.

> You stiff-necked people, uncircumcised in heart and ears, you always resist the Holy Spirit. As your fathers did, so do you. Which of the prophets did your fathers not persecute? And they killed those who announced beforehand the coming of the Righteous One, whom you have now betrayed and murdered, you who received the law as delivered by angels and did not keep it. (7:51–53).

Every word was true. The entire testimony was unimpeachable. Stiffnecked and uncircumcised, resisting the Holy Spirit, persecuting the prophets who prophesied of Christ and the murderers of the Just One! This was their condition. With this the testimony of Stephen is ended; more than that the testimony to the nation is now to be closed. No longer is the offer to be made to Jerusalem.

2. THE MARTYRDOM OF STEPHEN (VS. 54–60).

> Now when they heard these things they were enraged, and they ground their teeth at him. But he, full of the Holy Spirit, gazed into heaven and saw the glory of God, and Jesus standing at the right hand of God. And he said, "Behold, I see the heavens opened, and the Son of Man standing at the right hand of God." But they cried out with a loud voice and stopped their ears and rushed together[5] at him. Then they cast him out of the city and stoned him. And the witnesses laid down their garments at the feet of a young man named Saul. And as they were stoning Stephen, he called out, "Lord Jesus, receive my spirit." And falling to his knees he cried out with a loud voice, "Lord, do not hold this sin against them." And when he had said this, he fell asleep (vs. 54–60).

And now the awful storm breaks. The arrows of the truth of God carried by the power of God's Spirit had cut to the heart and they gnashed on him with their teeth. In their madness they were dumb. They did not find words to give vent to their burning hatred which Satan had kindled in their stubborn, unbelieving hearts. All they could do in their frenzy was to gnash with their teeth. It was not a sudden outburst but the tense rather shows that it was prolonged. In the midst of this wicked crowd, no longer the council but a murderous mob, stood Stephen. If his face shone like that of an angel in the beginning of his testimony, what glory must have rested upon him now? The heavenly glory into which he was so soon to enter must have been wonderfully reflected upon his face.

Three things are said of him. He was full of the Holy Spirit; he looked steadfastly into heaven seeing there the Glory of God, he saw Jesus standing on the right hand of God.

The Holy Spirit in his fulness was upon him. He had testified through him and now as they are gnashing their teeth, ready to seize him and to follow Satan, who is a murderer from the beginning, to the full extent of his power, Stephen stands in great calmness and peace. The Holy Spirit who possessed him so fully directed his gaze away from the earth upward into Heaven. He looked steadfastly into heaven. This is one effect of the filling of the Spirit, the heart occupation with heavenly things. But more than that he saw the glory of God and Jesus standing on the right hand of God. The unspeakable Glory shone out of the depths of heaven and in that Glory he saw Jesus standing on the right hand of God. He of whom he had borne such a good witness, whose blessed name he had glorified in his life and by his words and whom he soon was to glorify in his triumphant death was seen by him.

While we read in the Epistles that the Lord sat down, on the right hand of God, the attitude which tells of his finished work, we read here that he was seen standing. This is not a contradiction. We do not think it was because he was still waiting for Israel's repentance, ready to come back. He was seen standing because he had arisen from his seat to welcome into his own presence the faithful martyr.

This is the first manifestation of the glorified Christ, which we have on record. There are three of them only. He appeared here to Stephen. Then (oh! marvelous Grace!) he appeared to Saul, who consented to Stephen's death. Saul beheld him in that Glory, brighter than the noon-day sun and heard his voice. The last time the glorified Christ manifested Himself was to John in the island of Patmos. These three appearings of the glorified Christ present to our view the three aspects of his Second Coming. First he comes to welcome his own into his presence. He will arise and come into the air to meet his beloved co-heirs there. This is represented by the first appearing to Stephen, standing to receive

---

[5] Or *rushed with one mind*

him. Then Israel will behold Him, they who pierced him will see Him, like Saul of Tarsus beheld the Lord. Then he will appear as John saw Him, the One who judges the earth in righteousness.

And now after this great and glorious vision, Stephen bears testimony to it. "Behold, I see the heavens opened, and the Son of Man standing at the right hand of God" (7:56) he speaks, of the Lord as "Son of Man." This is the only time outside of the Gospel records, that we find this title of the Lord (aside from the Old Testament references in Hebrews 2).

But were not these familiar words to the frenzied council? Had they not heard One saying similar words? But a few weeks ago they had gazed upon Him, whom they hated and envied. The vision of that meek and lowly One must surely have come up before their eyes that very moment. And he had said in the presence of this very council, "But from now on the Son of Man shall be seated at the right hand of the power of God" (Luke 22:69). And here is the echo of that solemn word on account of which the Holy One was condemned. But it is more than an echo. It is the witness that the Son of Man is there at the right hand of God.

We do not read of an orderly trial which followed. All order was abandoned. Chaos and confusion reigned. They cried out with a loud voice, and stopped their ears and ran upon him with one accord. Stopping the ears is a frequent occurrence among orthodox Hebrews. We have talked with some of them and after pressing an argument about the Messiahship of Jesus, they would put their hands to their ears, as if to shut out any further argument.

The Sanhedrin[6] had been changed into a wild, furious, demon-possessed mob, bent on the murder of God's witness. One thing they do which was according to the law. They rushed him out of the city. Like the Lord Jesus Christ he was to suffer "outside the gate." The law required this (Lev 24:14; Num 15:35). And there they stoned Stephen. In this act they were lawbreakers for their own witness had been to the Roman authorities, "It is not lawful for us to put anyone to death" (John 18:31).

But they make a show of keeping the law. In Deuteronomy, it is written: "The hand of the witnesses shall be first against him to put him to death, and afterward the hand of all the people" (Deut 17:7). They had witnesses who began the awful work by casting stones upon him first. And that young Pharisee of Cilicia took a prominent part in this terrible scene. He was a prominent figure in it. Saul of Tarsus stands in the foreground. If he was a member of the council, which is more than probable, then he heard the whole testimony of Stephen and consented to his death. In Acts 22:20 we read that he said "I also was standing by." This may mean that he had charge over what occurred. One thing is certain, he was intimate with the witnesses. They took off their upper garments so as to be freed to strike hard, and deposited their garments at the feet of Saul.

And now the stoning began. The first thing Stephen did was to pray. He called upon the Lord God. His prayer was addressed to the Lord Jesus, into whose hands he committed his spirit.

Then he bowed his knees and with a loud voice he manifested the love of Christ by forgiving his murderers, "Lord, do not hold this sin against them" (7:60). This prayer was answered in the conversion of that young man, whose name was Saul, for the responsibility and guilt was upon him, inasmuch as he had consented to his death (8:1).

---

[6] Evans, "Sanhedrin," 1193–94; Burkill, "The Competence of the Sanhedrim," 80–96.

Then Stephen fell asleep. The mighty witness closed his eyes on earth. But what a moment it must have been when his spirit was received by him whose Glory and Person he beheld, and into whose hands he had committed his spirit.

God's gracious offer and Christ had now been fully rejected by the nation. Stephen, who bore this last witness, is a striking evidence of the transforming power of Christ. How much like the Lord he was!

he was filled with the Spirit, full of faith and power, and like the Lord he did great wonders and miracles among the people. Like Christ, he was falsely accused of speaking against Moses, the law and the temple, and of being a blasphemer. They brought him before the same council and did what they did with the Lord, bringing false witnesses against him. He gave witness to the truth of the confession, the Lord had given before the council, that he was to sit at the right hand of God. He beheld him there. The Lord Jesus committed his spirit in the Father's hands, and Stephen prayed that the Lord Jesus receive his spirit; and like the Lord he prayed for the forgiveness of his enemies. May the same power transform us all into the same image.

Chapter Eight

The final testimony to the rulers of the Jewish people had been given. It was rejected, and the Spirit-filled messenger killed. The last offer had therefore been completely rejected and the Gospel is now soon to be sent far hence to the Gentiles; those that are afar off are to be brought nigh. The eighth chapter is a transition chapter. The Gospel is preached in Samaria. The instrument used is not Peter or John, but Philip. We divide this chapter into five parts:

1. The first great persecution (vs. 1–3).

2. The preaching of the scattered believers. Philip in Samaria (vs. 4–8).

3. The events in Samaria (vs. 9–24).

4. The Gospel in many villages of Samaria (v. 25).

5. Philip and the Ethiopian Eunuch (vs. 26–40).

1. The First Great Persecution (vs. 1–3).

> And Saul approved of his execution.
>
> And there arose on that day a great persecution against the church in Jerusalem, and they were all scattered throughout the regions of Judea and Samaria, except the apostles. Devout men buried Stephen and made great lamentation over him. But Saul was ravaging the church, and entering house after house, he dragged off men and women and committed them to prison. (vs. 1–3).

The first sentence with which this chapter starts belongs to the preceding chapter. The young Pharisee, who soon takes the prominent place in this book, was in perfect agreement with the awful deed committed. He rejoiced. The death of Stephen was with his fullest approval. He took pleasure in it. He was an eye-witness to the entire suffering of Stephen from the moment the dispute took place to the time when the stones fell upon him outside of the city and his blood was shed. Later he refers to the scene, which must have been impossible for him to erase from his memory.

> And when the blood of Stephen your witness was being shed, I myself was standing by and approving and watching over the garments of those who killed him (Acts 22:20).

Concerning Saul the Lord said to Ananias, "For I will show him how much he must suffer for the sake of my name" (9:16). What was done to Stephen was done to Saul. The Jews and Saul with them, as we believe, disputed and resisted Stephen in the synagogue. The Jews disputed with Paul, resisted him, and rejected his testimony. Stephen was accused of blasphemy; so was Paul (19:37). Stephen was accused of speaking against Moses, the holy place and the customs; so was Paul (Acts 21:28; 24:6; 25:8; 28:17). They rushed upon Stephen with one accord and seized him. The same happened to Paul (Acts 19:29). Stephen was dragged out of the city. So was Paul (Acts 14:19). Stephen was tried before the Sanhedrin; so did Paul appear before the Sanhedrin. Stephen was stoned and Paul was stoned at Lystra (see Fig. 22). Stephen suffered martyrdom; so did Paul in Rome. And yet, with all the sufferings that Paul had to undergo, he rejoiced. His eyes rested constantly upon that glorious one, whom

Stephen, filled with the Holy Spirit, beheld in Glory. Later we hear him crying out from the prison in Rome, "That I may know him and the power of his resurrection, and may share his sufferings, becoming like him in his death" (Phil 3:10).

The first great persecution then broke out against the church in Jerusalem. The words of the Lord concerning his own, that they were to suffer and to be hated, were fully carried out. Saul was evidently the leader. Perhaps from the very scene of bloodshed he led forth a mob of people, like so many tigers, having seen blood. There is no detailed account of the persecution. They were driven out of Jerusalem. Houses were entered and men and women dragged out of them and put into prison. The Epistle to the Hebrews, no doubt, refers to this first great persecution.

> But recall the former days when, after you were enlightened, you endured a hard struggle with sufferings, sometimes being publicly exposed to reproach and affliction, and sometimes being partners with those so treated. For you had compassion on those in prison, and you joyfully accepted the plundering of your property, since you knew that you yourselves had a better possession and an abiding one. (Heb 10:32–34).

They were disgraced, flogged, their goods were taken from them and they were driven out of the city. All this they stood joyfully. There is no record of anyone appealing to the Roman law. How many believers would in our day endure such persecution! But even this was only the beginning. Hundreds of years followed of the most cruel and satanic persecutions in which uncountable numbers were tortured, cast into dungeons, starved to death, burned alive, sawn asunder, cast before wild animals; every conceivable cruelty was practiced upon Christians. But the roaring lion had to withdraw, defeated.

Saul is the leading figure in this great persecution. He ravaged and laid waste the church. What a miracle of grace to hear him later refer to his conduct,

> "I persecuted this Way to the death, binding and delivering to prison both men and women" (Acts 22:4). . . . And I said, "Lord, they themselves know that in one synagogue after another I imprisoned and beat those who believed in you. And when the blood of Stephen your witness was being shed, I myself was standing by and approving and watching over the garments of those who killed him." (22:19-20). . . . And I did so in Jerusalem. I not only locked up many of the saints in prison after receiving authority from the chief priests, but when they were put to death I cast my vote against them. And I punished them often in all the synagogues and tried to make them blaspheme, and in raging fury against them I persecuted them even to foreign cities. (26:10-11).

He called himself a blasphemer and a persecutor (1 Tim 1:13). What light these confessions of the great apostle shed upon the brief record here in our chapter. In the Epistle to the Galatians and in 1 Corinthians he declares that he persecuted the church of God (1 Cor 15:9; Gal 1:13). This should for once dispel the new teaching which has arisen, that the church did not come into existence till Paul had received the revelation concerning the church. That the church began on the day of Pentecost is frequently denied. But how could Paul persecute the church, if there was no church at all?

Then we see Stephen laid aside. His mangled body was carried by devout men to its resting place, while his spirit was in the presence of the Lord. These devout men were men like Joseph of Arimathea and Nicodemus. Their lamentations were a Jewish characteristic. The Hope of Glory was not known to them. Later even the Thessalonian Christians sorrowed as others, who have no hope (1 Thess 4:13). Then was made known that "blessed Hope," which should forever dispel the sorrow and lamentations of God's people. But that hope was unknown in the beginning of Acts.

2. THE PREACHING OF THE SCATTERED BELIEVERS. PHILIP IN SAMARIA (VS. 4–8).

> Now those who were scattered went about preaching the word. Philip went down to the city[1] of Samaria and proclaimed to them the Christ. And the crowds with one accord paid attention to what was being said by Philip when they heard him and saw the signs that he did. For unclean spirits, crying out with a loud voice, came out of many who had them, and many who were paralyzed or lame were healed. So there was much joy in that city. (vs. 4–8).

They were scattered abroad. Only the Apostles remained in Jerusalem (v. 1). This has been explained as a failure on the side of the twelve. It is incorrect; God guided them and kept them there. That they were not arrested and also put into prison may perhaps be explained by the fact that they were not Hellenists, but natives of the land. The persecution may have been the severest against the Grecian Jews.

And now for the first time we learn that "the blood of the martyrs is the seed of the church." "Those who were scattered went about preaching the word" (8:4). God permitted all these hardships, that the precious seed of his own Word might now be scattered abroad by the suffering saints. The Lord had said that they were to be his witnesses not only in Jerusalem, but also in Judea and in Samaria. This he accomplished by the suffering of his people. What a sight it must have been when they went north from Jerusalem! A stream of men, women and children, in bodily pain from the hands of cruel men, stripped of their belongings, pours forth from the gates of the city. They were cast upon the Lord as never before and the Lord became more real to their hearts. And then they went about preaching. Everyone was a preacher. The great head of the church, not some ecclesiastical council, some committee, which ordained them and gave them authority, but the Lord Himself sent them out as his witnesses. Alas! what a contrast with ecclesiasticism of today with its man-made rules, its crystallized forms, ordinations, recognitions, etc.

And such an exodus from the city, out of which the Lord had been led forth to suffer outside the gate, has been repeated over and over again in the history of the church with like gracious results in scattering the seed of the Word. We mention only the Waldenses and the Huguenots. Satanic powers produced the first great persecution. But the wrath of the enemy had to praise the Lord. Out of it all there was brought Glory to Himself.

And now Philip comes in view. He was not an Apostle, but a Grecian Jew, one of the seven which had been chosen to look after the poor. The first great missionary move was therefore not accomplished by apostolic authority, or apostolic leadership, nor by the decree of an apostolic council, but by the Lord Himself, who chose his own instrument and led him forth into the field.

And he led Philip to Samaria where he Himself had gone, yea, to the very city of Samaria, which is Sychar. There he had once gone on the weary journey, and tired on account of the way, "[he] was sitting beside the well" (John 4:6). The servant of the Lord Jesus Christ went the same road. What a comfort to remember when the servant is tired that he knows of this weariness. The Samaritans were not a race of strangers altogether, but they had Israelitish blood in them. They had claimed to possess the true law and the temple. A division was the result and they were hated. As we read in the Gospel of John, "Jews have no dealings with Samaritans" (John 4:9). The soil there, however, had been prepared. The Samaritans in large numbers had believed on Him, for the words of the woman with whom the Lord had that memorable

---

[1] Some manuscripts *a city*

conversation at Jacob's well. They invited the Lord to tarry, and many more believed on him and these said to the woman, "It is no longer because of what you said that we believe, for we have heard for ourselves, and we know that this is indeed the Savior of the world." (John 4:42). To these people Philip appeared and preached Christ. With one accord they listened to these things. Had he preached something else it would not have been so. The great message still is to preach Christ. Miracles also took place. Unclean spirits were driven out, many taken with palsies and that were lame were healed, so that there was great joy in that city. These miracles in Samaria were of special significance of which we shall hear in the verses which follow.

Philip did miracles in connection with preaching the Gospel. Unclean spirits are especially mentioned. They came out of many which were possessed by them. Like Judea, Samaria seems to have been much afflicted by demon possessions. The city where Philip preached and the miracles were done, rejoiced greatly. "There was much joy in that city" (8:8). Miracles were in order then because the Word of God was not yet complete. Now after the Revelation of God is complete, miracles are no longer a necessity. Faith rests upon the Word of God and not upon miracles. The verses which follow show that there was a special significance in the miracles done by Philip in Samaria.

3. THE EVENTS IN SAMARIA (VS. 9–13).

> But there was a man named Simon, who had previously practiced magic in the city and amazed the people of Samaria, saying that he himself was somebody great. They all paid attention to him, from the least to the greatest, saying, "This man is the power of God that is called Great." And they paid attention to him because for a long time he had amazed them with his magic. But when they believed Philip as he preached good news about the kingdom of God and the name of Jesus Christ, they were baptized, both men and women. Even Simon himself believed, and after being baptized he continued with Philip. And seeing signs and great miracles [2] performed, he was amazed (vs. 9–13).

A sinister person is now introduced in this historical account. Simon Magus, as he is called, was an instrument of Satan most likely used in a special way to keep the Samaritans in darkness and counteract the work of the Lord, which had been accomplished there (John 3). He had bewitched the Samaritans, who were much given to all kinds of superstitions. The superstitiousness of this people resulted in the fall of Pontius Pilate. About the year 35 AD., a deceiver had appeared in Samaria and claimed that the sacred vessels were hidden by Moses on Mount Gerizim and that he would discover them. A very large multitude followed him, but Pilate was there also with soldiers and drove the people away. Large numbers of them were killed. The Samaritans made a complaint to Vitellius, the proconsul of Syria, who had Pilate dispatched to Rome to be tried. Simon was one of the numerous persons who preached all kinds of evil and forbidden things. With his wicked sorceries he had ensnared the people. Suetonius, a Roman historian, who lived in the first part of the second century of our era, gives the information that the whole eastern countries were at that time overrun with all kinds of wonder-workers, astrologers, healers and necromancers. One of the greatest was Apollonius of Tyanaeus, who died about 97 AD. He was a great sorcerer and worker of miracles. His life and supposed miracles were often compared with those of our Lord. Satan had anticipated the coming of the Gospel and used this man to keep the Samaritans in bondage, to counterfeit the power of God, and to oppose the truth.

---

[2] Greek works of power

Simon used sorcery, and had amazed the Samaritans with his acts of sorceries. Satan revealed his powers through him, and Simon himself claimed to be some great one, perhaps the incarnation of some higher being. The people of Samaria had believed him and his lying wonders, and even called him "that man is the great power of God." he was a false prophet and his signs and miracles he did, sprung from an evil source. All this is full of significance. Satan still counterfeits the Power of God. For the end of this present age there is predicted the manifestation of Satan in all power and signs and lying wonders (2 Thess 2:9). As the age nears its close and with it the advent of the Lord Jesus Christ in power and glory, Satan with his host of demons becomes increasingly active, ensnaring the people and leading on into blindness those who reject the Gospel. As in the days of the Evangelist Philip, so now he uses men as his instruments. Simon Magus is reproduced in our days not only in persons who, deluded as they are, claim to be some great one, but in systems, such as Spiritualism, Christian Science and Millennial Dawnism.

The hour of deliverance came for the Samaritans when Philip preached the Word, concerning the Kingdom of God and the name of Jesus Christ. Signs and great miracles followed, and the Samaritans believed and were baptized. The miracles were done to show the power of God, to attest the preaching of the Gospel by Philip, and to expose the counterfeit powers of Simon. And he, like the sorcerers of Egypt, had to own that this was the power of God. He was amazed when he beheld the great miracles. But more than that, he also believed, was baptized and then continued with Philip. But his faith was not through the Word of God. God's word alone can produce faith in man, for faith cometh by hearing, and hearing by the Word of God. Simon was captivated by the miracles he had seen. He believed in the same way as the many of whom we read in John: "Now when he was in Jerusalem at the Passover Feast, many believed in his name when they saw the signs that he was doing" (John 2:23). But was this the true faith? Was this a saving faith? Are miracles necessary to believe? The last two verses of the second chapter of John answer these questions. "But Jesus on his part did not entrust himself to them, because he knew all people" (John 2:24).

He knew their believing on him was not in truth. And so Simon Magus believed in the miracles. He also submitted to water baptism from the hands of Philip, which completely disproves that unscriptural teaching that water baptism is a saving ordinance, and that the new birth takes place in that act. He continued with Philip. This also is significant. He kept close in the company of the evangelist, no doubt to watch him and see whether he could discover the secret of the power of Philip. In the truth, in the Word of God, that wicked man had absolutely no part. Philip did not discern him. The attitude of Simon and his outward profession must, therefore, have been very cleverly devised. The discovery, however, came when Peter and John appeared in Samaria.

> Now when the apostles at Jerusalem heard that Samaria had received the word of God, they sent to them Peter and John, who came down and prayed for them that they might receive the Holy Spirit, for he had not yet fallen on any of them, but they had only been baptized in the name of the Lord Jesus. Then they laid their hands on them and they received the Holy Spirit. Now when Simon saw that the Spirit was given through the laying on of the apostles' hands, he offered them money, saying, "Give me this power also, so that anyone on whom I lay my hands may receive the Holy Spirit." But Peter said to him, "May your silver perish with you, because you thought you could obtain the gift of God with money! You have neither part nor lot in this matter, for your heart is not right before God. Repent, therefore,

of this wickedness of yours, and pray to the Lord that, if possible, the intent of your heart may be forgiven you. For I see that you are in the gall[3] of bitterness and in the bond of iniquity." And Simon answered, "Pray for me to the Lord, that nothing of what you have said may come upon me." (vs. 14–24).

From Jerusalem, Peter and John were sent by the apostles to Samaria. The Holy Spirit had not been given to the Samaritans. After the two apostles had prayed for them and laid their hands on them, they received the Holy Spirit. This fact, that the Holy Spirit was given after the prayer of Peter and John, has led to erroneous teaching.

Ritualistic Christendom uses this passage in the defence of its traditional teachings of apostolic succession and different rites, which have no foundation in the Scriptures. A recent commentary on the Book of Acts makes the following remarks on these verses:

> The Apostles supposed that the Holy Spirit would be given in answer to prayer and the laying on of their hands. Their expectation was justified; *and the church has accepted this as the normal method.* Luke gives us, in all, four accounts of the outpouring of the Holy Spirit (Chap 2; 8; 10 and 19). On two occasions (Pentecost and Cornelius household) the gift itself was extraordinary. The two other occasions (Samaritans and disciples at Ephesus) were normal, and the gift was conveyed by prayer and the laying on of hands. These hands were apostolic; in the one case, those of Peter and John, in the other of Paul. Nowhere in the Acts is the laying on of hands by other than apostles mentioned in this connection; and it is evident from this incident that, although Philip was a prophet and one of the seven, although he preached the Word and baptized, yet he did not possess this power. We conclude then that, as Luke states it, *through the laying on of the hands of the apostles the Spirit is given.* We are justified then, in finding here the beginning of the church's rite of confirmation.[4]

Thus ritualism claims through the laying on of hands by men who are ordained through others, who likewise received ordination, and so back to the apostolic times to confer the gift of the Holy Spirit.

Another erroneous teaching, built on the apostles communicating the Holy Spirit to these new believers, is one which becomes more frequent and is the source of much confusion among sincere Christians. It is taught from this historical account that a person may be a believer without possessing the Holy Spirit. The reception of the Holy Spirit, it is claimed, is a work entirely distinct from conversion. A Christian believer may be saved for a long time and be entirely destitute of the Holy Spirit; in order to receive Him, the believer must seek the experience and receive the Spirit; this is a very widespread teaching. The case of the Samaritans is often quoted to uphold this teaching.

All these wrong interpretations and wrong teachings would be avoided if the dispensational character of this part of the Acts of the Apostles were recognized. We have no teaching concerning the Holy Spirit and how he is to be received in this passage. The doctrine of the Spirit and how the believer receives him and his work in the believer is not taught in the Acts of the Apostles. This is a historical account, and if one holds to this and to the fact that Samaria (John 4:19–24) had a controversy with Jerusalem, the coming of the Apostles from Jerusalem, and the withholding of the Holy Spirit from the Samaritans till Peter and John arrived, becomes plain at once.

---

[3] That is, a bitter fluid secreted by the liver; bile

[4] Richard Belward Rackham, *The Acts of the Apostles: An Exposition*, 7th ed. (London, U.K.: Methuen & Company, 1901), 117.

The Samaritan believers had to be identified with those in Jerusalem, so much the more because there was a schism between Samaria and Jerusalem. Samaria had denied both the city of Jerusalem and the temple. This had to be ended and could no longer be tolerated. It was therefore divinely ordered that the gift of the Spirit in *their* case should be withheld till the two apostles came from Jerusalem. This meant an acknowledgment of Jerusalem; if the Holy Spirit had been imparted to them at once it might have resulted in a continuance of the existing rivalry. And Peter is in the foreground and uses the keys here with the Samaritans as he did on the day of Pentecost with the Jews and later with the Gentiles. Nowhere in the church Epistles, in which the great salvation truths and blessings in Christ Jesus are revealed, is there a word said about receiving the Holy Spirit by the laying on of hands, or that one who has trusted in Christ and is born again should seek the gift of the Holy Spirit afterward. When we reach the nineteenth chapter of this book we shall follow this at greater length.

There is no record here that the gift of the Spirit was attended by outward signs, such as speaking in tongues. Some manifestation must have accompanied the gift, for Simon "saw" that the Holy Spirit was given by the apostles' hands. Then the wickedness of his heart was revealed when he offered them money for the same power to impart the gift. He is now completely uncovered. No work of God had been produced in his soul or he would not have uttered such wicked words. His whole desire was to get power and pay for it. He made merchandise of that which is the gift of God, and all for his own advantage and for vainglory. And this sin, which has been termed "Simony," is still alive in many different phases. One must think here in connection with Simon of the present day movement called "Christian Science." This system uses no doubt occult things and contains philosophical speculation, which were not unknown to Simon the Sorcerer. But to become a successful healer a certain sum of money must be paid. The secret of power to heal is sold. And what else could one say of the more subtle forms of this sin? And now the two Simons face each other, Simon Peter and Simon Magus. Peter at once detected the wicked heart of the man through whom the enemy of God had spoken. In holy indignation and condemnation Peter burst forth: "May your silver perish with you" (8:20). The sorcerer with his wicked heart thought that the Gift of God could be purchased with money. In this the aim was the Gospel itself. Salvation and all that is connected with it, including the Spirit, is the Gift of God, without money and without price; it cannot be earned nor bought. He had no part nor lot in this matter. And this is true of all who in the depravity of their hearts think of obtaining the power of God by what they do. He sees himself uncovered and exposed "in the gall of bitterness and in the bond of iniquity" (8:23) in spite of his outward profession, his baptism and association with Philip. And while Peter thus spoke these burning words against him, he also exhorted him to repentance and prayer. Simon Magus is a type of what apostate, self-centered, self-seeking Christendom is, as well as of that person who is the "son of perdition," the personal Antichrist. And what had Simon to answer? "And Simon answered, 'Pray for me to the Lord, that nothing of what you have said may come upon me.'" (8:24).

He was alarmed. He trembled like the demons, who believe and tremble. There is no confession from his lips, no self-judgment. He does not exhibit confidence in the Lord nor does he ask for forgiveness. He was not moved by repentance, but only by fear. We do not read anything again of him in the Word of God.

Much is reported of Simon the sorcerer by the most ancient sources, the writings of the so-called fathers. Justin Martyr, who was a native of Samaria, who lived about a hundred years later, tells us that Simon held the doctrines of Gnosticism (the same which have appeared in a modern garb in Christian Science) and that the Samaritans worshipped him as a divine being. Epiphanius declares that he claimed deity among the Samaritans and that he was a Messianic pretender. Other sources say that he became after this a greater enemy of the truth, and having lost his prestige in Samaria he went to Rome and there established a wicked movement, which became a gall and bitterness to the true believers there. That he should have met Peter again in Rome and found his end there is only a legend. It is certain that he did not repent.

But the Gospel stream was not arrested. The acts of the enemy came to naught. The roaring lion as exhibited in the Sanhedrin the first persecutions the more cunning deception of the counterfeit Simon, the sorcerer, all came to naught.

4. The Gospel in Many Villages of Samaria (v. 25).

> Now when they had testified and spoken the word of the Lord, they returned to Jerusalem, preaching the gospel to many villages of the Samaritans (v. 25).

The apostles had accomplished their mission. They are turning homeward. On that journey they carried out the divine commission to be his witnesses in Samaria. Many villages heard the Gospel from their lips and with joyful hearts they declared the good news. What stir it must have made! They followed the Lord who had gone through Samaria, and what joy it must have been in these Samaritan villages when these two Jews heralded the good news! This is the last thing reported of John in the Book of Acts. Besides the Epistle to Galatians we hear his name only mentioned in the Apocalypse.

5. Philip and the Ethiopian Eunuch (vs. 26–40).

> Now an angel of the Lord said to Philip, "Rise and go toward the south[5] to the road that goes down from Jerusalem to Gaza." This is a desert place. And he rose and went. And there was an Ethiopian, a eunuch, a court official of Candace, queen of the Ethiopians, who was in charge of all her treasure. He had come to Jerusalem to worship and was returning, seated in his chariot, and he was reading the prophet Isaiah. And the Spirit said to Philip, "Go over and join this chariot." So Philip ran to him and heard him reading Isaiah the prophet and asked, "Do you understand what you are reading?" And he said, "How can I, unless someone guides me?" And he invited Philip to come up and sit with him. Now the passage of the Scripture that he was reading was this:
>
> "Like a sheep he was led to the slaughter and like a lamb before its shearer is silent, so he opens not his mouth. In his humiliation justice was denied him. Who can describe his generation? For his life is taken away from the earth."
>
> And the eunuch said to Philip, "About whom, I ask you, does the prophet say this, about himself or about someone else?" Then Philip opened his mouth, and beginning with this Scripture he told him the good news about Jesus. And as they were going along the road they came to some water, and the eunuch said, "See, here is water! What prevents me from being baptized?"[6] And he commanded the chariot to stop, and they both went down into the water, Philip and the eunuch, and he baptized him. And when they came up out of the water, the Spirit of the Lord carried Philip away, and the eunuch saw him no more, and went

---

[5] Or *go at about noon*

[6] 36 Some manuscripts add all or most of verse 37: *And Philip said, "If you believe with all your heart, you may." And he replied, "I believe that Jesus Christ is the Son of God."*

on his way rejoicing. But Philip found himself at Azotus, and as he passed through he preached the gospel to all the towns until he came to Caesarea (vs. 26–40).

The last part of our chapter contains the most interesting account of the acts of Philip. Called by the Head of the church to go forth as an Evangelist to Samaria, after his work was finished in Jerusalem, he had been mightily used in preaching the Gospel. There is no record of the numbers who were saved. When the Gospel was preached in Jerusalem by Peter we hear of numbers (chs. 2:41; 4:4), because it was still an offer to the Jewish nation in connection with the promised Kingdom, but now as Jerusalem has rejected that offer and the Gospel goes forth to Samaria, and to the Gentiles, numbers are no longer mentioned. During this age the number of those who accept the Gospel and become members of the body of Christ, the church, is unknown. One of the sad features of present day Evangelism with its sensationalism are the reports of how many converts have been made, how many signed cards or promised to lead a better life. To what untruths and other evils such methods lead we need not to follow here.

Philip's ministry was greatly blest and so will every ministry still be used if it is done as under the Lord, in humility and dependence upon Himself. With such a successful field before him Philip might have settled down to strengthen the new converts and reach out after other places in Samaria. But the work of the Evangelist is to move about and preach the Gospel from place to place. Philip is commanded to change his place of testimony. The command was communicated to him by an angel of the Lord. It was a heavenly messenger who was used to direct his way.

The angel may not have appeared to Philip in visible form, for the text tells us that he spoke to him and does not mention anything else. His message informs Philip of the way he is to take. Later in the account when it is the question of imparting spiritual instruction and dealing with the eunuch not an angel, but the Spirit speaks to Philip. The direction of the angel calls Philip away from his pleasant field of labor into a lonely and desert road. How many objections he might have made to such a call. Why should he leave the populous city and villages of Samaria where the multitudes heard him gladly and go on a journey which would lead him into an uninhabited region and to a deserted city?[7] But Philip realized his place as a servant and that the servant's work is to be obedient to his Master. His Lord had been in Samaria and Philip had reaped what the Lord had sown. He had been sent to reap that upon which he had not bestowed any labor (John 4:36–38). And now the Lord called and he obeyed. He arose and went. Obedience to the Lord is a beautiful thing and must always result in blessing. Happy is the servant who can say "for I always do the things that are pleasing to him" (John 8:29 cf. 4:34; 6:38; 8:29). If this is the attitude and the heart's desire the Lord will direct and show us the way in which we are to go. Such a life of dependence on the Lord and obedience to the Lord is truly great and will bring an abundant harvest. The obedient Philip may also be looked upon as a type of the nation itself. Some day the remnant of Israel will go forth in obedience to the call of the Lord and publish good tidings. Then it will be fulfilled what is written in Isaiah.

> How beautiful upon the mountains are the feet of him who brings good news, who publishes peace,

---

[7] Gaza was deserted then. Gaza was a fortress in the extreme south of Palestine. It was destroyed by Alexander the Great in the fourth century before Christ. What was not destroyed by him was in the year 96 completely overthrown by the Maccabaean prince Alexander so that it was literally a desert.

who brings good news of happiness, who publishes salvation, who says to Zion, "Your God reigns." The voice of your watchmen—they lift up their voice; together they sing for joy; for eye to eye they see the return of the LORD to Zion (Isa 52:7–8).

But while the Lord had his eyes upon his toiling servant and directed him in the way, he also saw and knew the inquiring, hungry soul which traveled along that road towards Gaza. He knew his heart and his longing for the truth and then he brought Philip to meet this soul and through him he graciously brought light and blessing to the eunuch. And thus he works still. Oh! for more childlike confidence in his guidance! A blessed thing it is to watch his leadings and to see his hand in even the minutest things.

The person journeying, most likely in a caravan, on the road to Gaza, was a man from Ethiopia. He was a eunuch of great authority under Candace Queen of the Ethiopians; he was her treasurer. He had been in Jerusalem to worship, most likely to attend the feast of Pentecost and was sitting in his chariot reading the prophet Isaiah. Who Queen Candace was, and in what part of Ethiopia her kingdom existed is learned from the Roman writer Pliny, and the Greek geographer Strabo. Both declare that there were several queens by that name ruling over the Ethiopians. The head of her kingdom was Meroe.

The eunuch was one of those who looked to Jerusalem, for light and blessing and had gone there to worship. He returned unsatisfied, still a seeker. As eunuch he was by the law an outcast and could not enter the congregation of Israel; however blessings are promised to the eunuchs in the very book from which he was reading (Isa 56 :3–5). And then the Spirit directed Philip to join himself to the chariot. The Ethiopian read the book of Isaiah aloud and Philip's question addressed to him was, "Do you understand what you are reading?" (8:30) he was reading the Greek translation of that all important chapter, the fifty-third. He read of him who was led as a sheep to the slaughter and opened not his mouth. By his question the eunuch showed his ignorance in the Scriptures. He did not know that the passage had any reference to the Servant of the Lord, the Messiah of Israel.

> One would wonder that whilst he was at Jerusalem he should have heard nothing concerning Jesus. Or perhaps what he heard of him was the occasion of his studying at this time that passage in Isaiah's prophecy.[8]

It was then on that lonely road that Philip preached Jesus to him. He began at the same Scripture, which indeed is a good starting point. And the message Philip preached, showing Jesus as the One in whom these prophecies were fulfilled, was at once accepted by the seeking eunuch. He who by the law is excluded from the congregation of Israel is now received into another congregation, even joined to the Lord and added to the company which are saved. Nothing could hinder baptism, for he had believed; he himself asks to be baptized.

We have omitted the 37th verse. It does not belong into the text at all, but is an interpolation. The profession of faith put by this verse in the mouth of the Ethiopian anticipates Paul. The first time that Christ is preached that he is the Son of God is in Acts 9:20. Peter preached him as the rejected Jesus of Nazareth, raised from the dead and Philip simply preached Jesus. It was reserved for Paul to declare the fulness of the Gospel of the Son of God, that Gospel of which he writes to the Galatians "For I did not receive it from any man, nor was I taught it, but I received it through a

---

[8] John Lightfoot and Robert Gandell, *Horae Hebraicae et Talmudicae: Hebrew and Talmudical Exercitations upon the Gospels, the Acts, Some Chapters of St. Paul's Epistle to the Romans, and the First Epistle to the Corinthians* (Oxford, U.K.: Oxford University Press, 1859), 99.

revelation of Jesus Christ" (Gal 1:12). The best Greek manuscripts have not the verse, which speaks of the eunuch's confession that Jesus Christ is the Son of God. We do well to omit verse 37, as it is also done in the revised version.

The baptism takes place. Both Philip and the eunuch went down into the water and when they were come up out of the water the Spirit of the Lord caught away Philip and the eunuch saw him no more. Philip's mission was accomplished and now a miraculous event takes place. This is an interesting occurrence. The Greek word for "catching away" is used a number of times in the New Testament and means each time an action by power. It is found eleven times in the New Testament (Matt 11:12; 13:19; John 6:15; 10:12; 28. Acts 13:39; 23:10; 2 Cor 12:2,4; 1 Thess 4:17; Jude 23; Rev 12:5). It is interesting to see that in the account of Paul's rapture into the third heaven this word is used and also in the divine revelation concerning the coming of the Lord for his Saints (1 Thess 4:17). The catching away of Philip after the work was accomplished is a little type of what will take place some day by the mighty power of God, when all the living believers will be removed from the scene of their present labors. "Will be caught up together with them in the clouds to meet the Lord in the air" (1 Thess 4:17) this is the blessed and imminent future of all God's children.

And the eunuch? What became of him? Did he go to the queen and did he give up his treasurership and become a great Evangelist through whom all Ethiopia was converted? Tradition may tell us these things but the divine record is silent. The time was not then nor has it come since that time, that "Nobles shall come from Egypt; Cush shall hasten to stretch out her hands to God." (Ps 68:31); the fulfillment of this is reserved for the Millennial reign of Christ over the earth. The Holy Spirit has just one little sentence about the eunuch. But it is a most precious statement he makes concerning the Ethiopian [Cush] who had received the knowledge of the truth and had believed the Gospel. He "went on his way rejoicing" (8:39). He had Christ and well could he go on his way with joy unspeakable and full of glory. And, dear reader, this sentence should express the experience of every true believer. If we have Christ and are his and he is ours, if we know we are saved, and safe and have before us nothing but glory, then we too should go on our way rejoicing. Yea, even when trials and perplexities surround our path, the joy in the Lord must be our portion. Anything less dishonors the Lord and the Gospel.

Philip was found some 20 miles north of Gaza, at Azotus. From there he started out anew preaching the Gospel. In many cities his voice was heard, these coast cities were inhabited by many Gentiles and included larger places like Jamnia, Lydda, Joppa and Antipatris. The day of Christ will make known the labors and also the reward of this great Evangelist. Then he came to Caesarea. But did he stop with that? We know not. Twenty years later we shall find him there and Paul was then his guest.

Chapter Nine

The previous chapter may be looked upon in its main part as a parenthesis. The record now leads us back to the close of the seventh chapter and the person who was connected with the great tragedy enacted there is prominently brought before us. The witnesses of the wicked deed had laid down their clothes at a young man's feet, whose name was Saul. This is the first time this remarkable man is mentioned. We also learned that he was consenting to Stephen's death; he made havoc of the church and committed men and women to prison. While the scattered believers had carried the Gospel throughout Judea, Philip had gone down to Samaria and with great results preached the Gospel, and during the same time Peter and John preached in the Samarian villages, Saul carried on his work of persecution. This we learn from the opening verse of the present chapter: "And Saul, yet breathing out threatenings and slaughter against the disciples of the Lord, went to the high priest." The conversion of this great persecutor and his call by the risen and glorified Lord to be the Apostle to the Gentiles is the event which is next described. It is the greatest event recorded in Acts next to the outpouring of the Holy Spirit on the day of Pentecost.

Before we expound the most important account of Saul's conversion and point out its extremely interesting lessons, it may be in order to give a brief description of the young man, who takes the leading part in the remaining portion of the Book of Acts.

Saul was born in Tarsus, an old city, and the capital of Cilicia. In that city was situated a great university given mostly to the study of Philosophy. Josephus in agreement with Jewish literature identified the city with Tarshish, to which Jonah attempted to flee. Saul has often been called a "Hellenist," that is, a Grecian Jew. But this is easily answered by his own words, "a Hebrew of the Hebrews." he belonged to the sect of the Pharisees, and his father was likewise a member of the same class, for Saul called himself "a Pharisee, a son of Pharisees" (Acts 23:6). His bringing up was on the strictest Jewish order. All the observances of the law and the traditions of the elders were conscientiously followed by him. This fact he calls to mind when he wrote his great defense of the Gospel to the Galatians:

> For you have heard of my former life in Judaism, how I persecuted the church of God violently and tried to destroy it. And I was advancing in Judaism beyond many of my own age among my people, so extremely zealous was I for the traditions of my fathers (Gal 1:13-14).

He also witnesses of his life before the Grace and Power of God converted him, when he wrote to the Philippians:

> Circumcised on the eighth day, of the people of Israel, of the tribe of Benjamin, a Hebrew of Hebrews; as to the law, a Pharisee; as to zeal, a persecutor of the church; as to righteousness

under the law,[1] blameless (Phil 3:5-6).

This young Pharisee had a strong belief in the God of Israel, in his promises and the destiny of Israel. This belief manifested itself outwardly in a zeal for God.[2] While he was thus filled with pride of race, zeal for God, but without knowledge, striving to attain righteousness, to fulfill and obey the very letter of the law, he had an intense hatred of what he supposed to be disloyalty to the law. In Tarsus, his native city, he became fully acquainted with Greek customs, Greek life, literature, art and philosophy. The local industry of Tarsus was tent making. These tents were manufactured out of goat's hair. This trade the young Saul learned. Teaching boys a certain trade is an ancient Jewish custom. His family may have been very influential and wealthy. He had a married sister living in Jerusalem, who must have been very highly connected (Acts 23:16). Saul of Tarsus was furthermore a Roman citizen. This was a high honor and privilege. It could be bought for large sums of money. When Paul was about to be scourged he mentioned his Roman citizenship. The chief captain, a Greek by the name of Claudius Lysias (Acts 23:26), said: "The tribune answered, "I bought this citizenship for a large sum." Paul said, "But I am a citizen by birth" (Acts 22:28). The prisoner held a higher honor than the captain; no wonder Claudius Lysias was afraid. His family must have had the Roman citizenship conferred upon them as a mark of distinction or reward for some eminent service.

Saul received his religious education in Jerusalem. We listen again to his own words:

> I am a Jew, born in Tarsus in Cilicia, but brought up in this city, educated at the feet of Gamaliel[3] according to the strict manner of the law of our fathers, being zealous for God as all of you are this day (Acts 22:3).

Gamaliel was the greatest rabbi of the Pharisees, the president of the Sanhedrin. He was the son of Simon and grandson of the celebrated Hillel. We have found his name before in the fifth chapter. He was highly esteemed for his learning. The Talmud says, "When he died the honor of the Torah (law) ceased, and purity and piety became extinct" (*Seta* 15:18). At the feet of this great and learned man, Saul of Tarsus sat. That Saul was highly respected in Jerusalem and close to the leaders of the people, is seen by the letters entrusted to him and the commission to Damascus. He may have been even a member of the council, for "he voted."

> And I did so in Jerusalem. I not only locked up many of the saints in prison after receiving authority from the chief priests, but when they were put to death I cast my vote against them. (Acts 26:10).

It may be interesting to say a word on his outward appearance. He has frequently been pictured as a tall, handsome-looking man. But in 2 Corinthians 10:10 we read otherwise. The Corinthians were used to the athletic figures of the Greeks. Of Paul they said, "His letters are weighty and strong, but his bodily presence is weak, and his speech of no account" (2 Cor 10:10). A very old apocryphal book, dating back to the end of the first century, "*The Acts of Paul and Thecla (Acta Pauli et Theclae)*," has an interesting

---

[1] Greek *in the law*.
[2] The same zeal possessed him of which he speaks as possessing his brethren according to the flesh.

"Brethren, my heart's desire and prayer to God for Israel is, that they might be saved. For I bear them record that they have a zeal for God, but not according to knowledge. For they being ignorant of God's righteousness, and going about to establish their own righteousness, have not submitted themselves unto the righteousness of God" (Romans 10:1–3).

[3] Or *city at the feet of Gamaliel, educated*

description of his person, which may be genuine:

> A man of moderate stature, with crisp hair, crooked legs, blue eyes, large knit brows, and long nose, at times looking like a man, at times like an angel (*Acts Paul* 487).

And now we turn to the chapter before us. It is divided into five parts.

1. The Vision of Glory on the road to Damascus (vs. 1–9).
2. The Call to Ananias (vs. 10–16).
3. Saul filled with the Spirit, Baptized and Preaching Jesus, that he is the Son of God (vs. 17–22).
4. Saul Persecuted and back in Jerusalem (vs. 23–31).
5. Further Acts of Peter (vs. 32–43).

1. THE VISION OF GLORY ON THE ROAD TO DAMASCUS (VS. 1–9).

> But Saul, still breathing threats and murder against the disciples of the Lord, went to the high priest and asked him for letters to the synagogues at Damascus, so that if he found any belonging to the Way, men or women, he might bring them bound to Jerusalem. Now as he went on his way, he approached Damascus, and suddenly a light from heaven shone around him. And falling to the ground he heard a voice saying to him, "Saul, Saul, why are you persecuting me?" And he said, "Who are you, Lord?" And he said, "I am Jesus, whom you are persecuting. But rise and enter the city, and you will be told what you are to do." The men who were traveling with him stood speechless, hearing the voice but seeing no one. Saul rose from the ground, and although his eyes were opened, he saw nothing. So they led him by the hand and brought him into Damascus. And for three days he was without sight, and neither ate nor drank (vs. 1–9).

We behold then, this young Pharisee in the zenith of his hatred against the disciples of the Lord. He breathed out threatenings and slaughter. His aim was much like Haman the Agagite, who wanted all Jews exterminated; so Saul was bent on the extermination of the believers in the Lord.

The fact that he came to the high priest for letters to go to Damascus would show that he considered his work of persecution and scattering in Jerusalem about completed. There were several large synagogues in Damascus. As this city was in constant communication with Jerusalem, the Jews in Damascus must have heard much of the new and startling events which so recently had come to pass in Jerusalem. The day of Pentecost, in all probability, brought many Damascene Jews to Jerusalem, and perhaps some of them heard the message from Peter's lips. The good news was carried quickly in a short time; believers appeared in Rome at an early date, among them two, Andronicus and Junia, who were in Christ before Paul's conversion (Rom 16:7). Damascus had most likely a good number of Jews who believed in Jesus as the Christ. They had, however, not separated from the synagogue. The leader of them must have been Ananias, and of him Paul says later "a devout man according to the law, well spoken of by all the Jews who lived there" (22:12). The news of Saul's commission to arrest believers in the Lord Jesus Christ had also preceded him, for Ananias in his simplicity told the Lord, "and here he has authority from the chief priests to bind all who call on your name" (9:14). No doubt they must have earnestly prayed for deliverance from this great persecutor. He received his letters and went on his journey with a heart filled with burning hatred.

And now God's marvelous Grace and Power in salvation is to be manifested. Israel as a nation had rejected the offer and Stephen's death marked the end of that gracious offer. But God can manifest even greater riches of his Grace and display his great Love. Saul not alone belonged to the nation, which had rejected Christ, but shared in that rejection, but he was, so to speak, the heading up of all the hatred and malignity against the Christ of God. He personified the blindness, unbelief and hatred of the whole nation. He was indeed an enemy, the greatest enemy, the chief of sinners. Surely only Grace could save such a one, and Grace it is, which is now to be manifested in the conversion of Saul of Tarsus, the Grace, which he was to know first by the vision of the glorified Christ, and which he, ever after, was to proclaim and make known to others. And therefore he could say:

> But I received mercy for this reason, that in me, as the foremost, Jesus Christ might display his perfect patience as an example to those who were to believe in him for eternal life (1 Tim 1:16).

And we may also look upon the wonderful event which took place on the road to Damascus as a direct answer to Stephen's dying prayer and the first fruits of the blood of the first martyr. Stephen saw heaven opened; he beheld Jesus standing at the right hand of God; he saw the glory. We have mentioned before that Saul, the young Pharisee, stood by and beheld that uplifted face as it reflected the heavenly glory. He heard the words of Stephen testifying of this great vision and perhaps, as Stephen knelt down under the shower of stones, which fell upon him, he saw the dark face of the young Pharisee Saul, and then for him and all who shared in the vile deed, he prayed that Christ-like prayer, "Lord, do not hold this sin against them" (7:60). And now the heavens are opened once more. He, the chief of sinners, the religious Jew, who hated the name of Jesus and all who believed on Him, is now to gaze into the opened heavens and see not alone Glory and the Person of him whom he persecuted, but also to hear his voice. What infinite Grace! Stephen, the Saint of God, beheld an opened heaven and the Lord Jesus Christ, and the next who sees heaven opened and beholds the Lord and hears his voice is the chief of sinners.

What happened on the road to Damascus was unique. Saul's conversion is unlike any other conversion. Nor has such an event taken place since then. That it will be repeated on a larger scale in a future day is assured by the Word of Prophecy. The heavens will be opened once more. Out of the opened heavens there will again shine forth the Glory of the King of Kings, the Lord of Lords. In his Glory, he will appear the second time. And when he comes in the clouds of heaven there will be still his blinded people on earth, a remnant of them, and like Saul they will behold the glorious vision. Then will be fulfilled what is written in Zechariah:

> when they look on me, on him whom they have pierced, they shall mourn for him, as one mourns for an only child, and weep bitterly over him, as one weeps over a firstborn (Zech 12:10).

Saul must have seen the nail prints and the pierced side, as Thomas saw them, when the Lord appeared the second time. Of that second coming it is written,

> Behold, he is coming with the clouds, and every eye will see him, even those who pierced him, and all tribes of the earth will wail on account of him. Even so. Amen (Rev 1:7).

This is future. Those who pierced Him, his own, will see him in that day and that will mean a wonderful salvation for the whole nation, for all Israel living in that day. In John 19 We read in a number of passages that things were fulfilled when our Lord was crucified, but when it comes to the Scripture, "They will look on him whom they have pierced," the Holy Spirit avoids the word fulfilled and substitutes for it "again another Scripture says" (John 19:37).

The conversion of Saul is therefore a great type of the national conversion of the people Israel.

The vision itself which burst upon Saul on the road to Damascus is one of the greatest in the whole Bible. It has baffled unbelief. Infidels of all descriptions, French rationalists like Renan, reformed rationalistic Jews, and the worst of all, the advocates of the destructive Bible Criticism, have tried to explain the occurrence in some natural way.

Renan in his *Les Apotres* (the Apostles) says that it was an uneasy conscience with unstrung nerves, fatigue of the journey, eyes inflamed by the hot sun, a sudden stroke of fever, which produced the hallucination. And this nonsense is repeated to this day. Others of the critics have stated that it was a thunderstorm which overtook him, and that a flash of lightning blinded him. In that lightning flash he imagined that he saw Christ. This is preached by some of these critics, who occupy pulpits. Again, others have tried to explain his vision by some physical disease. Jews and others have declared that he suffered from Epilepsy, which the Greeks called "the holy disease." This disease, they say, put him into a state of ecstasy, which may have greatly impressed his Gentile hearers. In such an attack he imagined to have seen a vision and heard a voice. All these and other opinions are puerile inventions emanating from the Father of lies. The fact is, the conversion of Saul is one of the great miracles and evidences of Christianity.

After we have learned the importance and significance of the conversion of Saul of Tarsus, as well as the typical and prophetic aspect of the event, we shall now examine the event in its details.

The ninth chapter does not contain the full record of what happened on the road to Damascus. The Apostle Paul himself relates twice his own experience in chapter 22:5–16 and in chapter 26:12–18. He also mentions his conversion briefly in 1 Corinthians 15:8, Galatians 1:15–16 and I Timothy 1:12–13. The three accounts of Saul's conversion are not without meaning. The one before us in the ninth chapter is the briefest and is simply the historical account of the event as it had to be embodied in the Book of the Acts, as history. The account in the twenty-second chapter was given by Paul in the Hebrew tongue; it is the longest statement and was addressed to the Jews. The account in the twenty-sixth chapter was given in presence of the Roman governor Festus and the Jewish king Agrippa, therefore addressed to both Jews and Gentiles. But are there not discrepancies and disagreements in these three accounts? Such has been the claim from the side of men who reject the inspiration of the Bible. There are differences, but no disagreements. These differences in themselves are the evidences of inspiration. The differences, however, are simply in the manner in which the facts of the event are presented. We shall point out all this when we come to these accounts.

It was near Damascus, when suddenly there shone round about the great persecutor of the church of God a light out of heaven. Nothing is said in this record here of the time of the day when this happened. In the third account in this book, the Apostle mentions the part of the day when it took place: "At midday, O king, I saw on the way a light from heaven, brighter than the sun, that shone around me and those who journeyed with me" (Acts 26:13). It was in the time of the day when the sun shone brightest. Its glaring rays fell upon the road upon which Saul and his companions were journeying on. Saul was pushing onward in his madness, eager to reach the city in which further demonstrations of his hatred were to be given, when suddenly a far brighter light than the light of the mid-day sun shone round about him and his companions. The light fell out of heaven and was the Glory of the Lord of Glory. On the field of Bethlehem the Glory of the Lord shone round about the shepherds, but here it is the shining forth of the Glory of him who had died and had risen from the dead, the Glory of Him, who entered into heaven and sat down at the right hand of God. And Saul under that Glorylight, fell to the earth; it was too much for a human being to stand. He laid prostrate on the ground. Those who were with him likewise fell down, for Paul in his account says that they all fell to the earth (ch. 26:14).

This is one of the alleged discrepancies. While in his account Paul declares that the whole company fell down, the record here states that the men, who journeyed with him stood speechless (v. 7). In our present chapter the companions of Paul are seen standing while Paul tells us later they fell down. This is claimed to be a disagreement. Even some careful expositors like Dean Alford have found a difficulty here. But why should there be any difficulty at all? Paul's narratives of what happened to him contain the complete account. He tells us that they were all fallen to the ground when this glory-light shone out of heaven. This fact is omitted in the historical account here. We see those who journeyed with Saul standing speechless, after the Lord had spoken to him. It does not say that they stood when the light shone upon them. That would have been impossible. If the band, which had gone after the Lord in the garden to take him captive, fell backward when the Man of humiliation had uttered his majestic "I am" (John 18:6), how much more must these have fallen to the ground, when the heavenly Glory burst upon them. The text here tells us that the companions of Paul were so amazed at what had happened that they had lost temporarily the power of speech They had fallen to the ground but now had arisen and stood speechless.

But Saul had heard a voice out of that bright light. The voice spoke in the Hebrew tongue. This we learn from Paul's address before Festus and Agrippa. The voice calls him by name. He is fully known to him who speaks out of heaven. All along in all his work of evil, his persecutions and the hatred he exhibited against those who believed on Christ, that eye had seen him and followed him. He had kept silent. He did not interfere in the wicked work Saul had done; but now he kept silence no longer. But more than that, Saul beheld the Lord Himself. In that great light which shone about him, in that opened heaven, he saw Him, who had spoken, the Man in Glory. The Lord Jesus Christ appeared to him. The Son of God in the Glory of the Father was revealed to Saul. Though the record here is silent about the actual vision, it Is clearly seen from other Scriptures that such was the case. Ananias later addressed Saul and said, "Brother Saul, the Lord Jesus who appeared to you on the road" (9:17). From another verse in our chapter (9:27), we learn that Barnabas said "how on the road he had seen the Lord, who spoke to him." Then in Chapter 26:16, the Lord Himself spoke to Saul: "I have appeared to you." A more direct testimony is found from the Apostle in 1 Corinthians 15, where, after mentioning the different witnesses of the resurrection, Paul says:

> Last of all, as to one untimely born, he appeared also to me. For I am the least of the apostles, unworthy to be called an apostle, because I persecuted the church of God (1 Cor 15:8–9).

He saw the Lord in all his resurrection Glory and this, besides the direct call, constituted him an Apostle, for he was now a fit witness to the resurrection of Jesus Christ. "Am I not free? Am I not an apostle? Have I not seen Jesus our Lord? Are not you my workmanship in the Lord?" (1 Cor 9:1). Did he know the Lord in person when he walked on the earth? Saul was in Jerusalem at that time; he must have seen him there. 2 Corinthians 5:16 seems to indicate this.

And now that voice, which had spoken with so much tenderness on earth, the voice he had refused to hear, spoke to him from glory: "Saul, Saul, why are you persecuting me?" And he said, "Who are you, Lord?" And he said, "I am Jesus, whom you are persecuting."[4]

And what a meeting it was which thus took place on the road to Damascus! The Lord who had died for that nation (John 11:51), and he who was the culmination of all the hatred of the nation, who hated him without a cause, were now face to face. his eyes gazed upon that figure in Glory, his ears heard the words which fell from his lips. The words which came out of heaven were not the words of a stern Judge. It was the voice of a gracious, loving Saviour and Lord, the same who had once called in the garden to fallen man, "Where are you"? Saul, the persecutor of the church of God, had deserved wrath. Instead of judgment and wrath, Grace, infinite and unfathomable Grace, meets him. That Grace, which he was the chosen instrument to proclaim from henceforth in all its unlimited riches, he must taste first of all. That Grace which flows from the risen and glorified Saviour is first of all manifested in his own case. The possibilities of Grace, the riches of Grace, are indeed fully demonstrated in the great event on the Damascus road. Triumphantly he declared afterwards:

> The saying is trustworthy and deserving of full acceptance, that Christ Jesus came into the world to save sinners, of whom I am the foremost. But I received mercy for this reason, that in me, as the *foremost*, Jesus Christ might display his perfect patience as an example to those who were to believe in him for eternal life (1 Tim 1:15-16).

---

[4] The words which follow in the Authorized Version "It is hard for thee to kick against the pricks. And he trembled and astonished said, Lord what wilt Thou have me to do?" must be omitted here. They do not belong into the historical account as given by Luke. They were inserted later from chapters 22 and 26, where they are in the right place. No Greek manuscript contains them. Alford, *The NT for English Readers*, 1:710.

"Saul, Saul, why are you persecuting *me*?" The voice had spoken out of heaven. How could he answer that question? It was unanswerable. From the trembling lips of the young Pharisee there comes the question, "Who are you, Lord?" The person he beholds, shining out of heaven surrounded by the glory-light, which of old dwelt in the midst of Israel, can be none other but the Lord. And so the prostrate Saul addresses him as Lord. And the Lord answers him in his loving Grace, "I am Jesus, whom you are persecuting." The full and awful truth now flashes upon the trembling questioner. The Jesus, who went about doing good, and healing all that were oppressed of the devil (Acts 10:38), who was crucified, who was rejected by the nation, the Jesus, whom dying Stephen beheld, into whose hands he had committed his spirit, that Jesus, whom he hated and whose followers he had so cruelly persecuted, is the Lord. The Man, who hung on a cross reckoned among the evil-doers, who died that shameful death, lives and is the Man in Glory at the right hand of God. Marvellous revelation as it burst upon the collapsed persecutor in the simple answer, "I am Jesus, whom you are persecuting."

What was he then with all his boasting law-keeping? Who was he, the Hebrew of the Hebrews, as touching the law, a Pharisee and the son of a Pharisee? Nothing less than an enemy of God and the chief of sinners. In that Glory from above, in that voice, which spoke and declared Himself as Jesus the Lord, the blindness, wickedness and enmity of Israel and the flesh as well, were fully discovered.

But if we were to enlarge, it would be necessary to cover all the blessed God-breathed teachings of the Gospel as contained in the Pauline Epistles. The Gospel he preached, which he called "my Gospel," this Gospel of Grace and Glory, the Holy Spirit so blessedly teaches in the great doctrinal Epistles penned through the Apostle Paul, is contained in a nutshell in the event on the road to Damascus. To the Galatians Paul wrote later in his wonderful defense of that Gospel:

> For I would have you know, brothers, that the gospel that was preached by me is not man's gospel.[5] For I did not receive it from any man, nor was I taught it, but I received it *through a revelation of Jesus Christ.* (Gal 1:11-12).

That Gospel, which he received was first revealed in that Glory-flash out of heaven; it is the Gospel of the Glory of the blessed God. Man has no part nor share in it, but it is all of God, all of Grace.

But in the first chapter of Colossians Paul tells us that he is not only the minister of the Gospel but that another ministry was given to him, the ministry of the church, which is his body. The two, the Gospel of Grace and the truth concerning the church, the mystery hidden in former ages go together and are inseparably connected. God tells out in the two the completeness and riches of his grace in Christ Jesus. In the Epistle to the Ephesians, well termed "the rich Epistle," the Holy Spirit blends into a marvellous gem the two Gospel and Church truth. And here the man in the dust of the highway, the chosen vessel, learns for the first time the great revelation he was to make known. Listen to him as he writes from the Roman prison:

> For this reason I, Paul, a prisoner for Christ Jesus on behalf of you Gentiles— assuming that you have heard of the stewardship of God's grace that was given to me for you, how the mystery was made known to me by revelation, as I have written briefly. When you read this, you can perceive my insight into the mystery of Christ, which was not made known to the sons of men in other generations as it has now been revealed to his holy apostles and prophets by the Spirit (Eph 3:1–5).

That mystery is the church as the body of Christ. Every believing sinner is a member of the body of Christ. Christ in Glory, the Lord, who spoke to Saul in the way, is the Head of that body, the church. Christ is in each member of his body, his life is there; and every believer is in Christ. "You in Me and I in you." And this great hidden mystery too flashes forth in this wonderful event, for the first time. "Saul, Saul, why are you persecuting *me*? . . . I am Jesus, whom you are persecuting." The poor, hated, despised Nazarenes, whom the mad, Jewish zealot Saul of Tarsus had driven out of Jerusalem: put into prison and delivered to death, were one with the Lord in Glory. They were identified with him and he with them. Their persecution meant his persecution, in their affliction he was afflicted. They were members of his body and that body was in existence.

The Lord commanded Saul to arise and go into the city where "you will be told what you are to do" (9:6). The men then had also arisen and had lost the power of speech "hearing the voice but seeing no one." We remember years ago how a poor, blinded Jew attended our Gospel meetings and among his claims that the New Testament contradicted itself, he would cite the statement here about the companions of Saul and Paul's statement that they "did not understand the voice of the one who was speaking to me" (22:9). He called this a disagreement. The far more blinded Higher Critics make the same assertion. But there is no disagreement. Luke in his brief account tells us that the men heard a voice. But Paul tells us that "hearing the voice but seeing no one." They did not hear the conversation, they heard the sound of a voice but the voice itself was unintelligible to them. John 12:28–29 explains it perfectly. The Son of God heard the Father's voice. The people who stood by heard the sound waves and some declared that it was thunder, others

---

[5] Greek *not according to man*

that an angel had spoken. Only the Son heard what the Father had said. So here. The men heard the sound of the voice, but what was said they did not hear; Saul alone understood the words of the heavenly speaker.

Then Saul arose. He is obedient at once. It is the first act of obedience he yields to him whose bond servant he had become through his wonderful grace. But when his eyes were opened, he saw no man. The vision of the Lord and his Glory had blinded his eyes and his companions had to take him by the hand and lead him. What a change had taken place! The self-sufficient, boasting Pharisee, who had pressed on towards Damascus, had become as helpless as a child. He who led others was now obliged to be led. We wonder what became of the letters he carried from the high priest. Perhaps he flung them at once from his person.

The blindness which had come upon him has also its spiritual significance. It indicates the result of the vision of Glory in his own life. He was blind to the things down here. It is said of an astronomer who had looked too long into the light of the sun that he became blind. However, it was not darkness, which enshrouded him; but the brilliant orb of the sun in the heavens ever dazzled before his eyes. Wherever he looked he saw the sun. If he awoke in the darkest night the fiery ball of the sun was the object before his eyes. And Paul after his glory experience had but one object, Christ in Glory and the Glory of Christ. He truly like the disciples on the mount of transfiguration "saw no one but Jesus only" (Matt 17:8). The Gospel of Grace and Glory of the Son of God must blind our eyes to the things which are seen.

Three days Saul was without sight, nor did he eat and drink. He was passing through a grave like Jonah. What must have been his feeling and his experience during these three days? Shut up in darkness; what soul exercise must have been his portion! But he was secure in the hands of Him, of whom he was soon to testify, "who loved me and gave himself for me" (Gal 2:20).

2. THE CALL TO ANANIAS (VS. 10–16).

> Now there was a disciple at Damascus named Ananias. The Lord said to him in a vision, "Ananias." And he said, "Here I am, Lord." And the Lord said to him, "Rise and go to the street called Straight, and at the house of Judas look for a man of Tarsus named Saul, for behold, he is praying, and he has seen in a vision a man named Ananias come in and lay his hands on him so that he might regain his sight." But Ananias answered, "Lord, I have heard from many about this man, how much evil he has done to your saints at Jerusalem. And here he has authority from the chief priests to bind all who call on your name." But the Lord said to him, "Go, for he is a chosen instrument of mine to carry my name before the Gentiles and kings and the children of Israel. For I will show him how much he must suffer for the sake of my name (vs. 10–16).

And now the Lord, who had in such grace met Saul on the road to Damascus, goes before him to the city. An humble disciple lived there; he was a devout man according to the law, having a good report of all the Jews, who lived in that city (Acts 22:12). This devout follower of the Lord Jesus Christ had a vision which concerned Saul. Rackham has well said, "The Lord Jesus as master of the house must, so to speak, complete arrangements for adding Saul to his household."[6] What a great change had been wrought! Perhaps someday, in the presence of the Lord, when all hidden things will be made manifest, we may find that Saul's hatred was aimed especially against Ananias, who must have been the leader of the assembly in Damascus. Saul had set out to bind Ananias and all that call on the name of the Lord, and put them into

---

[6] Rackham, *The Acts of the Apostles*, 134.

prison. But Ananias hears now that he is to go to Saul instead and seek him, who had come to seek and persecute them. It was the Lord who spoke to Ananias in the vision. The childlike and calm answer this disciple gave to the Lord is an evidence of the simplicity and reality of his prayer life. The Lord gave him the directions where to find him. He was to inquire in the house of Judas in the street, which is called Straight. But the Lord furthermore told Ananias that Saul likewise had a vision. "Behold, he is praying" (9:11) was the cheering message the Lord gave of him. It was the manifestation of the new life in Saul. In answer to the prayer of Saul prayer, no doubt for light and deliverance the Lord had given him the vision. He saw Ananias coming in and putting his hand on him, that he might receive sight. "A pair of visions, which mutually correspond, as the visions of Ananias and Saul in this instance, removes all suspicion of treacherous phantasy."[7]

That Ananias was chosen for this mission is very significant. The Samaritans, as we learned in Chapter 7, had to wait till Peter and John came from Jerusalem, before the Holy Spirit came upon them. One would expect that the Apostles were equally needed in the case of Saul of Tarsus. Peter, John nor any of the other Apostles, however, are mentioned in connection with Saul's conversion, baptism and the gift of the Holy Spirit. In their place an humble, unknown disciple is called by the Lord to act. And yet Saul was called an Apostle and chosen to be the greatest of the Apostles. Ritualistic Christendom, with its claims of apostolic succession and authority, finds this hard to explain. Paul's apostleship was "not from men nor through man, but through Jesus Christ and God the Father, who raised him from the dead" (Gal 1:1). Jerusalem and the Apostles there had nothing whatever to do with his case. One who was not an Apostle at all, whose name is not mentioned again in the Bible, was the chosen instrument to lay his hands on Saul of Tarsus. Here then we have the first indication of what the apostleship of Paul was to be. It was three years after all this had transpired that he went up to Jerusalem to see Peter; and then it was not for any confirmation of his apostleship.

Ananias answered the Lord. The evil reputation of Saul had preceded him to Damascus. Perhaps some of the suffering believers, who had been forced to leave Jerusalem, found a refuge in Damascus. And Ananias in a simple and natural way tells the Lord all about it. The task laid upon him seems too great and he acquaints the Lord with what he had heard about this man. This, has been declared, was a foolish thing. Of course, the Lord knew all about Saul; he knew far better the evil work he had accomplished than Ananias could ever know. Further-more the Lord had told Ananias that Saul was praying; why then should he protest against the call and speak thus to one who is omniscient? While unbelief had its share in it and the weakness of the flesh is seen, it is likewise something which brings cheer to our hearts. The Lord in his graciousness does not rebuke Ananias for his unbelieving reply. He bears with the weakness of his servant and condescends to make known to him the future destiny of the praying Saul. And we, too, fail so much in our prayers, doubting and fearing, when we are addressing Him, who is the omnipotent and omniscient Lord, so reluctant to follow unquestioning his gracious directions. Have we not found him as loving and condescending as Ananias did?

And the Lord takes his servant into his own confidence; he tells him about Saul and

---

[7] Bengel, *Gnomon of the New Testament*.

what is in store for him. He is a chosen vessel and the Name, which is above every other name, is to be made known by him to Gentiles, Kings and the children of Israel. It is significant that the children of Israel are mentioned last, while the Gentiles are in the foreground. While Paul the Apostle preached to the Jews and went into their synagogues, his mission was to the Gentiles as the Apostle of the Gentiles. His sufferings for his Name's sake are likewise announced by the Lord. And here we must not forget that the same Lord, who knew all about Saul and his life as it was to be, is our Lord, too, and knows us, plans for us, as he knew him and did with him, who delighted to call himself, "the chief of sinners." What comfort we should take from this fact!

3. SAUL FILLED WITH THE SPIRIT, BAPTIZED AND PREACHING JESUS, THAT HE IS THE SON OF GOD (VS. 17–22).

> So Ananias departed and entered the house. And laying his hands on him he said, "Brother Saul, the Lord Jesus who appeared to you on the road by which you came has sent me so that you may regain your sight and be filled with the Holy Spirit." And immediately something like scales fell from his eyes, and he regained his sight. Then he rose and was baptized; and taking food, he was strengthened.
>
> For some days he was with the disciples at Damascus. And immediately he proclaimed Jesus in the synagogues, saying, "He is the Son of God." And all who heard him were amazed and said, "Is not this the man who made havoc in Jerusalem of those who called upon this name? And has he not come here for this purpose, to bring them bound before the chief priests?" But Saul increased all the more in strength, and confounded the Jews who lived in Damascus by proving that Jesus was the Christ. (vs. 17–22).

The Lord had said to Ananias "go." So Ananias departed. He followed the Lord obediently. Directed by Him, he soon found the stricken Saul in the place, which the vision had revealed to him. The two, Saul of Tarsus and Ananias are now face to face. Saul does not see his visitor, for he is still blind, but he was patiently waiting for him to come, for the Lord had told him all about his coming and even revealed his name. And Ananias saw before himself the former persecutor of the Church of God (Gal 1:13) in a helpless condition. They do not need to be introduced to each other. The Lord had done this. Ananias addresses Saul and the way he does it is extremely precious. "*Brother Saul*," he said as he put his hands on him, "the Lord Jesus who appeared to you on the road by which you came has sent me so that you may regain your sight and be filled with the Holy Spirit." he addressed him as brother. The work had been accomplished and the young Pharisee, who had seen the Lord was indeed now "a loved brother." The Grace of God is strikingly illustrated in this. There was no confession to Ananias, no rebuke nor accusation, nothing from the side of Saul of Tarsus; Grace had saved him and made of him a brother in the Lord. And now his blindness is removed under the laying on of hands; he received his sight. When we reach Chapter 22, Paul's account of this scene, we shall find additional information of what transpired then. Here the record is brief. The laying on of the hands of this disciple [8] of the Lord most likely was the moment when not only Saul's eyes were opened, but when he was also filled with the Holy Spirit. Ananias had delivered the message to him that he should be filled with the Holy Spirit and though it is not directly stated here that this filling took place at once in connection with the opening of his eyes, it is perfectly right to

---

[8] The learned Dr. Lightfoot in his *Horae Hebraicae* puts the following questions without answering them. "Could Ananias therefore confer the Holy Spirit? This seemed the peculiar prerogative of the Apostles; could therefore a private disciple do this to an Apostle? By the imposition of his hands could he impart the gift of tongues and prophecy?"

assume that such was the case. We discover a variety of modes of the filling with the Spirit.

On Pentecost no hands were laid on anyone, but the statement there made was, Repent, be baptized and ye shall receive the gift of the Holy Spirit. The Samaritans had been baptized, but for a special reason (stated in our exposition) they had to wait till Peter and John came from Jerusalem and laid their hands upon them. Cornelius and his household were not baptized, nor had hands been laid upon them, when the Holy Spirit fell upon them. The disciples at Ephesus (Acts 19) were baptized and only after Paul laid his hands upon them came the Holy Spirit upon them. Paul must have received the Spirit first, then he arose and was baptized. Why these different modes? If there had been uniformity in every case it would have resulted in the belief that in order to receive the Holy Spirit, the same uniform method must be followed. This was to be avoided. It must be remembered that all these cases in Acts were unique, falling into the transition stage. The Epistles, however, teach that the Holy Spirit is received by all who believe in the Lord Jesus Christ; "believed in him, were sealed with the promised Holy Spirit" (Eph 1:13) is the order now.

Saul after this was certain days with the disciples which were at Damascus. Who can describe the happy times in the Lord they must have had! What hymns of praise they must have sung to the Lord for the riches of his Grace, so wonderfully manifested in the salvation of Saul! "And immediately he proclaimed Jesus in the synagogues, saying, 'He is the Son of God'" (9:20). The word *"immediately"* teaches us something. It is the word which occurs some thirty-five times in the Gospel of Mark, the Gospel record, which shows Christ as the perfect servant. The word "immediately" manifests the Lord's prompt and untiring service, which he rendered to his Father. And Saul begins his witness for the Lord with "immediately." Of all the Apostles he was the most prompt in his service, laboring more than all the others. The glorious vision on the Damascus road, the sight of the Man in Glory and his oneness with Him, as made known to him by revelation, produced this marvellous service in the life of the converted persecutor of the Church. We, too, if we have the Lord ever before our hearts may have our "immediate" service.

And what a sensation was produced as he went from synagogue to synagogue and delivered his message! Perhaps as he entered the synagogues his brethren welcomed him most heartily. Had he not done, according to their view, such a good work in Jerusalem? They hated that Name, too, and were glad that Saul had come to bind the believers in Christ and bring them to Jerusalem to be dealt with by the chief priests of the nation. But how great must have been their consternation when the celebrated Pharisee and persecutor opened his lips and preached the very name they despised and hated. As he continued in this work in the synagogues his strength increased. The testimony he gave established him and was a blessing to his own soul. The Jews dwelling in Damascus, and their numbers were very large, were confounded. His preaching was exclusively concerning the Lord Jesus, who had been crucified; and he proved that this is the very Christ. The question of the Messiah promised to Israel was then agitating the hearts and minds of all Jews, as it does still among those Jews, who still believe in the Law and the Prophets. And what a preacher Saul must have been! he had a remarkable knowledge of the Old Testament Scriptures. The Holy Spirit filling him illuminated the many Messianic prophecies and in the power of the Spirit these were applied as being fulfilled in Him, whose name they had refused to accept. He began his great witness bearing in the synagogues in Damascus. Later we read of the method he used, so effectually. "reasoned with them from the Scriptures, explaining and proving that it was necessary for the Christ to suffer and to rise from the dead, and saying, 'This Jesus, whom I proclaim to you, is the Christ'"[9] (Acts 17:2–3). The one who hung on the cross, whose tomb was found empty on the third day, who had been seen by his disciples after his passion, whom they declared to be risen from the dead, who had left the earth and ascended into heaven, whose resurrection had been fully proven by the Coming of the Holy Spirit and by many signs and miracles, Saul had seen and heard his voice. Therefore he preached Jesus that he is the Son of God. Up to this time this name of the risen Lord had not been preached. It would have been very natural for Peter to refer to his former confession of Christ at Caesarea Philippi, where he said, "You are the Christ, the Son of the living God;" (Matt 16:16) but it was not for Peter to preach Jesus thus. Saul had seen the rejected One in Glory and this demonstrates him the Son of God by resurrection from the dead, the great and blessed foundation truth of the Gospel.

4. SAUL PERSECUTED AND BACK IN JERUSALEM (VS. 23–31).

When many days had passed, the Jews[10] plotted to kill him, but their plot became known to Saul. They were watching the gates day and night in order to kill him, but his disciples took him by night and let him down through an opening in the wall,[11] lowering him in a basket.

And when he had come to Jerusalem, he attempted to join the disciples. And they were all afraid of him, for they did not believe that he was a disciple. But Barnabas took him and brought him to the apostles and declared to them how on the road he had seen the Lord, who spoke to him, and how at Damascus he had preached boldly in the name of Jesus. So he went in and out among them at Jerusalem, preaching boldly in the name of the Lord. And he spoke and disputed against the Hellenists.[12] But they were seeking to kill him. And when the brothers learned this, they brought him down to Caesarea and sent him off to Tarsus.

So the church throughout all Judea and Galilee and Samaria had peace and was being built up. And walking in the fear of the Lord and in the comfort of the Holy Spirit, it multiplied. (vs. 23–31).

The Holy Spirit has not given us a record of the "many days" mentioned in the 23rd verse. During these many days he made a journey to Arabia (see Fig. 9). The first chapter in Galatians tells us of this fact. "Nor did I go up to Jerusalem to those who were apostles before me, but I went away into Arabia, and returned again to Damascus" (Gal 1:17). This is the only time his journey into Arabia is mentioned in the Bible. How long he spent there and what he did there is unrevealed. It is incorrect to say he spent three years in Arabia (see Fig. 9); in Galatians the statement is made that three years after his return to Damascus he went to Jerusalem. This does not mean that he was for three years in Arabia. Most likely as other great men of God went to the desert, Saul likewise sought Arabia for quietness, meditation and prayer. His reappearing in Damascus was the signal for an outbreak against him. He had confounded the Jews before he went into Arabia, and now with still greater power he was ready to continue

---

[9] This is still the right way in arguing with the Jews. First, showing from the Scriptures the predictions concerning Christ. Secondly, showing their fulfilment in the person of our Lord. And to this arguing from Scripture came the powerful argument of his own experience. He had seen the Lord.

[10] The Greek word *Ioudaioi* refers specifically here to Jewish religious leaders, and others under their influence, who opposed the Christian faith in that time

[11] Greek *through the wall*

[12] That is, Greek-speaking Jews

The Acts of the Apostles

9. Petra was the capital of the Arabian kingdom of the Nabataeans under Roman control until it became a Roman province in AD 106. Paul likely have visited it during his stay in Arabia, since the Nabataean king, Aretas IV tried to seize Paul (2 Cor 11:32).

his God-given message. The Jews then took counsel to kill him. It is the first act of persecution and suffering recorded in this wonderful life of suffering for Christ's sake. He is starting with when the Lord had said, "For I will show him how much he must suffer for the sake of my name" (9:16). But the plot was discovered by Saul. He knew himself in the hands of the Lord. That glorious Lord, whom he had seen, was his shield and he guarded his servant, as he still keeps his servants by his power. The plot was the work of Satan, who had become aroused on account of the great victory the Lord had achieved in translating the persecutor from the power of darkness into his own kingdom (Col 1). He could not wrest him from Christ, so he would silence his testimony here; but this Satan could not do.

The Jews had the gates watched; but by night he was let down by the wall in a basket. Paul refers to this later:

> At Damascus, the governor under King Aretas was guarding the city of Damascus in order to seize me, but I was let down in a basket through a window in the wall and escaped his hands (2 Cor 11:32–33).

According to his statement in the chapter which relates his sufferings, this experience of having to leave Damascus as a fugitive was a very humiliating one. What a contrast with the anticipated entrance into Damascus, when he had left Jerusalem to persecute the church and his flight from Damascus to go to Jerusalem! This first visit to Jerusalem took place three years after his conversion. Why did he not return at once? Flesh and blood indeed must have suggested this to him. He was a courageous man. Nothing would have pleased him better than to return at once to the city he loved so well and preach the Name he once despised. But he did not confer with flesh and blood, nor did he go up to Jerusalem to them which were Apostles before him (Gal 1:16–17). It had to be so to prove that he had his apostleship apart from Jerusalem. This is the reason why this historical account is embodied in the first chapter of the Epistle to the Galatians. In his defence of the Gospel contained in that Epistle he shows first that he is an Apostle and how he became an Apostle. The twelve in Jerusalem had nothing to do with it. But when he arrived there he was treated with suspicion. Evidently the testimony he had given so faithfully in Damascus was not fully known in the church in Jerusalem. Could it be possible that this young Pharisee, who but three years ago had scattered the believers in the city, put them into prison and had them maltreated in every way and killed, was now truly a believer? This distrust surely was a sign of weakness in the disciples. Instead of believing the Grace of God, which had wrought so mightily in Saul, and rejoicing that he which persecuted them in times past, now preached the faith he once destroyed, they were afraid of him. This must have humbled him much. But he who had become the recipient of such Grace and delighted to call himself the chief of sinners, was gracious, and we hear no complaint from his side on account of the distrust of the disciples. We meet again Barnabas; it is the same of whom we read in the closing verses of chapter 4. Barnabas, whose name means "son of consolation," was all this to Saul. He took him and introduced him to the Apostles, and told out the story of Grace more fully.

But we must again examine the historical record contained in the Apostle's own words in Galatians 1. There we learn the details of this visit. He did not see all the Apostles, but only Peter and James, the Lord's brother. The other Apostles he did not see. This detailed statement is made to show that no council of the Apostles was called before which (according to ecclesiastical rules in our day) Saul had to appear to receive the sanction of the Apostles upon his own Apostleship, a kind of ordination. He did not need this; the Lord had called and ordained him. He was an Apostle, not of men, neither by man, but by Jesus Christ.

he abode with Peter, was Peter's guest. He had come especially to get better acquainted with Peter. Perhaps he wanted Peter to tell him about the Lord, the blessed words he had heard from Him, the miracles he had done. The Gospel records were then not in existence. What a happy time they must have had together!

he abode with Peter fifteen days. His time in Jerusalem was well used. He spoke boldly in the name of the Lord Jesus. He also disputed with the Hellenist Jews. He did the same work which Stephen was occupied with when he was ushered before the council. For all we know it was the same synagogue which he sought out, the man who hailed from Tarsus in Cilicia. And if, as we showed in our exposition of the sixth chapter, Saul was one of those who disputed with Stephen, what a sensation it must have made in the synagogue, when this same Saul arose to perpetuate the mighty work Stephen had left to enter into the Lord's Own presence! But Stephen's fate threatened Saul. "But they were seeking to kill him" (9:29). The brethren knew of it and brought him to Caesarea and sent him forth to Tarsus, his own native city. The reason why Saul readily consented to this is learned from chapter 22:17–21:

> And it came to pass, that, when I was come again to Jerusalem, even while I prayed in the temple, I was in a trance; And saw him saying to me, Make haste, and get thee quickly out of Jerusalem: for they will not receive thy testimony concerning me. And I said, Lord, they know that I imprisoned

and beat in every synagogue them that believed on thee: And when the blood of thy martyr Stephen was shed, I also was standing by, and consenting to his death, and kept the raiment of them that slew him. And he said to me, Depart: for I will send thee far hence to the Gentiles (Acts 22:17–21).

He received then in that trance-message his commission. Not Jerusalem and Judea was to be the scene of his activity, but the territory outside of the land; not the Jews' Apostle he was to be, but the Apostle to the Gentiles. "Depart: for I will send thee far hence to the Gentiles" (9:21). When later Paul in self-will stepped upon the territory the Lord had told him to leave, he got into great difficulty and became a prisoner. As a result of Saul's conversion, the 31st verse says, "the church throughout all Judea and Galilee and Samaria had peace." The word "churches," in the KJV however, must be changed into "church" (ESV). The translation of church in the plural is founded upon later manuscripts. There were many local churches or assemblies in Judea, but it was but *one* church, as there is but one church to-day. *The* church then had rest. The believers walked in the fear of the Lord and comfort of the Holy Spirit. Increase marked this happy condition.

5. Further Acts of Peter (vs. 32–43).

> And it came to pass, as Peter passed throughout all quarters, he came down also to the saints which dwelt at Lydda. And there he found a certain man named Aeneas, which had kept his bed eight years, and was sick of the palsy. And Peter said to him, Aeneas, Jesus Christ maketh thee whole: arise, and make thy bed. And he arose immediately. And all that dwelt at Lydda and Saron saw him, and turned to the Lord.
>
> Now there was at Joppa a certain disciple named Tabitha, which by interpretation is called Dorcas: this woman was full of good works and alms deeds which she did. And it came to pass in those days, that she was sick, and died: whom when they had washed, they laid her in an upper chamber. And forasmuch as Lydda was nigh to Joppa, and the disciples had heard that Peter was there, they sent to him two men, desiring him that he would not delay to come to them. Then Peter arose and went with them. When he was come, they brought him into the upper chamber: and all the widows stood by him weeping, and shewing the coats and garments which Dorcas made, while she was with them. But Peter put them all forth, and kneeled down, and prayed; and turning him to the body said, Tabitha, arise. And she opened her eyes: and when she saw Peter, she sat up. And he gave her his hand, and lifted her up; and when he had called the saints and widows, he presented her alive. And it was known throughout all Joppa; and many believed in the Lord. And it came to pass, that he tarried many days in Joppa with one Simon a tanner (vs. 32–43).

The ninth chapter closes with further acts of the Apostle Peter. It seems Peter made a kind of visitation, going from place to place. Two miracles happened in this connection. The healing of Aeneas and the raising up of Tabitha, who had died. The significant fact in connection with one of these miracles is that it was an answer to prayer. The one was healing and restoration, the other resurrection from the dead. Both miracles are of deep symbolical meaning. The Gospel was about to go forth to the Gentiles. Peter was to use again the keys of the kingdom of heaven in preaching to the household of Cornelius. Before this takes place the two miracles happened. They are significant in the place we find them, upon the threshold of the great event, the Gentiles to hear the Gospel. But why are they significant?

A commentator on these miracles says:

> The record of these two miracles at this point makes us fancy that Luke saw in them a double sign of the great event to which they were the preface, viz., the gift of the Gentiles of *repentance to life* (11:18). For they are complimentary: 1. The healing of Aeneas denotes the restoration of activity; and in the parallel sign of the Lord, the healing of the palsied man at Capernaum, this is associated with the forgiveness of sins (Luke 5:17–26; Matt 9:2–8, Mark 2:3–12). 2. The raising of Dorcas denotes the gift of life; and it shows the need of it for the pious such as Dorcas, as for the

innocent like Jairus' daughter, whom the Lord raised. In Aeneas then we may see symbolized the healing of those Gentiles who are sick with sin; in Dorcas the giving of life to those Gentiles who, though full of good works, "are aliens from the life of God because of the ignorance that is in them (Luke 8:41–56; Matt 9:18–26; Mark 5:22–43)" (Eph 4:18).[13]

Peter tarried in Joppa in the house of Simon the tanner. Was he breaking with his Jewish law and customs? Tanning made necessary the handling of skins taken from unclean animals. It was, therefore, as a trade considered unclean by the Jews.

But for the great work Peter had to do in opening the door of the Kingdom to the Gentiles he had to be prepared in a special way.

---

[13] Rackham, *The Acts of the Apostles*, 143–44.

Chapter Ten

In Ephesians 2:11–18, we read the blessed words concerning the Grace of God to the Gentiles.

> Therefore remember that at one time you Gentiles in the flesh, called "the uncircumcision" by what is called the circumcision, which is made in the flesh by hands—remember that you were at that time separated from Christ, alienated from the commonwealth of Israel and strangers to the covenants of promise, having no hope and without God in the world. But now in Christ Jesus you who once were far off have been brought near by the blood of Christ. For he himself is our peace, who has made us both one and has broken down in his flesh the dividing wall of hostility by abolishing the law of commandments expressed in ordinances, that he might create in himself one new man in place of the two, so making peace, and might reconcile us both to God in one body through the cross, thereby killing the hostility. And he came and preached peace to you who were far off and peace to those who were near. For through him we both have access in one Spirit to the Father (Eph 2:11-18).

Up to this time in the Book of Acts we have seen nothing of this gracious purpose, the blessed result of the finished work of Christ on the cross. Jerusalem heard the Gospel first. Once more the good news of the Kingdom was preached with a full offer of forgiveness to the Jews. God was willing to blot out their transgressions and to make good all he had promised to the nation. Many signs and miracles had been done in Jerusalem in demonstration of the resurrection from the dead of the Prince of Life, whom they had crucified. We have seen how the seventh chapter in this book marks the close of that special offer to Jerusalem. Immediately after the death of Stephen, the Gospel was carried into Judea and Samaria. In Samaria a people heard and accepted the glad tidings. They were a mixed race and practiced circumcision and obeyed parts of the law. In the ninth chapter the conversion of Paul is recorded and the Lord makes known that the persecutor of the church is to be the chosen vessel to bear his name before the Gentiles. Paul, however, was not chosen to open first the door to the Gentiles as such, but Peter, the Apostle of the circumcision. A new work is given him to do, which was indeed a strange work for a Jew. He was to go to the Gentiles, whom the Jews considered unclean. It was unlawful for a Jew to join himself to any Gentile; an insurmountable barrier divided them. As we read in the words quoted from the Epistle to the Ephesians, Gentiles were "alienated from the commonwealth of Israel and strangers to the covenants of promise" (Eph 2:12). For this reason the Jews considered the Gentiles as unclean, common, spoke of them as dogs, and had no intercourse with them. It is of interest to notice that Peter tarried in Joppa; from this old city he is to be sent forth to preach the Gospel to Cornelius and his household. Centuries ago another Jew had come to Joppa with a solemn message from his God, which he was commissioned to bear far hence to the Gentiles. Jonah, the prophet, took a ship from Joppa and refused obedience to the divine call.

But here is one who is obedient to the heavenly vision and who is to bring a higher message to the Gentiles, the good news of a free and full salvation. That Peter, the Apostle of the circumcision, was chosen for this great errand, was an important hint that the middle wall of partition had been broken down and that believing Jews and Gentiles were to form one new man. Yet with the vision he had which opened the way for Peter to go to the Gentiles; and the great results he had witnessed when Cornelius and his household believed, and the Holy Spirit fell upon them, the Apostle Peter could later in Antioch put up the same wall of partition which he knew was broken down.

> For before certain men came from James, he was eating with the Gentiles; but when they came (Jews from Jerusalem) he drew back and separated himself, fearing the circumcision party.[1] (Gal 2:12).

He then built again the things he had destroyed.

The events of the tenth chapter are divinely pre-arranged; and both Cornelius and those with him, who were to hear the Gospel, and Peter the messenger, are prepared for it. Peter is divinely prepared and instructed to go, Cornelius is divinely prepared to send and to hear.

We divide the chapter into five parts:

1. Cornelius of Caesarea and his Preparation (vs. 1–8).

2. The trance-vision of Peter in Preparation for his Mission (vs. 9–16).

3. Peter with Cornelius at Caesarea (vs. 17–33).

4. Peter Preaching the Gospel to the Gentiles (vs. 34–43).

5. The interrupted Message (vs. 44–48).

---

[1] Or *fearing those of the circumcision*

CHAPTER TEN

1. Cornelius of Caesarea and his Preparation to hear the Gospel (vs. 1–8).

At Caesarea there was a man named Cornelius, a centurion of what was known as the Italian Cohort, a devout man who feared God with all his household, gave alms generously to the people, and prayed continually to God. About the

10. Roman centurion (Lat. *centurio*; Gr.: κεντυρίων). These military officers usually commanded 80 men in their unit, although senior officers usually commanded cohorts. Tower of David Museum, Jerusalem.

ninth hour of the day[2] he saw clearly in a vision an angel of God come in and say to him, "Cornelius." And he stared at him in terror and said, "What is it, Lord?" And he said to him, "Your prayers and your alms have ascended as a memorial before God. And now send men to Joppa and bring one Simon who is called Peter. He is lodging with one Simon, a tanner, whose house is by the sea." When the angel who spoke to him had departed, he called two of his servants and a devout soldier from among those who attended him, and having related everything to them, he sent them to Joppa (vs. 1–8).

11. Remains of the ancient Roman aqueduct at Caesarea Martima.

The city in which Cornelius dwelt is mentioned first, and it will not be out of place to give some information about that ancient city. It must not be confounded with another Caesarea, of which we read in the Gospel, Caesarea Philippi (see Fig. 24). The Caesarea here was situated between Joppa and Dora (see Fig. 11, 41). Augustus, the Emperor, gave this city to Herod; he made a most beautiful city out of it, spending immense sums of money. It was a Gentile city, though many Jews live there also. Cornelius was a centurion, who was at the head of a band, which was known by the name of "the Italian band."

A legion in the Roman army had 6,000 men. Each legion was divided into 10 cohorts of 600 each, and a cohort was divided into six centuries, that is, a hundred men in each century. Cornelius was a centurion (see Fig. 10, 42), he had charge of one of these subdivisions of a cohort.

Of another centurion we read in the Gospels. He was in character much like Cornelius, for it is said of him "for he loves our nation, and he is the one who built us our synagogue" (Luke 7:5). It is striking that two centurions, soldiers of rank, should be so prominently mentioned in connection with the Gospel. The Holy Spirit had done a gracious work in both of these Gentile soldiers. Cornelius must have been a man of authority. His name indicates this, for he belonged to the house to which also belonged the Scipios and Sulla. He was well known to the whole Jewish nation (v. 22); he also had a large circle of friends in Caesarea. But he had more than a good report. He was a devout man, one that feared God with all his house, and who showed his piety by almsgiving and by prayer. It is stated that he "prayed continually to God" (10:2). He belonged to that class of Gentiles who, illumined by the Holy Spirit, had turned to God from idols, to serve the true and the living God. He was godly and a converted man before Peter ever came to him and preached the Gospel in his house. It is wrong, therefore, to speak of the event described in this chapter as the conversion of Cornelius. Nor was he a proselyte who had become circumcised and accepted Judaism. Of salvation through the Lord Jesus Christ for himself and the blessed assurance of that salvation he knew nothing.

It was at the ninth hour when Cornelius had a divine visitation. He was praying (10:30) when a man stood before him in bright clothing. It seems Cornelius observed the Jewish hours of prayer; the ninth hour was 3 P.M., the time of the evening oblation. The appearing of the angel filled Cornelius with fear. The angel brought him the assurance that God had

---

[2] That is, 3 p.m.

heard his prayers and that his good works were pleasing to God. They sprung from faith.

The angel also gave him the directions for sending to Peter, and where Peter was to be found, with whom he lodged and where his lodging house was located. Peter was to tell him what he ought to do. From this we may gather that his prayer must have been to God for light and guidance. How blessed and full of comfort all this is! The Lord observed this devout centurion, he heard his prayers. His eye was upon Peter likewise and he knew his movements. And this is still the case. His loving, watching eye is upon all who are His. He still directs and guides those who depend on Him. What honor to serve such a Lord! Yet how little our poor, failing hearts enter into all this. How often we doubt and fear when faith should rejoice and praise.

Cornelius called at once two of his household servants and a devout soldier, and after he had acquainted them with the divine message and direction he had received, he sent them to Joppa, and they in due time reached their destination. While they were inquiring for Simon the tanner's house at the seaside, the chosen messenger had his vision.

2. THE TRANCE-VISION OF PETER IN PREPARATION FOR HIS MISSION (VS. 9–16).

> The next day, as they were on their journey and approaching the city, Peter went up on the housetop about the sixth hour[3] to pray. And he became hungry and wanted something to eat, but while they were preparing it, he fell into a trance and saw the heavens opened and something like a great sheet descending, being let down by its four corners upon the earth. In it were all kinds of animals and reptiles and birds of the air. And there came a voice to him: "Rise, Peter; kill and eat." But Peter said, "By no means, Lord; for I

---

[3] That is, noon

12. An inscription on a theatre seat in the Miletus theatre that states "Place of the Jews, who are also called God-fearing." Cornelius is mentioned as a God-fearer (Acts 13:16; 26).

> have never eaten anything that is common or unclean." And the voice came to him again a second time, "What God has made clean, do not call common." This happened three times, and the thing was taken up at once to heaven (vs. 9–16).

The messenger needed a preparation as well as Cornelius. As a Jew, though filled with the Spirit, he needed a special revelation to send him forth to the Gentiles. On the day of Pentecost he had declared: "For the promise is for you and for your children and for all who are *far off*, everyone whom the Lord our God calls to himself" (2:39). Those "afar off" are the Gentiles. Peter then did not realize the far-reaching meaning of this utterance. And when he heard from the Lord's own lips the great commission to preach the Gospel to every creature, he little understood that it meant the Gentiles. Had someone demanded suddenly of Peter before this event occurred, that he should go and associate with Gentiles, enter their houses and speak to them concerning Christ, he would have drawn back in astonishment, if not in horror. But now the hour is come when it is to be known that indeed the middle wall of partition is broken down. Peter had tarried many days in Joppa. Nothing is said of further service he rendered in that city. He may have been waiting on the Lord for guidance. The messengers of Cornelius were nearing Joppa when Peter went up upon the housetop to pray, about the sixth hour. He still maintained Jewish forms. He had not yet broken his fast and while on the flat roof he fell into a trance. The vision he saw, coming out of the opened heaven, was a vessel like a great sheet. The four corners were together and thus the sheet was let down upon the earth. The sheet contained clean and unclean animals.

The voice from heaven demanded that Peter should kill and eat. And he who rebuked his Lord while on earth, there at Caesarea Philippi, when he said, after the Lord announced his coming passion, "Far be it from you, Lord!"[4] (Matt 16:22), does so here again on the housetop of Caesarea. He said, "This shall never happen to you." He protests that he had never eaten anything common or unclean. The voice came again the second time, telling him, "What God has made clean, do not call common." (10:15). Thrice the same thing was done, and then straightway the vessel was received up into heaven. It returned to the place from which it had been lowered. And what is the meaning? The vessel is the type of the church. The four corners represent the four corners of the earth. The clean animals it contained, the Jews; the unclean, the Gentiles. But all in that vessel are cleansed. The Grace of God in the Lord Jesus Christ has cleansed those who are in Christ. "You were washed, you were sanctified, you were justified in the name of the Lord Jesus Christ and by the Spirit of our God" (1 Cor 6:11). Jew and Gentile believing, redeemed by blood, saved by Grace, washed and sanctified, are put into one body. What the great Apostle to the Gentiles wrote to the Ephesians is here made known in a vision.

> This mystery is[5] that the Gentiles are fellow heirs, members of the same body, and partakers of the promise in Christ Jesus through the gospel (Eph 3:6).

The vessel came down from heaven and disappeared there. This reveals the heavenly origin and the heavenly destiny of the church. The church is a heavenly revelation, and, as the vessel disappeared in heaven, so will the church someday be taken up into heaven to enter upon her heavenly destination. Such are the lessons which this vision clearly teaches.

3. Peter with Cornelius at Caesarea (vs. 17–20).

> Now while Peter was inwardly perplexed as to what the vision that he had seen might mean, behold, the men who were sent by Cornelius, having made inquiry for Simon's house, stood at the gate and called out to ask whether Simon who was called Peter was lodging there. And while Peter was pondering the vision, the Spirit said to him, "Behold, three men are looking for you. Rise and go down and accompany them without hesitation,[6] for I have sent them." (vs. 17–20).

Peter was in doubt about the vision. What did it mean? Did it mean that all distinction between clean and unclean animals was to be abolished and that the great dietary instructions divinely given through Moses were to be abandoned? Perhaps the words of the Lord came back to him, when he had said, "do you not see that whatever goes into a person from outside cannot defile him" (Mark 7:18) he was deeply exercised about the vision to know its deeper meaning. But the Lord Himself had the interpretation of his vision ready for Peter. Just at that moment the messengers of Cornelius, who had asked their way to

---

[4] Or "[May God be] *merciful to you, Lord!*"

[5] The words *This mystery is* are inferred from verse 4.

[6] Or *accompany them, making no distinction*

CHAPTER TEN

Simon's house at the seaside, had arrived at the gate. God was arranging everything, even in the smaller details. His purpose and plan could not fail, nor can it ever fail. Nothing could hinder that which was to be accomplished. And so it is still. *We need to fear no failure, nor do we need to worry, if we are in his plan.* And when these men were inquiring for Simon, surnamed Peter, whether he lodged there, Peter was still in deep thought on the vision. He did not hear the calling of the men at the gate. But another One spoke to him: "the Spirit said to him, 'Behold, three men are looking for you. Rise and go down and accompany them without hesitation, for I have sent them'" (10:20). The Holy Spirit now begins his directions. The words reveal the truth of the personality of the Holy Spirit in a very striking way. "I have sent them" is what the Holy Spirit declares. And he who sent the three men to summon Peter to Caesarea, also commanded Peter to arise and to go with them without any hesitation.

> And Peter went down to the men and said, "I am the one you are looking for. What is the reason for your coming?" And they said, "Cornelius, a centurion, an upright and God-fearing man, who is well spoken of by the whole Jewish nation, was directed by a holy angel to send for you to come to his house and to hear what you have to say." So he invited them in to be his guests.
>
> The next day he rose and went away with them, and some of the brothers from Joppa accompanied him. (vs. 21–23).

How great must have been Peter's astonishment, when he faced suddenly the three Gentiles at the gate. But could he doubt after such a vision? Was not the presence of these three men, uncircumcised, unclean Gentiles, an explanation of the vision? The Holy Spirit furthermore had told him that they were sent by Himself and that he was to go with them. And the men now told him what had happened to Cornelius, the devout centurion, and that an angel of God had directed him to Peter. The full light must have flashed upon the Apostle of the circumcision. He called them in and lodged them. This was certainly breaking away from Jewish customs. On the next morning we see a company leaving Joppa. Peter was not like Jonah, who fled from Joppa, but he leaves in obedience to the divine call, accompanied by certain brethren and the three messengers of Cornelius.

> And on the following day they entered Caesarea. Cornelius was expecting them and had called together his relatives and close friends. When Peter entered, Cornelius met him and fell down at his feet and worshiped him. But Peter lifted him up, saying, "Stand up; I too am a man." And as he talked with him, he went in and found many persons gathered. And he said to them, "You yourselves know how unlawful it is for a Jew to associate with or to visit anyone of another nation, but God has shown me that I should not call any person common or unclean. So when I was sent for, I came without objection. I ask then why you sent for me."
>
> And Cornelius said, "Four days ago, about this hour, I was praying in my house at the ninth hour,[7] and behold, a man stood before me in bright clothing and said, 'Cornelius, your prayer has been heard and your alms have been remembered before God. Send therefore to Joppa and ask for Simon who is called Peter. He is lodging in the house of Simon, a tanner, by the sea.' So I sent for you at once, and you have been kind enough to come. Now therefore we are all here in the presence of God to hear all that you have been commanded by the Lord." (vs. 24–33).

While the company was journeying on towards the city, Cornelius, who had called together his kinsmen and near friends, was waiting for the heaven-sent messenger. With eager anticipation, longing for the blessed truth he was to hear, he waited for Peter's arrival. And then he came. No sooner did Cornelius see Peter than he fell down at his feet and worshipped. This happened outside of Cornelius' house, perhaps at a distance

---

[7] That is, 3 p.m.

from it. The first act he did was to fall at the Apostle's feet and to do him divine honor. In this he betrayed his heathen training. Remembering the vision of the angel he looked upon Peter as deserving the greatest honor. But Peter would not tolerate this for a moment. Lifting Cornelius up, he said, "Stand up; I too am a man." What Cornelius did was an act of worship. The same word Satan used when he demanded that the Lord Jesus Christ should fall down and worship him. God alone is to be worshipped. Such reverence which Cornelius did is not to be rendered to a mere man nor to an angel (see Rev 19:10 and 22:9). "Worship God;" the Apostle John is told as he fell at the feet of the angel which showed him the things he saw. Some Christians have declared that even the Lord Jesus Christ should not be worshipped. But this is a serious mistake. The Lord Jesus Christ is God and worship belongs to him. "That all may honor the Son, *just as they honor* the Father. Whoever does not honor the Son does not honor the Father who sent him" (John 5:23). But what a contrast between Peter and those who claim to be the successors of Peter! That wicked man-made priesthood, which in its assumption has been the corruption of Christianity, demands honor and reverence from man. The pope and the priests accept reverence from man, which belongs only to the Lord. Ritualism, whether in Romish, Greek or Protestant form, always exalts a man and looks upon sinful man as having authority and therefore entitled to honor and worship. "his Worship," "his Grace," "his Reverence," "his Eminence," "his Holiness," etc., are the titles attached by ritualistic Christendom to men. For this there is no authority whatever in the Word of God. Peter's action here repudiates the whole thing. His Epistle in which by the Spirit of God he teaches the priesthood of *all* believers and not once mentions anything about himself, as holding a place above the other believers, is a complete refutal of traditional Christendom. Indeed, Ritualism is a return to heathenish customs; it is idolatry. Such is the teaching of Galatians 4:9–11.

Then Peter went with Cornelius into the house, telling him of how God had in the vision on the house top delivered him from the traditional Jewish prejudices and that he had now full liberty to enter into the house of a non-Jew and did no longer consider such an act unlawful. Asking Cornelius for what intent he had sent for him, the centurion rehearses once more the answer which God had sent him, when he had prayed. He closes his address to Peter with those familiar words, "Now therefore we are all here in the presence of God to hear all that you have been commanded by the Lord" (10:33). How beautiful all this is and how comforting to the heart! In his days upon the earth our Lord had said: "And I have other sheep that are not of this fold. I must bring them also, and they will listen to my voice. So there will be one flock, one shepherd" (John 10:16). Here in his own blessed way the risen Christ accomplishes what he predicted. The other sheep are the Gentiles, the one fold (flock)[8] is the church and the one shepherd over all the Lord Jesus Christ. He was the actor in this great event. He drew Cornelius and spoke to him. And he is still the same Lord, who adds to his flock. He still calls the other sheep.

Cornelius and his kinsmen knew the messenger was sent of God and that the message he brings was God's message. Peter knew he was sent and that souls had been

---

[8] Not *fold* as the Authorized Verion has it. Judaism was a fold, but Christianity, according to the New Testament, knows nothing of a fold, but there is *one* flock.

prepared to hear the message. How blessed the meetings of God's people might be if such were always the case, and the servant of Christ were conscious in dependence on the Lord as his messenger, sent of God, and if those who come to hear, came expecting God's own message for their souls.

4. Peter Preaching the Gospel to the Gentiles (vs. 34–43).

> So Peter opened his mouth and said: "Truly I understand that God shows no partiality, but in every nation anyone who fears him and does what is right is acceptable to him. As for the word that he sent to Israel, preaching good news of peace through Jesus Christ (he is Lord of all), You yourselves know what happened throughout all Judea, beginning from Galilee after the baptism that John proclaimed: how God anointed Jesus of Nazareth with the Holy Spirit and with power. He went about doing good and healing all who were oppressed by the devil, for God was with him. And we are witnesses of all that he did both in the country of the Jews and in Jerusalem. They put him to death by hanging him on a tree, but God raised him on the third day and made him to appear, not to all the people but to us who had been chosen by God as witnesses, who ate and drank with him after he rose from the dead. And he commanded us to preach to the people and to testify that he is the one appointed by God to be judge of the living and the dead. To him all the prophets bear witness that everyone who believes in him receives forgiveness of sins through his name" (vs. 34–43).

There is a great difference between Peter's address to the Gentiles and his previously reported addresses to the Jews. The word repentance so prominent in his witness to Jerusalem is absent entirely. These words of Peter may be divided into three parts:

1. The remarks introductory to the Gospel. Peter declares that he perceives that God is not a respecter of persons. This statement was made already in the Old Testament (See Deut 10:17; 2 Chr 19:7 and Job 34:19). The Holy Spirit brings this to Peter's remembrance. Peter had previously looked upon God as a respecter of persons, but his experience had convinced him that such was not the case. The same truth is very significantly mentioned in the opening chapters of Romans, the chapters which so clearly prove that there is no difference, but that all, Jews and Gentiles, have sinned and come short of the glory of God. In Romans we read: "but glory and honor and peace for everyone who does good, the Jew first and also the Greek. For God shows no partiality" (2:10–11). The same truth Peter states here: "but in every nation anyone who fears him and does what is right is acceptable to him" (10:34). However, this does not mean, as it is so often declared, that the heathen's natural light and acquired morality renders him acceptable in the sight of God. The fear of God and the working of righteousness is not the product of the natural heart, but the work of God Himself. Such work is not confined to the Jewish soul but is done also through grace in the Gentiles. This is the meaning of the statement. Peter adds something which is often overlooked. He tells Cornelius and his friends that they were not ignorant of the Word which God sent to the children of Israel, preaching peace by Jesus Christ, who is Lord of all. They knew of all this and had heard of it in some way. The blessing was in possession of the children of Israel. For this reason the centurion must have loved the nation Israel and did good to them. But he had no assurance that that which was preached to Israel was to be enjoyed by him, nor did Peter realize it till God revealed it to him that the Gentiles were to be sharers of it.

2. Then Peter explains that word and briefly rehearses the facts concerning Jesus of Nazareth. God had anointed him with the Holy Spirit and with power. God was with Him. It was demonstrated by what he did, going about doing good and healing all that were oppressed by the devil. They had been witnesses of all this. In a brief sentence

Peter mentions the death of Christ, that they slew him and hanged him on a tree. Then follows the declaration of his resurrection. God raised him up the third day. But he was not seen by all the people, but only by those whom God had chosen; who did eat and drink with Him.

With what interest the centurion and those with him must have listened to this blessed message, much of which was known to them by hearsay, but here stood Peter, one of the eye witnesses of all this which had happened. One directly sent by God was telling out all this in their presence. But he was a Jew, who spoke these words. They were Gentiles. What meaning had all this for them? The third part of Peter's address makes this clear. It brings the blessed Gospel of Christ home to their hearts.

3. The Apostle speaks next of the fact that Christ had given them a commission. He commanded them to preach to the people and to testify that it is he which God ordained to be the judge of quick and dead. But the centurion and his company could not take any comfort in this preaching. Who else were the people but the Jewish people to whom that risen One had given commandment to preach. The Holy Spirit might have worded his message in another way, which would have revealed the truth in a general way. He might have said that the Lord had given a commission which said: "Go into *all* the world and proclaim the gospel to the *whole* creation" (Mark 15:16). From this they might have reasoned, we are creatures of God, therefore the Gospel is for us. He chose another, a more precious way, a way which was to bring blessing to Peter's heart as well. The truth flashed at once into Peter's heart and mind as he spoke.

> To him, [he declares,] all the prophets bear witness that *everyone* who believes in him receives forgiveness of sins through his name (10:43).

Some have made the statement that Peter and the other Apostles were not obedient to the Lord's command when they tarried in Jerusalem, that; it was the Lord's will for them to spread the Gospel among the Gentiles at once. Instead of carrying out the commission they abode in that city. However, this view is incorrect. They acted according to God's will. Peter did not realize the full meaning of the Lord's purpose until the proper time had come for it and then the power of God made it clear to Him. It was revealed to Peter as he spoke these words that there was indeed no difference, that God is no respecter of persons. The truth so fully revealed in a doctrinal way in Romans 3:22 that the righteousness of God, by faith in Jesus Christ is to *all* and upon *all* them that believe, Jew and Gentile, bursts upon the Apostle of the circumcision through divine illumination. Blessed and precious sentence, which Peter uttered "*everyone* who believes in him receives forgiveness of sins through his name." Yes, *everyone*, it is the word which tells out the meaning of the Gospel for a lost and guilty world. "*Everyone*" the Lord had used it Himself knowing the blessed results of his work on the cross.

> For God so loved the world,[9] that he gave his only Son, that whoever believes in him should not perish but have eternal life (John 3:16).

And when God closes his Holy Word on the last page, he must tell a sinful world once more that blessed word God's own redeemed people love so well. "Let the one who is thirsty come; let the one who desires take the water of life without price" (Rev 22:17).

The great truth has been spoken for the first time. The full and free good news of salvation through his Name has been

---

[9] Or *For this is how God loved the world*

offered for the first time to Gentiles. What is the result?

5. THE INTERRUPTED MESSAGE (VS. 44–48).

> While Peter was still saying these things, the Holy Spirit fell on all who heard the word. And the believers from among the circumcised who had come with Peter were amazed, because the gift of the Holy Spirit was poured out even on the Gentiles. For they were hearing them speaking in tongues and extolling God. Then Peter declared, "Can anyone withhold water for baptizing these people, who have received the Holy Spirit just as we have?" And he commanded them to be baptized in the name of Jesus Christ. Then they asked him to remain for some days (vs. 44–48).

Peter's message was suddenly interrupted. He intended to continue; he had only begun to speak (11:15) when he was arrested. The Holy Spirit fell on all them which heard the Word. Cornelius and those with him had been ignorant of this very fact, which Peter had made known. They heard that all this salvation, the remission of sins, was for them and in that moment as they heard the Word they believed and as soon as they believed, the very moment they accepted this blessed message, the Holy Spirit fell on them. It was then demonstrated that the gift of the Holy Spirit is given by hearing of faith. The apostle of the Gentiles wrote later to the foolish Galatians, who were falling from grace by going back under the law, "let me ask you only this: Did you receive the Spirit by works of the law or by hearing with faith?" (Gal 3:2). Even so in this blessed Gospel the sealing with the Spirit and much else is received in believing. Something new had taken place. On Pentecost it meant water baptism as a condition of receiving the Holy Spirit (Acts 2:38) and the remission of sins; In Samaria the Apostles, Peter and John, according to the wisdom of God, had to lay on hands, but here without water baptism and laying on of hands the Holy Spirit came upon the Gentiles. Nor was there any process of seeking, surrendering, examining themselves, giving up, praying for it, but by hearing of faith, in believing the message of the Gospel the Holy Spirit fell on them. And to show that every barrier between Jew and Gentile had been removed, that nothing inferior had been bestowed upon Gentiles, than that which came upon the believing Jews on the day of Pentecost, Cornelius, his kinsmen and friends spoke with tongues and magnified God. It was the conclusive evidence that Gentiles, uncircumcised and unbaptized, received the Holy Spirit like the Jews. "While Peter was still saying these things, the Holy Spirit fell on all who heard the word." (10:44).

Water baptism follows. Up to this chapter water baptism preceded the gift of the Holy Spirit. This shows the place water baptism holds on the ground of grace. Water baptism has no place in the proclamation of the Gospel of Grace. It is not a means of grace, nor a sacrament. Peter, however, does not slight nor ignore baptism. "Can anyone withhold water for baptizing these people?" Then he commanded them to be baptized in the name of the Lord. This shows that not Peter himself did this act; it is therefore not a ministerial thing. This, too, was done here in anticipation of what should be made of baptism through "ordained men" who claim apostolic succession.

Peter was requested to tarry with the happy company certain days. No doubt he must have fulfilled their request. What blessed intercourse they must have had!

CHAPTER ELEVEN

The present chapter we divide into four parts:

1. Peter's defence in Jerusalem and its result (vs. 1–18).

2. The Foundation of the Church in Antioch (vs. 19–21).

3. Barnabas sent to Antioch (vs. 22–26).

4. The Prophecy of Agabus (vs. 27–30).

1. PETER'S DEFENCE IN JERUSALEM AND ITS RESULTS (VS. 1–18).

1Now the apostles and the brothers[1] who were throughout Judea heard that the Gentiles also had received the word of God. So when Peter went up to Jerusalem, the circumcision party[2] criticized him, saying, "You went to uncircumcised men and ate with them." But Peter began and explained it to them in order: "I was in the city of Joppa praying, and in a trance I saw a vision, something like a great sheet descending, being let down from heaven by its four corners, and it came down to me. Looking at it closely, I observed animals and beasts of prey and reptiles and birds of the air. And I heard a voice saying to me, 'Rise, Peter; kill and eat.' But I said, 'By no means, Lord; for nothing common or unclean has ever entered my mouth.' But the voice answered a second time from heaven, 'What God has made clean, do not call common.' This happened three times, and all was drawn up again into heaven. And behold, at that very moment three men arrived at the house in which we were, sent to me from Caesarea. And the Spirit told me to go with them, making no distinction. These six brothers also accompanied me, and we entered the man's house. And he told us how he had seen the angel stand in his house and say, 'Send to Joppa and bring Simon who is called Peter; he will declare to you a message by which you will be saved, you and all your household.' As I began to speak, the Holy Spirit fell on them just as on us at the beginning. And I remembered the word of the Lord, how he said, 'John baptized with water, but you will be baptized with the Holy Spirit.' If then God gave the same gift to them as he gave to us when we believed in the Lord Jesus Christ, who was I that I could stand in God's way?" When they heard these things they fell silent. And they glorified God, saying, "Then to the Gentiles also God has granted repentance that leads to life." (vs. 1–18).

Peter had tarried certain days with the happy company in Caesarea, no doubt, telling them more of the Lord, of his life and miracles, his death and resurrection. How blessed this fellowship must have been! It fully demonstrated that the middle wall of partition had been broken down and that the believing Jews and Gentiles were one in Christ Jesus. But the report of his action and that the Gentiles had received the Word of God reached the apostles and brethren in Judea. Instead of creating rejoicing over what God had done, contention arose and the danger of a division was imminent. Failure is seen once more. Murmurings had arisen before (ch. 6); but here party spirit showed itself for the first time. This subtle work of the flesh (Gal

---

[1] Or *brothers and sisters*
[2] Or *Jerusalem, those of the circumcision*

5:20)³ was ready to make a rend among the brethren. We must bear in mind that two classes of Jews composed the assemblies in Jerusalem and in Judea. The Hellenists and the more strict Palestinian Jews. To the latter class belonged many Pharisees and the large number of priests, who had believed. These were all zealous for the law (Acts 21:20).

These still looked upon the Gentiles as unclean. Their belief was that a Gentile in order to be saved had to submit to circumcision and become a Jew. Years later we find them very outspoken about this in the record of the first church council held in Jerusalem. Publicly they stated "it is necessary to circumcise them and to order them to keep the law of Moses" (Acts 15:5). Here the party spirit asserts itself and the dissenters are called "the circumcision party," which means that some of them pressed circumcision and the law unduly, for all the Jewish believers were of the circumcision. Gradually they became a strong party in the church. Striking it is, too, that Peter is praised later "for his apostolic ministry to the circumcised," (Gal 2:8) and later his action in Antioch, so inconsistent with the events in Caesarea, brought forth the divine rebuke through the apostle of the Gentiles (Gal 1:14). The eating with the Gentiles was the one point of accusation here.

> They seem to have heard the fact, without any circumstantial detail; and, . . . from some reporter, who gave the objectionable part of it, as it is not uncommon in such cases, all prominence.⁴

Peter's answer is most instructive. He does not refer to his apostolic authority. He might have reminded them of the fact that the Lord at another Caesarea had committed to him "the Keys of the kingdom of heaven," (Matt 16:19) and that in virtue of this commission he had acted. But no reference to that is made at all by him. Nor does he go to his fellow apostles to lay the matter before them. His defence consists in a rehearsal of what had taken place. We do not need to follow this again, as we have already done so in the previous chapter. The statements given proved irresistible. Here were facts which were unanswerable. They heard these things, they held their peace. But more than that, they began to praise instead of strife; they glorified God. Gratefully they acknowledged that God had granted to the Gentiles repentance to life. In the course of time this wonderful opening of the door to the Gentiles was forgotten and "those of the circumcision" became a strong party. Peter but briefly refers in Acts 15 to that, which he so fully describes here.

2. The Foundation of the Church in Antioch (vs. 19–21).

> Now those who were scattered because of the persecution that arose over Stephen traveled as far as Phoenicia and Cyprus and Antioch, speaking the word to no one except Jews. But there were some of them, men of Cyprus and Cyrene, who on coming to Antioch spoke to the Hellenists⁵ also, preaching the Lord Jesus. And the hand of the Lord was with them, and a great number who believed turned to the Lord (vs. 19–21).

The nineteenth verse connects with Chapter 8:4. The great persecution had scattered the believers. Philip had been the chosen instrument to bring the gospel to Samaria. That had to be reported first. And now we are to learn what others did and where they proclaimed the blessed Gospel. They went to Phoenice. This was a strip of coast land some 120 miles long. Tyre and Sidon were

---

³ The words translated in Galatians 5:20 by "seditions, heresies," means "disputes, schools of opinion."

⁴ Alford, *The NT for English Readers*, 1:726–26.

⁵ Or *Greeks* (that is, Greek-speaking non-Jews)

cities of Phoenice. There the Gospel was preached and with blessed results, which appear later in this book (21:4–7; 27:3). Cyprus was closely connected with Phoenice. Many ships sailed constantly from the Phoenician ports to that island. Barnabas and Mnason (21:16) were from Cyprus (see Fig. 14). Then others must have gone along the coast and reached Antioch. They all preached to the Jews only. But some of these evangelists were men of Cyprus and Cyrene who, when they came to Antioch, preached the Lord Jesus to the Greeks, that is to the Gentiles. A great number of these turned to the Lord and believed. Antioch comes into prominence as the other great center of Christianity, second only to Jerusalem. Here the preaching to the Gentiles was begun and fully recognized by the church in Jerusalem.

From here the great missionary movement of the apostolic age started. Here Saul appears again to take from now on, as the apostle of the Gentiles, a leading part. In Antioch, furthermore, the disciples were called "Christians" for the first time. In Jerusalem, this name was unknown; they were termed "the sect of the Nazarenes." All this brings out the great importance as the center of Christianity on Gentile ground. This importance has led some to see in Antioch the place where the church began to come into existence. It is denied that the day of Pentecost was the day that the church was empowered for service, but the claim is made that the church began in Antioch. This is a far-fetched theory, which lacks scriptural support. We have already shown that Pentecost was the day on which the church received power. No event like the baptism of the Holy Spirit took place in Antioch, but Antioch shared in that which had happened in Jerusalem. The Antiochan Gentile believers were simply added by the same Spirit to the church, the foundations of which are the apostles and prophets, Jesus Christ Himself being the chief cornerstone (Eph 2:20). Antioch itself was an influential city founded by Seleucus Nicator in 300 B. C. It was a beautiful city situated on the river Orontes, with marvellous scenery. It was a luxurious, voluptuous city, steeped in the greatest immoralities. Here the Gospel was to be manifested as the power of God to salvation.

It is a very striking contrast with what goes before in this great historical book that the instruments used in preaching the Gospel to the Antiochenes, and in the establishment of the church among them, are not named. The true character of the church, independent of any human, earthly authority, dependent on him who is Head over all, is indicated in this fact. And yet, as we shall see directly, the new departure had to be acknowledged and recognized in Jerusalem. It needed, however, not apostles to lay their hands upon them, so that they might receive the Holy Spirit.

3. BARNABAS SENT TO ANTIOCH (VS. 22–26).

> The report of this came to the ears of the church in Jerusalem, and they sent Barnabas to Antioch. When he came and saw the grace of God, he was glad, and he exhorted them all to remain faithful to the Lord with steadfast purpose, for he was a good man, full of the Holy Spirit and of faith. And a great many people were added to the Lord. So Barnabas went to Tarsus to look for Saul, and when he had found him, he brought him to Antioch. For a whole year they met with the church and taught a great many people. And in Antioch the disciples were first called Christians. (vs. 22–26).

CHAPTER ELEVEN

The wonderful work done in Antioch, the assembling of large numbers of Greeks, who had turned to the Lord, induced the church in Jerusalem to send forth Barnabas. The church in Jerusalem felt a responsibility towards this new evidence of the power of their risen and glorified Lord. They wanted to know in Jerusalem if the reports were true, and if true the assembly had to be recognized as such. This shows that the Oneness of the church, though not yet fully made known by revelation, was nevertheless realized through the Holy Spirit. And that a blessed relationship existed between the assembly in Jerusalem and the one in Antioch, is seen by Peter's visit in that city, when in the liberty wherewith Christ, has made us free, he ate with these believing Gentiles and enjoyed fellowship with them (Gal 2:11–12). Barnabas was well fitted for the mission. However, he does not come as an apostolic delegate, to baptize, to confirm or to admit these new believers into some fellowship, but his mission was simply to see if "the report of this" was true. And if true the recognition of these Gentile believers had to follow.

Barnabas when he came saw the grace of God. He saw that a genuine work of the Holy Spirit had been accomplished. This filled his heart with joy. His exhortation was that with purpose of heart they should cleave to the Lord. Nothing else was needed. These Gentile believers were the Lord's and as such they were to cleave to the Lord. The unity with the fellow believers in Jerusalem was with this recognized. Barnabas did not remain idle while he was in Antioch. The Holy Spirit used him mightily. The exhortations of the good Barnabas, full of the Holy Spirit and of faith, resulted in a great crowd which was added to the Lord. This latter expression is the same as used in chapter 2:42 and 47.

But here was a great field; a strong man was needed. No angel nor heavenly vision

13. Imperial bronze portrait of Roman emperor Claudius (10 BC–54 AD; r. 41–54 AD). National Archaeological Museum of Spain, Madrid.

points out that man. Barnabas knew him, and guided by the indwelling Spirit, the Son of consolation, for this is the meaning of Barnabas, departs to go to the nearby Tarsus to find Saul. Saul was his man. Barnabas had introduced him to the apostles and there can be no question at all that Barnabas knew from Saul's lips and experience, that he had been called by the Lord to preach to the Gentiles. He found him in Tarsus. Patiently Saul must have waited for the right moment when his life's work should begin. That time had now come. We see them together in Antioch for a whole year; they assembled themselves with the church, and taught much people. A brief sentence tells us that these Gentiles,

Page | 135

who had become believers in the Lord, were first called Christians in Antioch.

The movement had attracted the attention of the outsiders. The Jews, it is certain, did not give this name, but the Gentiles invented it. Antioch was famous for its readiness to jeer and call names; it was known by its witty epigrams. So they coined a new word, "*Christianoi*" Christians. It is used exclusively by outsiders, as seen in the case of Agrippa, also see 1 Peter 4:16. Jews and Gentiles alike were called by this name, "Christians," so that it bears testimony to the oneness of Jew and Gentile in Christ.

4. THE PROPHECY OF AGABUS (VS. 27–30).

> Now in these days prophets came down from Jerusalem to Antioch. And one of them named Agabus stood up and foretold by the Spirit that there would be a great famine over all the world (this took place in the days of Claudius). So the disciples determined, every one according to his ability, to send relief to the brothers[6] living in Judea. And they did so, sending it to the elders by the hand of Barnabas and Saul" (vs. 27–30).

An additional proof is found in these verses of the intercourse and fellowship, which existed between the assembly in Jerusalem and the assembly in Antioch. Prophets came to Antioch from Jerusalem. This is the first time that New Testament prophets are mentioned. They came as a gift of the Lord to his church next to the apostles. Many were prophets in the early days of Christianity. However, their gift must not be limited to predictions. Anyone who speaks of divine things out of the fullness of a heart, which is in blessed communion with God, prophesies. These spiritual gifts were led from Jerusalem to Antioch to minister there. Prominent among them is Agabus.[7] He made a prediction that a great famine should soon come. It came during the days of Claudius Caesar (see Fig. 13). Then follows a precious action, which clearly shows again the blessed fellowship and unity of the church. Then the disciples, every man according to his ability, determined to send relief to the brethren which dwelt in Judea. The church in Jerusalem was poor, the disciples in Antioch were more blessed with earthly things. And now, according to their ability, it was an individual matter, they gave. They sent temporal gifts to Jerusalem from which they had received so much spiritual blessing. Barnabas and Saul carried the fellowship to the elders of the assembly in Jerusalem.

---

[6]

[7] The same Agabus who appears in 21:11.

Chapter Twelve

With this chapter we reach the conclusion of the second part of this book. Jerusalem had heard the second offer concerning the Kingdom and mercy was ready even for the murderers of the Prince of Life. But that offer was rejected. Stephen's testimony followed by his martyrdom marked the close of that second offer to the city where our Lord had been crucified. Then broke out a great persecution and they were scattered abroad except the Apostles. With the eighth chapter we saw the Gospel preached in Judea and Samaria. From our last chapter we learned that others who were driven out of Jerusalem preached the Word in Phoenice, Cyprus and Antioch. In this second section of the Book of Acts the conversion of Saul, the Apostle to the Gentiles, Peter's acts and his preaching to Cornelius, the foundation of the church in Antioch as a second great center of Christianity, are reported. The twelfth chapter, with which this part of Acts closes, is an interesting one. It is not only interesting on account of the historical information it contains, but also because of its dispensational foreshadowing. Once more we are introduced to Jerusalem and see another great tribulation. The wicked King is reigning over the city. James is killed with the sword, while Peter is imprisoned but wonderfully delivered; the evil King, who claimed divine power and worship, is suddenly smitten by the judgment of the Lord. Then the Word grew and multiplied, Barnabas and Saul returned from Jerusalem to Antioch, from where the great missionary operations were soon to be conducted. The events in Jerusalem, James' martyrdom under King Herod, Peter's imprisonment and deliverance, as well as the fate of the persecuting King foreshadow the events with which this present age will close. After the true church is taken from the earth, that is when 1 Thessalonians 4:16–17 is fulfilled, the great tribulation will take place. While great tribulation and judgment will come upon the whole world, the great tribulation will come upon the Jewish people who have returned in part to their own land. In the midst of the masses of unbelieving Jews, there will be found a remnant of God-fearing Jews (see Fig. 12), who are converted and bear testimony to the truth. A wicked King, the man of sin, the false Messiah, will then be in power in Jerusalem. Part of that Jewish remnant will suffer martyrdom; these are represented by James, whom Herod, the type of the Antichrist, slew. Another part will be delivered as Peter was delivered. Herod's presumption and fate clearly points to that of the Antichrist (2 Thess 2:3–8). All this may well be kept in mind as we study this chapter in detail.

1. The great persecution of the church by Herod Agrippa I (vs. 1–5).

2. The miraculous deliverance of Peter (vs. 6–17).

3. The Presumption and Judgment of King Herod (vs. 18–23).

4. Barnabas and Saul returning to Antioch (vs. 24–25).

1. The Great Persecution of the Church by Herod Agrippa I (vs. 1–5).

> About that time Herod the king laid violent hands on some who belonged to the church. He killed James the brother of John with the sword, and when he saw that it pleased the Jews, he proceeded to arrest Peter also. This was during the days of Unleavened Bread. And when he had seized him, he put him in prison, delivering him over to four squads of soldiers to guard him, intending after the Passover to bring him out to the people. So Peter was kept in prison, but earnest prayer for him was made to God by the church. (vs. 1–5).

The second great persecution broke out. It was about that time when the events had taken place with which the previous chapter closed. Herod, the King, mentioned here is known in history as Herod Agrippa 1. He was the grandson of Herod the Great. First he had the tetrarchy of Philip (Luke 3:1), then he received the territory of Herod Antipas, Galilee and Peraea; lastly through political intrigue he added to his Kingdom Judea and Samaria (Josephus *Ant.* 19.8.2). Much of his time was spent in Rome, where he lived extravagantly. When he came to Jerusalem he tried in every possible way to gain the good will of the Jews by an outward observance of the law and defense of their customs. The persecution of the church was no doubt inspired by the desire to gain favour with the Jews. As far as the historical account goes, it seems his hatred was exclusively directed against the Apostles; James was killed by the sword. This James was the brother of John, one of the three disciples who are specially mentioned in the Gospels. With his younger brother John and Peter, he had witnessed the raising of Jairus' daughter, had been on the mount of transfiguration and in Gethsemane. No record is given of his work as an Apostle nor anything about his trial; the details of his martyrdom are also passed over. He was put to death in the same way as John the Baptist, beheaded with the sword. This mode of death was looked upon by the Jews as the most disgraceful. The Talmud makes this statement and informs us that this punishment was used in case someone misled the people to worship other gods. Whether this was the accusation or not which was brought against James, we do not know. The two sons of Zebedee, James and John, had desired to sit at the right and at the left hand in his Kingdom. The Lord had answered them, after their declaration that they could drink the cup that he was to drink of, and had said, "You will drink my cup, but to sit at my right hand and at my left is not mine to grant, but it is for those for whom it has been prepared by my Father" (Matt 20:23), and here is the fulfillment of this prediction in the life of James. He is the first Apostle who died and the only Apostle of whose death we have an account given in the New Testament. That no record is given of the details of his suffering and death is also significant. Well has one said:

> In days of ardent faith and also of expectation of the Lord's speedy return, death sank into its true place as simply a change of condition; it was but a falling asleep. Accordingly instead of dwelling with morbid interest on the painful details of the martyr's sufferings, the church pressed forward to reap with joy the harvest of their blood.[1]

The bloody deed pleased the Jews and the wicked King stretched out his hand against Peter and put him into prison. Peter was the only remaining Apostle in Jerusalem. This seems to be clear from verse 17. Peter requests that his deliverance be made known to James (the Lord's brother) and to the brethren. His fellow Apostles, the ten, are not mentioned by him. They were away from Jerusalem at that time. That one of the twelve had been taken away and the others, with the exception of Peter, were not in Jerusalem, is a hint that their work in connection with the nation was ended.

---

[1] Rackham, *The Acts of the Apostles*, 174.

Peter was put into prison for the third time. The wonderful deliverance of the same man as recorded in chapter 4 must have been still vividly in the minds of many of the Jews and it may have led to the great caution exercised in this imprisonment. Four quaternions of soldiers guarded him. He was in the inner ward. A soldier was on each side and he was bound with two chains and the keepers before the door kept the prison. Thus he was kept in that prison. Cruel Herod would stamp out the Nazarenes and Peter was to share James' fate.[2]

"But earnest prayer for him was made to God by the church" (12:5). Of this Herod knew nothing; with this fact the cruel despot did not reckon. Nothing is said of prayer having been made for James. Perhaps his martyrdom was a sudden event. Or it may have been that the Holy Spirit indicated at once that James was to glorify the Lord by his death and no prayer could then be made for his release. The church held a prayer-meeting and it was a prolonged prayer-meeting. However, the word translated "without ceasing" (KJV) means "intensely." It was an intense prayer meeting and of course was therefore carried on without ceasing. The prayer-meeting was held in a private house, as we shall see later. One member suffered and so all suffered. Prayer was their refuge; they were led into it by the Holy Spirit.

2. THE MIRACULOUS DELIVERANCE OF PETER (VS. 6–17).

Now when Herod was about to bring him out, on that very night, Peter was sleeping between two soldiers, bound with two chains, and sentries before the door were guarding the prison. And behold, an angel of the Lord stood next to him, and a light shone in the cell. He struck Peter on the side and woke him, saying, "Get up quickly." And the chains fell off his hands. And the angel said to him, "Dress yourself and put on your sandals." And he did so. And he said to him, "Wrap your cloak around you and follow me." And he went out and followed him. He did not know that what was being done by the angel was real, but thought he was seeing a vision. When they had passed the first and the second guard, they came to the iron gate leading into the city. It opened for them of its own accord, and they went out and went along one street, and immediately the angel left him. When Peter came to himself, he said, "Now I am sure that the Lord has sent his angel and rescued me from the hand of Herod and from all that the Jewish people were expecting."

When he realized this, he went to the house of Mary, the mother of John whose other name was Mark, where many were gathered together and were praying. And when he knocked at the door of the gateway, a servant girl named Rhoda came to answer. Recognizing Peter's voice, in her joy she did not open the gate but ran in and reported that Peter was standing at the gate. They said to her, "You are out of your mind." But she kept insisting that it was so, and they kept saying, "It is his angel!" But Peter continued knocking, and when they opened, they saw him and were amazed. But motioning to them with his hand to be silent, he described to them how the Lord had brought him out of the prison. And he said, "Tell these things to James and to the brothers."[3] Then he departed and went to another place. (vs. 6–17).

A few hours before Herod intended to carry out his wicked scheme the prayer of the church was answered. Peter was sleeping between the two soldiers, in all probability chained to each, so as to make another escape an impossibility. And why did Peter sleep so peacefully? It was not the sleep of exhaustion, but must have been the result of a calm mind trusting in the Lord. Perhaps

---

[2] Four Herods are mentioned in the New Testament. All are types of the Anti-Christ and all were energized by Satan. - Herod the Great who had the children of Bethlehem killed. - The Herod who killed John the Baptist. - The Herod who slew James, - The Herod Agrippa before whom Paul stood and preached.

[3] Or *brothers and sisters*

he remembered in that prison the words which the risen Lord had addressed to him at the shore of the lake Tiberias: "when you are old, you will stretch out your hands, and another will dress you and carry you where you do not want to go" (John 21:18). Thus the Lord had spoken, signifying thereby by what death he should glorify God. He was not yet old. He knew his Lord was greater than poor, miserable Herod. Peter rested in the Lord and in his gracious word to him. Oh! that God's people might know the calm rest of faith. Our lives are in his hands. He is over us and no enemy can harm us; nothing can touch us without his will.

An angel appeared and delivered Peter. The chains fell from his hands. The light of glory shone in the prison. He obeyed the angel, following him as in a dream. The first and second ward passed, they came to the iron gate, which opened by itself. Outside in the street the angel departed. Then Peter realized that the Lord had sent an angel to deliver him. No further comment on the details of this miracle is necessary. In spite of all the precautions, Peter was delivered, and once more the prison was empty. Still on Kingdom ground an angel was seen. Through this age the ministry of angels is hidden. This book closes with another prisoner, Paul, in Rome; no angel was sent to lead him forth. And ever after there have been unaccountable prisons in which the children of God suffered for Christ and for righteousness sake, but the heavens were silent and did not interfere. Thousands were tortured and dragged out a miserable existence in prison till death released them, and, though prayers ascended for their deliverance, no answer came. This has been a mystery to not a few and has been one of the taunts of infidelity. But one of the characteristics of the present age are the closed heavens.[4] They will not be closed forever. James' death and Peter's deliverance foreshadow the death of future Jewish saints during the tribulation and the miraculous deliverance of others.

Once more Peter goes to his own company. They are gathered in the house of Mary, the mother of John. The Mary here is the mother of John Mark, and she is here introduced for the first time in the Book of Acts; she was the aunt of Barnabas. The house must have been a large one, for there was a court-yard. In the spacious house a goodly number of believers were gathered, engaged in prayer. No leader was there, for we read that James and the brethren were absent. It was, as we say, an informal gathering, but the Holy Spirit was the leader. Perhaps they were still on their knees when Peter knocked for admission. The maid Rhoda (Rose) hastened to the gate. Gladness filled her heart when she recognized Peter's voice. For joy she forgot all about that latch at the gate, and instead of opening to Peter she ran back to the house to communicate the good news. She must have interrupted the prayers of the assembled company. The prayer had been answered and praise was now in order. Alas! there was no response from their side. Instead of believing that Peter had been delivered, they looked upon the happy, beaming face of Rhoda and said, "You are out of your mind." Not one of the company believed that Peter had been released. Rhoda was the one who believed that it was Peter. And this is undoubtedly the reason why her name is mentioned in this book. The poor maid, perhaps a slave girl, pleased God because she had faith. While there was great earnestness in that prayer meeting,

---

[4] We recommend to our readers the excellent book by Sir Robert Anderson "The Silence of God." It deals with this question.

when the prayer was answered, unbelief manifested itself.

When Rhoda could not be shaken in her belief that it was really Peter, the company tried to explain the knocking in a spiritualistic way. "It is his angel," they said. This is generally believed to mean that it was his "guardian angel." Upon this expression, much of the belief in guardian angels is founded. However, it is far-fetched to do so. They meant by this expression, the disembodied spirit of Peter. They thought that he had been martyred and that it was a kind of spiritualist manifestation of the fact. But the door was at last opened, and Peter stood safe and sound in their midst; then they were astonished.

After making known how he was delivered, he departed and went into another place. This left James, the Lord's brother, in Jerusalem. The other Apostles had gone and Peter makes likewise haste to leave Jerusalem. Surely this marks the conclusion of this transition period. Where did Peter go? We do not know. Roman Catholicism declares that he went to Rome. There is absolutely no proof for it, but all is against it. Peter never saw Rome. Paul wrote his Epistle to the Romans in 54, and there we learn that at that time no Apostle had visited that city. We see Peter back in Jerusalem in chapter 15, and it is clear that he had not followed work among the Gentiles. He continued to hold to the gospel of the circumcision (Gal 2:7–8).

3. THE PRESUMPTION AND JUDGMENT OF KING HEROD (VS. 18–23).

> Now when day came, there was no little disturbance among the soldiers over what had become of Peter. And after Herod searched for him and did not find him, he examined the sentries and ordered that they should be put to death. Then he went down from Judea to Caesarea and spent time there.
> Now Herod was angry with the people of Tyre and Sidon, and they came to him with one accord, and having persuaded Blastus, the king's chamberlain,[5] they asked for peace, because their country depended on the king's country for food. On an appointed day Herod put on his royal robes, took his seat upon the throne, and delivered an oration to them. And the people were shouting, "The voice of a god, and not of a man!" Immediately an angel of the Lord struck him down, because he did not give God the glory, and he was eaten by worms and breathed his last (vs. 18–23).

The escape of Peter was soon discovered, and the soldiers, being responsible with their lives, according to Roman law, were of course greatly distressed. Herod sought for his prisoner, but he was beyond his reach. The keepers were put to death by the king. He followed the footsteps of his cruel grandfather, who had the children of Bethlehem killed.

He then left Jerusalem for Caesarea, where he had a magnificent palace. Some difficulty existed between him and the people of Tyre and Sidon. The Phoenician cities were dependent on Palestine for food, as their land was but a narrow strip along the seacoast. They were therefore forced to make peace, which they did through Blastus, their friend and the king's chamberlain. Most likely the interest of Blastus was gained by a bribe. It also seems that Herod must have cut off the supply of the Phoenicians. They could not buy nor sell. Thus they were forced to bow before the king. In all this, he appears as a type of the man of sin, whose character Herod foreshadows.

Then a day came when an audience was granted to the people. The king appeared in royal apparel. Josephus, the Jewish historian, informs us that his garment was made of the brightest silver, which, with the sunlight falling upon it, dazzled the eyes of the multitude. He sat on

---

[5] That is, trusted personal attendant.

his throne, the bema, or judgment seat. Then he made an oration, most likely announcing to the ambassadors of Tyre and Sidon that he was now reconciled. The scene must have been a brilliant one. The people were carried away by the magnificent spectacle and flattering oration of the king, and cried out it is, "the voice of a god, and not of a man!" No doubt the aim of Herod was this very acclamation. He had planned it all. The zenith of his glory seemed reached. Monarchs were then deified, and Augustus, the emperor, was also worshipped. He gave not the glory to God, but usurped his Glory, and the result was a sudden judgment.

What happened to Herod is mentioned by Josephus. He, however, tries to shield the king, though he speaks of Herod's wickedness. He says that sudden pains attacked him, which were produced by the sight of an owl, a bird he dreaded, and which was seen sitting on one of the ropes of the awning of the theatre. The Word of God gives us the true account. It was the angel of the Lord that smote him, and he was eaten of worms. A most awful and loathsome disease took hold of him, and literally he was eaten, after a few days, of Worms.

> He was seized with violent internal pains, and carried to his palace. There he lingered five days in extreme agony; being eaten of worms, the cause of his intestine disorder (Josephus *Ant.* 19.8).

The coming antichrist, too, will claim divine honors and assume the place of God. His end is foreshadowed in Herod's awful fate and the place which is beyond, "where their worm does not die" (Mark 9:48).

4. Barnabas and Saul Returning to Antioch (vs. 24–25).

> But the word of God increased and multiplied. And Barnabas and Saul returned from [6] Jerusalem when they had completed their service, bringing with them John, whose other name was Mark. (vs. 24–25).

Nothing could hinder the victorious progress of the Word of God. It grew and was multiplied. Herod's removal by divine judgment must have had an influence for the truth. Then Barnabas, having been in Jerusalem, went back to Antioch, and John Mark accompanied him. The last verse connects closely with the beginning of the third great part of the book.

---

[6] Some manuscripts *to*.

Chapter Thirteen

The thirteenth chapter is the beginning of the third part of this book. The second great center of Christianity comes to the front. It is no longer Jerusalem, but the city of Antioch. The gospel which had been preached in Jerusalem, in Judea and Samaria, which Cornelius and his house had heard, and accepted, is now in a special manner to go far hence to the Gentiles. The city in which the first great Gentile church had been established is the starting point. Peter, so prominent in the first twelve chapters of our book, is no longer the leading actor. He is mentioned only once in this second part of the Book of Acts. In the fifteenth chapter in connection with the council in Jerusalem, his voice is heard once more. The special work in connection with the kingdom of heaven, in opening the door to the Jews and Gentiles (Acts 2 and chapter 10) had been accomplished by him. Now he disappears from our view, though he continued to exercise his apostleship in connection with the circumcision (Gal 2:7). Paul, the great Apostle of the Gentiles, instead appears upon the scene and his wonderful activity is described in the remaining part of the book. The opposition and blindness of the Jews in a continued rejection of the gospel becomes fully evident throughout this section and the book itself closes with the testimony against them: "herefore let it be known to you that this salvation of God has been sent to the Gentiles; they will listen" (Acts 28:28). Besides this we shall find in these chapters the acts of the Holy Spirit in the call and sending forth of the chosen instruments in the way he guided them, how he filled them, opened doors, and manifested his gracious power in the salvation of sinners and the establishment of the church. We also find the acts of the enemy in opposing the progress of the gospel and in its perversion.

We divide the present chapter into four parts:

1. The divine choice and call. Barnabas and Saul separated to the work (vs. 1–3).

2. The beginning of the journey and the first events in Cyprus (vs. 4–12).

3. The Gospel in Galatia. Paul's address in the synagogue (vs. 13–41).

4. The Gospel rejected by the Jews; they turn to the Gentiles (vs. 42–52).

1. THE DIVINE CHOICE AND CALL. BARNABAS AND SAUL SEPARATED TO THE WORK (VS. 1–3).

> Now there were in the church at Antioch prophets and teachers, Barnabas, Simeon who was called Niger,[1] Lucius of Cyrene, Manaen a lifelong friend of Herod the tetrarch, and Saul. While they were worshiping the Lord and fasting, the Holy Spirit said, "Set apart for me Barnabas and Saul for the work to which I have called them." Then after fasting and praying they laid their hands on them and sent them off. (vs. 1–3).

The time was towards the spring of the year 46. The picture unfolded in these few words is as important as it is precious. The new

---

[1] *Niger* is a Latin word meaning *black*, or *dark*.

start is about to be made. The whole assembly was undoubtedly moved by the Spirit of God and impressed with the fact that an important work was now to be begun. The men who are mentioned were some of the gifts of the Lord in the assembly. Five names are given, the first being Barnabas and the last Saul, but the last, he who delighted to call himself "the very least of all the saints," (Eph 3:8) was through the Grace of God to take the first and prominent place. Then there was Lucius of Cyrene, an evangelist, Simeon, called Niger, who may have been an Ethiopian. Alongside of him stands the name of one who moved in the highest circles, a foster brother of Herod, Manaen. Grace had not only saved them, but had given them gifts "to equip the saints for the work of ministry, for building up the body of Christ" (Eph 4:12). They were together as a waiting company. Just as in the beginning of this book we behold a waiting company, so in the beginning of the second part we find believers waiting. But there is a marked difference. The waiting disciples in chapter 1 waited for the coming of the Holy Spirit. He came on the day of Pentecost. The waiting ones in Antioch waited, not for his coming, but for the Holy Spirit, who indwelt them, to speak and make his wishes known.

They ministered to the Lord and fasted. The Greek word for ministering is "*Leitourgia*," from which comes the word Liturgy. Ritualism claims from this the scripturalness in using a set form in service. It has been stated that the assembled company remembered the Lord, when they were together in this way, and that it was then, when the Holy Spirit spoke. The argument used from ritualistic sides is the fact that the Greek church still calls the Communion "The Liturgy." From this the conclusion is derived that they were together remembering the Lord in the breaking of bread. This is, of course, far-fetched. However, it is true that in the Lord's Supper Christian believers minister to the Lord in the highest sense of the word. Whenever it is done in the power of the Spirit as a true act of worship, it is the exercise of our holy priesthood. We then offer up spiritual sacrifices, the sacrifice of praise to God, that is, the fruit of our lips. While we are comforted in the remembrance of his dying love, He, too, receives a portion from us and beholds then his inheritance in his saints and thus we minister to Him.

The ministry to the Lord from the side of the gathered ones here was no doubt praise and prayer. They waited on the Lord. The Lord grant to every reader this conception of prayer, that it is a ministry to our blessed Lord in glory, and that he delights to receive such service from our feeble hearts and lips!

They were not in a hurry to rush into the new departure. They had formed no plans, had appointed no committee. Alas! all that which is so prominent in our modern day Christian activities is entirely absent in this great book of the beginning of the church on earth, and that which is most prominent in the divine record, dependence on the Lord and definite guidance by the Holy Spirit, is almost entirely absent today. In our present day great movements we hear men, money and methods emphasized, and, in great banquets and conventions, an enthusiasm is stirred up, which is but the expression of self-confidence and self-reliance. In the eyes of the world, the simple gathering in Antioch did not look like a great movement; but it was great because the Holy Spirit was the Person who started it and guided in it. And he loves humility, self-emptiness. If we cannot reproduce all this in our day, let us as individuals, called to serve the Lord Jesus Christ, serve and walk in dependence upon Himself, and trust in the guidance of the Holy Spirit. The fasting mentioned was most likely specially appointed.

And it was then, while they were ministering to the Lord, that the Holy Spirit spoke. This is one of the strong passages from which we learn the Personality and Divinity of the Holy Spirit. Another most important fact is brought here before us. All spiritual Christians long for a continued guidance by the Spirit. If we walk in the Spirit, then we are guided by the Spirit. This is a simple truth. And yet often the children of God are perplexed. Some have followed impressions, or inner voices, which they thought were the voice of the Holy Spirit, but they were deceived. The important hint here is this "*While* they were worshiping the Lord and fasting, the Holy Spirit said" (13:2). When we cast ourselves in dependence on the Lord, when we wait on him and minister to Him, then we may expect confidently the Holy Spirit to speak. In his speaking here at this occasion we learn that he is on earth to be the guide for the church. He is come to take charge of the affairs of the church. The right to choose for service, to call and to send forth, belongs to Him. This is put into the foreground. The whole transaction rested with the Holy Spirit. The words he spoke were brief. "Set apart for me Barnabas and Saul for the work to which I have called them" (13:2). Two of the assembled gifts were separated to him to undertake a special work. True Christian ministry is the exercise of a spiritual gift, which is of the Holy Spirit. The exercise of that gift in a practical way is to be under the control of the same blessed Person. The service rests not in the hands of the servant for self-choosing, nor in the hands of the church, but with the Holy Spirit.

And immediately after the Holy Spirit had thus spoken they acted in obedience to the divine call, laid hands upon them, and let them go. This action has been wrongly interpreted as an ordination. Hence we have the teaching and practice in evangelical Christendom of ordaining men to go out as missionaries, or ordaining them as pastors of churches or evangelists. Such an ordination is not taught here. It is not taught anywhere in the New Testament Scriptures. The authority to preach the Gospel cannot be conferred by one man upon another man, but it is "not from men nor through man" (Gal 1:1). No man nor set of men, according to the New Testament, can give the authority to preach the Word of God. That is a gift from him and, we state it again, the gift must be exercised through the guidance of the Holy Spirit. This is the teaching of the New Testament. How the professing church has departed from this teaching and how much of the confusion and ruin in Christendom about us is the result of this departure, is only too evident. Multitudes of men have entered into and are today in, what is called "the Christian ministry," ordained by some session or conference, whom the Holy Spirit never called and set apart to Himself. And the conditions are far worse in the denominations in which ordination in the form of apostolic succession is used to put man into the place of a "priest" in the church.

Now Barnabas and Saul needed no ordination whatever by which they were authorized to fill a certain office and preach the Word. They were both preachers and teachers. How could they be ordained to an office if they were in it for a good while? If they were to be ordained to something higher than the office of a prophet and teacher, it must have been the place of an apostle. But that could not be, for Paul was already an apostle.

But what did it mean when they laid hands on them? One of their number had uttered that which was the voice of the Holy

The Acts of the Apostles

Spirit. The assembly or church had heard this call. They accepted it as from the Holy Spirit and were obedient to it. Then by the laying on of hands they expressed outwardly their fellowship and identification with the two who had been set apart to do the work to which the Holy Spirit had called. They had nothing to do with their work but to wish them the blessing of the Lord showing their fellowship in it.

This is seen by the last sentence in the third verse that states they: "sent them off." That is "They let them go." The church, or the elders of the church, did not so much send them away, for the very next verse guards against such a thought, for it tells us "being sent out by the Holy Spirit" (13:4). But they did sent them with their blessings.

2. The Beginning of the Journey. The First Events in Cyprus (vs. 4–12).

> So, being sent out by the Holy Spirit, they went down to Seleucia, and from there they sailed to Cyprus. When they arrived at Salamis, they proclaimed the word of God in the synagogues of the Jews. And they had John to assist them. When they had gone through the whole island as far as Paphos, they came upon a certain magician, a Jewish false prophet named Bar-Jesus. He was with the proconsul, Sergius Paulus, a man of intelligence, who summoned Barnabas and Saul and sought to hear the word of God. But Elymas the magician (for that is the meaning of his name) opposed them, seeking to turn the proconsul away from the faith. But Saul, who was also called Paul, filled with the Holy Spirit, looked intently at him and said, "You son of the devil, you enemy of all righteousness, full of all deceit and villainy, will you not stop making crooked the straight paths of the Lord? And now, behold, the hand of the Lord is upon you, and you will be blind and unable to see the sun for a time." Immediately mist and darkness fell upon him, and he went about seeking people to lead him by the hand. Then the proconsul believed, when he saw what had occurred, for he was astonished at the teaching of the Lord (vs. 4–12).

They set forth under the guidance of the Holy Spirit, who had called them to this

14. Salamis from southwest with a view of the remains of the gymnasium and Therme. It is believed that after Paul and Barnabas separated (Acts 15:36-40) that Barnabas remained on Cyprus until his death.

service and to Him, and not to men they looked. The first place mentioned is Seleucia. This was a fortified city, some fifteen miles from Antioch. No report is given of any work done in this city. The island of Cyprus, visible from the seacoast at Seleucia, the home of Barnabas, was the place they were guided to by the Spirit. The nearest port to Seleucia is Salamis (see Fig. 14); this they reached. Salamis had a large Jewish population and Barnabas and Saul preached the Word in the synagogues. John Mark is mentioned as being along as their helper. Some take it that he was to baptize the converts, but there is no evidence for it. He was simply an attendant, who assisted them in different ways, perhaps in preparing the simple meals and looking after other matters, so that Barnabas and Saul might give themselves unhindered to the preaching of the Word. No record is given of the result of the testimony in Salamis. Nor is there anything said of their labors throughout the island. The Holy Spirit in giving us the narrative did not report their activity in detail, because he wanted the event in Paphos to take the prominent and first place in this first journey of the Apostle to the Gentiles.

15. Inscription of Sergius Paulus, the proconsul in Paphos, Cyprus, housed in the Yalvac Museum, Pisidian Antioch. Some scholars suggest that: "L[ucius] Sergius Paulus the younger, son of L[ucius]" may be the son of the elder Sergius Paulus, the proconsul of Acts 13. The name of Sergius Paulus (*nomen*, name of tribe) was certainly known in Cyprus.

And a significant event it was. There they found a sorcerer, a false prophet, a great instrument of Satan, ready to oppose the Gospel as it now was to be preached to the Gentiles. Such evil persons, the special instrument of the enemy, appear repeatedly in this book and always when the Gospel was carried in some new region. In Samaria it was Simon Magus, In Macedonia the damsel with the familiar spirit, Here it is the sorcerer, Bar-Jesus. He was a Jew and his name means "Son of Jesus." The Cyprian name he carried was Elymas, which is not Greek and may mean "The Wise." Paphos was a wicked city of a very bad reputation; Aphrodite, the goddess Venus, was worshipped in a magnificent temple. It was a stronghold of Satan and he had his man there to oppose the messengers of God sent forth by the Holy Spirit. This false prophet with his significant name, a Jew, yet practicing the evil things of Oriental occultism, was in close connection with Sergius Paulus (see Fig. 15), the deputy of that country.[2] he was most likely attached to the household of the deputy. Sergius Paulus was a searcher for the truth, for he called for the two Apostles to hear the Word of God from their lips. Then the Satanic opposition from the side of Elymas was brought out. It was an important moment, for it was the first time that the doctrine of Christ was presented to the Roman world. Satan through Elymas withstood the Apostles in their testimony and sought to keep Sergius Paulus from the faith. Then Paul, filled with the Holy Spirit, set his eyes on him. Just in the moment when Satan's power came into play the Holy Spirit filled the messenger to overcome the wicked devices of the false prophet and pronounce judgment upon him. As in the case of Simon Magus, so here the Holy Spirit uncovers the true character of the impostor. He is a child of the devil and not a "Bar-Jesus," a son of Jesus, the Saviour. He claimed to be a prophet, in reality he was an enemy of all righteousness. He had perverted the right ways of the Lord and continued in this evil work. Then divine judgment is pronounced upon Elymas. "You will be blind and unable to see the sun for a time" (13:11). The judgment was executed at once. A mist and darkness fell on him and he went about seeking someone to lead him by the hand. Sergius Paulus then believed, being astonished at the doctrine of the Lord. There can be no question but Sergius Paulus was truly converted. If it be said that he was astonished at the sudden judgment, a doubt might be raised, but he was astonished at the *doctrine* of the Lord. Signs are for the Jews, but the Gentile needs no sign.

---

[2] On the Sergius Paulus Inscriptions see David E. Graves, *Biblical Archaeology: An Introduction with Recent Discoveries That Support the Reliability of the Bible*, vol. 1 (Toronto, Ont.: Electronic Christian Media, 2014), 212–14.

This false prophet, the Jew Bar-Jesus, Elymas the sorcerer, is a type of apostate Judaism, which has turned away from the truth, rejected the Gospel and perverts the right ways of the Lord. Such Judaism became after rejecting the offer of God's mercy.

As Elymas tried to keep the Word of God from the Roman Sergius Paulus (see Fig. 15), so the Jews tried to keep from the Gentiles the Gospel, which they themselves had rejected. The judgment which fell upon the Sorcerer is likewise significant. Blindness has been put judicially upon the Jews and without a leader they are groping around in the darkness. This judicial blindness was repeatedly predicted by the prophets. We find it mentioned in Isaiah 6:9–10. Their eyes were to be shut. Our Lord quotes this twice and each time in connection with his rejection in Matthew 13:15 and John 12:40. Then the Apostle Paul uses these words for the last time in the New Testament. See Acts 23:25–28. The Salvation of God was sent to the Gentiles after the Jews refused to accept it, and the Jews were blinded. But the blindness is not permanent. "A partial hardening [blindness] has come upon Israel, until the fullness of the Gentiles has come in" (Rom 11:25). Corresponding to this is the blindness of Elymas, which was to be "for a time." Israel's time is this present age. When to this age is over, the judicial blindness, the veil which is upon their hearts, will be removed.

That this incident is the first one reported in the beginning of the great missionary movement is in full keeping with the scope of the Book of Acts. Of equal significance is it that for the first time, and that in connection with this incident, the name of Paul is mentioned. Some have suggested that he took the name in honor of Sergius Paulus, but that is incorrect. Paul is a Roman name, and means "little." Later he writes of himself as "the very least of all the

16. A colonnaded street in the ancient city of Perga of Pamphylia (in modern Turkey).

saints," (Eph 3:8). He took the lowest place and the name, which signifies this comes now into prominence. Barnabas is taking the second place; not Barnabas and Saul, but Paul and Barnabas is now the order.

After the significant incident in Paphos, the judicial blindness of Elymas and the faith of the Gentile deputy in the doctrine of the Lord, the Apostle Paul and his company loosed from Paphos. "Now Paul and his companions set sail from Paphos and came to Perga in Pamphylia. And John left them and returned to Jerusalem" (13:13). Paul occupies now the prominent place. As soon as Perga (see Fig. 16) was reached, John the helper, who had gone forth with them from Antioch, deserted them. It was a desertion, for later we find the statement that he departed from them from Pamphylia, and went not with them to the work (15:38). No reason is given why John turned back. Was it on account of the dangers or the hard labor! Or was it cowardice! The reason of his return was most likely of a different nature. He was still greatly attached to Jerusalem. His Hebrew name is mentioned only in this chapter and not the Gentile, the Roman, Mark. Perhaps he could not fully endorse the complete association with the Gentiles and turned back to Jerusalem to be in fellowship with them who were of the circumcision and "zealous for the law"

17. Ruins of ancient Pisidian Antioch.

(21:20). No matter what was the motive, he did leave them. It was failure on his part and for a long time John Mark had evidently little or no service. He was unprofitable. Blessed is the information we receive from the Second Epistle to Timothy by the Apostle Paul. He requested Mark's presence in Rome. "Get Mark and bring him with you, for he is very useful to me for ministry" (2 Tim 4:11). He had been restored, seen his error and judged himself. There can be no question, but John Mark is the writer of the Gospel of Mark, in which the perfect servant of God, the Lord Jesus Christ is portrayed in his unfailing service. What encouragement we should take from this! One who failed in service and was graciously restored, then chosen to write the Gospel of the Servant.

3. THE GOSPEL IN GALATIA. PAUL'S ADDRESS IN THE SYNAGOGUE OF ANTIOCH (VS. 13–15).

> Now Paul and his companions set sail from Paphos and came to Perga in Pamphylia. And John left them and returned to Jerusalem, but they went on from Perga and came to Antioch in Pisidia. And on the Sabbath day they went into the synagogue and sat down. After the reading from the Law and the Prophets, the rulers of the synagogue sent a message to them, saying, "Brothers, if you have any word of encouragement for the people, say it" (vs. 13–15).

They reached another Antioch (see Fig. 17). It was situated in Pisidia. The region into which they now carried the Gospel was also known as Galatia. This district was settled by Gauls, Celtic invaders, who had left about 278 B. C. Southern Europe, and took possession of parts of Asia Minor. In 189 BC, they were subdued by Rome and the Kingdom of Galatia was formed, which comprised besides Galatia proper a number of other provinces, including Pisidia. From the Epistle to the Galatians we know that the Apostle Paul preached the Gospel there and founded the different churches. The record of his visit and work is contained in the 13th and 14th chapter, beginning with Antioch in Pisidia. Antioch had, like other cities at that time, a number of Jews, and therefore a synagogue. To this place they went on the Sabbath, and took their place among the other attendants. The order of service as carried on in orthodox synagogues of today is about the same as in the synagogues of the first century. The "Hear O Israel!" the so-called "*Shema*" (a recitation of Deut 6:4–9), prayers and the reading of a prescribed portion of the Pentateuch, and a similar portion from the Prophets, called the "*Haftorah*." After the reading of those portions, exhortation was in order. It was at this point that the rulers requested the visiting brethren, of whom they may have heard as teachers, to speak if they had any word of exhortation. The rulers addressed them as Brethren. Gentiles who feared God had likewise access to the synagogue and a number were present on that Sabbath day.

> So Paul stood up, and motioning with his hand said:
> "Men of Israel and you who fear God, listen. The God of this people Israel chose our fathers and made the people great during their stay in the land of Egypt, and with uplifted arm he led them out of it. And for about forty years he put up

with[3] them in the wilderness. And after destroying seven nations in the land of Canaan, he gave them their land as an inheritance. All this took about 450 years. And after that he gave them judges until Samuel the prophet. Then they asked for a king, and God gave them Saul the son of Kish, a man of the tribe of Benjamin, for forty years. And when he had removed him, he raised up David to be their king, of whom he testified and said, "I have found in David the son of Jesse a man after my heart, who will do all my will." Of this man's offspring God has brought to Israel a Savior, Jesus, as he promised. Before his coming, John had proclaimed a baptism of repentance to all the people of Israel. And as John was finishing his course, he said, "What do you suppose that I am? I am not he. No, but behold, after me one is coming, the sandals of whose feet I am not worthy to untie."

"Brothers, sons of the family of Abraham, and those among you who fear God, to us has been sent the message of this salvation. For those who live in Jerusalem and their rulers, because they did not recognize him nor understand the utterances of the prophets, which are read every Sabbath, fulfilled them by condemning him. And though they found in him no guilt worthy of death, they asked Pilate to have him executed. And when they had carried out all that was written of him, they took him down from the tree and laid him in a tomb. But God raised him from the dead, and for many days he appeared to those who had come up with him from Galilee to Jerusalem, who are now his witnesses to the people. And we bring you the good news that what God promised to the fathers, this he has fulfilled to us their children by raising Jesus, as also it is written in the second Psalm,

"You are my Son, today I have begotten you."[4] And as for the fact that he raised him from the dead, no more to return to corruption, he has spoken in this way, "I will give you the holy and sure blessings of David."[5] Therefore he says also in another psalm, "You will not let your Holy One see corruption."[6]

For David, after he had served the purpose of God in his own generation, fell asleep and was laid with his fathers and saw corruption, but he whom God raised up did not see corruption. Let it be known to you therefore, brothers, that through this man forgiveness of sins is proclaimed to you, and by him everyone who believes is freed[7] from everything from which you could not be freed by the law of Moses. Beware, therefore, lest what is said in the Prophets should come about:

"'Look, you scoffers, be astounded and perish; for I am doing a work in your days, a work that you will not believe, even if one tells it to you.'"[8] (vs. 16–41).

We have before us an intensely interesting record. Whether this is a full report or a condensed report of the address of the Apostle we do not know for certain. We incline to the belief that it is a report in full of what Paul spoke. It corresponds in different ways to Peter's preaching to the Jews, yet it differs from Peter's message in regard to the Gospel. As we have seen Peter's preaching was addressed to the Jews and he offered forgiveness of sins to them who repent and are baptized. But Paul utters a truth for the first time, which Peter did not declare. He said: "by him [Christ] everyone who *believes* is *freed* from everything from which you could not be freed by the law of Moses" (13:39). It is justification by faith he now preaches. We have in his first recorded utterance the Keynote of the two great Epistles, dictated by the Holy Spirit to the Apostle Paul; the great doctrinal Epistle to the Romans and the controversial Epistle to the Galatians, the defence of his Gospel. The discourse of the Apostle contains three parts.

1. A historical retrospect, which forms the introduction of his address (vs. 17–25).

---

[3] Some manuscripts *he carried* (compare Deuteronomy 1:31).
[4] Psalm 2:7
[5] Isaiah 55:3
[6] Psalm 16:10

[7] Greek *justified*; twice in this verse.
[8] Habakkuk 1:5

2. The proclamation of the Gospel of the Son of God (vs. 26–40).

3. The solemn warning (vs. 40–41).

He addressed the Jews present as Israel, the covenant Name, and the assembled Gentiles "you that fear God." he traces rapidly the history of the people Israel, the background of the Gospel he is to preach. God had *chosen* their fathers, *exalted* the people, *delivered* them out of Egypt, he carried them through the wilderness and *suffered*[9] their manners. He furthermore *destroyed* their enemies and gave them an inheritance. In Exodus 4:22 it is written, "Israel is my firstborn son" and in Hosea 11:1 we read: "When Israel was a child, I loved him, and out of Egypt I called my son." It is this history of Israel as the firstborn son the Apostle sketches rapidly. In the promised land they had judges, a prophet and a King. While he mentions Saul, the Son of Cis, reminding them of the failure involved in his case, he speaks more fully of David as the one whom God raised up, in whom he was pleased, who was to fulfill all his will. At once he mentions Him, who according to the flesh is the seed of David (Rom 1:3). The connection with David is obvious. The three facts mentioned by Paul concerning David find their fulfillment in the promised Saviour, the Son of David. He was raised up by God (vs. 23, 30, 33 and 34); God gave him testimony "This is my beloved Son, with whom I am well pleased" (Matt 3:17; Mark 1:11), he alone could "fulfill all his will." So Paul speaks of the Lord Jesus Christ as the promised One, raised up to Israel as a Saviour. The preaching of John before this Saviour came, calling all the people of Israel to repentance is the concluding paragraph of the first part of the Apostle's address.

In the second part of his address he preached the Gospel to them. He addressed the assembled congregation as men and brethren, children of the stock of Abraham; the Gentiles present he also mentioned "those among you who fear God" (13:26). Then without further delay he uttered the fact of the Gospel, "to us has been sent the message of this salvation." One is reminded of the Lord Himself, when in the synagogue of Nazareth he said: "today this Scripture has been fulfilled in your hearing" (Luke 4:21). How eagerly the gathered company must have listened to what was about to be announced. The cross of Christ, the death of the promised Saviour and the circumstances of his death are immediately proclaimed. There is no salvation apart from the cross of Christ. The word of this salvation he preached to them centers not in the earthly life of the Lord Jesus Christ, but in his death on the cross. Like Peter, the Apostle to the Gentiles emphasizes the fact that they that dwelt at Jerusalem and their rulers knew him not. The reason of their ignorance was because they knew not the voices of the prophets. Ignorance of the written Word led to the rejection of the living Word. It is still so today in Judaism and Christendom. They read every Sabbath the prophecies concerning the Messiah, his rejection and his work, and they fulfilled these predictions in condemning Him. His death on the cross was therefore a fulfillment of Scripture. No cause of death was found in Him. He was delivered into the hands of the Gentiles. All was fulfilled by them, which was written of Him; all the sufferings of Christ as the Lamb of God were accomplished on the tree.[10] he was

---

[9] A better rendering is "he nursed them."

[10] Peter used the word "tree" and Paul writing to the Galatians said: "Christ hath redeemed us from the curse of the law, being made a curse for us, for it is written: Cursed is everyone that hangeth on a tree." (Gal 3:13).

taken down and laid in a sepulchre. His death on the cross was thus briefly pictured by the speaker. And then he announced next to the fact of his death, fully proven by his burial in a sepulchre, that God raised him from the dead. It is the order Paul follows here which he later writes to the Corinthians.

> For I delivered to you as of first importance what I also received: that Christ *died* for our sins in accordance with the Scriptures, that he was *buried*, that he was *raised* on the third day in accordance with the Scriptures (1 Cor 15:3–4).

The proofs of resurrection that he was seen many days are also briefly mentioned. Then he declared the good tidings. As an evangelist he announces what had been accomplished in the death and resurrection of Christ. It is a beautiful and concise statement of Him, who had been raised up in incarnation, and who is by resurrection from the dead the Son of God. The promise made to the fathers had been gloriously fulfilled. The Second Psalm had predicted this raising up. God sent his Son into the world. On a certain day he entered as the Begotten One into the world. After he had died he became the First Begotten from the dead, destined as such to be the King upon the holy hill of Zion, and to receive the nations for his inheritance. He could not see corruption. This, too, had been predicted in the Psalms (Ps 16). The similarity of this first reported evangelistic message of Paul with Peter's is again seen at this point. But he also speaks of him as the Pious One, the Holy and Gracious One, in whom now are found the faithful mercies of David.

And then he pressed it all home to their hearts and consciences.

> Let it be known to you therefore, brothers, that through this man forgiveness of sins is proclaimed to you, and by him everyone who believes is freed from everything from which you could not be freed by the law of Moses (13:38–39).

This is the great climax reached. He did not once mention the word repentance. He has nothing to say of baptism. He did not exhort them to do the best they could or to live under that law, which they had. The Law of Moses could not justify them. The Epistle to the Galatians, most likely read by those in Antioch who heard Paul speak, enlarges upon this fully. Justification from all things is offered now by faith in Jesus Christ. *All that believe are justified of all things* is the blessed message of the Gospel of Grace which Paul preached and which is not after man, but by the revelation of Jesus Christ (Gal 1:11–12).

How simple the message was. All had been done by Christ. He died the Just One for the Unjust; he who knew no sin had been made sin. Forgiveness of sins and a perfect justification from all things is now ready for Jews and Gentiles from the side of a just God, who can be righteously the Justifier of him, who believeth in Jesus. And this simple Gospel, this perfect way of salvation is still to be preached. It is the power of God to salvation; what a model for the true Gospel address Paul's discourse in the synagogue of the Pisidian Antioch is (see Fig. 17)! Then in the third part, in the concluding words, he gives a solemn warning. This must likewise be attached to every true Gospel testimony. The warning is taken from the Prophet Habakkuk (1:5). It is addressed by the Prophet to "those among the Gentiles." The passage warns against unbelief. The message may be accepted or rejected. The work which God worked in Habakkuk's day was judgment by the Chaldean invasion. It came upon them that believed not. Judgment would surely come upon them if they believed not and rejected the offer of the Gospel. A few years later Paul wrote to the Thessalonians concerning the Jews,

> by hindering us from speaking to the Gentiles that they might be saved—so as always to fill up the

measure of their sins. But wrath has come upon them at last! (1 Thess 2:16).

The destruction of Jerusalem and the dispersion of the nation was the punitive work God worked for those who believed not. Well does every Gospel preacher if he gives the solemn warning that

> whoever believes in the Son has eternal life; whoever does not obey the Son shall not see life, but the wrath of God remains on him (John 3:36).

There is a judgment work coming for all that believe not when the Lord Jesus shall be revealed from heaven with his mighty angels in flaming fire taking vengeance on them that know not God, and that obey not the Gospel of our Lord Jesus Christ.

4. The Gospel rejected by the Jews; they turn to the Gentiles (vs. 42–52).

> As they went out, the people begged that these things might be told them the next Sabbath. And after the meeting of the synagogue broke up, many Jews and devout converts to Judaism followed Paul and Barnabas, who, as they spoke with them, urged them to continue in the grace of God.
>
> The next Sabbath almost the whole city gathered to hear the word of the Lord. But when the Jews saw the crowds, they were filled with jealousy and began to contradict what was spoken by Paul, reviling him. And Paul and Barnabas spoke out boldly, saying, "It was necessary that the word of God be spoken first to you. Since you thrust it aside and judge yourselves unworthy of eternal life, behold, we are turning to the Gentiles. For so the Lord has commanded us, saying,
>
> > 'I have made you a light for the Gentiles, that you may bring salvation to the ends of the earth.' "[11]
>
> And when the Gentiles heard this, they began rejoicing and glorifying the word of the Lord, and as many as were appointed to eternal life believed. And the word of the Lord was spreading throughout the whole region. But the Jews [12] incited the devout women of high standing and the leading men of the city, stirred up persecution against Paul and Barnabas, and drove them out of their district. But they shook off the dust from their feet against them and went to Iconium. And the disciples were filled with joy and with the Holy Spirit. (vs. 42–52).

18. Statue of St. Paul in front of the facade of the Basilica of Saint Paul Outside-the-Walls, Rome.

The offer had been made. Were the Jews in the dispersion to accept it or to oppose the Gospel and reject its gracious invitation? It seems as if a deep impression was created. How else could it have been after hearing such a perfect and able presentation in the power of the Holy Spirit. The request was made that they would speak again a week later. Many Jews and proselytes followed the two messengers. The exhortation of the Apostles that they should continue in the grace of God seems to imply that some had accepted the offer of the Gospel.

But during the week the enemy did his work. The whole city came together the next Sabbath. Large numbers of Gentiles, many of whom had never before entered the synagogue, crowded in to hear the Word. This was too much for the Jews. Jealousy and envy filled their hearts. It came to a riotous opposition. Paul was again the

---

[11] Isaiah 49:6

[12] Greek *Ioudaioi* probably refers here to Jewish religious leaders, and others under their influence, in that time.

preacher, and not alone did they speak against the truth as preached by him, but they contradicted and blasphemed. What Elymas, the sorcerer, had done as an individual, the type of the blinded Jew, the Jews did in Antioch. Once more Paul with Barnabas pronounces the word of condemnation. The offer of salvation was refused and now the Jews, judging themselves unworthy of eternal life by unbelief, the Apostles said, "we are turning to the Gentiles" (13:46). Scripture is fully on their side in this action, for the prophet had declared,

> It is too light a thing that you should be my servant to raise up the tribes of Jacob and to bring back the preserved of Israel; I will make you as a light for the nations, that my salvation may reach to the end of the earth. (Isa 49:6).

While the Jews blasphemed and rejected, the Gentiles were glad and glorified the Word of the Lord. As many as were ordained to eternal life believed.

> The Jews had judged themselves unworthy of eternal life; the Gentiles, as many as were *disposed* to eternal life, believed. By whom so disposed, is not here declared; nor need the word be in this place further particularized. We know that it is God who worketh in us the will to believe, and that the preparation of the heart is of Him, but to find in this text preordination to life asserted, is to force both the word and the context to a meaning which they do not contain.[13]

All who accept the Gospel by faith are ordained to eternal life. The good news spread rapidly throughout all Galatia. All this brought out still more fully the jealousy and fierce antagonism of the unbelieving Jews. They used certain women of the higher classes, no doubt the wives of the rulers of the city. These women were devout; they went to the synagogue. Through these women and the chief men of the city a successful persecution of the Apostles was raised and they had to suffer. Nothing is mentioned of suffering here, but Paul mentions it to Timothy (See 2 Tim 3:11). They were expelled from that region.

The banished Apostles must have known the Word of the Lord about persecutions and shaking the dust off their feet (Matt 10:14). They did this and passed on to Iconium. The disciples they left behind were filled with joy and with the Holy Ghost.

---

[13] Alford, *The NT for English Readers*, 1:745.

CHAPTER FOURTEEN

The concluding ministry of the first missionary journey of the apostles, their sufferings and testimony, as well as their dangers and return to Antioch, are the events recorded in this chapter.

1. The work in Iconium and the persecution of the Apostles (vs. 1–7).

2. Their testimony in Derbe and Lystra, the healing of the impotent man and what followed (vs. 8–18).

3. The stoning of Paul and further ministries (vs. 19–24).

4. The Return to Antioch (vs. 25–28).

1. THE WORK IN ICONIUM AND THE PERSECUTION OF THE APOSTLES (VS. 1–7).

> Now at Iconium they entered together into the Jewish synagogue and spoke in such a way that a great number of both Jews and Greeks believed. But the unbelieving Jews stirred up the Gentiles and poisoned their minds against the brothers.[1] So they remained for a long time, speaking boldly for the Lord, who bore witness to the word of his grace, granting signs and wonders to be done by their hands. But the people of the city were divided; some sided with the Jews and some with the apostles. When an attempt was made by both Gentiles and Jews, with their rulers, to mistreat them and to stone them, they learned of it and fled to Lystra and Derbe, cities of Lycaonia, and to the surrounding country, and there they continued to preach the gospel. (vs. 1–7)

Iconium was a Phrygian town, bordering on Lycaonia. Later it became a very influential city, the capital of Lycaonia proper and a center of Christianity in that region. It is also known through an apocryphal book, *The Acts of Paul and Thecla*. The heroine, Thecla, is said to have lived in Iconium and that she was converted by the preaching of Paul.[2] Once more the Apostles sought out the synagogue to preach the Gospel there. Jews and Greeks were present to listen to their testimony. It is a *far-fetched theory*, which claims that they preached nothing but the kingdom in the different synagogues. The preaching of the Apostles is not reported here, but we may take it for granted that the clear and simple Gospel testimony delivered by the Apostle Paul in the synagogue of Antioch was repeated in Iconium (see Fig. 19). The message was wonderfully blessed and owned of God. They spake so that not only a few, but a great multitude of Jews and Greeks believed. But the acts of the enemy followed at once. He could not permit such a powerful and successful testimony to go on unhindered. Once more the Elymas character of the unbelieving Jews is brought out. They stirred up the Gentiles, those who had no sympathy with the synagogue, and made their minds evil affected against the brethren.

But the messengers of the Lord could not be driven from the scene before their

---

[1] Or *brothers and sisters*

[2] The whole story is an invention. Tertullian has shown that it is a fictitious story written by a certain Presbyter, who was a great admirer of the Apostle Paul. The Presbyter was disciplined for his writing.

testimony was finished. How long they remained is not stated. It was a "long time" they abode there, and with much boldness they spoke the Word of God. And the Lord added his seal to the faithful testimony of his servants. Signs and wonders were done by their hands. By these God demonstrated once more to the unbelieving Jews in the dispersion that Jesus is the Christ. The entire city seems to have been divided. When it came to actual persecutions, and both the unbelieving Jews and unbelieving Gentiles made ready to stone them, and the plot became known, they left Iconium and fled to Lystra (see Fig. 22) and Derbe. No doubt this was the will of the Lord and they followed his guidance. That it was not cowardice or self-protection is seen by the fact that a short time after they returned to Iconium (14:21).

2. Their testimony in Derbe and Lystra: the healing of the impotent man (vs. 8–18).

> Now at Lystra there was a man sitting who could not use his feet. He was crippled from birth and had never walked. He listened to Paul speaking. And Paul, looking intently at him and seeing that he had faith to be made well,[3] said in a loud voice, "Stand upright on your feet." And he sprang up and began walking. And when the crowds saw what Paul had done, they lifted up their voices, saying in Lycaonian, "The gods have come down to us in the likeness of men!" Barnabas they called Zeus, and Paul, Hermes, because he was the chief speaker. And the priest of Zeus, whose temple was at the entrance to the city, brought oxen and garlands to the gates and wanted to offer sacrifice with the crowds. But when the apostles Barnabas and Paul heard of it, they tore their garments and rushed out into the crowd, crying out, "Men, why are you doing these things? We also are men, of like nature with you, and we bring you good news, that you should turn from these vain things to a living God, who made the heaven and the earth and the sea and all that is in them. In past generations he allowed all the nations to walk in their own ways. Yet he did not leave himself without witness, for he did good by giving you rains from heaven and fruitful seasons, satisfying your hearts with food and gladness." Even with these words they scarcely restrained the people from offering sacrifice to them. (vs. 8–18).

The two cities Lystra and Derbe were in Lycaonia proper. The people inhabiting these places were called Barbarians; they heard the Gospel next. No synagogue was located in Lystra, for there were not enough Jews there to form one. However, we know that a pious Jewess had her residence in Lystra (see Fig. 22). Her name was Eunice. She had been married to a Greek, who had died. Her son was Timothy, and she lived with her mother, Lois. From Acts 16:1–3 we learn that Eunice had believed. The mother was also a believer (2 Tim 1:5). Eunice taught her son the Scriptures. We do not know from the report in our chapter that Paul then came in touch with her, but we fully believe this must have been the case and that the apostles perhaps lodged in her house.

And now another lame man is healed by the power of God. He had been crippled from his mother's womb and had never walked. He heard the Word. Faith came to his heart by hearing, and the Apostle Paul, beholding him, perceived that he had faith

19. A Roman sarcophagus from Iconium (ca. 250-260 AD) depicting the labors of Hercules in the Archaeological Museum, in Konya.

---

[3] Or *be saved*

20. Head of Mercury wearing winged petasus, on a bronze Semuncia coin (215–211 BC).

to be healed. Then Paul spoke the word and the Lord answered by healing the lame man so that he leaped and walked. The miracle created a great stir among the people, and they cried out in their own language, "The gods have come down to us in the likeness of men" (14:11). The mythological superstitions took hold of them, and they imagined that the two apostles, Barnabas and Paul, were some of their gods who had taken on human form.

In Barnabas they imagined to see Jupiter (see Fig. 21) and in Paul, who did the most talking, Mercurius (see Fig. 20).[4] But the two apostles did not know what all the commotion meant, for they did not understand the Lycaonian language.[5] The temple of Jupiter or Zeus, as this god is called in the Greek language, was outside of the city. From there the priests brought oxen with garlands, ready to bring sacrifices to the newlydiscovered gods. It was then

21. Marble statue of Jupiter (Late 1st cent AD). Drapings, cepter, Eagle, and Victory are made of painted plaster dating to the 19th cent. Hermitage, St Petersburg, Russia.

that the apostles heard of it, and rending their clothes, ran among the people to stop their foolish endeavors. These servants of the Lord Jesus Christ did not want honors from men, as if they were some great ones. The people tried to idolize them, but they abhorred these wicked proceedings. The enemy lurked behind this, no doubt, but the grace of God gave to the apostles the power to act as they did. How much of such idolizing is going on in modern days; how men, professedly the servants of the Lord, seek and love the honor and praise of men, is too evident to be mentioned. Seeking honor from men and having delight in the applause of the "religious world" is a deadly thing, for it dishonors Christ, to whom all honor and glory is due. And how much of all this there is in the present day! It is but the result of not giving the Lord Jesus Christ the preeminence.

---

[4] The story is told by Ovid of Jupiter and Mercury, who disguised themselves as mortals and visited the region looking for hospitality but none was found until a poor woman named Baucis took them in and fed them. When the wine was miraculously refilled she identified them as gods (Ovid *Meta.* 8. 626-724).

[5] They did not possess therefore the miraculous gift of languages and understood not what was said. This answers the statements made by those who believe in the restoration of the "gift of tongues," that speaking in tongues is the evidence of the baptism with the Holy Spirit.

The Acts of the Apostles

Powerful were the words which the two men of God addressed to the poor Pagans. They did not preach what they were not capable of understanding. They came right down to their level. They showed them the wickedness of idolatry which puts the creature into the place of the Creator. The message was suited to them and to their needs and paved the way for the Gospel testimony.

> We also are men, of like nature with you, and we bring you good news, that you should turn from these vain things to a living God, who made the heaven and the earth and the sea and all that is in them (14:15).[6]

Yet even with these burning words they were almost unable to restrain the people from carrying out their purpose.

3. The Stoning of Paul and further ministries (vs. 19–24).

> But Jews came from Antioch and Iconium, and having persuaded the crowds, they stoned Paul and dragged him out of the city, supposing that he was dead. But when the disciples gathered about him, he rose up and entered the city, and on the next day he went on with Barnabas to Derbe. When they had preached the gospel to that city and had made many disciples, they returned to Lystra and to Iconium and to Antioch,

---

[6] "What is notable, I think, especially for all those engaged in the work of the Lord, is the variety in the character of the apostolic addresses. There was no such stiffness as we are apt to find in our day in the preaching of the gospel. Oh, what monotony! what sameness of routine, no matter who may be addressed! We find in Scripture people dealt with as they were, and there is that kind of an appeal to the conscience which was adapted to their peculiar state. The discourse in the synagogue was founded on the Jewish scriptures, here to these men of Lycaonia there is no allusion to the Old Testament whatever, but a plain reference to what all see and know - the heavens above them and the seasons that God was pleased from old to assign round about them, and that continual supply of the fruits of his natural bounty of which the most callous can scarce be insensible." Kelly, *Lectures Introductory to the Study of the Acts*, 108.

22. Inscription with the name Lystra. The inscription includes the full Roman name *Colonia Iulia Felix Gemina Lustra*. Konya museum.

> strengthening the souls of the disciples, encouraging them to continue in the faith, and saying that through many tribulations we must enter the kingdom of God. And when they had appointed elders for them in every church, with prayer and fasting they committed them to the Lord in whom they had believed. Then they passed through Pisidia and came to Pamphylia. (vs. 19–24).

Jews from Antioch and Iconium (see Fig. 19) suddenly appeared in Lystra (see Fig. 22). Not satisfied to make opposition to the apostles and to stir up strife in their own cities, they followed after these men. Word must have reached them of their success in Lystra. They came to stir up the Lycaonians. What evil things they said against the two servants of God may well be imagined. They persuaded the people that they were not gods; they must have branded them as deceivers and worse. The mass of people who were ready to worship Barnabas and Paul changed quickly and stoned Paul. Most likely the fury turned against him because he had been instrumental in healing the crippled man. As the stones fell upon him, must he not have remembered Stephen? And may he not have prayed as Stephen did? And after they thought him dead, they dragged his body out of the city. But the Lord, who had announced such suffering for him, had watched over his servant. He

was in his own hands, as every child of God is in his care. The enemy who stood behind the furious mob, as he stood behind the attempt to sacrifice to them, would have killed Paul. But he could not touch Paul's life, as he was not permitted to touch the life of another servant of God, Job (Job 2:6). The Lord's omnipotent hand shielded Paul, and when the disciples stood round about the apparent dead body, he arose and came into the city. This sudden recovery was supernatural. He refers in 2 Corinthians 11:25 to this stoning, "Once I was stoned." Another reference to Lystra we find in his second Epistle to Timothy: "my persecutions and sufferings that happened to me at Antioch, at Iconium, and at Lystra—which persecutions I endured; yet from them all *the Lord rescued me*" (2 Tim 3:11). Blessed be his name, he is the same Lord still and will deliver them that trust in Him.

The next day finds Paul and Barnabas at Derbe, a small town, some thirty miles from Lystra. Here he preached the Gospel to the entire city and taught many. In chapter 20:4 we have Gaius of Derbe mentioned, who in all probability was a fruit of the apostles' testimony in that city. From Derbe they returned to Lystra without fear, and also revisited Iconium (see Fig. 19) and Antioch of Pisidia (see Fig. 17). The divine purpose in this was to confirm, to establish the disciples. They had to suffer persecution in these places, and so the apostles exhorted them to continue in the faith and assured them: "that through many tribulations we must enter the kingdom of God" (14:22). The Kingdom of God, however, must not be confounded with the kingdom of heaven, which is another term and has another meaning. That they retraced their steps and looked after those who had believed to help them on in the truth and strengthen their faith, is of much importance. Modern evangelism, aiming at big things and large crowds, has lost sight of this. We find in our days but few evangelists who return to the same places to help those who believed and to establish their souls. Besides this the two apostles looked to the proper order for the assemblies. "They had appointed elders for them in every church" (14:23) that is; "they chose elders." It was not done when the apostles had first labored in these places, for time was necessary to show who was gifted and qualified for the office of an elder. It is true the apostles looked after this personally, and later Paul commissioned Titus and Timothy to appoint elders. But the Holy Spirit also has given in the Epistles, for the church throughout the age, the marks of true New Testament eldership. It is the Holy Spirit who calls and fits elders for their work in the assembly, and the assembly, having the Scriptures to show the fitness for the office, must recognize such. Confusion, division and disorder in many assemblies are often the result of having ignored this fact. Those who are gifted for oversight must exercise this gift.

23. The old harbor of Attalia (modern Antalya, Turkey).

After they had accomplished this important and needful work, commending them also in prayer to the Lord, they passed through Pisidia and came to Pamphylia.

4. THE RETURN TO ANTIOCH (VS. 25–28).

And when they had spoken the word in Perga, they went down to Attalia, and from there they sailed to Antioch, where they had been commended to the grace of God for the work that they had fulfilled. And when they arrived and gathered the church together, they declared all that God had done with them, and how he had opened a door of faith to the Gentiles. And they remained no little time with the disciples. (vs. 25–28).

No report is given of the result of the preaching at Perga. From there they went to the seaport Attalia (see Fig. 23), and then they returned to the starting point, Antioch, from where they had been called to do the work, and which they had, through the grace of God, fulfilled. They had been gone for about eighteen months. The church in Antioch was gathered together to hear the wonderful story of God's grace and power. What a blessed time they must have had together when Paul and Barnabas related what God had done! What praise and joyful exclamations must have welled forth from the hearts and lips of God's people as they listened how the Lord had opened the door of faith to the Gentiles! And there Paul and Barnabas abode in blessed fellowship with the disciples.

CHAPTER FIFETEEN

A very critical time had now arrived for the church. An important question had to be settled. That Gentiles can be saved and salvation must be extended to the Gentiles had been fully demonstrated. The Apostle of the circumcision, Peter, had been used to preach the Gospel to a company of God-fearing Gentiles (see Fig. 12). Evangelists had gone to Antioch and the great Gentile center had there been founded. Paul and Barnabas had completed their great missionary journey and numerous assemblies of Gentiles, saved by Grace, were formed. The question of the salvation of Gentiles could no longer be raised. But we remember from the eleventh chapter of this book, that when Peter returned to Jerusalem, they that were of the circumcision contended with him. They objected to Peter going to men uncircumcised and eating with them. But those of the circumcision had not been fully satisfied with the status of the believing Gentiles. What about circumcision in their case? Should they not also keep the Law? In other words, the question of the relation of the believing Gentile to the Law and to circumcision had to be determined.

This question was but the natural outcome of the situation in the beginning of this age. To make this clear we quote from another:

> Wherever the Jews went in the Gentile world, their presence gave rise to two conflicting tendencies. On the one hand, the Jew possessed the knowledge of the one true God; and amidst the universal corruption, idolatry and superstition of the ancient world this saving knowledge exercised a powerful attraction. The synagogues of the Jews became the center of a large body of seekers after truth, whether actually circumcised proselytes or simply God-fearing Gentiles.
>
> On the other hand, this knowledge was enshrined in a law, which imposed upon the Jews a number of distinctive customs and observances and these separated them from the rest of mankind and made a real coalescence impossible. Four characteristics in particular struck the Gentiles, the absence of all images or emblems of the deity in Jewish worship, the observance of the Sabbath, abstinence from unclean meat and especially swine's flesh, and circumcision. This last was sufficient in itself to prevent the world from adopting Judaism.
>
> But the law of uncleanness caused the Jew on his side to look upon the Gentiles with contempt, as unclean, and put an effectual bar on any real fellowship. The Gentiles in their turn readily paid back Jewish exclusiveness with an ample interest of ridicule and hatred. This double relation to the Gentiles divided the Jews themselves into two schools.
>
> On the one side were those who with some consciousness of the brotherhood of common humanity were striving to remove barriers and to present the Jewish faith to the world in its most spiritual and philosophic aspect. Such were the Hellenists of Alexandria.
>
> On the other side, the salvation of the Gentiles was inconceivable to the genuine Hebrew, and this was the attitude of mind which prevailed in Judea. There the Hebrews were growing more and more rigid; instead of lowering, they were raising the fence around the law and trying to make the barrier between Jew and

Gentile absolutely impassable.[1]

From this situation it is easily seen what an important question it was which had to be faced. We must likewise remember that the great controversial Epistle, the divinely inspired defence of the Gospel of the Apostle Paul, the Epistle to the Galatians, was then not written. We shall have to turn to this Epistle in connection with the chapter before us. The interesting account has five parts:

1. The false teachers from Judea; Paul and Barnabas sent to Jerusalem (vs. 1–5).
2. The Council in Jerusalem (vs. 6–21).
3. The result made known (vs. 22–29).
4. The Consolation brought to Antioch (vs. 30–35).
5. Paul and Barnabas separate (vs. 36–41).

1. THE FALSE TEACHERS FROM JUDEA; PAUL AND BARNABAS SENT TO JERUSALEM (VS. 1–5).

> But some men came down from Judea and were teaching the brothers, "Unless you are circumcised according to the custom of Moses, you cannot be saved." And after Paul and Barnabas had no small dissension and debate with them, Paul and Barnabas and some of the others were appointed to go up to Jerusalem to the apostles and the elders about this question. So, being sent on their way by the church, they passed through both Phoenicia and Samaria, describing in detail the conversion of the Gentiles, and brought great joy to all the brothers.[2] When they came to Jerusalem, they were welcomed by the church and the apostles and the elders, and they declared all that God had done with them. But some believers who belonged to the party of the Pharisees rose up and said, "It is necessary to circumcise them and to order them to keep the law of Moses." (vs. 1–5)

It was a happy scene in Antioch with which the previous chapter closed. But the enemy never leaves God's people undisturbed in their happiness and peace. The disturbing element were certain men, who came from Judea. Their names are not made public, but they were the instruments of Satan. From verse 24 in this chapter it is evident they came from Jerusalem and perhaps some of the Judaizing leaders sent them on this errand. What a message it was they brought! "Unless you are circumcised according to the custom of Moses, you cannot be saved." (Acts 15:1). Here were large numbers of Gentiles who had accepted the Gospel and having believed were saved. Furthermore, they had the gifts in their midst, apostles, evangelists and teachers. The Holy Spirit had manifested his blessed power again and again in the growing assembly. And now, after all these gracious blessings and enjoyment of salvation, these men appear from Judea and taught them "Unless you are circumcised according to the custom of Moses, you cannot be saved" (15:1). No doubt they cited the fact of the believing Jews in Judea and Jerusalem and that circumcision was a divine institution. They came as teachers professing authority.

How great must have been the consternation among these Gentile believers when they heard this message! But Paul and Barnabas detected the subtle work of the enemy. No small dissension and strife arose, with many questionings. Paul then must have already thundered forth his great word in Galatians: "But even if we or an angel from heaven should preach to you a gospel contrary to the one we preached to you, let him be accursed" (Gal 1:8). The Gospel he preached had nothing to do with the law nor with circumcision. But the question had been introduced and brought discussion into the Antiochan Church; it had to be settled.

It was determined that Paul and Barnabas and certain other of them should go up to Jerusalem to the Apostles and

---

[1] Rackham, *The Acts of the Apostles*, 240.
[2] Or *brothers and sisters*; also verse 22

elders about this question. The second chapter in Galatians must here be considered for it gives additional information on this visit to Jerusalem. "Then after fourteen years I went up again to Jerusalem with Barnabas, taking Titus along with me. I went up because of a revelation" (Gal 2:1–2). From this we learn it was fourteen years after his previous visit to the city of his fathers, that Titus accompanied him, and that he had a revelation from the Lord about this visit to Jerusalem. Perhaps Paul was reluctant to proceed to Jerusalem. His Gospel was not received from nor linked with Jerusalem. Why should he go to Jerusalem in defense of that Gospel? But he tells us in the second chapter of Galatians that his journey to Jerusalem was by revelation. This may have been by some strong intimation given by the Holy Spirit or by a direct word from the Lord Himself. And Titus, whom he took along was a Greek, a pure Gentile, and as such uncircumcised. The reason must have been to present in Titus a specimen of what the Grace of God and the gifts of the Holy Spirit can do for a Gentile.

The whole assembly had sympathy with the journey. They brought the delegation on their way. The travel to Jerusalem was not in idleness. In Phoenice and Samaria they declared everywhere the conversion of the Gentiles, most likely a rehearsal of what God had done on their great missionary journey. Everywhere the brethren rejoiced. From this it is clearly seen that the great majority of the Christians in Phoenice and Samaria were in full sympathy with that Gospel which Paul preached, and opposed to the Judaizing teachers.

When they reached Jerusalem the Church received the delegates. Apostles and elders besides the other members of the church were present. In their presence they told out once more what it had pleased God to do through them. In Galatians, Paul writes,

> I went up because of a revelation and set before them (though privately before those who seemed influential) the gospel that I proclaim among the Gentiles, in order to make sure I was not running or had not run in vain (Gal 2:2).

This is not in contradiction with the historical account in this chapter. He gave an explanation of that Gospel he had received by revelation to the Apostles and Elders privately. But in the Church they simply spoke of the fact how the Lord had guided them and opened such a wide door among the Gentiles and how many of them had believed on the Lord Jesus Christ. A protest from the side of the Judaizing Pharisees was at once raised. These may have been the teachers who went to Antioch, and who most likely followed the deputation from Antioch to Jerusalem. They demanded that it was needful to circumcise them (the Gentiles) and to command them to keep the law of Moses. What happened immediately after this interruption is learned from Paul's own account in Galatians. Titus must have been present and the Pharisees objected to him as an uncircumcised Gentile. But Paul in the contention opposed them, and that successfully. "But even Titus, who was with me, was not forced to be circumcised, though he was a Greek" (Gal 2:3). Paul calls these Judaizing teachers "false brothers" and speaks of his opposition he made to them.

> "Yet because of false brothers secretly brought in—who slipped in to spy out our freedom that we have in Christ Jesus, so that they might bring us into slavery—to them we did not yield in submission even for a moment, so that the truth of the gospel might be preserved for you" (Gal 2:4–5).

This was followed by a council in which the important question of Salvation without the law was to be considered.

2. THE COUNCIL IN JERUSALEM (VS. 6–21).

The apostles and the elders were gathered together to consider this matter. And after there had been much debate, Peter stood up and said to them, "Brothers, you know that in the early days God made a choice among you, that by my mouth the Gentiles should hear the word of the gospel and believe. And God, who knows the heart, bore witness to them, by giving them the Holy Spirit just as he did to us, and he made no distinction between us and them, having cleansed their hearts by faith. Now, therefore, why are you putting God to the test by placing a yoke on the neck of the disciples that neither our fathers nor we have been able to bear? But we believe that we will be saved through the grace of the Lord Jesus, just as they will."

And all the assembly fell silent, and they listened to Barnabas and Paul as they related what signs and wonders God had done through them among the Gentiles. After they finished speaking, James replied, "Brothers, listen to me. Simeon has related how God first visited the Gentiles, to take from them a people for his name. And with this the words of the prophets agree, just as it is written,

> "After this I will return, and I will rebuild the tent of David that has fallen; I will rebuild its ruins, and I will restore it, that the remnant[3] of mankind may seek the Lord, and all the Gentiles who are called by my name, says the Lord, who makes these things known from of old."[4]

Therefore my judgment is that we should not trouble those of the Gentiles who turn to God, but should write to them to abstain from the things polluted by idols, and from sexual immorality, and from what has been strangled, and from blood. For from ancient generations Moses has had in every city those who proclaim him, for he is read every Sabbath in the synagogues (vs. 6–21).

That which is written in Galatians 2:6–10 took place in the private conference which Paul and Barnabas had with the Apostles and not in the council as reported here. James, Cephas and John, the three pillars of the Church in Jerusalem, then gave to Paul and Barnabas the right hand of fellowship. The larger council followed afterward. This first reported church council is a most interesting event. How different from the Church councils of the present time, with their political trickeries and machinery, their unscriptural division of God's people into clergy and laity, the making of laws and rules and their voting by ballot!

The Apostles and Elders were present, but also the multitude (v. 12). There was perfect liberty in disputation. It has not pleased the Holy Spirit to give us an account of the debate which was carried on. Peter rose up and delivered the first address to the council. This is the last time his name appears in the Book of Acts. As the Apostle of the circumcision, and used first to give the Gospel to the Gentiles, he was the right person to be heard. To this fact he refers at once. The Holy Spirit had been given to the Gentiles as he had been bestowed upon the believing Jews. After these well-known facts were stated before the multitude, Peter speaks of the law as a yoke which neither the fathers nor they were able to bear. "But we believe that we will be saved through the grace of the Lord Jesus, just as they will" (15:11). He declares that to force the Gentiles to submit to circumcision and to keep the law of Moses is nothing less than to tempt God. Peter, the acknowledged Apostle of the circumcision, is used by the Holy Spirit to show the error of the demand of the Judaizing teachers. Gentiles had heard the Gospel, believed the Gospel, and upon that God gave them his greatest gift, next to the unspeakable gift, the Holy Spirit. The law was a yoke for them and their fathers and they could not bear it. As Jews they expected salvation, not by the keeping of the law nor by circumcision, but through grace. The argument was complete. The law and circumcision should not be put upon the Gentiles. The cross of Christ has made a

---

[3] Or *rest*
[4] Amos 9:11–12

complete end of the law. To go back to the law and mix law with that grace by which we are saved, is an evil thing.

After Peter's address the multitude kept silence. It was the evidence that every heart gave full assent to what Peter had so tersely stated. The Judaizing element seems to have been completely silenced. It was the guidance of the Holy Spirit which brought Barnabas and Paul to their feet. They told once more the interesting story of their labors among the Gentiles and restated what miracles and wonders God had wrought. And after the multitude had listened to this additional testimony of how God in grace had visited the Gentiles, there was another period of silence. What a contrast with the tumult and disorder one sees in modern general church councils, general conferences, and assemblies! In these councils of Christendom everybody tries to be heard and there is a sinful ambition for leadership, which sometimes does not stop short of the most abominable schemes. If we call this gathering in Jerusalem the first church council, then it did not even have a president. The president was the Holy Spirit; he guided and directed the affairs of this important meeting.

How long the silence lasted we do not know. Perhaps many hearts were lifted up in prayer and in praise, thanking God for what he had done. The voice of James broke the silence. Through the Spirit of God he made a most important declaration. It has rightly been called the divine program. It is significant that in this first great gathering in Jerusalem, the Holy Spirit lays down the exact plan of how God works in this present age and what will follow after the special purpose of God in this age is accomplished. And this great truth of the dispensations, so necessary to understand the Word of God, is almost unknown today. What would Christendom be if the divine plan and program as uttered by James were believed? How different the work of the great denominational gatherings, if the dispensational facts so prominent in the whole Bible and so fully stated here, were taken into consideration! Worldliness, departure from the truth, and confusion have come in because this divine program has been forgotten and ignored.

We give an analysis of the words of James. From Simeon's word spoken in their hearing, it was fully demonstrated that God visits the Gentiles, to take out of them a people for his name. This, then, is the starting point:

1. God visits the Gentiles, to take out of them a people for his name.

It is a remarkable fact that, in the quotation, James (evidently the prominent and venerable leader of the Hebraic party) does not use the Hebrew text, but the Septuagint, that is the Greek version of the Old Testament, which brings out the call of the Gentiles more fully. In doing so he was clearly led by the Holy Spirit.

And this calling out from the Gentiles a people for his name is the special purpose of God in this age. Peter's testimony, followed by that of Barnabas and Paul, had fully demonstrated that God had begun this blessed work. And the Apostle Paul teaches later "this mystery is that the Gentiles are fellow heirs, members of the same body, and partakers of the promise in Christ Jesus through the gospel" (Eph 3:6). Now that people taken out, called by the Gospel, the Gentiles who are fellow-heirs, are the church. The word "church," in the Greek, is *ecclesia*—which means "an out calling." This out calling still goes on and will go on till the church is completed.

There seems to be a tendency in our days among certain Bible teachers to make everything as much as possible Jewish. They tell us that there is nothing about the church in the Gospels nor in the Book of Acts. They want us to believe that the seven church messages in Revelation have nothing to do with this present age, but that these seven churches will come into existence during the great tribulation. Again the Olivet discourse has nothing to do, so they tell us, with our age; it all refers to the Jews. But these fanciful teachers with their speculative theories, which they do not get from the Word of God, but bring there, have even declared that the word of James must be read in another light. It has been stated that the visitation of the Gentiles to take of them a people for his name, as declared by James, has no reference at all to this present age nor to the formation of the church. According to this far-fetched theory that visitation of which James spoke almost 1900 years ago will take place in the future. (!) It is not surprising that some good people who adopt such novel and strange expositions, if they can be called that, should become confused. The visitation of the Gentiles began after Israel had rejected God's offer. Cornelius and his house, as well as those reached by the evangelists (Acts 11:20), and the multitudes called out by the preaching of Paul and Barnabas are in view here. All those believing Gentiles constituted with believing Jews the one body, the church. This visitation of the Gentiles through the Gospel of Grace still goes on. What then, is next in the divine program?

2. *"After this I will return."* In the Hebrew text of Amos 9:11–12 these words are not found. Nor does James state that they are written in that passage, which he partially quotes from the Greek translation (Septuagint). He said, "with this the words of the prophets agree, just as it is written, 'After this I will return' " (15:15-16).

The Lord announces his return to his people in these words, "I will return." This return of the Lord to turn graciously to his people Israel is written not merely in one of the prophets, but in the prophets. They all announce this great coming event. Now, according to the statement of James, the Gentiles must be visited first; a people (the church) is to be taken out of them. After this is accomplished and the full number, which constitutes the church, is called out, the Lord will return. It is not his coming for the saints, as revealed in 1 Thessalonians 4:16–18, but his visible Return in power and glory, of which the prophets speak.[5] That during the end time the Gospel of the Kingdom will be preached among the nations (Matt 24:14), a work which will begin after the true church has been removed from the earth, is elsewhere revealed in the Scriptures; but that this work during the great tribulation should be that of which James speaks exclusively is an extremely fanciful conception. The Gentiles had been and were to be visited for the out calling of a people for his name and *after* this the Second Coming of the Lord Jesus Christ will take place.

3. Next we read of what will be the result of the coming of the Lord. "I will rebuild the tent of David that has fallen; I will rebuild its ruins, and I will restore it" (15:16). This is of course only one of the results of the Return of the Lord. The Kingdom will be established as promised in the Davidic covenant. The divine announcement made to Mary the Virgin concerning our Lord will then be fully accomplished.

> And the Lord God will give to him the throne of his father David, and he will reign over the house of Jacob forever, and of his kingdom there will be no end (Luke 1:32–33).

---

[5] The Coming of the Lord for his Saints, who are to be raised from the dead, and with the living believers to be caught up in clouds to meet the Lord in the air, is nowhere revealed in the prophetic books of the Old Testament, although Paul explains this mystery to the church.

This, likewise, is announced by the prophets that such a restoration of Israel, the Kingdom as a theocracy, is to take place. All the prophets predicted the coming establishment and glory of the Kingdom in connection with the visible manifestation of the Lord out of heaven.

4. "That the remnant of mankind may seek the Lord, and all the Gentiles who are called by my name, says the Lord, who makes these things known from of old" (15:17–18). The Gentiles, yea, all of them, will be brought to a knowledge of the Lord after the tabernacle of David has been set up. The Gentiles will seek the Lord after he has come back. There will not be another "out calling," but the nations will turn to the Lord and the glory of the Lord will cover the earth as the waters cover the sea. This fourth part of the divine program as given through James corresponds with the vision which Isaiah saw:

> It shall come to pass in the latter days that the mountain of the house of the Lord shall be established as the highest of the mountains, and shall be lifted up above the hills; and *all the nations shall flow to it* (Isa 2:2). . . In that day the root of Jesse, who shall stand as a signal for the peoples—of him shall the nations inquire, and his resting place shall be glorious (Isa 11:10). . . Behold, you shall call a nation that you do not know, and a nation that did not know you shall run to you, because of the Lord your God, and of the Holy One of Israel, for he has glorified you (Isa 55:5). . . From new moon to new moon, and from Sabbath to Sabbath, all flesh shall come to worship before me, declares the Lord (Isa 66:23).

And all this wonderful plan God had laid from the beginning of the world.

The important truths contained in James' utterance are the following:

> God gives the Gospel to the Gentiles, through the preaching of the Gospel, a people is called out for his Name. The church is this out called people. The Lord Jesus Christ returns after God's purpose in this age has been accomplished. The result of his return will be the setting up of the tabernacle of David, that is, the promised Kingdom. After he has come again the nations of the world will seek the Lord.

World-conversion, according to this divine program laid down in the Jerusalem council, cannot take place till the Lord has returned.

James likewise stated that these Gentiles who had turned to God should not be troubled. The burden of the law was not to be laid upon them; nor should they have anything to do with circumcision. Four things he mentioned from which the Gentiles should be requested to abstain from pollution of idols, from fornication, from things strangled, and from blood. These things were partially connected with idolatry, especially fornication. Immoralities were at the bottom of the worship of different idols. But these regulations were not based upon the law of Moses, but upon the covenant made with Noah and as such binding upon the Gentiles (Gen 9:4).

3. THE RESULT MADE KNOWN (VS. 22–29).

> Then it seemed good to the apostles and the elders, with the whole church, to choose men from among them and send them to Antioch with Paul and Barnabas. They sent Judas called Barsabbas, and Silas, leading men among the brothers, with the following letter: "The brothers, both the apostles and the elders, to the brothers[6] who are of the Gentiles in Antioch and Syria and Cilicia, greetings. Since we have heard that some persons have gone out from us and troubled you[7] with words, unsettling your minds, although we gave them no instructions, it has seemed good to us, having come to one accord, to choose men and send them to you with our beloved Barnabas and Paul, men who have risked their lives for the name of our Lord Jesus Christ. We have therefore sent Judas and Silas, who themselves will tell you the same things by word of mouth. For it has seemed good to the Holy Spirit and to us to lay on you no greater burden than these

---

[6] Or *brothers and sisters*; also verses 32, 33, 36

[7] Some manuscripts *some persons from us have troubled you*

requirements: that you abstain from what has been sacrificed to idols, and from blood, and from what has been strangled, and from sexual immorality. If you keep yourselves from these, you will do well. Farewell." (vs. 22–29).

After the important decision had been reached in the Jerusalem council, the result had to be made known to those who were troubled. This was done through a document in the form of a letter, which was addressed to the brethren of the Gentiles in Antioch, Syria and Cilicia. The whole assembly was of one mind in this matter. Barnabas and Paul, with other chosen men, were commissioned to carry this message to the brethren. The two chosen were Judas, surnamed Barsabas, a Hebrew, and Silas. The latter must have been a Grecian Jew, a Hellenist, for his name, Silvanus, is Latin, and we know that he possessed the Roman citizenship. This we learn from chapter 16:37. The document reveals the wisdom which is from above, that wisdom of which James speaks later in his Epistle. "But the wisdom from above is first pure, then peaceable, gentle, open to reason, full of mercy and good fruits, impartial and sincere" (Jam 3:17). The letter sent to the Gentile brethren bears these blessed marks. It is a most wonderful document, brief and extremely tactful. Much might have been said in the denunciation of these false teachers, but all this is carefully avoided and only the most essential matter is presented. And yet it is firm and decisive. How different from present day ecclesiastical rulings, letters concerning the question of fellowship, etc., with their bitter party spirit and unchristian rejection of brethren! The Hebrew element could not be offended at what the council had decided upon, though circumcision and law-keeping were mentioned as not necessary to salvation. On the other hand, the two brethren from Antioch, Barnabas and Paul, were praised for their conduct: "men who have risked their lives for the name of our Lord Jesus Christ" (15:26). Such a loving acknowledgment must have had a very salutary effect upon the much disturbed Antiochian assembly. All was done by the guidance of the Holy Spirit, who indeed had indicated all along that circumcision was not necessary for Gentiles, for he had come upon the uncircumcised; therefore the statement - "For it has seemed good to the Holy Spirit and to us."

4. The Consolation brought to Antioch (vs. 30–35).

> So when they were sent off, they went down to Antioch, and having gathered the congregation together, they delivered the letter. And when they had read it, they rejoiced because of its encouragement. And Judas and Silas, who were themselves prophets, encouraged and strengthened the brothers with many words. And after they had spent some time, they were sent off in peace by the brothers to those who had sent them. [8] But Paul and Barnabas remained in Antioch, teaching and preaching the word of the Lord, with many others also (vs. 30–35).

It is a most blessed and happy scene described in these verses. The assembly in Antioch must have been much in prayer while Paul and Barnabas were absent; eagerly they waited for their return. As soon as they had arrived the multitude of Christians came together for a general meeting. The letter then was read and the result was great joy. It was a great consolation to receive such a loving message. But Judas and Silas had been enjoined to "tell you the same things by word of mouth," (15:27) that is, orally. They now discharged their commission. They both were prophets, and exhorted the brethren with many words. The gift of a prophet is here described. It is exhortation and speaking for the edification of God's people. Through these exhortations the

---

[8] Some manuscripts insert verse 34: *But it seemed good to Silas to remain there*

assembly was confirmed, that is, more fully established. No doubt their chief exhortation must have been "eager to maintain the unity of the Spirit in the bond of peace" (Eph 4:3). They abode in Antioch for some time and then, perhaps after another assembly gathering, they were permitted to return to the Apostles in Jerusalem in peace, or rather, *with peace*. From Galatians 2:10 we gain the additional information that the three of whom Paul writes as the pillars, James, Cephas, and John, had made a request which was not embodied in the letter read to the assembly. "Only, they asked us to remember the poor, the very thing I was eager to do" (Gal 2:10). Most likely this request was not forgotten and the poor in Jerusalem were generously remembered by the large assembly in Antioch and the money sent to the Apostles.

There is some doubt about the genuineness of verse 34. Most manuscripts omit the statement about Silas. The preceding verses show that both Judas and Silas were let go to return to the Apostles. Silas, however, must have returned to Antioch, for we find him there according to verse 40 of this chapter. The blessed activity of Paul and Barnabas was renewed in Antioch. They taught and preached the Word of the Lord with many others. What liberty they must have then enjoyed and what gracious results the Lord must have given from this ministry! But the controversy was not altogether overcome. Peter some time later visited Antioch, a visit not mentioned in the Book of Acts. We read of it in Galatians 2:11–14. Paul was then likewise present and withstood Peter to the face when he refused to eat with the Gentiles and build again what he had destroyed. Peter's visit must have taken place shortly after the return of Paul and Barnabas to Antioch.

5. PAUL AND BARNABAS SEPARATE (VS. 36–41).

> And after some days Paul said to Barnabas, "Let us return and visit the brothers in every city where we proclaimed the word of the Lord, and see how they are." Now Barnabas wanted to take with them John called Mark. But Paul thought best not to take with them one who had withdrawn from them in Pamphylia and had not gone with them to the work. And there arose a sharp disagreement, so that they separated from each other. Barnabas took Mark with him and sailed away to Cyprus, but Paul chose Silas and departed, having been commended by the brothers to the grace of the Lord. And he went through Syria and Cilicia, strengthening the churches (vs. 36–41).

The second great journey of the Apostle Paul had an unfortunate beginning. It started with the separation of the two who had so blessedly worked together and whose joined work had so graciously been owned by the Lord. Human failure and shortcoming were at the bottom of it. It is evident from the inspired record, that there was no waiting before the Lord and no dependence on the guidance of the Holy Spirit in connection with this new start. How different from the first journey! *Then* the whole assembly was ministering to the Lord and the Holy Spirit said, "Set apart for me Barnabas and Saul" (13:2). *Here* prayer is not mentioned, nor does the Holy Spirit indicate a new work for the two messengers and as a result the two are separated, not to fresh service, but from each other. Paul said, "let us return and visit the brothers in every city where we proclaimed the word of the Lord, and see how they are" (15:36). His great love for the brethren prompted this action. His heart longed for them, but it was nevertheless his own will and desire, and not according to the mind of the Holy Spirit. The great work the Lord had for his servant was not to go over the same route and in a kind of inspection tour, visiting every place again, but to carry the Gospel into other regions and evangelize new cities and provinces. To go again with Barnabas, from place to place, places already visited, was Paul's plan; the Lord's plan was another. And how much self choosing in service for God there is in our days! How little true waiting on the Lord and dependence on the Holy Spirit! Many servants who should carry the Gospel into needed fields and teach the Word to those who are destitute of the truth, confine themselves to a small circle of churches and minister exclusively to these. "Let us return and visit the brothers" but what about the other members of the same body and the many cities where the Gospel is greatly needed? The servant of Christ, whether he is evangelist or teacher, must exercise this gift under the Lord, directed by his Spirit. Paul suggested to another servant, to Barnabas, what he thought he should do. How could he know what the Holy Spirit meant Barnabas to do?

Barnabas was quite ready to fall in line with Paul's suggestion. Nothing is said that they bowed their knees together and asked the Lord first, whether it was his will that they should go again. Soon it became evident that the action was not sanctioned by the Lord. Barnabas had a will of his own, and was determined to take John Mark along. Paul refused this request. He did not care to be associated with one who had failed in his service. A sharp contention followed, and Barnabas and Paul were separated from each other. Barnabas took Mark and sailed away into Cyprus (see Fig. 14). What their service was is not reported in this book. Such contention and separation of beloved brethren was surely not the work of the Holy Spirit. It was the result of not asking counsel of the Lord. But God overruled it all in the end and brought good out of this failure, as he only can in his unfathomable grace. It may be possible that another reason was also connected with this separation. Both John Mark and Barnabas may have had leanings toward the Hebrew side in the matter of the keeping of the law; while Paul stood firmly for what he had so earnestly contended for in Jerusalem. That this may have been the case is suggested in Galatians "And the rest of the Jews acted hypocritically along with him, so that *even Barnabas was led astray by their hypocrisy*" (Gal 2:13). But this break of fellowship in service, the subtle work of the enemy, was not permanent.

Paul mentions Barnabas in 1 Corinthians 9:6, and of Mark's restoration and Paul's love for him we read in Colossians 4:10 and 2 Timothy 4:11.

Paul then chose Silas. He took the place of Barnabas in this second journey. The assembly fully recognized the choice of Paul and the brethren commended them both to the grace of God. Paul went through Syria and Cilicia first confirming the churches, which does not mean the so-called man-made rite of confirmation, but he taught them more fully, and thus they were confirmed in the truth and established.

CHAPTER SIXTEEN

Before we follow the second missionary journey of the Apostle Paul, it may not be out of place to give a little chronological table of the life of this chosen instrument, beginning with his conversion down to the close of the second journey. This will help in reviewing the remarkable activity of the great apostle to the Gentiles and put before us the events from Chapter 9–18 in a concise form.

ca. AD. 36	Conversion of Saul of Tarsus (Acts 9).	
36–39	At Damascus-Preaching in the synagogue. His journey into Arabia. Returns to Damascus and flees from Damascus.	
	his **FIRST** visit to Jerusalem; three years after his conversion. Back to Tarsus (Acts 9:23–26. Gal 1:18. 39–40).	
39–30	Rest of the Jewish Churches (Acts 9:31).	
	Paul preaches the gospel in Syria and Cilicia (Gal 1:21).	
	A period of uncertain length. During this time he probably experienced many of the perils and sufferings which he recounts to the Corinthians (2 Cor 11).	
40–43	he is brought from Tarsus to Antioch by Barnabas; and remains there a year before the famine (Acts 11:26).	
44	Paul's **SECOND** visit to Jerusalem, with the collection (Acts 11:30).	
45	he returns to Antioch (Acts 12:2–5).	
	Paul's FIRST missionary journey with Barnabas to Cyprus, Antioch in Pisidia, Iconium, Lystra. Returns to Antioch, Derbe.	
46–49	Labors a long time in Antioch.	
	Dissension and disputation about circumcision (Acts 14, 15:1, 2).	
	Paul's **THIRD** visit to Jerusalem with Barnabas, fourteen years after his conversion (Gal 2:1).	
50	They attend the council at Jerusalem (Acts 15).	
	Return of Paul and Barnabas to Antioch, with Judas and Silas (Acts 15:32–35).	
	Paul's **SECOND** missionary journey with Silas and Timothy. From Antioch to Syria, Cilicia, Derbe, Lystra, Phrygia, Galatia, Troas. Luke joins him (Acts 16:10).	
51	Entrance of the Gospel into Europe (Acts 16:11–13).	
	Paul visits Philippi, Thessalonica, Berea, Athens, Corinth. Spends a year and six months at Corinth (Acts 18:11).	
52	First Epistle to the Thessalonians written. Second Epistle to the Thessalonians written.	
53	Paul leaves Corinth and sails to Ephesus (Acts 18:18, 19).	
54	Paul's **FOURTH** visit to Jerusalem at the feast. His return to Antioch	

The second missionary journey of Paul is now before us and the divine record is full of interest. The sixteenth chapter shows the pr ogress of the Gospel from Asia to Europe. We divide this chapter into four parts:

1. In Derbe and Lystra: Timothy chosen and circumcised by Paul (vs. 1–5).

2. The Holy Spirit forbids the preaching of the Word in Asia (vs. 6–8).

3. The vision of the man of Macedonia and the journey there (vs. 9–12).

4. The Gospel in Europe. Events in Philippi (vs. 13–40).

1. IN DERBE AND LYSTRA: TIMOTHY CHOSEN AND CIRCUMCISED BY PAUL (VS. 1–5).

> Paul[1] came also to Derbe and to Lystra. A disciple was there, named Timothy, the son of a Jewish woman who was a believer, but his father was a Greek. He was well spoken of by the brothers[2] at Lystra and Iconium. Paul wanted Timothy to accompany him, and he took him and circumcised him because of the Jews who were in those places, for they all knew that his father was a Greek. As they went on their way through the cities, they delivered to them for observance the decisions that had been reached by the apostles and elders who were in Jerusalem. So the churches were strengthened in the faith, and they increased in numbers daily. (vs. 1–5).

Derbe and Lystra, familiar to us from the first missionary journey, are visited again. In Lystra, Paul had healed the cripple, and there he must have met the Jewess Eunice, who lived with her mother, Lois, and whose son was Timothy. Eunice was a believer and so was the grandmother of Timothy (2 Tim 1:5). He had brought up in the Holy Scriptures (2 Tim 3:15). The young man had an excellent report by the brethren of Lystra and Iconium (see Fig. 19). The Holy Spirit moved the Apostle to have Timothy to go forth with him. The Epistles to Timothy shed more light on this. In first Timothy 1:18 we read: "This charge I entrust to you, Timothy, my child, in accordance with the prophecies previously made about you, that by them you may wage the good warfare." Timothy had been marked out by the Holy Spirit through the gift of prophecy as the proper companion of the Apostle. No mention is made in the record before us of the laying on of hands. However, we read of it in the Epistles to Timothy.

> Do not neglect the gift you have, which was given you by prophecy when the council of elders laid their hands on you (1 Tim 4:14). . . For this reason I remind you to fan into flame the gift of God, which is in you through the laying on of my hands (2 Tim 1:6).

This laying on of hands by the elders and by the Apostle Paul must have been done in Lystra. The circumcision of Timothy is prominently mentioned. Paul circumcised him, and the reason of this act "because of the Jews who were in those places" (16:3). This action of Paul has been often condemned as an action which was not according to the mind of the Spirit. We do not think such was the case at all. That Paul's act in circumcising Timothy must have produced a stir among the Gentile Christians can easily be imagined. But recently their minds had been agitated about circumcision. The message of the false leaders "Unless you are circumcised according to the custom of Moses, you cannot be saved" (15:1)—was still fresh in their memories. And now Paul himself circumcised one whose father was a Greek. Paul's teaching on circumcision was well known; he was the apostle of the uncircumcision. Did not this action side him with the law keepers and the Judaizers? But looked upon in the right way, all these charges of inconsistency and going back to the law fall down. The law has nothing to say about the circumcision of the offspring of mixed marriages. It is well known that, if

---

[1] Greek *He*
[2] Or *brothers and sisters*; also verse 40

there was a mixed marriage (i.e., between a Jew and a Gentile), the law would have nothing to say to the offspring.

> Legally, the Jewish father could not own his own children born of a Gentile mother, or *vice versa* (see Ezra 10). Now Timothy being the offspring of such a marriage, there could be no claim, even if there was license to circumcise him; and Paul condescends out of grace to those who were on lower ground, and stops their mouths most effectually.[3]

His act then was not according to Law, for circumcision in Timothy's case was not commanded but it was done on the ground of grace; he did not want to put a stumbling block into the way of the Jews. First Corinthians gives the fullest reason for this act of the Apostle:

> To the Jews I became as a Jew, in order to win Jews. To those under the law I became as one under the law (though not being myself under the law) that I might win those under the law (1 Cor 9:20).

We see then the apostolic band, Paul, Silas and Timothy, going through the different cities making known the decrees of the apostles and elders at Jerusalem, that is, what had been agreed upon concerning the relation of believing Gentiles to the law. How needful this was for these Galatian churches! These Galatians were by nature fickle-minded and unstable. When Paul was with them they were ready to pluck out their eyes and give them to the apostle (Gal 4:15); some time later they were only too ready to listen to the Judaizing teachers and Paul had to write them: "I am astonished that you are so quickly deserting him who called you in the grace of Christ and are turning to a different gospel" (Gal 1:6). The effect of the ministry of the apostle and the declaration of the decision of the Jerusalem council resulted in the strengthening of the churches and in an increased membership.

2. THE HOLY SPIRIT FORBIDS THE PREACHING OF THE WORD IN ASIA (VS. 6–8).

> And they went through the region of Phrygia and Galatia, having been forbidden by the Holy Spirit to speak the word in Asia. And when they had come up to Mysia, they attempted to go into Bithynia, but the Spirit of Jesus did not allow them. So, passing by Mysia, they went down to Troas. (vs. 6–8).

They travel on throughout Phrygia and Galatia. Though there is no record given of work done here, it does not mean that they were idle and had no testimony for the multitudes. But suddenly their plans of evangelization were halted by the voice of the Holy Spirit. He forbade them to preach the Word in Asia. Their intention was to reach now the large province of Asia[4] with its flourishing cities. But the Holy Spirit entered a protest against this plan. He did not want to have the Word preached *at that time* in Asia. Later Paul spent three years in the capital of the province, in Ephesus, and all Asia heard the Word. Then they reached the northern part of the province, Mysia; obedient to the voice of the Holy Spirit, they did not speak the Word. They then expected to reach Bithynia, which borders the Black Sea, but the Spirit of Jesus suffered them not. He would not let them go there. Bithynia heard the Word at another time, perhaps through Peter, for his first Epistle is addressed to the strangers throughout Pontus, Galatia, Cappadocia, Asia and *Bithynia*. Christianity became so strong in that province at the beginning of the second century that idol worship was seriously affected.[5]

---

[3] Kelly, *Lectures Introductory to the Study of the Acts*, 125.

[4] At that time a large territory of Asia Minor along the Aegean Sea was called "Asia."

[5] From a letter of the Roman governor Pliny.

But the Holy Spirit had his own time and ways for giving the Gospel to these provinces. This shows clearly that the Holy Spirit must guide and direct in service. How he arrested the messengers and suffered them not to proceed is not stated. They followed his guidance obediently. How necessary it is for the servant of Christ, be he an evangelist or a teacher, to depend on the Holy Spirit for a direction! Waiting on the Lord and then to go forth guided by his Spirit is the true way of a successful ministry. He must point out the way and the places and the time when and where the precious Word is to be spoken. Such humble reliance upon the direction of the Holy Spirit is but little known in our days. The great movements of our times seem to place more stress on organization, widespread advertising methods and financial support, than on the presence and guidance of the Holy Spirit. The servants of the Lord Jesus Christ ministering the Gospel and the Word in the end of this present evil age need the guidance of the Holy Spirit as much as the apostle in the beginning of the age. And the Holy Spirit is today the same as he was then, when he suffered them not to minister in Asia and in Bithynia. We also call attention to the true rendering "the Spirit of *Jesus* did not allow them." The blessed Lord walked on earth in the power of the Spirit and now the same Spirit who led him while on earth, leads and guides his own into service.

In this action of the Holy Spirit he assumed once more his authority, which, as we saw, was not fully recognized in the beginning of the second missionary journey, as he was recognized when Paul went forth the first time. He had to be held back from going in self-choosing to places which were not then to be visited. Thus kept back from ministry in Bithynia they turned towards the seacoast and came to Troas. This seaport was located opposite the European Continent and Macedonia was the nearest province. Not permitted to preach in Asia, held back from ministry in Bithynia, a double course was open to the apostle, either to go back to Antioch or to cross over to Europe.

3. THE MACEDONIAN CALL (VS. 9–12).

> And a vision appeared to Paul in the night: a man of Macedonia was standing there, urging him and saying, "Come over to Macedonia and help us." And when Paul[6] had seen the vision, immediately we sought to go on into Macedonia, concluding that God had called us to preach the gospel to them.
>
> So, setting sail from Troas, we made a direct voyage to Samothrace, and the following day to Neapolis, and from there to Philippi, which is a leading city of the[7] district of Macedonia and a Roman colony. We remained in this city some days. (vs. 9–12).

The Lord, who had kept them back by his Spirit from going into the provinces, which were not to be reached at that time, now makes his will known where they were to go. All the uncertainty and perplexity which had rested upon the little company is now to be lifted. That there was deep soul exercise and continued prayer we may well surmise. They cast themselves completely on the Lord and he now directs them. Paul had a vision during that night. He beheld a man from Macedonia, whom he must have recognized as such by his dress or some other way and he prayed him "Come over to Macedonia and help us." And after he had seen the vision they immediately decided to cross over into Macedonia. They had gathered first by spiritual intelligence that the meaning of the vision was that the Lord called them to preach the Gospel in that land. All this is full of encouragement to God's servant. If we only learn to wait and trust in Him, he will direct our steps.

---

[6] Greek *he*
[7] Or *that*

Chapter Sixteen

24. Philippi's forum and basilica B seen from the acropolis.

However, the vision Paul had must not be taken as the common mode of guidance, nor as something which was to be repeated. We are to walk in faith and not by sight, and faith does not want sight, nor expects visions to know the will of the Lord. The prophecy of Joel in which dreams and visions are mentioned does not concern the present age at all. The people who claim to have visions and dreams now, as a result of a greater outpouring of the Holy Spirit, are generally, if not always the subjects of delusion. When a Christian is fully obedient to the Holy Spirit and the Spirit of God fills him, he does not want and does not need visions and dreams. The vision Paul had was an extraordinary event. It was unexpected and unasked for.

According to the so-called *Bezan* text[8] they found in the harbor a ship sailing the next morning. This may have been the case, for the text shows that there was no delay in their departure. Whenever the Lord calls to a service he also opens the way providentially. The tenth verse is interesting for another reason. The pronoun is now changed from "they" to "we." From this we learn that Luke, the beloved physician and the chosen instrument to write this historical book, joined the party. He does not mention his name at all, but keeps himself completely in the background. May we profit by this beautiful example of humility! From Samothracia they came to

---

[8] A Greek MS. of the Gospels and Acts Written in the 6th Century, which came into possession of Beza the scholar and reformer. It has many variations from the ordinary text.

The Acts of the Apostles

Neapolis and from thence to Philippi (see Fig. 24, 25).

Philippi, the first European city in which the Gospel of the Son of God was preached, is described as the chief city of that part of Macedonia and a colony (verse 12). This city had been founded by Philip of Macedon, to keep the wild Thracians in check, which were the neighbors of the Macedonians. In 42 BC, a decisive battle was fought during the Roman civil wars, and Philippi was made a Roman colony and settled with soldiers. It was mostly inhabited by Roman citizens. It was a city filled with idolatry. The presence of Lydia of Thyatira gives the hint that a trade in purple must have existed there. No synagogue was located in the city. The events which transpired here are given in detail and occupy the rest of this chapter.

4. The Gospel in Europe: the conversion of Lydia (vs. 13–15).

> And on the Sabbath day we went outside the gate to the riverside, where we supposed there was a place of prayer, and we sat down and spoke to the women who had come together. One who heard us was a woman named Lydia, from the city of Thyatira, a seller of purple goods, who was a worshiper of God. The Lord opened her heart to pay attention to what was said by Paul. And after she was baptized, and her household as well, she urged us, saying, "If you have judged me to be faithful to the Lord, come to my house and stay." And she prevailed upon us. (vs. 13–15).

They may have arrived quite early in the week and waited for the sabbath. But there was no synagogue in the city, since the Apostle and his companions to find the few Jews in that city went out of the city by the rivers ide, where prayer was wont to be made. The river was the small stream Gangites. It was the custom of the Jews to go to the riverside or to the sea for prayer, most likely on account of the different washings commanded by the law. Of this we read already in Ezra (8:15, 21). Many other sources speak of this custom. The Apostle and his associates found a company of women gathered there. We wonder if Paul looked for the man whom he had seen in his vision. But there was no man present; only a company of women. But these messengers were not discouraged by the humble audience, the first which ever gathered in Europe to hear the Gospel. They did not despise the small things but were ready to speak to the few women who had come together for prayer. Paul spoke to them. His words are not given, but he had one theme, the Gospel of Grace, and of this and the Lord Jesus Christ, his death on the cross and his resurrection he assuredly spoke. Among the women was Lydia, a seller of purple, of the city of Thyatira, which was situated in the province of Asia, where the door had been closed. Lydia was a worshipper of God. She had turned to the true God and had dropped idolatry. She was a pious soul earnestly seeking after the truth; this piety was seen in her seeking out on the sabbath those who worship the Lord. She was, like Cornelius, converted, but had no knowledge of salvation, because she knew nothing of the Lord Jesus Christ.

And then the Lord opened the heart of Lydia. A blessed word this is. He Himself must open the doors of the hearts of the hearers. Human hands could not do this; the power belongs to him alone, unless the Lord goes before and prepares the hearts for the reception of the truth and removes the bars, all efforts are in vain. May those who go forth to preach the Gospel look to the Lord to open the he arts of the hearers, and when precious souls accept the truth, let us give the praise and the glory to him and not to the evangelists. Alas! how much work is being done m which the Lord has no share, in which he and his Spirit is dishonored. There is also a special significance in the fact that Lydia was from Thyatira. It is more than possible that she carried the Gospel to her native city in Asia. An assembly was there and from the words of our Lord in the message to Thyatira (Rev 2:18—29) we learn that another woman corrupted Christianity there.

> "But I have this against you, that you tolerate that woman Jezebel, who calls herself a prophetess and is teaching and seducing my servants [9] to practice sexual immorality and to eat food sacrificed to idols" (Rev 2:20).

Such a woman had sprung up in Thyatira, the opposite from the gentle Lydia with her beautiful experience and Christian character. Prophetically, Jezebel in Thyatira stands for Rome, "the woman clothed in purple and scarlet."

The baptism of herself and her household followed immediately, and having had her heart opened, she now opened her house to Paul and his companions. She besought them and, evidently a rich woman, she showed great humility—"If you have judged me to be faithful to the Lord" (16:15). And they abode in her house. She fully identified herself with the messengers of the Lord, and must have shown them great kindness. Her house became the home of Paul, Silas, Timothy and Luke, and the gathering place of the assembly in Philippi (v. 40). No doubt later in sending fellowship from Philippi to the Apostle (Phil 4:14—16) she had a large share in this. Thus the blessed fruits of the Spirit were abundantly revealed.

5. PAUL AND SILAS IN PRISON (VS. 16–24)

> As we were going to the place of prayer, we were met by a slave girl who had a spirit of divination and brought her owners much gain by fortune-telling. She followed Paul and us, crying out, "These men are servantse of the Most High God, who proclaim to you the way of salvation." And this she kept doing for many days. Paul, having become greatly annoyed, turned and said to the

---

[9] Greek *bondservants*

25. The ancient theatre of Philippi, Macedonia.

> spirit, "I command you in the name of Jesus Christ to come out of her." And it came out that very hour. (vs. 16–18.)

The second event in Philippi is the deliverance of the damsel, possessed with the spirit of Python. The enemy is now coming to the front once more. He could not leave the entrance of Europe by the Gospel unchallenged and so he begins his work. He comes in the garb of an angel of light and appears as a friend of the servants of Christ, seemingly ready to help the cause of the Apostle. A damsel, most likely a slave girl, had a spirit of divination, or, as the word is in the original, of Python. Python was the name, supposedly, of a great dragon at Delphi, slain by Apollo. She had masters over her and brought them much gain by her soothsaying. She was what is called today, a medium, possessed by a demon. Such the spiritualistic mediums are, if they are not outright frauds, who deceive their dupes by clever tricks. And it is a startling and solemn fact that some of the leading educators, college professors, literary men and even so-called clergymen are seeking after these demon-possessed girls and women and pay them well for their damnable practices. Of course this goes under the name of "scientific investigation" or "psychical research."

The girl here was possessed by a spirit. This was fully recognized by the people of Philippi as well as by the Apostle. Alford remarks:

All attempts to explain away such a narrative as this by the subterfuges of Rationalism is more than ever futile.[10]

Another commentary on Acts suggests that the damsel was probably a ventriloquist! Through this cunning demon Satan tried to hinder the work by assuming a friendly relation towards the servants of the Lord Jesus Christ. She followed Paul and his three helpers and announced before them the fact that they are the servants of the most high God and that they show the way of salvation. This she did many days. That demon spoke the truth, though he could not confess Christ as Lord and Saviour. Instead of calling them deceivers and warning against the Gospel they brought, this evil spirit *applauded* them. Instead of assailing the work in an open fashion, he appears as if he would help it along and that by flattery. His attempt was to support outwardly the work of the Gospel by this loud-mouthed advertising and then to hurt it at the same time. But the Gospel does not need such support. Nor does it need the support of the world, behind which Satan stands as ruler, prince and god. The support and applause of the world does not further the Gospel, but it is the most deceptive hindrance of it Satan has ever invented. And how much of all this we see at the present time! How often evangelistic movements with their great schemes seek the alliance and assistance of the daily press, which is generally antichristian, to help along the work of the Gospel by giving to it prominence in the eyes of the world; and other facts we leave unmentioned. The world is always the world and friendship with it must mean enmity to God. Such was the attempt of Satan here to ally himself with the servants of Christ and then to spoil them. How well he has succeeded in Christendom of to-day!

But Paul would not accept this testimony. He ignored the attempt at first and goes on his way without paying any attention to the wild cries of the damsel. At last he was grieved and then in the blessed name of the Lord Jesus Christ he commanded the demon to come out of her. And he came out the same hour.

> But when her owners saw that their hope of gain was gone, they seized Paul and Silas and dragged them into the marketplace before the rulers. And when they had brought them to the magistrates, they said, "These men are Jews, and they are disturbing our city. They advocate customs that are not lawful for us as Romans to accept or practice." The crowd joined in attacking them, and the magistrates tore the garments off them and gave orders to beat them with rods. And when they had inflicted many blows upon them, they threw them into prison, ordering the jailer to keep them safely. Having received this order, he put them into the inner prison and fastened their feet in the stocks. (vs. 19–24).

The enemy having failed in his wily attempt now shows himself in his true character. The masters of the damsel who was delivered from the evil spirit, were just as much in Satan's power as the demon-possessed girl. Through these men Satan now opposes the progress of the Gospel by force. Paul and Silas are rushed into the marketplace before the magistrates.

The accusation was that they taught an unlawful religion. Paul's preachings of course aimed at the idol worship of Rome and of Augustus. In this at least the accusation was true. But the offence of the two men appeared in a worse light, when it was announced that both Paul and Silas were Romans. To proclaim another religion was paramount with treason. Of course the motives presented before the judges were false and a mere pretence. But Satan succeeded in stirring up the multitudes. The mass of people rose up against them. The

---

[10] Alford, *The NT for English Readers*, 1:762.

Magistrates also joined in and stripped the two messengers of the Lord of their clothes. This was considered a great shame and insult and they must have felt it keenly. Paul refers to it in his Epistle to the Thessalonians

> But though we had already suffered and been shamefully treated at Philippi, as you know, we had boldness in our God to declare to you the gospel of God in the midst of much conflict (1 Thess 2:2).

Then in that condition they were severely whipped, many stripes were laid on them. This is one of the beatings with rods to which Paul refers in 2 Corinthians 11:25 "Three times I was beaten with rods." The shame and severe pain from this beating must have been almost unbearable. Then they were cast into the prison and the jailer was especially charged to keep them safely. This individual felt his responsibility and to make them doubly secure he put their feet into the stocks. And thus stripped of the clothes, with lacerated and bleeding backs, their feet were encased in the cruel stocks. The cruelty of man producing such suffering was the work of the enemy. They suffered in patience and the Holy Spirit filling them gave them strength to suffer unjustly.

6. The Philippian Jailer Converted (vs. 25–28)

> About midnight Paul and Silas were praying and singing hymns to God, and the prisoners were listening to them, and suddenly there was a great earthquake, so that the foundations of the prison were shaken. And immediately all the doors were opened, and everyone's bonds were unfastened. When the jailer woke and saw that the prison doors were open, he drew his sword and was about to kill himself, supposing that the prisoners had escaped. But Paul cried with a loud voice, "Do not harm yourself, for we are all here." (vs. 25–28).

Evening comes on and when midnight is reached strange sounds are heard in the dungeon. Curses and vile language are the familiar tones with weeping and gnashing of teeth, which sounded through these miserable Roman prisons. But now the voice of singing is heard. Player and Praise come from the cell of the two imprisoned evangelists. At midnight Paul and Silas prayed and sang praises to God. The prisoners heard them. No doubt the prayer and praise was fully on the line of the blessed Gospel; they must have praised God for the Lord Jesus, that he suffered for their sins and had saved them. They knew the Lord was with them and the joy of the Lord burst forth in these songs in the night. "Who gives songs in the night" (Job 35:10). How this was verified in their case and what a testimony it was. Sufferings like theirs we know no longer; and alas! if some suffering is the lot of some Christians, or a little tribulation comes, there is often murmuring and doubting instead of rejoicing and praising the Lord.

And *suddenly* there came an answer. The Lord answered the prayers of his suffering servants by an earthquake. He intervened in their behalf in an extraordinary manner. Rationalism has tried either to make it appear as if this was a coincidence or ignored the earthquake completely.[11]

God shook the whole place when they were still praising Him. The doors were opened, the bonds of the prisoners were loosed, but the prison itself did not fall. This may be explained by the fact that this prison, like other Roman prisons consisted in excavations in a rocky hillside. The prisoners were chained to the walls and the cave cells were shut by wooden doors with heavy bolts. These burst open and the fetters of the prisoners dropped to the

---

[11] Renan in his work does not even mention the earthquake. Ernest Renan, *Saint Paul* (Paris, France: Calmann Lévy, 1888).

ground. The Lord set the prisoners free. But how many dungeons there have been since then with their uncountable victims with tortured limbs, parched tongues and feverish brow, prisoners who, too, like Paul and Silas, prayed and praised. But no answer came to deliver them. No earthquake opened the doors; they died the death of martyrs-and heaven was silent to their pleas: After God's Revelation is completed the heavens are silent, and God expects man to believe his Word. A day is coming when once more there will be intervention from above in the affairs of this world.

The jailer was awakened by the shock and was ready to kill himself, seeing that his prisoners had been liberated, for he was responsible, according to the Roman law, with his life for the prisoners. But Paul's loud cry "Do not harm yourself, for we are all here" kept him from piercing himself with his own sword. Satan would have rushed the jailer into eternity by suicide; but God had something else for the poor Roman heathen.

> And the jailer[12] called for lights and rushed in, and trembling with fear he fell down before Paul and Silas. Then he brought them out and said, "Sirs, what must I do to be saved?" And they said, "Believe in the Lord Jesus, and you will be saved, you and your household." And they spoke the word of the Lord to him and to all who were in his house. And he took them the same hour of the night and washed their wounds; and he was baptized at once, he and all his family. Then he brought them up into his house and set food before them. And he rejoiced along with his entire household that he had believed in God.
>
> But when it was day, the magistrates sent the police, saying, "Let those men go." And the jailer reported these words to Paul, saying, "The magistrates have sent to let you go. Therefore come out now and go in peace." But Paul said to them, "They have beaten us publicly, uncondemned, men who are Roman citizens, and have thrown us into prison; and do they now throw us out secretly? No! Let them come themselves and take us out." The police reported these words to the magistrates, and they were afraid when they heard that they were Roman citizens. So they came and apologized to them. And they took them out and asked them to leave the city. So they went out of the prison and visited Lydia. And when they had seen the brothers, they encouraged them and departed. (vs. 29–40).

The sudden event, the fact that the prisoners had not escaped, the assurance from Paul that they were all there, and perhaps the singing and the prayers of the Apostles, which he may have heard, all carried conviction to his soul. We see him at the Apostle's feet a trophy of God's Grace, a witness to the power of God and an evidence that the wrath of the enemy must praise Him. "Sirs, what must I do to be saved?" was the all important question which concerns him now more than the few prisoners or even his own physical life. The Grace of God had changed the poor jailer into a thoroughly awakened soul. The answer to the anxious soul is not slow in coming, "Believe in the Lord Jesus, and you will be saved, you and your household." And upon this they spake to him the Word of God, the story of Christ, the blessed Gospel of trusting on him who died on the cross. Only believing, nothing to do, for God had done it all in his own Son. This is the Gospel of Grace, that a free and full salvation is given to the sinner in simply believing on the Lord Jesus Christ. It is the same way of salvation to-day as it was then. Everyone who denies and rejects it has no hope and is a lost soul.[13]

---

[12] Greek *he*

[13] And how God's way of salvation is rejected in these days is frightful. Salvation by character, a bloodless Gospel is the present day substitute. Thus a certain preacher taught some months ago in a popular monthly "Salvation is not an instantaneous act whereby the sinner is assured of deliverance from hell

And the promise was not only to the jailer, but also to his house. This is a blessed truth alas! too often overlooked by Christian parents or ignored through false teaching. The promise of course is conditional. No one can be saved except by personal faith in a personal Saviour. The Christian home stands for much according to New Testament. The husband is to love his wife even as Christ also loved the Church, and gave Himself for it, so that the husband represents Christ. The wife is to submit under the husband, as the church is subject to the Lord, and the children are to obey the parents in the Lord (Eph 5:22–33; 6:1). The exhortation is given to the fathers, "bring them up in the discipline and instruction of the Lord" (Eph 6:4). We can bring our children to the Lord and as we bring them up according to divine instruction we have full assurance that they shall be saved.

Not alone did the jailer hear the Word of the Lord, but also all that were in his house, which no doubt meant his household, wife and children and all who belonged to him. And after he had washed their stripes he and all his were baptized straightway. There was no delay with water baptism.

In washing their stripes and welcoming Paul and Silas to his home, setting meat before them, the jailer showed the works which follow faith. And faith had brought joy to his heart. He rejoiced, believing in God with all his house.

The morning brought an order from the magistrates that these men should be dismissed. But Paul now demands to be heard. These magistrates ha d dealt in an unjust manner and they had to acknowledge their fault as well as the rights of the Gospel. He demanded that they come themselves and fetch them out of prison, inasmuch as they had beaten them uncondemned, and the men whom they had treated in this way were Romans. When the magistrates heard the message they feared. According to Cicero, to bind a Roman was a crime, to scourge him a scandal, to kill him a homicide. It was one of the most valued privileges of Roman citizenship, this immunity from corporal punishment. The cry *civis Romanus sum* (I am a Roman citizen) brought even among Barbarians help and safety. They came therefore out to the prison and besought them, desiring that they should depart out of the city. In this action they acknowledged the wrong they had done. But they were not in a hurry to leave. They first entered the house of Lydia and saw the brethren, whom they comforted. Then they departed. Luke stayed behind in Philippi. The blessed fruit of the ministry of Paul and Silas formed the beginning of the first assembly in Europe, to which later from Rome the Apostle addressed that precious Epistle of Christian life and experience.

---

and enjoyment of heaven, but a lifelong process." Such a statement sweeps the entire Gospel away.

Chapter Seventeen

Three cities in which the Gospel is next preached are before us in this chapter. But there is a marked difference between these three places. In Thessalonica there was much hostility, the result of the success of the Gospel. In Berea a more noble class of Jews were found. Their nobility consisted in submission to the Scriptures, the oracles of God, and in a ready mind. There was a still greater blessing among the Jews and the Gentiles. In Athens the Apostle Paul met idolatry, indifference and ridicule.

    1. The Gospel in Thessalonica (vs. 1–9).

    2. The Gospel in Berea (vs. 10–15).

    3. Paul in Athens (vs. 16–34).

1. The Gospel in Thessalonica (vs. 1–9).

> Now when they had passed through Amphipolis and Apollonia, they came to Thessalonica, where there was a synagogue of the Jews. And Paul went in, as was his custom, and on three Sabbath days he reasoned with them from the Scriptures, explaining and proving that it was necessary for the Christ to suffer and to rise from the dead, and saying, "This Jesus, whom I proclaim to you, is the Christ." And some of them were persuaded and joined Paul and Silas, as did a great many of the devout Greeks and not a few of the leading women. But the Jews[1] were jealous, and taking some wicked men of the rabble, they formed a mob, set the city in an uproar, and attacked the house of Jason, seeking to bring them out to the crowd. And when they could not find them, they dragged Jason and some of the brothers before the city authorities, shouting, "These men who have turned the world upside down have come here also, and Jason has received them, and they are all acting against the decrees of Caesar, saying that there is another king, Jesus." And the people and the city authorities were disturbed when they heard these things. And when they had taken money as security from Jason and the rest, they let them go. (vs. 1–9).

No record is given of work done on the way to Thessalonica. Under the guidance of the Holy Spirit the blessed messengers of the cross made for the influential capital of the province, knowing that they would find a goodly number of Jews there and a synagogue where they could preach. Thessalonica was one of the most influential cities in those days. Even to-day it is a city of almost 100,000 inhabitants and its ancient name is still to be traced in its present one, that is, Saloniki, the second largest city in European Turkey. It has an excellent location on the Aegean Sea and by a direct road, the Egnatian way, had communication with the capital of the Roman Empire. It was one of the free cities of the Empire and had its own constitution. This was democratic, its authority resting with the Demos, the people. The chief magistrates were called Politarchs, as we would call them now, city fathers or rulers. This word is used by Luke in verses 6 and 8. As it is not found at all in classical literature, certain Bible critics accused the writer of the Book of Acts of inaccuracy and impeached

---

[1] Greek *Ioudaioi* probably refers here to Jewish religious leaders, and others under their influence, in that time; also verse 13.

26. Politarch inscription from the gateway in Thessalonica now displayed in the British Museum (BM Inscriptions 171). Older English versions obscure Luke's accuracy in using this specific term by tranlating it "Rulers of the city" (AV) and "City authorities" (RSV).

in this way the inspiration of the book. But like all other criticism, this charge has come back upon the critics. There is in the British Museum to-day a stone block in which the word "Politarch" is chiseled (see Fig 26). The stone was taken from a triumphal arch, which stood in Thessalonica in the first century and which was preserved till 1867, when it was destroyed. The one stone block containing an inscription was transferred to the famous British Museum. The inscription is translated as follows:

> The Politarchs being Sopater, son of Cleopatra, and Lucius Pontius Secundus, Aulus Arius Sabinus, Demetrius son of Faustus, Demetrius son of Nicopolis, Foilus son of Parmenio also called Meniscus, Caius Agilleius Potitus.[2]

It is intensely interesting to find that some of these names are mentioned in Acts 20:4.

In this city the missionaries entered, and Paul at once sought out the synagogue. This was his custom. For three Sabbath days, or, as the margin has it, weeks, he ministered the Word to the Jews. And now we have before us a very interesting record.

> he reasoned with them from the Scriptures, explaining and proving that it was necessary for the Christ to suffer and to rise from the dead, and saying, "This Jesus, whom I proclaim to you, is the Christ" (17:2–3).

---

[2] On the Politarch Inscription see Graves, *Biblical Archaeology Vol 1: An Introduction*, 1:214.

From this we may learn important lessons. His mode of approaching the Jews here as well as elsewhere was not in a regular discourse in the form of a sermon or a lecture. It was just a converse, a discussion permitting questions and giving answers. It was teaching in a conversational way and the Scriptures were the foundation of it. Of course, the Old Testament is meant by the name Scriptures, for the New Testament Scriptures were not yet in existence. Such reasonings suited the Jewish mind well. It is still the best way in which to approach the Jew with the Gospel. The method which Paul followed is by far the best. He opened the Scriptures. The Law, the Prophets and the Writings [3] were opened by him in reference to the Messiah, whom God had promised to them. He quoted the great Messianic prophecies. He must have turned to the Psalms and opened that blessed book in its many predictions. No doubt the different types as given in the tabernacle and its worship, the sacrifices and offerings, the Passover and deliverance out of Egypt, the brazen serpent and other events were rehearsed by him. But the argument and reasoning was altogether on the Person of the Messiah. He showed that the Scriptures teach that the promised Christ had to suffer and to die and rise again from the dead. Then after he had established this fact, independent of who that promised Messiah is, he pressed home another fact, namely, that Jesus whom he preached is that Christ. How powerful this reasoning must have been and under the Holy Spirit; it brought conviction to their hearts. Some believed. But the greater success was among the devout Greeks, such as had abandoned idolatry, who were attendants at the

---

[3] The Old Testament in Hebrew is divided into three parts. *Torah*, the Law; *Nevijm*, the Prophets; *Kethuvim*, the Writings - such as Proverbs, Psalms, Job, etc.

27. The imperial family at the sacrifice of thanksgiving, depicted on the Arch of Galerius in Thessalonica. The faces have been chiselled off possibly as a *damnatio memoriae*.

synagogue. A great multitude with many of the chief women believed. But many of these Greeks, as we learn from the Epistle to the Thessalonians, were converted directly from idolatry (see Fig. 27), "how you turned to God from idols to serve the living and true God" (1 Thess 1:9).

As servants the Apostle and his companions had perfect liberty to enter these synagogues to deliver the message. This liberty still belongs to all who are servants of the Lord Jesus Christ. The servants at Christ have perfect freedom to go wherever the Lord opens a door to preach the Gospel.[4]

Another interesting fact is learned concerning the activity of the apostle in Thessalonica from the two Epistles, which he addressed some time after to the Thessalonians. These were the first Epistles Paul wrote. From these we learn that the Apostle not only preached the Gospel, but also taught the Thessalonian believers prophetic Truths and emphasized the Second Coming of Christ and the events connected with it. In the Second Epistle he reminds them of his oral teaching. "Do you not remember that when I was still with you I told you these things?" (2 Thess 2:5). He told them that they were to wait for his Son from heaven (1 Thess 1:10); that there would be the falling away first and the man of sin be revealed before the day of the Lord could come (2 Thess 2:3–7) as well as other truths. He did therefore not think, as it is said so often in our days, that dispensational truths were too deep for these new converts and babes in Christ. Nothing in God's Word is too deep for those who are born again and are indwelt by the Holy Spirit. This apostolic method is absolutely necessary to open up the Truth of God and lead newborn saints into it. One of the reasons of present day conditions among those who are no doubt saved, is the lack of dispensational teachings, which the Apostle Paul had so closely linked with the preaching of the Gospel in Thessalonica.

But the enemy was soon aroused in the city. Once more the acts of the enemy through the unbelieving Jews are recorded. He resorts to the same tactics as at Philippi to stir up the mob of the city. The rabble stormed the house of Jason, where the Apostle and Silas lodged. Their intention was to drag the two before the people. Failing to find these, they drew Jason and some other brethren before the Politarchs. Then the usual tumult ensued and the accusation was shouted out:

> These men who have turned the world upside down have come here also, and Jason has received them, and they are all acting against the decrees of Caesar, saying that there is another king, Jesus (17:6-7).

The enemy gave a testimony in this accusation to the power and influence of Christianity. The accusation that they opposed Caesar's decrees and claiming that another is King, namely Jesus, must have sprung from the fact that the dispensational

---

[4] We emphasize this because there are some ultra separationists who form little sects, claiming to be the church. They forbid their preachers and teachers to enter church buildings of the different denominations and have even put some out of their fellowship because they preach the Gospel in a church.

teaching Paul gave had reached the people in a distorted way. Persecution set in, and from the Epistles to the Thessalonians we learn that the church there had much tribulation. So severe became the troubles that the Thessalonians were greatly disturbed when false teachers spread the report that they were facing the great tribulation. To set their minds at rest on this question the apostle wrote his second Epistle. The rulers here took security of Jason and the others and then let them go.

2. THE GOSPEL IN BEREA (VS. 10–15).

> The brothers [5] immediately sent Paul and Silas away by night to Berea, and when they arrived they went into the Jewish synagogue. Now these Jews were more noble than those in Thessalonica; they received the word with all eagerness, examining the Scriptures daily to see if these things were so. Many of them therefore believed, with not a few Greek women of high standing as well as men. But when the Jews from Thessalonica learned that the word of God was proclaimed by Paul at Berea also, they came there too, agitating and stirring up the crowds. Then the brothers immediately sent Paul off on his way to the sea, but Silas and Timothy remained there. Those who conducted Paul brought him as far as Athens, and after receiving a command for Silas and Timothy to come to him as soon as possible, they departed. (vs. 10–15).

Paul and Silas were immediately sent away by night. What had become of Timothy? he is not at all mentioned in connection with this visit to Thessalonica nor do we hear anything from him since he joined Paul and Silas at Lystra. However from this we must not conclude that he had left them. There is sufficient evidence that he was with them in Thessalonica. Both Epistles to the Thessalonians are from Paul and Sylvanus and Timothy (1 Thess 1:1; 2 Thess 2:1). This is conclusive evidence that he was with Paul and Silas. (Silas is the same as

---

[5] Or *brothers and sisters*; also verse 14.

Silvanus). From these Epistles is also gained the information that Paul and most likely also his companions worked with their own hands (1 Thess 2:9; 2 Thess 3:8). And now we find them in the City of Berea, some 40 miles from Thessalonica. This city had a magnificent situation at the foot of a mountain range. It is still a good sized city, known by the name of Verna. As soon as they arrived in the city, they went to the synagogue and here they found evidently prepared ground. The Jews they found are described as "more noble than those in Thessalonica" (17:10). The word noble does not mean, as some have said, a kind of aristocracy, but it consisted in a ready mind to receive and test by the Scriptures what the messengers of the Lord had to say. They searched the Scriptures daily, whether those things were so. They were anxious to know the truth and in searching the Word they compared Scripture with Scripture. Alas! How little of this readiness of mind and searching the Scriptures one finds among the modern Jews. Many have rejected their own Scriptures and the orthodox Jews are sadly ignorant of the oracles of God, while the Talmudical sayings, the oral traditions of the elders and the paraphrases have worked told mischief. Only when the judicial blindness which rests upon them will be removed, the veil which is upon their hearts (2 Cor 3:13–15) will they see him of whom Moses and the Prophets spake. But the neglect of the Bible is as marked, if not greater, in nominal Christendom. May we search the Scriptures daily.

Therefore, because they had a ready mind and searched the Scriptures, many believed. And to the Berean assembly there were also added Gentiles "not a few Greek women of high standing as well as men" (17:12).

Satan, however, knows no rest. When an effectual door is opened, then the adversaries begin. News of Paul and Silas preaching in Berea reached Thessalonica and Satan brought his willing instruments, the unbelieving Jews, to Berea to stir up the people. It was thought best by the brethren, no doubt after prayer and direction from the Lord, to send Paul away. Silas and Timothy remained there.

3. Paul in Athens (vs. 16–21).

> Now while Paul was waiting for them at Athens, his spirit was provoked within him as he saw that the city was full of idols. So he reasoned in the synagogue with the Jews and the devout persons, and in the marketplace every day with those who happened to be there. Some of the Epicurean and Stoic philosophers also conversed with him. And some said, "What does this babbler wish to say?" Others said, "He seems to be a preacher of foreign divinities"—because he was preaching Jesus and the resurrection. And they took him and brought him to the Areopagus, saying, "May we know what this new teaching is that you are presenting? For you bring some strange things to our ears. We wish to know therefore what these things mean." Now all the Athenians and the foreigners who lived there would spend their time in nothing except telling or hearing something new. (vs. 16–21).

The exact route which Paul took is uncertain. Some of the noble brethren of Berea conducted him, showing thereby their courtesy as well as love for the servant of the Lord Jesus Christ. When they parted the Apostle sent through them a message to Silas and Timothy to come to him with all speed. And now we behold our great Apostle in the wonderful city of Athens, the capital of Greece. Well has Rackham said:

> Paul at Athens, Paul the Jew of Tarsus in the city of Pericles and Demosthenes, of Sophocles and Euripides, of Socrates and Plato that is a situation to which our pen cannot attempt to do justice: Nor is it less difficult adequately to estimate the place of Athens in the Roman Empire. For at this date Athens was still the intellectual and artistic capital of the world. It was also a religious capital, for it was the stronghold of the Greek mythology, which was generally accepted as the most authentic account of the gods and their history.[6]

What a great city it must have been! What splendor in art and architecture the eyes of the apostle must have beheld! Here the great masterpieces of the greatest masters in architecture and sculpture were to be seen. And then the memories of the past and the great philosophical leaders and their different schools.

Socrates, Plato and Aristotle had moved and taught in this city and the proud Athenians had erected upon their philosophies different schools. It was furthermore a great religious city, full of idols. Xenophon said of Athens: "The whole of it is one great altar, one sacrifice and votive offering to the gods."[7] One artist tried to outdo the other with filling streets and temples with idol statues. But at the same time this great city was on the road to degeneracy. The Athenians lived on the glories of the past, both in art and philosophy. Of this verse 21 bears a striking witness.

Paul in walking through the streets of the city and seeing it wholly given to idolatry was very much stirred in him; he was provoked. He did not halt to examine the temples and great masterworks. Behind the much praised masterpieces he beheld the corruption and wickedness of the human heart.

Not alone was his own spirit provoked in him, but the Holy Spirit stirred him to witness against it. In the synagogues, first of all, he disputed with the Jews and the devout persons, Greeks who had turned away from idols, and in the market daily, he spoke with those that met him. The market

---

[6] Rackham, *The Acts of the Apostles*, 301.

[7] Rackham states quoted by Wetstein from Xenophon; but I have been unable to verify the quotation. Ibid., 302.

28. View of Athens (Attica, Greece) from Acropolis hill – Stoa of Athens where Paul likely stood before the Areopagus (city coucil) who were in charge of admission of new deities into the Athenian pantheon.

was the *Agora*, an open square in the heart of the city. On its sides stood the public buildings what we would call City Hall, courthouses and the temples of different gods. Here also numerous shops were found, and, like in our country towns it was the place of buying and selling, for the people from the country came in with their wares. When business hours were over then the gossipers began. It was the place where new opinions were expounded, where philosophers and traveling orators found a ready audience. From classical literature we learn, that Socrates 450 years before moved in this very place and spoke to individuals and by severe questionings tried to destroy their self confidence and explain his philosophy. But in Paul a greater than Socrates was moving around the Agora, questioning and reasoning with all who would listen. Soon he came across some Epicureans and Stoics. The Epicureans were Materialists. They believed in a certain sense in gods, but held in their belief something like the atomic theory of present day science. They denied a life after death. The Stoics held a belief in a supreme being. They believed that in the Universe there existed an omnipresent spirit and of this spirit the human spirit was a part. The modern Pantheism was their creed. Yet they were religious. But they were extremely self-righteous and proud. The Stoics were much like the Pharisees, while the Epicureans represent the Sadducees of Judaism. With some of these philosophers the Apostle met. As they listened to him they termed him a babbler.[8] Others were more serious and charged him with being a setter forth of strange gods. For this very thing Socrates had been put to death. But we are not left in ignorance of what Paul preached. He knew but one theme, Jesus and the resurrection.

So one day they took hold on him and brought him to Areopagus (see Fig. 28, 29). The Areopagus was a court corresponding to the Roman Senate. Here he had a representative audience of philosophers, leading citizens and a large number of the gossipers, the folks who spent their time in nothing else, but either to tell or to hear some new thing. Here was their opportunity. Standing before the Athenian Court Areopagus (see Fig. 14, 15) he is told in a polite way to defend himself of the accusation made against him. "May we know what this new teaching is that you are presenting? For you bring some strange things to our ears. We wish to know therefore what these things mean" (17:21).

> So Paul, standing in the midst of the Areopagus, said: "Men of Athens, I perceive that in every way you are very religious. For as I passed along and observed the objects of your worship, I found also an altar with this inscription, 'To the unknown god.' What therefore you worship as unknown, this I proclaim to you. The God who made the world and everything in it, being Lord of heaven and earth, does not live in temples

---

[8] The Greek word is *Spermalogos*, translated, a seed picker. It was a slang word used to describe the people who frequented the Agora and picked up, like birds, a little here and there.

made by man,[9] nor is he served by human hands, as though he needed anything, since he himself gives to all mankind life and breath and everything. And he made from one man every nation of mankind to live on all the face of the earth, having determined allotted periods and the boundaries of their dwelling place, that they should seek God, and perhaps feel their way toward him and find him. Yet he is actually not far from each one of us, for:

"'In him we live and move and have our being';[10] as even some of your own poets have said, "'For we are indeed his offspring.'"[11]

Being then God's offspring, we ought not to think that the divine being is like gold or silver or stone, an image formed by the art and imagination of man. The times of ignorance God overlooked, but now he commands all people everywhere to repent, because he has fixed a day on which he will judge the world in righteousness by a man whom he has appointed; and of this he has given assurance to all by raising him from the dead."

Now when they heard of the resurrection of the dead, some mocked. But others said, "We will hear you again about this." So Paul went out from their midst. But some men joined him and believed, among whom also were Dionysius the Areopagite and a woman named Damaris and others with them. (vs. 22–34).

The address of the great apostle is one of unusual tact and wisdom. If he became to the Jews as a Jew, here he becomes to the Grecian philosophers as a philosopher. He makes use of both the Epicureal and Stoic philosophy as far as he can and avoids as much as possible what might stumble them. He starts with the belief in God as the omnipresent and immanent Creator, the Ruler and Keeper of the Universe. This he could back up by quotations from their own poets. After this ground work he speaks of judgment to come, and introduced him who is the Judge, and the fact of his resurrection.

Let us examine this discourse in its different parts. It has three parts:

1. The Introduction (vs. 22–23).

2. Who the Unknown God Is (vs. 24–29).

3. The Message From God (vs. 30–31).

The Introduction (vs. 22–23).

He addressed them by the usual phrase, "Men of Athens." The charge he brings against them is not superstition. What he said was that the Athenians were a very religious people, given to the worship of many deities. It was a wise statement. It would be well if some Gospel preachers would profit by it. In preaching the Gospel to Romanists or to the Jews one does well not to antagonize their customs, but to avoid such controversies. Paul had found in Athens an altar with a strange inscription, "to the unknown god."[12] How this altar came to be in Athens is not known. It certainly bore witness to the fact that the true God was an unknown God to the Athenians. In this fact the Apostle found the true starting point. The human heart can set up gods and altars, beginning with the likeness of man, then of birds, quadrupeds and reptiles (Rom 1:22), but the true God the human heart with its vain reasonings cannot discover. He can only be known from revelation. And Paul is now in the presence of this illustrious audience to make known the unknown God. "What therefore you worship as unknown, this I proclaim to you" (17:23).

Who the Unknown God Is (vs. 24–29).

He unfolds the truth of God as a Person. He is a personal God and as such he made the world and all things therein. This truth was not owned by the Epicureans or the Stoics. The Epicureans with their atomic

---

[9] Greek *made by hands*
[10] Probably from Epimenides of Crete.
[11] From Aratus's poem "Phainomena."

[12] Other ancient authorities speak of the existence of such altars in Athena. For instance, Philostratus and Lucian.

theory, that the universe came together by itself, and the Stoics with their cold Pantheism denied this fundamental truth. This bold announcement effectively set aside the philosophical babblings of these wise men, and these few words completely answer the modern Materialists and Pantheists. With the next sentence Paul lays bare the follies of paganism. As Lord of heaven and earth, because he is the Creator, he does not dwell in temples made with hands, nor can he be worshipped with men's hands as though he needed anything. In this statement he leaned towards the expressions used by the Epicureans, who declared that the divine nature is self sufficiency and needs nothing from us. But at the same time he rebukes the Stoics by showing that God giveth to all life, and breath and all things. He is the Preserver as well as the Creator. Next Paul shows that God created man and that all nations of men are made by him of one blood. This was not believed in paganism. Polytheism was closely connected with the conception that the different races came into existence in different ways. The various races therefore had different racial gods. The Greeks had divided the world into two classes, Greeks and Barbarians. That they, the proud Greeks, had sprung from the same stock as the Barbarians must have humbled them greatly. It rebuked their national pride. All the Apostle said to the cultured Greeks, the great philosophers was elementary. The most simple truth about God and the origin of man could not be discovered by the keenest intellect. How all this bears out the divine statement in Romans:

> For although they knew God, they did not honor him as God or give thanks to him, but they became futile in their thinking [reasonings], and their foolish [senseless] hearts were darkened. Claiming to be wise [philosophers], they became fools (Rom 1:21–22).

29. Mars Hill or Hill of Ares (Areopagus), Athens, Greece.

And furthermore Paul states that God is the governor over the nations. He has set the bounds of their habitations. The creature is to seek after the Lord, if haply they might feel after him and find Him, though he be not far from everyone of us. All this, and that in him we live and move and have our being, is in connection with God as Creator, that he is the giver of life and breath and all things. The creature is sustained by Him. Then in connection with this he quotes from their own poets. "As even some of your own poets have said, 'For we are indeed his offspring'" (17:28). Two Greek poets had spoken thus, Cleanthus and Aratus. Aratus was a Stoic. Thus he used the expressions of their own poets against themselves. These poets had more wisdom than the philosophers. In quoting this sentence from the poets Paul presses home the truth that man in his nature is the creation of God, created in the image of God. But where has man drifted to? Idolatry in its wicked foolishness is exposed. The Godhead has been made like to gold, or silver, or stone, graven by art and man's device. It uncovered the miserable folly into which their reasonings had led them. How significant that in cultured Athens the great Apostle had to come down to the most elementary things of the truth.

The Message From God (vs. 30–31).

Their sin of idolatry had been uncovered and now the apostle brings a message to their hearts. He calls the times of their boasted philosophies and progress "the times of ignorance," and assures them that God has overlooked it, passed it by. But now he calls to repentance.

he aims at their conscience to awaken them to the sense of need to turn away from idols to the true God. God sends to all one message, be they Jew or Gentiles, Greeks or Barbarians, to repent. And then he states the reason. A day is appointed in which he will judge the world in righteousness. The one through whom God will judge is a Man ordained by Him; then follows the declaration of the resurrection of this Man. The day of judgment here does not mean a universal judgment (a term not known in Scripture) nor the great white throne judgment. The judgment here does not concern the dead at all, but it is the judgment of the habitable world. It is the judgment which will take place when the Man whom God raised from the dead, our Lord Jesus Christ comes the second time. His resurrection is the assurance of it.

But why did the apostle not press home the Gospel and speak of the forgiveness of sins? They were not ready for this. He talked to them as philosophers to stir up their consciences.

As soon as they heard of the resurrection of the dead, it was enough for most of them. Some began to mock. They plainly proved that they were far from the condition to hear more of salvation. Others said, as Felix said later, We will hear thee again of this matter. But even this testimony was not in vain. Some clave to him and believed. No doubt he took these apart and instructed them in God's way of salvation. Among them is mentioned a member of the Areopagus, Dionysius, the Areopagite. Tradition says that he became the leader of the Athenian Assembly.

Chapter Eighteen

From Athens Paul journeyed to Corinth. This was the capital of Achaia and a short distance from Athens. It was a different city altogether. Corinth was then a great commercial center and had a cosmopolitan character. Here the Apostle settled down for one year and six months and Silas and Timothy joined him here. It was one of the most immoral cities then in existence. The grossest immoralities were here practiced in connection with religion. In different ways this chapter is an interesting one. Besides working at his trade as tentmaker and preaching the Gospel, he wrote by inspiration in Corinth the two Epistles to the Thessalonians and the Epistle to the Romans.

1. In Corinth with Aquila and Priscilla. His testimony and separation from the Jews (vs. 1–8).

2. Encouragement from the Lord in a vision (vs. 9–11).

3. Paul and Gallio (vs. 12–17).

4. From Corinth to Ephesus and Antioch. The second journey ended (vs. 18–22).

5. Establishing disciples in Galatia and Phrygia (v. 23).

6. Apollos, the Alexandrian (vs. 24–28).

1. Paul in Corinth with Aquila and Priscilla (vs. 1–8).

After this Paul[1] left Athens and went to Corinth.

---

[1] Greek *he*

And he found a Jew named Aquila, a native of Pontus, recently come from Italy with his wife Priscilla, because Claudius had commanded all the Jews to leave Rome. And he went to see them, and because he was of the same trade he stayed with them and worked, for they were tentmakers by trade. And he reasoned in the synagogue every Sabbath, and tried to persuade Jews and Greeks.

When Silas and Timothy arrived from Macedonia, Paul was occupied with the word, testifying to the Jews that the Christ was Jesus. And when they opposed and reviled him, he shook out his garments and said to them, "Your blood be on your own heads! I am innocent. From now on I will go to the Gentiles." And he left there and went to the house of a man named Titius Justus, a worshiper of God. His house was next door to the synagogue. Crispus, the ruler of the synagogue, believed in the Lord, together with his entire household. And many of the Corinthians hearing Paul believed and were baptized. (vs. 1–8).

For the first time Aquila and his wife Priscilla are now mentioned. They appear as prominent characters in the Epistles. Paul was guided to them and abode with them, for like himself, they were tent-makers, an occupation which reminds one of the pilgrim character of the child of God. Aquila was a native of Pontus, who had settled in Rome. Both he and his wife Priscilla may have been believers, when Paul met them, though the record speaks of him as a Jew. If they had become believers as a result of becoming acquainted with the Apostle the record of this fact would have appeared in this chapter. Perhaps they had heard and believed the Gospel in Rome. A persecution against the Jewish race had

30. Synagogue inscription displayed in the Archaeological Museum of Ancient Corinth (ID 123).

broken out in Rome and they with many others were banished from the city. Rome hated the Jews, many of whom had settled in the city. Tiberius had sent some 4000 Roman Jews into an unhealthy country, in hope that the fever there would destroy them, and Claudius in the year 49 had banished them entirely from the capital of the Roman Empire. The Roman biographer and historian Suetonius [2] in his life of Claudius gives the reason for the harsh edict of the Emperor Claudius because "since the Jews constantly made disturbances at the instigation of Chrestus" (*Cl.* 5.25.4 [Rolfe]). The word "Chrestus" means undoubtedly "Christos," that is Christ.

This interesting couple had established themselves in Corinth, and what a joy it must have been to the Apostle when he was led to their home. How sweet their fellowship must have been as they toiled together and spoke one to another about the Lord! From the same chapter we learn that after Paul's ministry had terminated they went to Ephesus (v. 19). From First Corinthians 16:19 we learn that they were still there when that Epistle was written. But in writing to the Romans Paul says, "greet Prisca and Aquila, my fellow workers in Christ Jesus" (Rom 16:3), so that they had wandered back to Rome and were in happy fellowship with the Roman assembly. Second Timothy 4:19 tells us that once more they were back in Ephesus where Timothy had his abode. "Greet Prisca and Aquila, my fellow workers in Christ Jesus" (Rom 16:3). They were indeed strangers and pilgrims, but blessed to know that their wanderings were directed by the Lord. Priscilla is mostly mentioned before Aquila, from which we may learn that she, like other notable women of apostolic days, "fellow workers in Christ Jesus."

It is significant that here it is prominently mentioned that the Apostle worked at his trade as tentmaker. He had also done so in Thessalonica.

> For you remember, brothers, our labor and toil: we worked night and day, that we might not be a burden to any of you, while we proclaimed to you the gospel of God (1 Thess 2:9; 2 Thess 3:8).

He labored at Ephesus. "You yourselves know that these hands ministered to my necessities and to those who were with me" (Acts 20:34). From this we learn that he also supported his fellow helpers. Corinth was a wealthy city. He did not take anything whatever from the Corinthians, of which he reminds them in both of his Epistles. In this way he illustrated most blessedly the gift of God, the Gospel, without money and without price. What a contrast with the trafficking in spiritual things we behold about us in our days! And yet it is equally true that the Lord has ordained "that those who proclaim the gospel should get their living by the gospel" (1 Cor 9:14).

It seems that Paul followed the same method of work as he did in Thessalonica. First, he reasoned in the synagogue every Sabbath and persuaded the Jews and the Greeks (v. 4). This must have been altogether on Old Testament ground, showing the divine predictions concerning Christ. When Silas and Timothy arrived, then he was greatly pressed in spirit and testified to the Jews more fully that Jesus is the Christ. That there was blessed fruit we

---

[2] he lived during the reign of Hadrian in the beginning of the second century.

learn from his Epistles to the Corinthians. He himself baptized Crispus and Gaius and the household of Stephanas (1 Cor 1:14–16). And he was with them in weakness, and in fear, and in much trembling. His speech was far different from the one he had used in addressing the philosophers of Athens.

> And I was with you in weakness and in fear and much trembling, and my speech and my message were not in plausible words of wisdom, but in demonstration of the Spirit and of power (1 Cor 2:3–4).

His presence was humble to them. "I who am humble when face to face with you (2 Cor 10:1). His bodily presence, these Corinthians said, is weak, and his speech contemptible (2 Cor 10:10). It is possible that he was greatly depressed. Silas and Timothy brought him good news from the Thessalonians:

> But now that Timothy has come to us from you, and has brought us the good news of your faith and love and reported that you always remember us kindly and long to see us, as we long to see you—for this reason, brothers, in all our distress and affliction we have been comforted about you through your faith (1 Thess 3:6–7).

He must have written the first Epistle to the Thessalonians immediately after the arrival of Silas and Timothy. They also may have brought to Paul the fellowship from the saints in Philippi, which may have reached Thessalonica after Paul had left (Phil 4:15, 16). Opposition from the side of the Jews followed after the bold declaration that Jesus is the Christ. Not alone did they reject the Gospel but they blasphemed. Alas! this blaspheming is still heard among the Jews, whenever the full claims of the Lord Jesus Christ are pressed upon their consciences. For the second time Paul declares that he will go to the Gentiles.

Next we behold the Apostle of the Gentiles in the house of a devout Gentile named Justus. His house was next to the synagogue. Here the Lord's special blessing rested upon the testimony, for the chief ruler of the synagogue, Crispus, with his house, as well as many other Corinthians, believed on the Lord. His baptism as well as the others by the Apostle himself we have already mentioned.

2. ENCOURAGEMENT FROM THE LORD IN A VISION (VS. 9–11).

> And the Lord said to Paul one night in a vision, "Do not be afraid, but go on speaking and do not be silent, for I am with you, and no one will attack you to harm you, for I have many in this city who are my people." And he stayed a year and six months, teaching the word of God among them. (vs. 9–11).

It is blessed to see when this encouraging vision took place. Paul had been greatly depressed, and fear and trembling, as seen from the first Epistle to the Corinthians, had taken hold on him. The good news from Thessalonica had cheered him and the conversion of Crispus and the other Corinthians encouraged him much. But he needed a direct encouragement from the Lord. The Lord knew all which awaited his faithful servant. He knew of the plot to bring him before the judgment seat of the deputy of the province. The Lord wanted his servant to be without anxiety and assured him that no man could set on him or hurt him. He also told him that he had much people in Corinth. Perhaps if this vision had not been given to Paul at this time he might have been tempted to leave Corinth, but now he felt authorized to continue for a year and six months. A strong assembly was gathered. As we do not write on the Corinthian Epistles we cannot follow the most interesting theme of the condition of the Corinthian church. But the Epistles mention that the majority of believers were composed of the poorer class. Of another class were Crispus, the once chief ruler of the synagogue, Stephanas and Gaius, who were given to hospitality and therefore must have been people of means; Chloe, a lady who had many servants; Erastus, who held a responsible position, and others. Then there were present diversities of gifts, the gift of tongues being prominent and responsible for certain disorders. After the Apostle had left, divisions came in and the leaven of vainglory and worldliness, even to immoralities, got in amongst them and did its dreadful work.

3. Paul and Gallio (vs. 12–17).

> But when Gallio was proconsul of Achaia, the Jews[3] made a united attack on Paul and brought him before the tribunal, saying, "This man is persuading people to worship God contrary to the law." But when Paul was about to open his mouth, Gallio said to the Jews, "If it were a matter of wrongdoing or vicious crime, O Jews, I would have reason to accept your complaint. But since it is a matter of questions about words and names and your own law, see to it yourselves. I refuse to be a judge of these things." And he drove them from the tribunal. And they all seized Sosthenes, the ruler of the synagogue, and beat him in front of the tribunal. But Gallio paid no attention to any of this (vs. 12–17).

Gallio was deputy, or proconsul of Achaia This proves the accuracy of the record before us. Achaia up to the year 44 was united to the province of Macedonia. But the Emperor Claudius restored Achaia as a province and it had then its own proconsul. We know from Roman historians a good deal of the personality of Gallio.

> he came from a Spanish family which had won for itself a distinguished place in Roman letters and society. Annaeus Seneca, his father, was a well known rhetorician, Seneca the Stoic and tutor of Nero was his brother, and the poet Lucan his nephew. His own name was originally M. Annaeus Novatus, but having been adopted by Lucius Junius Gallio he also adopted his name. He had attained the highest office in the state, the consulship. But he was best known by his amiable

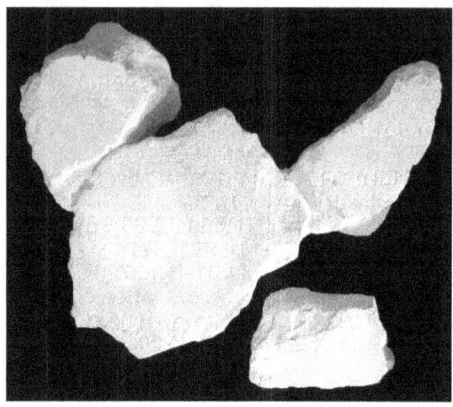

31. The Gallio inscription from the Temple of Apollo in Delphi, Greece.

character; "sweet Gallio," Statius calls him, and Seneca speaks of him "as one who could not be loved enough. (Pliny *Nat.* 31:33; See fig. 3).[4]

Before this man the Jews brought Paul, accusing him that he persuades men to worship God contrary to law. The Satanic attempt, however, laid not so much in the accusation as in the insurrection these Jews made. The whole Jewish community was stirred up by them to impress Gallio with the seriousness of the offence. And the accusation itself was couched in deceptive terms. It reads as if Paul had done something against the Roman law. This is exactly what they meant to do, namely, to constitute the Apostle a transgressor of the law of the Roman Empire. But Gallio was too keen for them. He at once recognized the deception. It was their own Jewish law about which they were disturbed. So without even listening to Paul, what he had to say for himself, he settled the case at once by a few well chosen words and then drove them out of the court. Then the Greeks who had witnessed the whole scene turned against the Jews. They had their spokesman in Sosthenes, the chief ruler of

---

[3] Greek *Ioudaioi* probably refers here to Jewish religious leaders, and others under their influence, in that time; also verses 14 (twice), 28.

[4] On the Gallio Inscription see Graves, *Biblical Archaeology Vol 1: An Introduction*, 1:215–16.

32. The *bema* or platform in the agora of Corinth. This is where Gallio, the Roman proconsul of Achaia, accused Paul in Acts 18 and dates to AD 44.

the synagogue. He must have taken the place of Crispus, who had believed on the Lord. Upon him the Greeks fell and gave him a good beating. And Gallio had nothing to say to this. Sosthenes deserved all he got.

If the Sosthenes who is mentioned in the opening verse of the first Epistle of the Corinthians is the same, then he profited immensely by his experience. Paul addresses him as a brother. We believe he is the same person, for the Grace of God delights to take up such characters and show in them what Grace can do.

4. PAUL RETURNS TO ANTIOCH: THE SECOND JOURNEY ENDED (VS. 18–22).

> After this, Paul stayed many days longer and then took leave of the brothers[5] and set sail for Syria, and with him Priscilla and Aquila. At Cenchreae he had cut his hair, for he was under a vow. And they came to Ephesus, and he left them there, but he himself went into the synagogue and reasoned with the Jews. When they asked him to stay for a longer period, he declined. But on taking leave of them he said, "I will return to you if God wills," and he set sail from Ephesus.
>
> When he had landed at Caesarea, he went up and greeted the church, and then went down to Antioch. (vs. 18–22).

---

[5] Or *brothers and sisters*; also verse 27

The great Apostle was not in a hurry to leave Corinth; he tarried there a good while. "Whoever believes will not be in haste" (Isa 28:16). When the Lord's own time arrived he took his leave of the brethren and sailed from the port of Corinth, Cenchrea, for Syria. The only companions mentioned are Priscilla and Aquila. The interesting item is the statement concerning the vow and the cutting of the hair. To whom does it refer? Did Aquila or Paul make the vow? Many able expositors believe that Aquila is meant, while others contend that it was Paul who had made the vow. Those who believe that Aquila is in view, call attention to the fact that the name of his wife Priscilla precedes his name and that in this way Aquila is marked out as the person who made the vow. But if the reader turns to Romans 16:3 and 2 Timothy 4:19, he will find that Priscilla is named first, so that this argument does not hold good. Inasmuch as the Apostle Paul is the prominent figure in the account, the statement must refer to him. Every vow made a visit to the temple in Jerusalem necessary (Num 11:1–21). But we learn that Aquila remained in Ephesus and did not go to Jerusalem. It is not necessary to charge The Apostle on account of this vow with an out and out violation of the great truths so fully taught in the Epistle to the Galatians. To the Jews he became as a Jew and under the law (1 Cor 9:19–23); and no doubt he made certain concessions in this direction. Some Christians seem to look upon the great Apostle as almost infallible in his actions and repudiate the thought that he could have made a mistake. The great Epistles he wrote *are* infallible, for the Holy Spirit is the author of them, but no such perfection can be claimed for his Christian life and walk. He too was "a man with a nature like ours" (Jam 5:17) and we shall find how faithfully and yet how tenderly the Holy Spirit reveals in the next chapters his actions in self will.

Ephesus, which was closed by divine authority (16:6) in the beginning of this journey, is now reached by the Apostle. It was a fine city known not only by its great commerce and as the capital of the Roman province Asia, but also by the great temple of Artemis. Models of this temple were made to be carried along for a charm or to be placed in houses (see 19:24). Ephesus had a very large Jewish population. They were wealthy and influential. The Jewish historian Josephus mentions the fact that the Roman government, as well as the citizens of Ephesus, accorded to them special privileges in the free observance of their customs. Paul soon entered the synagogue and reasoned with the Jews. The request to stay longer was denied by him. We surely see haste here instead of calmness and waiting on the Lord. Having not consented to remain, he bade them farewell, promising them to return, if it be God's will. The reason given for his haste was his desire to reach Jerusalem to keep this feast, which was Pentecost. Why he did not stay with such an opportunity and then telling the Jews of the absolute necessity of visiting Jerusalem is indeed strange. What follows reveals still greater haste with no record at all of what he did in Jerusalem or what was accomplished by him. He sailed from Ephesus, landed at Caesarea and went up, which means Jerusalem, he saluted the church and went down to Antioch. Thus ended the second missionary journey. Perhaps an intense love for his brethren in Jerusalem, his deep yearning for them, led him in this course.

5. Establishing disciples in Galatia and Phrygia (v. 23).

> After spending some time there, he departed and went from one place to the next through the region of Galatia and Phrygia, strengthening all the disciples. (v. 23).

This work was next laid upon his heart and with it the third journey began. The account is very brief but if we read the Epistle to the Galatians we can well understand how needful and important this work was. Judaizing teachers had invaded the churches which had been founded in large numbers. Their teaching was of the most pernicious kind. They taught the observance of the law and its works as being absolutely necessary for salvation. They perverted the Gospel of Grace and preached that Gospel which had the divine anathema upon it, because it sets aside that blessed finished work of Christ on the Cross.

> For if righteousness were through the law, then Christ died for no purpose (Gal 2:21). . . You are severed from Christ, you who would be justified by the law; you have fallen away from grace (Gal 5:4).

Their teaching was extremely bold, for they repeated the false teaching which had been brought before the council in Jerusalem, "Unless you are circumcised according to the custom of Moses, you cannot be saved" (Acts 15:1). At the same time they had impeached the apostolic authority of Paul. The Galatian Christians, who had been so loving and tender towards Paul, so that if it had been possible they would have plucked out their own eyes to give them to the apostle, the same people were now being moved against Paul and the Gospel he had preached to them. The Epistle to the Galatians was undoubtedly written during the Apostle's second visit to Ephesus and it shows that perhaps immediately after the recorded visit in this chapter the Judaizing element increased in strength. Most likely the news of the grave danger which was then threatening the Galatian churches had reached him in Antioch.

6. Apollos the Alexandrian (vs. 24–28).

> Now a Jew named Apollos, a native of Alexandria, came to Ephesus. He was an eloquent man, competent in the Scriptures. He had been

instructed in the way of the Lord. And being fervent in spirit,[6] he spoke and taught accurately the things concerning Jesus, though he knew only the baptism of John. He began to speak boldly in the synagogue, but when Priscilla and Aquila heard him, they took him aside and explained to him the way of God more accurately. And when he wished to cross to Achaia, the brothers encouraged him and wrote to the disciples to welcome him. When he arrived, he greatly helped those who through grace had believed, for he powerfully refuted the Jews in public, showing by the Scriptures that the Christ was Jesus. (vs. 24–28).

This is an extremely beautiful incident. A new preacher appeared among the Jews in Ephesus, Apollos the Alexandrian. He is described as an eloquent man and mighty in the Scriptures. In Alexandria, Philo, the great Hellenistic Jewish Philosopher, had flourished. He was born about 20 BC and died after the year 40 AD. He introduced Platonism into Judaism. In all probability Apollos was one of his disciples, but he accepted that which Philo did not believe. He had come most likely in touch with disciples of John the Baptist and had been baptized with John's baptism to repentance. He knew that Jesus is the Messiah, knew the facts of his earthly life and the miracles he did. Of the meaning of his death and resurrection Apollos knew nothing, nor had he any knowledge of the Holy Spirit. The entire truth of the Gospel of Grace was unknown to Him. He "spoke and taught accurately the things concerning Jesus" (18:25), that is, the things concerning Jesus. Yet this little knowledge he had concerning him who had appeared in the midst of his people, in whom he believed as the Messiah and King of Israel, set his soul on fire. With his great knowledge in the Scriptures, such as the learned Jews possess, he spoke boldly in the synagogue, proving, no doubt, from the Law and the Prophets, that Jesus is the Messiah. Yet how limited was his message. What difficulties must have arisen in his mind! What questions, which he could not answer! Nearly twenty years had gone since that blessed Person, in whom he believed, had disappeared, and that Kingdom which Jewish hope and expectation associates with the King Messiah had not been manifested, and the promises given through the Prophets had not found their fulfilment. Yet he continued to speak boldly concerning the things of Jesus.

But God did not leave him long in this condition. The Lord had guided him to Ephesus, and the same Lord had arranged it so that Priscilla and Aquila remained in Ephesus. He had a service for them. Both Priscilla and Aquila listened to him and must have been made glad by the courageous testimony of Apollos. They felt at once how little he really knew of the Lord, and they did not turn away from him, but sought him out and took him in to expound to him the way of God more perfectly. And the great, eloquent preacher on whose lips hung the multitudes, was humble enough to sit at the feet of a tent-maker and his wife and receive instructions from them. How little of the patience of Aquila and Priscilla and the humility of Apollos we see in our days! If some humble Christian would go now to some great and eloquent preacher to show him the way of God more perfectly, what answer would he receive? And how often towards those who are inferior in spiritual knowledge those who are well taught show but little patience. Instead of condemning such who are ignorant of the truth we should seek them out in a loving way and lead them on.

His deeper knowledge of the Lord, the truth of his death on the cross, his presence in Glory at the right hand of God closed his ministry in Ephesus. The Jews in large numbers may listen to an eloquent man, even if he proves from the Scriptures that

---

[6] Or *in the Spirit*

Jesus is the Messiah, but the preaching of the cross is the great stumbling block. It is still so in our day.

Apollos went to Corinth and became a great blessing to the assembly there. Mightily he convinced the Jew, publicly showing by the Scriptures that Jesus was the Christ. What a blessed factor he became in the Corinthian church is seen from the testimony of the Holy Spirit through Paul in the first Epistle to the Corinthians. "I planted, Apollos watered, but God gave the growth" (1 Cor 3:6). But there likewise was a faction of the Christians calling themselves after this great preacher, "I am of Apollos." Later he left Corinth and returned to Ephesus and was very reluctant to return to Corinth, though Paul had invited him to do so.

> Now concerning our brother Apollos, I strongly urged him to visit you with the other brothers, but it was not at all his will[7] to come now. He will come when he has opportunity (1 Cor 16:12).

As he was such an humble man, it is probable that he refused to return for fear of attracting the people to himself, as it had been the case already.

---

[7] Or *God's will for him*

Chapter Nineteen

The chapter which we have reached is as interesting as it is important. In the foreground stands another manifestation of the Holy Spirit, when he came upon the twelve disciples of John and they spake with tongues. This is followed by extraordinary blessings and the manifestation of the power of God and the power of Satan. The acts of the Holy Spirit and of Satan are very pronounced in this chapter. Then the chapter is important because Paul's first step towards Jerusalem is recorded. We divide the chapter in five parts.

1. The second visit of Paul to Ephesus. The twelve disciples of John (vs. 1–7).

2. The Apostle's continued labors. The separation of the disciples. The Province Asia evangelized (vs. 8–10).

3. The Power of God and the Power of Satan (vs. 11–20).

4. Paul plans to go to Jerusalem and to visit Rome (vs. 21–22).

5. The opposition and riot at Ephesus (vs. 23–41).

1. The second visit of Paul to Ephesus (vs. 1–7).

And it happened that while Apollos was at Corinth, Paul passed through the inland[1] country and came to Ephesus. There he found some disciples. And he said to them, "Did you receive the Holy Spirit when you believed?" And they said, "No, we have not even heard that there is a Holy Spirit." And he said, "Into what then were you baptized?" They said, "Into John's baptism." And Paul said, "John baptized with the baptism of repentance, telling the people to believe in the one who was to come after him, that is, Jesus." On hearing this, they were baptized in[2] the name of the Lord Jesus. And when Paul had laid his hands on them, the Holy Spirit came on them, and they began speaking in tongues and prophesying. There were about twelve men in all. (vs. 1–7).

Once more Paul appears in Ephesus and is brought now in touch with certain disciples. Some have taken them to have been the fruit of Apollos' labors in Ephesus. If that had been the case and Apollos knew them, he certainly would have imparted to them the knowledge his own soul so richly enjoyed through the instructions of the godly Priscilla and Aquila. As Ephesus was a large city it is not surprising that the twelve disciples were not known to Paul during his first and very brief visit, nor to Priscilla and Aquila. When Paul met these disciples he must have been impressed with some lack in them. Perhaps the joy and peace which should characterize every true Christian was completely absent in them and therefore the Apostle asked at once a very vital and fundamental question: "Did you receive the Holy Spirit when [since] you believed?" But the word "since" has more the thought of "when." Upon this little word "since" certain preachers and Bible teachers have

---

[1] Greek *upper* (that is, highland)

[2] Or *into*

built their unscriptural theory that the Holy Spirit must be definitely received in a second experience, which they either term a "second blessing", "baptism of the Holy Spirit" or by some other name. According to these teachers a person may be a Christian, a true disciple, saved by Grace and yet be entirely destitute of the Holy Spirit. The word "since" is always emphasized by these men. "Did you receive the Holy Spirit when you believed?" (19:2). You must get the Holy Spirit after you have believed and accepted the Lord Jesus Christ. Then a lot of rules how to surrender and to receive the Holy Spirit are given. All this is wrong. If the word "when" is simply understood, this whole misconception would disappear.

Paul makes the gift of the Spirit a test of true discipleship. If they were true believers they received the Holy Spirit *when* they believed, that is when they accepted the Lord Jesus Christ as their Saviour. If they did not receive the Holy Spirit then it is an evidence that they did not believe. "Anyone who does not have the Spirit of Christ does not belong to him" (Rom 8:9).

But were these disciples whom Paul met Christian disciples? Not at all. They knew nothing whatever of Christianity. Their knowledge about the person of Christ was more limited than the knowledge which Apollos possessed. The questions put by the Apostle brings out the fact that they knew nothing whatever of the gift of the Holy Spirit and that they had been baptized with John's baptism to repentance. This is how far their creed went: of Christ and his great redemption work they knew nothing whatever. Though the record does not give an account of it Paul must have preached Christ and the Gospel to those twelve disciples. Then they believed and were baptized in the name of the Lord Jesus.[3] After the laying on of hands the Holy Spirit came on them and they spake with tongues and prophesied. These were the outward signs. They were then sealed by the Holy Spirit and added by him as members to the body of Christ, the church.

This is the last time in this book that we read that the Holy Spirit was given and that they spoke with tongues. It is well to review the few times reported in this historical book, when the Holy Spirit was communicated to the different companies of believers.

1. On the day of Pentecost. The one hundred and twenty were filled with the Holy Spirit and spoke with other tongues. No laying on of hands is mentioned here. They were all Jews who received the Holy Spirit on that day (Acts 2).

2. Peter and John went to Samaria. The Samaritans had believed and had been baptized in the name of the Lord Jesus, but the Holy Spirit had not been given to them. The reason was explained by us in the exposition of Chapter 8. Peter and John laid their hands on them and they received the Holy Spirit. Nothing is said that they prophesied or spoke in tongues.

3. While Peter preached the Gospel to Cornelius and his house the Holy Spirit fell on them which heard the Word. They spoke with tongues and praised God (Acts 10).

4. The last record in our present chapter. Jews in the dispersion receive the Holy Spirit by the laying on of hands by the Apostle Paul. In every case it is the same Holy Spirit, the promise of the Father, who came down from heaven on the day of Pentecost. It would be incorrect to say that he came anew from heaven, when the

---

[3] This is the only case of rebaptism recorded in Acts. Notice that it was not Christian baptism with which they had been previously baptized in water.

Samaritans, the Gentiles and the twelve disciples received Him. He came to this earth on the day of Pentecost and no other coming was necessary. It is unscriptural to speak of "another outpouring" of the Holy Spirit or pray for a new baptism with the Spirit. But the different records show different manifestations of the same Spirit upon different groups of people, Jews, Samaritans and Gentiles.

That all this is not to be repeated is obvious. Apostles communicated the Spirit by laying on of hands. There are no more apostles and apostolic authority, unless some one believes in that ridiculous, if not evil, doctrine of apostolic succession. That Paul here laid on his hands and the Holy Spirit was given to these twelve men just as the Samaritans received the Spirit after the laying on of hands of Peter and John, proved him to be an Apostle just as much as they. This is striking, for the enemies of Paul, the Judaizing teachers, which were corrupting the Galatian churches, vigorously denied the authority of the Apostle Paul.

But the Holy Spirit is no longer communicated in this extraordinary way, but by the hearing of faith, and every child of God possesses him as the indwelling guest. Our endeavor is not to seek more of Him, but to let him take possession of us, for which he has come to our hearts when we believed on the Lord Jesus Christ. To seek the so-called "gift of tongues" as a sign that we have the Holy Spirit, is a morbid condition and a dangerous desire.

2. THE APOSTLE'S CONTINUED LABORS. THE SEPARATION OF THE DISCIPLES. THE PROVINCE OF ASIA EVANGELIZED (VS. 8–10).

> And he entered the synagogue and for three months spoke boldly, reasoning and persuading them about the kingdom of God. But when some became stubborn and continued in unbelief, speaking evil of the Way before the congregation, he withdrew from them and took the disciples

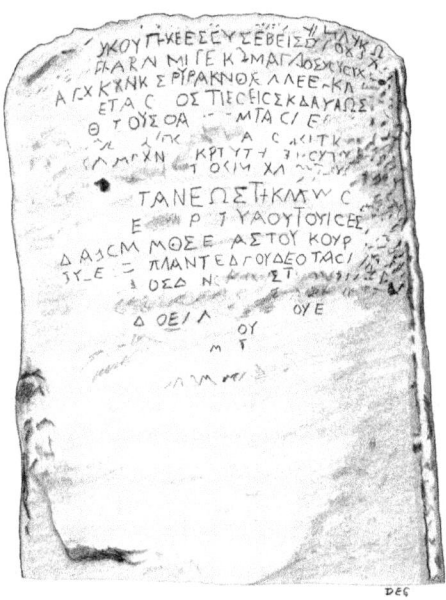

33. Drawing of a pillar in Ephesus with the name Tyrannius inscribed on it, dating from the first century AD.

> with him, reasoning daily in the hall of Tyrannus.[4] This continued for two years, so that all the residents of Asia heard the word of the Lord, both Jews and Greeks. (vs. 8–10).

Paul continued to labor in the synagogue, but matters had now to reach a climax. For three months he disputed with the Jews. The great theme was the Kingdom of God, which means more than the teaching concerning that Kingdom, which is promised to Israel and which some day will be established. No doubt it entered largely into the disputings of the Apostle with the Jews, but it was not confined to that phase of the Kingdom. Jews who believe their own Scriptures and still hold to the Jewish hope are quite willing to listen to arguments touching the realization of this hope; but if the Kingdom of God is preached which is not meat and drink, but righteousness, and peace, and joy in the Holy Spirit (Rom

---

[4] Some manuscripts add *from the fifth hour to the tenth* (that is, from 11 a.m. to 4 p.m.).

14:17) they oppose this and harden their hearts. This deeper message of the Gospel was not received by the multitude of Jews. Some hardened themselves and were disobedient and spoke evil of that way. Separation from this unbelieving and disobedient mass was the next step. In this way the assembly in Ephesus was formed. A number of brethren were also with Paul in Ephesus. His own hands ministered to his own necessities and to them that were with him (Acts 20:34). The same information we gain from the Epistle to the Galatians, which Paul wrote from Ephesus with his own hand (Gal 1:2). These companions of Paul were Timothy and Erastus, Gaius and Aristarchus, two brethren of Thessalonica, Titus, Tychicus and Trophimus (Acts 19:22, 29; Acts 20:4; 2 Cor 7:6). Then there were Aquila and Priscilla and a number of converts. The first fruit was undoubtedly Epaenetus[5] (Rom 16:5), also Onesiphorus and his house (2 Tim 1:16), Hymenaeus, Alexander, Phygellus and Hermogenes of whose bad record we read in I Timothy 1:20 and 2 Timothy 1:15. The assembly had elders and of them and the Apostle's faithful labors we shall read more in the next chapter. The record here tells us that the work was continued in the school of one Tyrannus (see Fig. 33), some large building obtained for that purpose. Most likely the assembly itself met elsewhere. Then the entire province of Asia of which Ephesus was the capital heard the Word of the Lord Jesus, both Jew and Greeks. A blessed work of evangelization was done.

3. The Power of God and the Power of Satan (vs. 11–20).

And God was doing extraordinary miracles by the hands of Paul, so that even handkerchiefs or aprons that had touched his skin were carried away to the sick, and their diseases left them and the evil spirits came out of them. Then some of the itinerant Jewish exorcists undertook to invoke the name of the Lord Jesus over those who had evil spirits, saying, "I adjure you by the Jesus whom Paul proclaims." Seven sons of a Jewish high priest named Sceva were doing this. But the evil spirit answered them, "Jesus I know, and Paul I recognize, but who are you?" And the man in whom was the evil spirit leaped on them, mastered all[6] of them and overpowered them, so that they fled out of that house naked and wounded. And this became known to all the residents of Ephesus, both Jews and Greeks. And fear fell upon them all, and the name of the Lord Jesus was extolled. Also many of those who were now believers came, confessing and divulging their practices. And a number of those who had practiced magic arts brought their books together and burned them in the sight of all. And they counted the value of them and found it came to fifty thousand pieces of silver. So the word of the Lord continued to increase and prevail mightily. (vs. 11–20).

Ephesus was a stronghold of Satan. Here many evil things both superstitious and satanic were practiced. Books containing formula for sorcery and other ungodly and forbidden arts were plentiful in that city. The Jews themselves were contaminated with these evil practices. God was pleased to perform special miracles by the hands of Paul. Handkerchiefs and aprons he had used healed the sick and drove out demons. Rationalists and higher critics explain these miracles as being simply superstitions.

But in this and similar narratives Christian faith finds no difficulty whatever. All miraculous working is an exertion of the direct power of God; a suspension by him of his ordinary laws; and whether he will use *any* instrument in doing this, or *what instrument*, must depend altogether on his own purpose in the miracle-the effect to be produced on the recipients, beholders, or bearers.[7]

---

[5] Correct reading is "who is first fruits of Asia unto Christ" not Achaia as in the Authorized Version.

[6] Or *both*

[7] Alford, *The NT for English Readers*, 1:782.

CHAPTER NINETEEN

God wanted to bear witness to his messenger and his message that they were of him and therefore he manifested here his extraordinary power. But this power was not in Paul nor were such manifestations to continue. They ceased. That which claims to be a continuation in the Romish church (relics, most of them spurious, for which claim is made that they possess miraculous powers) is nothing but superstition and fanaticism. Equally fanatical are the present day claims of a certain class of Christians, that the apostolic Pentecostal gifts are being restored. It is a foolish thing, to say the least, if some of these misguided people imitate what is recorded here in connection with the great Apostle, and send handkerchiefs about, claiming that they actually have cured sickness.

That this manifestation of the power of God in this most remarkable way was likewise needed to bring to naught the evil powers of darkness, which were so active in Ephesus, is revealed in what follows. Jewish instruments of Satan in the person of the sons of Sceva, a chief priest, men who were sorcerers and dealt in magic, were in Ephesus. This is the fourth time we read of such satanic instruments. The first was Simon Magus. This subtle instrument claimed to be converted and tried to buy the power of the Holy Spirit with money. Elymas, or Bar Jesus, was the second, and he opposed the Gospel, going forth to the Gentiles, a type, as we pointed out in our exposition, of the Jewish nation in their opposition and blindness. In Philippi a damsel with the spirit of Python had cried after Paul and through her the enemy had tried his work. The seven sons of Sceva tried to imitate the power of God as it was manifested through Paul; but they knew not the Lord Jesus Christ. They were professional exorcists travelling from place to place and preaching the expulsion of evil spirits. All kinds of mysterious things were used by these exorcists; the use of different names of God in driving out the evil spirits were especially resorted to. The so-called *Kabbala* and many parts of the Talmud are full of these mysterious things of magic. In some cases no doubt there was reality, as we learn from Matthew 12:27.

The sons of Sceva used the name of Jesus over a man who had an evil spirit. "I adjure you by the Jesus whom Paul proclaims" (19:13). They used simply the name of Jesus and avoided the name Lord. The effect was disastrous. The demon acknowledged that he knew Jesus and Paul, but "who are you?" The man with fury, energized by the superhuman strength of the demon, overcame the two, tore their clothes so that naked and wounded they had to flee from the house. The demon turned against them. A worse fate will some day befall those, who use the name, which is above every other name, without being His.

> Then a demon-oppressed man who was blind and mute was brought to him, and he healed him, so that the man spoke and saw. And all the people were amazed, and said, "Can this be the Son of David?" (Matt 12:22–23).

The punishment which had fallen upon the sons of Sceva made a profound impression upon the whole city and that blessed name which is above every other name was magnified. Many of those who had believed seemed to have been secretly attached to these curious arts that is, magical things. They were deeply convicted of this sin and then confessed the evil deeds of darkness. But more than that, they brought their parchments and rolls which contained the magical formulas, incantations and adjurations. These formulas and written amulets had at that time a world-wide reputation and were known by the name "*Ephesia gramata*" the Ephesian letters. They brought them together and burned them before all men. Some eight thousand dollars' worth of manuscripts was quickly consumed by the flames. A greater fire would result if the evil books, books on Occultism, Spiritualism, especially that wicked work, which is placed alongside the Bible, the textbook of "Christian Science" Science and Health, and others were piled up to be burned. But such a day is coming when the fire shall consume these evil works of darkness. A great victory had been gained over the power of Satan. "So the word of the Lord continued to increase and prevail mightily" (19:20).

4. PAUL PLANS TO GO TO JERUSALEM AND VISIT ROME (VS. 21–22).

> Now after these events Paul resolved in the Spirit to pass through Macedonia and Achaia and go to Jerusalem, saying, "After I have been there, I must also see Rome." And having sent into Macedonia two of his helpers, Timothy and Erastus, he himself stayed in Asia for a while. (vs. 21–22).

We reach now a critical point in the labors of the great Apostle. The 21st verse marks an important change, which introduces us to the last stage of the recorded acts of Paul in this historical account. *Rome* is the goal, which looms up before him. "I must also see Rome." And he saw Rome, but not in the way as he purposed in his spirit, but as the prisoner of the Lord. His journey begins now towards that great city and at the close of the book we find him there a prisoner, "proclaiming the kingdom of God and teaching about the Lord Jesus Christ with all boldness and without hindrance" (28:31). The story of his journey to Jerusalem, a journey in which he perseveres though repeatedly warned by the Spirit of God, his arrest in Jerusalem, his trials and addresses before the Jews, before Felix, Festus and King Agrippa, his voyage to Rome and shipwreck and arrival in Rome are the contents of the remaining part of our book. The record of great victories of the Gospel and its spread by the Apostle to the Gentiles comes suddenly to an end and we see that

34. Erastus inscription which some claim refers to the Erastus mentioned by Paul in Romans 16:23 and Luke in Acts 19:22.

Gospel he preached opposed by Judaism and legalism as well as by the great world-power Rome. The great apostle with his God-given, heavenly-revealed Gospel of the Glory is shut up in Rome. It is nothing less than a great prophecy of what was to happen to that Gospel.

A recent writer on the Book of Acts calls this part of the book, "the passing and passion of Paul."[8] He sees a correspondency between the Lord and Paul. Like our Lord, Paul was accused by the Jews and delivered by them into the hands of the Gentiles. The Lord had said of Paul, "for I will show him how much he must suffer for the sake of my name" (Acts 9:16). He had sufferings and afflictions in many ways throughout the years of his great activity. In his second Epistle to the Corinthians he rehearses these.

> Five times I received at the hands of the Jews the forty lashes less one. Three times I was beaten with rods. Once I was stoned. Three times I was shipwrecked; a night and a day I was adrift at sea; on frequent journeys, in danger from rivers, danger from robbers, danger from my own people, danger from Gentiles, danger in the city, danger in the wilderness, danger at sea, danger from false brothers; in toil and hardship, through many a sleepless night, in hunger and thirst, often without food,[9] in cold and exposure" (2 Cor 11:24– 27).

But now the time of his special sufferings were drawing near. Of this fact

---

[8] Rackham, *The Acts of the Apostles*, 358.
[9] Or *often in fasting*

the Holy Spirit testified directly (Acts 20:23; 21:11).

The question has often been raised how the purposing of Paul in the spirit to go again to Jerusalem is to be understood. Is the word "spirit" to be written with a capital "S" or not? In other words, did he purpose in the Spirit of God after prolonged prayer, to go up to Jerusalem? Did the Holy Spirit guide him to take up to the city of his fathers the contributions from Achaia and Macedonia for the poor saints? (Rom 15:25–26). It could not have been the Spirit of God who prompted him to go once more to Jerusalem, for we find that during the journey the Holy Spirit warned him a number of times not to go to Jerusalem. These warnings were not heeded, but they prove conclusively that Paul purposed in his own spirit. He was called to evangelize; to continue to preach the glorious Gospel, and it was a turning aside from the great ministry committed to him. But behind his burning desire to go up to Jerusalem stood the mighty constraint of love for his own beloved brethren. How he did love them and how his heart, filled with the love of God, yearned over them! This love is so fully expressed in his Epistle to the Romans.

> I am speaking the truth in Christ—I am not lying; my conscience bears me witness in the Holy Spirit—that I have great sorrow and unceasing anguish in my heart. (Rom 9:1–2). . . Brothers, my heart's desire and prayer to God for them is that they may be saved (Rom 10:1).

This holy love and courage prompted him to say, when once more his brethren had besought him by the Spirit not to go up to Jerusalem,

> What are you doing, weeping and breaking my heart? For I am ready not only to be imprisoned but even to die in Jerusalem for the name of the Lord Jesus (Acts 21:13).

And the Lord in his mercy, who knows the motives of the heart, overruled the error of his servant. Later from the prison in Rome, Paul could write in his joyous Epistle to the Philippians.

> I want you to know, brothers,[10] that what has happened to me has really served to advance the gospel, so that it has become known throughout the whole imperial guard[11] and to all the rest that my imprisonment is for Christ (Phil 1:12–13).

All things, even our mistakes, must work together for good. Before we can follow Paul on his last journey to Jerusalem, we have to consider the account of the riot which took place in Ephesus.

5. THE OPPOSITION AND THE RIOT AT EPHESUS (VS. 23–41).

> About that time there arose no little disturbance concerning the Way. For a man named Demetrius, a silversmith, who made silver shrines of Artemis, brought no little business to the craftsmen. These he gathered together, with the workmen in similar trades, and said, "Men, you know that from this business we have our wealth. And you see and hear that not only in Ephesus but in almost all of Asia this Paul has persuaded and turned away a great many people, saying that gods made with hands are not gods. And there is danger not only that this trade of ours may come into disrepute but also that the temple of the great goddess Artemis may be counted as nothing, and that she may even be deposed from her magnificence, she whom all Asia and the world worship."
>
> When they heard this they were enraged and were crying out, "Great is Artemis of the Ephesians!" So the city was filled with the confusion, and they rushed together into the theater, dragging with them Gaius and Aristarchus, Macedonians who were Paul's companions in travel. But when Paul wished to go in among the crowd, the disciples would not let

---

[10] Or *brothers and sisters*. The plural Greek word *adelphoi* (translated "brothers") refers to siblings in a family. In New Testament usage, depending on the context, *adelphoi* may refer either to men or to both men and women who are siblings (brothers and sisters) in God's family, the church; also verse 14

[11] Greek *in the whole praetorium*

THE ACTS OF THE APOSTLES

him. And even some of the Asiarchs,[12] who were friends of his, sent to him and were urging him not to venture into the theater. Now some cried out one thing, some another, for the assembly was in confusion, and most of them did not know why they had come together. Some of the crowd prompted Alexander, whom the Jews had put forward. And Alexander, motioning with his hand, wanted to make a defense to the crowd. But when they recognized that he was a Jew, for about two hours they all cried out with one voice, "Great is Artemis of the Ephesians!"

And when the town clerk had quieted the crowd, he said, "Men of Ephesus, who is there who does not know that the city of the Ephesians is temple keeper of the great Artemis, and of the sacred stone that fell from the sky?[13] Seeing then that these things cannot be denied, you ought to be quiet and do nothing rash. For you have brought these men here who are neither sacrilegious nor blasphemers of our goddess. If therefore Demetrius and the craftsmen with him have a complaint against anyone, the courts are open, and there are proconsuls. Let them bring charges against one another. But if you seek anything further,[14] it shall be settled in the regular assembly. For we really are in danger of being charged with rioting today, since there is no cause that we can give to justify this commotion." And when he had said these things, he dismissed the assembly. (vs. 23–41).

The Ephesian Gentiles became greatly agitated through the influence of the prince of the power of the air, the spirit of darkness, which worked in them (Eph 2:2). The result was the great riot. Richard B. Rackham writes:

> Fully to appreciate the incident, a more detailed account of Ephesus is required. At Ephesus there met together four authorities.
>
> 1. The supreme authority of Rome represented by the proconsul. For judicial purposes the provinces were divided into shires (conventus), each with its assize town. In the province Asia Ephesus was the chief assize town;

35. Reproduction of the Ephesian Greek goddess Artemis (Roman goddess *Diana*). She was the goddess of the hunt, wild animals, childbirth, virginity, and twin of Apollo. Homer describes Artemis "of the Wilds" (*Agrotera*) and "Mistress of Animals" (*Potnia Theron, Il.* 21.470) and she is often depicted as a huntress carrying a bow and arrow (Ovid *Metam.* 3.251). The Ephesian depiction of Artemis was unique with multiple breasts, sometimes identified by scholars as bull testicles, pomegranates, or eggs and wearing a long cloak of bees. There seemed to be similar attributes with Cybele (an Anatolian mother goddess), including being served in the Temple by female slaves, young virgins, and eunuch priests.

> and accordingly court days (v. 38) were kept there, when justice was administered by the pro-consul.
>
> 2. The city itself, like Athens, was 'free' and it retained its Greek constitution, which was democratic in form. There was a Senate, to which

---

[12] That is, high-ranking officers of the province of Asia.

[13] The meaning of the Greek is uncertain.

[14] Some manuscripts *seek about other matters*.

power gravitated in imperial times. But nominally Ephesus was still governed by the Demos or People (v. 30) assembled in their Ecclesia or assembly. "An Ecclesia was held three times a month and these meetings were the regular or ordinary assemblies (v. 32), but an extraordinary assembly could be convened as on the present occasion. Where, as in cities of the empire, the powers of such an assembly were limited to purely domestic and formal matters, the substantial authority would fall into the hands of its secretary-the official who summoned and dismissed the assembly (v. 41), kept the minutes and acted as chairman. Thus the secretary of the assembly or town clerk (v. 35), would naturally be one of the magnates of the city; and this we find to have been the case from the inscriptions, in which the secretary often appears as also holding the highest office, such as the Asiarchate."

3. The Asiarchate was a provincial office. Each province had a council composed of delegates from the chief cities. Their chief business was the supervision of the provincial worship of the emperor, a cult, which furnished, besides a test of royalty, a bond of unity for the empire. A temple and altar to Rome and the emperor were erected in some city and the common worship of the province was celebrated there with games and festivals. "The president of the common council acted as high priest and presided over these festivities and games, which were given at his expense. In return, he enjoyed the title of 'Ruler of the province' Asiarch (the one over the province Asia), Galatarch over Galatia, etc. The Asiarchs of verse 31, then, were such high priests of the aristocracy and plutocracy of Asia. There is a difficulty in the use of the plural, for as a rule there was only one Ruler for a province. It has been suggested that the Ruler retained the designation as an honorary title after his period of office. But a better explanation is to be found in the exceptional prosperity of Asia.[15]

The great temple, that of Diana (Artemis), was likewise in Ephesus. Excavations of this temple have been made in the past and numerous inscriptions bear witness to the goddess and the worship connected with it. Her name is found in

36. Recreation of the Artemision, Temple of Artemis, as it would have looked at Ephesus. This model is at Miniatürk Park, Istanbul, Turkey.

those inscriptions to have been exactly that, which the mob used, "the Great Diana." The usual invocations to these goddesses were "Great Diana" or *Artemis*, the word used in the Greek. In other inscriptions she was called "the most great goddess." The temple of itself was a magnificent structure. Some parts may be seen in the British Museum. The structure was about 420 feet long and nearly 250 wide. Hundreds of persons, such as priests, eunuchs, temple wardens, virgin priestesses, were in connection with the temple. The temple was stored with rich treasures of gold and silver. A large part of the city lived on the trade, which had been created by the existence of the great temple and the thousands of pilgrims which flocked to the idolatrous festivities and games. There was a guild of silversmiths, and they manufactured shrines of Artemis and most likely all kinds of souvenirs, little models of the temple and the goddess. Demetrius was the leader of this guild and in the meeting he called, he stated before the silversmiths that they well knew that this seemingly religious craft is the source of their wealth. Quite a confession this silversmith made. And it is not different in the great "world religion" though it may have the name of Christian attached to it. The same selling of idolatrous objects, rosaries, candles, statues, blessed (?)

---

[15] Rackham, *The Acts of the Apostles*, 362–63.

The Acts of the Apostles

objects and many other things by which money is obtained under the cover of religion.

But Demetrius also bears witness to the great influence of the Gospel. "This Paul has persuaded and turned away a great many people, saying that gods made with hands are not gods" (19:26). How active Paul must have been and his testimony was backed up with the power of God. Not alone was the craft of the silversmith in great danger, but the great Diana and the temple was in danger of collapse under the preaching of the tentmaker of Tarsus. It may have been a well-plotted scheme when the company of silversmiths in fury rushed out of their meeting room into the streets and shouted at the top of their voices. "Great is Artemis of the Ephesians." The whole city was aroused. Gaius and Aristarchus, the Macedonian companions of Paul, were dragged into the theatre. This was an enormous place, being able to shelter about 25,000 persons. Paul himself was ready to face the angry mob, but the disciples opposed him and even some of the friendly Asiarchs cautioned him against assuming such a risk. The whole assembled company was an unruly mob, the great majority, perhaps, did not know what they had come for. Then the Jews put forward one of their orators to address the mob, one Alexander. But he could not bring in a word. He was known as a Jew, and the Jews hated idolatry.

For two hours the wild cry of the demonized multitude continued, "Great is Artemis of the Ephesians." Then the town clerk appeared. He settled the whole question in a very diplomatic way. First he stated the popular superstition that the image of Artemis fell down from Jupiter. Then he exhorted them to quietness, and after some sound advice and showing the danger that the superior Roman officers might hold them responsible for their

37. Restored Library of Celsus, Ephesus. The relief in the foreground is reminiscent of the elements of armor given in Ephesians 6:13–17, including the belt, breastplate, greaves for the feet, shield, helmet and sword. While the Library was only completed in 135 AD and was not present in Paul's day, the relief may have existed earlier, as it was not attached to the structure.

riotous behavior, he dismissed the assembly.[16] What might have happened if Paul had gone in person to the theatre may only be guessed at. God in his mercy shielded his servants, and the Devil was completely defeated in his efforts. In the beginning of the next chapter, we find the Apostles once more in Macedonia and Achaia.

---

[16] The Greek for assembly is *ecclesia*, "the out called ones." This word is also used for the church. The ecclesia "of the Ephesian mob was called out by the silversmiths." the "ecclesia" of "the Lord Jesus Christ is called out by the Holy Spirit."

Chapter Twenty

With this chapter we follow the Apostle in his eventful journey to Jerusalem. We divide the chapter into four parts:

1. Paul in Macedonia (vs. 1–2).
2. Eutychus Raised from the Dead (vs. 3–12).
3. The journey from Troas to Miletus (vs. 13–16).
4. The farewell to the Ephesian Elders (vs. 17–38).

1. Paul in Macedonia (vs. 1–2).

> After the uproar ceased, Paul sent for the disciples, and after encouraging them, he said farewell and departed for Macedonia. When he had gone through those regions and had given them much encouragement, he came to Greece. (vs. 1–2).

The record before us is very brief. Some have thought the reason is the fact that the Apostle had turned aside from his given ministry and therefore the Holy Spirit had nothing to report. We do believe that this is correct. The object of the Spirit of God is now to lead us rapidly forward to the last visit of the Apostle to Jerusalem, therefore much is passed over in the untiring service and labors of the great Man of God. After the uproar was over in Ephesus Paul embraced the disciples and departed to go into Macedonia. It is the first farewell scene on this memorable journey. He must have visited Philippi, Thessalonica, Berea and perhaps other cities. Besides giving them much exhortation, he received their fellowship for the poor saints in Jerusalem. In this he was fulfilling the request which had been made at the council in Jerusalem. James, Cephas and John had there asked Paul and Barnabas "to remember the poor, the very thing I was eager to do" (Gal 2:10). From Macedonia Paul passed on into Greece (Achaia).

2. Eutychus Raised from the Dead (vs. 3–12).

> There he spent three months, and when a plot was made against him by the Jews[1] as he was about to set sail for Syria, he decided to return through Macedonia. Sopater the Berean, son of Pyrrhus, accompanied him; and of the Thessalonians, Aristarchus and Secundus; and Gaius of Derbe, and Timothy; and the Asians, Tychicus and Trophimus. These went on ahead and were waiting for us at Troas, but we sailed away from Philippi after the days of Unleavened Bread, and in five days we came to them at Troas, where we stayed for seven days.
>
> On the first day of the week, when we were gathered together to break bread, Paul talked with them, intending to depart on the next day, and he prolonged his speech until midnight. There were many lamps in the upper room where we were gathered. And a young man named Eutychus, sitting at the window, sank into a deep sleep as Paul talked still longer. And being overcome by sleep, he fell down from the third story and was taken up dead. But Paul went down and bent over him, and taking him in his arms, said, "Do not be alarmed, for his life is in him." And when Paul had gone up and had broken bread and eaten, he

---

[1] Greek *Ioudaioi* probably refers here to Jewish religious leaders, and others under their influence, in that time; also verse 19.

conversed with them a long while, until daybreak, and so departed. And they took the youth away alive, and were not a little comforted. (vs. 3–12).

Three months were spent by him in Achaia, but we hear nothing of his labors there. Corinth was the place where he tarried. The Jews, who well remembered the defeat before Gallio, the deputy of Achaia (18:12), laid in wait for him as he was about to sail across to Syria. The plot was aimed at Paul's life, which most likely had been planned to be accomplished on board of ship, he intended to take from the port of Corinth, Cenchrea. Instead of sailing from there, he returned to Macedonia. Seven brethren accompanied him, and went before into Asia to wait at Troas for Paul and Luke. Sopater (the same as in Romans 16:21), was of Berea. Two were from the assembly in Thessalonica, Aristarchus and Secundus, Gaius was from Derbe, Timothy and the two of Asia, Tychicus and Trophimus. The last-named was left sick in Miletus (2 Tim 4:20).

From the little word "we" in verse 6, we learn that Luke, the beloved physician, and the penman, used by the Holy Spirit to write this book, joined the Apostle. He had not been with Paul for about seven years. The last "we" was found in Philippi (Acts 16:16) and here in Philippi it is used again. It is more than probable that Luke spent the greater part of his time in that city.

After a brief stay in Philippi and a five days' voyage, they came to Troas, where they found that the other brethren had arrived before them. In Troas the whole company tarried for seven days. Here something occurred which is of interest and importance. In verse 7 we find a description of how the disciples there kept the first day of the week. We have here the fact stated that the disciples including the apostolic company, came together on the first day of the week. This is the blessed day, which followed the Sabbath, the day on which our

38. Remains of the ancient bath (Therme) of Herodes, at Aleaxandria Troas.

ever-blessed Lord rose from the dead, the day on which he manifested Himself to his disciples and appeared in their midst (John 20:19). For this reason the first day of the week is called "the Lord's day" (Rev 1:10). And it is right that we call the day of New Testament worship not Sabbath, for it is not the Sabbath; the Sabbath is the seventh day and if we were under the law, we would be obliged to keep that day in the strictest way. Nor should we call the day "Sunday," for it is named after the Sun god, but if we say "the Lord's day," we speak scripturally. It is a blessed day of privilege. And what glorious memories are connected with that day! If God's people are really in the Spirit, all the wonderful and blessed truths and facts of our redemption in the Lord Jesus Christ crowd in upon the soul. The Lord Jesus Christ rose from the dead on that day and this glorious truth points back to the cross, where he died, the Just for the unjust, and gave his life for a ransom for many. He is risen and lives; this directs the heart upward to the place of glory, where, at the right hand of God we see Jesus, who was made a little lower than the angels, crowned with glory and honor. The blessed hope that we shall see him as he is and be like Him, is closely connected with this. And these great facts and wonderful truths are the incentives and objects of true Christian worship.

And on the first day of the week the disciples in Troas came together. There was only one company. The sad division into sects and parties was then wholly unknown. But why did they gather together? Did the news that the Apostle Paul was in their midst bring them together? Did they come to hear the mighty man of God preach a great sermon? No. But we read that the disciples came together not a mixed multitude, but as disciples to break bread. This was their first object in the gathering on the first day of the week. The statement one meets occasionally that the breaking of bread meant that they had a meal together is so superficial and unwarranted that we need not to argue about it. The breaking of bread means the Lord's Supper. "Do this in remembrance of Me" our blessed Lord had requested his disciples, and this request was re-stated by the Apostle Paul. In 1 Corinthians 11:23–26, we read:

> For I received from the Lord what I also delivered to you, that the Lord Jesus on the night when he was betrayed took bread, and when he had given thanks, he broke it, and said, "This is my body which is for [2] you. Do this in remembrance of me."[3] In the same way also he took the cup, after supper, saying, "This cup is the new covenant in my blood. Do this, as often as you drink it, in remembrance of me." For as often as you eat this bread and drink the cup, you proclaim the Lord's death until he comes.

He had received this of the Lord, no doubt in a direct revelation, and he delivered it as his message to the churches. That blessed memorial feast the Lord Jesus Christ instituted on the night he was betrayed is to be kept by his own redeemed people "until he comes." Can there be anything more precious than this? What is all service and sacrifice in service, in comparison with the response to his request

---

[2] Some manuscripts *broken for*.
[3] Or *as my memorial*; also verse 25.

ere he went to the cross, "do this in remembrance of Me"? What memories flood the soul when in the power of the Spirit of God this feast is kept! All the marvellous facts of our redemption are proclaimed at the Lord's table. His coming into the world, his death on the cross and the infinite worth of that death, what has been accomplished by it, the new and living way which has been made into the Holiest, his resurrection, his presence as Priest in glory, his coming again, all these and much more cluster around the Lord's table.

The question has often been raised, How often should the Lord's supper be kept? There is no command whatever about the frequency of the observance of this blessed ceremony. From Acts 2 we learned that in the beginning of the church it was kept daily. The Holy Spirit brought the Lord's request at once before the hearts of the company of believers and so strong was the love for the Lord that they remembered him daily in the breaking of bread.

The passage before us carries with it the impression that it was the custom of the disciples to come together to remember the Lord on the first day of the week. The Lord's day and the Lord's supper belong together and there can be no doubt that the early church celebrated that feast of love each Lord's day.

If we had been present in Troas that Lord's day we would have witnessed a meeting of praise and worship. After some disciple had given thanks for the bread and for the wine, these emblems of his great love were passed around among the gathered company.

After the breaking of bread was over, Paul preached to them. However, the word preached must be understood here as "discoursed." It was not the preaching of the Gospel to an unsaved company, for such had not gathered to remember the Lord. No unsaved person has a place at the

The Acts of the Apostles

Lord's table. Only believers being present, Paul addressed them. It has not pleased the Holy Spirit to report this discourse. Following the remembrance of the Lord what blessed truths must have been brought out by the great Apostle! The address was not like the modern day "sermonette" of fifteen or twenty minutes: "he prolonged his speech until midnight" (20:7).

The meeting place was an upper chamber and many lights were burning. All at once a young man, Eutychus, fell down from the third loft and was taken up dead. He sat in a window and had fallen in a deep sleep till he fell from that height to the ground. Through Paul's embrace he was raised to life. Life had not gone out of the body and Paul declared that his life (soul) was in him. The functions of life were restored and the bonds between soul and body were re-established. The incident has been much used in an allegorical way. Some see in Eutychus the type of a believer who has fallen asleep spiritually and fallen, and who is restored. Others read the history of the church in this event.

Paul then partook of the bread (which in verse 11 means the simple eating of bread and no longer the Lord's supper) and talked a long while, till the day dawned, when he departed.

3. The Journey from Troas to Miletus (vs. 13–16).

> But going ahead to the ship, we set sail for Assos, intending to take Paul aboard there, for so he had arranged, intending himself to go by land. And when he met us at Assos, we took him on board and went to Mitylene. And sailing from there we came the following day opposite Chios; the next day we touched at Samos; and[4] the day after that we went to Miletus. For Paul had decided to sail past Ephesus, so that he might not have to spend

---

[4] Some manuscripts add *after remaining at Trogyllium*.

39. The visible area of the synagogue in Miletus next to the colossal circular Harbor Monument (63 BC). Paul may have met the Ephesian elders here.

time in Asia, for he was hastening to be at Jerusalem, if possible, on the day of Pentecost. (vs. 13–16).

The company then took ship to sail to Assos, but Paul made the journey of over 20 miles on foot. He wanted to be alone like Elijah as well as others. What thoughts must have passed through his mind! What burdens must have been upon his heart! What anxieties in connection with that coming visit to Jerusalem!

No doubt as he walked along, he stepped along in prayer in communion with the Lord, unhindered and undisturbed by his fellow laborers. How well it is if we follow his example and the examples of all the other great men of God, above all the example of our Lord, and be alone, alone with God.

> For us this is often a wise thing. To be alone, apart from men, but alone with God, where we can think of Him, of ourselves and of the work as he sees it. Alone where in his presence responsibility is felt, instead of activity before men. This communion with Him, as his servants, gives and sustains a blessed confidence in Him, an intimacy of soul with Him, full of goodness and of grace.

And how the heart of the child of God yearns for such an intimacy with God! The enemy of our souls ever tries to keep us from this. Well it is if we tear ourselves loose from our choicest friends and fellowship of saints and service, to seek his presence, to be alone.

They took him in at Assos, which they reached before the Apostle had arrived. Nothing but the route is here described. Ephesus looms up. But it seemed impossible for the hurrying Apostle, who was determined to reach Jerusalem at Pentecost, to visit the beloved city. When Miletus was reached he was but thirty miles from Ephesus.

4. Paul's address to the Elders of Ephesus (vs. 17–38).

From Miletus, Paul sent to Ephesus and called the elders of the church. The remaining part of this chapter contains his great farewell address to the Ephesian elders and through them to the church located there. Two great speeches by the Apostle have so far been reported in this book. The first was addressed to the *Jews* in Antioch of Pisidia (see Fig. 17; Acts 13:16–41). The second was addressed to the *Gentiles* in Athens (ch. 17). The address here in our chapter is to the *church*. It is of very great and unusual interest and importance. He speaks of himself, his own integrity and recalls to them his ministry. He declares his own coming sufferings and his determination not to count his life dear, but to finish his course with joy. He warns the church concerning the future apostasy and the appearance in their midst of false teachers. But we must study the great address in detail.

> Now from Miletus he sent to Ephesus and called the elders of the church to come to him. And when they came to him, he said to them:
>
> "You yourselves know how I lived among you the whole time from the first day that I set foot in Asia, serving the Lord with all humility and with tears and with trials that happened to me through the plots of the Jews; how I did not shrink from declaring to you anything that was profitable, and teaching you in public and from house to house, testifying both to Jews and to Greeks of repentance toward God and of faith in our Lord Jesus Christ. And now, behold, I am going to Jerusalem, constrained by[5] the Spirit, not knowing what will happen to me there, except that the Holy Spirit testifies to me in every city that imprisonment and afflictions await me. But I do not account my life of any value nor as precious to myself, if only I may finish my course and the ministry that I received from the Lord Jesus, to testify to the gospel of the grace of God. And now, behold, I know that none of you among whom I have gone about proclaiming the kingdom will see my face again. Therefore I testify to you this day that I am innocent of the blood of all, for I did not shrink from declaring to you the whole counsel of God. Pay careful attention to yourselves and to all the flock, in which the Holy Spirit has made you overseers, to care for the church of God,[6] which he obtained with his own blood.[7] I know that after my departure fierce wolves will come in among you, not sparing the flock; and from among your own selves will arise men speaking twisted things, to draw away the disciples after them. Therefore be alert, remembering that for three years I did not cease night or day to admonish every one with tears. And now I commend you to God and to the word of his grace, which is able to build you up and to give you the inheritance among all those who are sanctified. I coveted no one's silver or gold or apparel. You yourselves know that these hands ministered to my necessities and to those who were with me. In all things I have shown you that by working hard in this way we must help the weak and remember the words of the Lord Jesus, how he himself said, 'It is more blessed to give than to receive.'"
>
> And when he had said these things, he knelt down and prayed with them all. And there was much weeping on the part of all; they embraced Paul and kissed him, being sorrowful most of all because of the word he had spoken, that they would not see his face again. And they accompanied him to the ship. (vs. 17–38).

The entire address contains the characteristic phrases so generally employed

---

[5] Or *bound in*
[6] Some manuscripts *of the Lord*
[7] Or *with the blood of his Own*

by the apostle. These phrases used by Paul or in connection with him are often found in the Book of Acts:

- *Lying in wait*, or *plots* (9:24, 20:3; 23:30);
- *house to house* (8:3);
- *faith in the Lord Jesus* (24:24, 26:18);
- *and now behold* (13:11);
- *bound in the spirit* (19:21);
- *afflictions* (14:22);
- *course* (13:25);
- *I am pure* (18:6);
- *the counsel of God* (13:36);
- *appointed* (19:21);
- *perverse* (13:8, 10);
- *the Word of his Grace* (14:3). Compare 1 Thess 1:5, 9 with verse 18 in this chapter.
- *Serving the Lord* (Rom 12:11);
- *humility of mind* (Col 2:18);
- *tears* (2 Cor 2:4);
- *profitable* (1 Cor 10:23);
- *Jews and Greeks* (Rom 1:16);
- *finish my course* (Phil 3:12, 2 Tim 4:7);
- *ministry which I received* (Col 4:17, Romans 1:5, Eph 3:7, Col 1:23, 25, 1 Tim 1:12);
- *from the Lord* (Gal 1:12, 1 Cor 9:23);
- *see my face* (Col 2:1);
- *admonish* (Rom 15:14, Col 1:28, 3:16);
- *covet* (Rom 7:7);
- *these hands ministered* (1 Cor 4:12, 1 Thess 2:9, 2 Thess 3:8);
- *laboring* (1 Thess 5:12, 1 Tim 5:17);
- *help the weak* (1 Thess 5:14, 1 Cor 12:28);
- *remember* (Gal 2:10, Eph 2:2, Col 4:18, etc.).

How many elders (*presbyters*) had come to Miletus is not stated. Their office and their work is given in verse 28. They are overseers (*episcopi*), and the Holy Spirit appointed them to feed the church of God. Ritualistic churches claim that the office of a presbyter and a bishop, an overseer, are distinct; but such a distinction which is claimed does not exist. It is also incorrect to say that because there are no more Apostles, there can be no more elders. This is as erroneous as if one would say the gifts of evangelists, pastors and teachers have ceased.

The word "bishop" overseer describes the work of an elder the word "presbyter" an elder, that is one mature in years and experience, not a novice (1 Tim 3:6).

As long as the true church is on earth these gifts and elders are also in existence and they must be recognized.

The address of the Apostle Paul falls into four parts:

1. A rehearsal of his integrity and faithfulness in ministry (vs. 19–21).

2. The announcement of his anticipated sufferings and his determination to endure (vs. 22–27).

3. The charge to the elders and the warning (vs. 28–31).

4. The final word (vs. 32–35).

1. A Rehearsal of his integrity and faithfulness in ministry (vs. 19–21).

First then we find a rehearsal of his integrity and faithfulness in his ministry. On account of the prominence given to himself and his labours the Apostle Paul has been charged with egotism and that his address was not spoken by inspiration. Such, however, is not the case at all. One might just as well charge the Apostle with egotism in writing his different Epistles in which the personal element is often so predominant. The fact is that God has been pleased to make this great man a pattern in every way. When he refers thus to himself he was led by the Holy Spirit to manifest the Grace of God in his own life as a devoted servant of the Lord Jesus Christ. He had arrived in Ephesus in the spring of 51 just four years previous. He was among them, as he loved to call himself, as the servant of the Lord, serving Him. And how he served the Lord! These things he mentioned. With all humility of mind. From 2 Corinthians 10:1 and verse 10 we learn that his bodily presence was unattractive and base. Paired with an humble bodily appearing was humble-mindedness. "Have this mind among yourselves, which is yours in Christ Jesus[8]" (Phil 2:5), thus he wrote by the Holy Spirit and the life of Christ had produced this very mind, the leading characteristic of which is humility, in the great Apostle. He mentions the many *tears*, with which he was amongst them. Our beloved Apostle was a man of many tears; he wept much and watered the seed with his tears. The affection and anguish of his heart brought forth tears and under such deep exercise he wrote his Epistles. "For I wrote to you out of much affliction and anguish of heart and with many tears" (2 Cor 2:4). Of the enemies of the cross of Christ he spoke with weeping (Phil 3:18). And he also served among them surrounded with *temptations* and *dangers*. How few such servants we find in our present days! Men are called great servants if they can organize great campaigns, reach thousands, address constantly large audiences and make a great name for themselves and have their photographs exhibited as often as possible. This is man's pattern of a great servant. But here we have a servant of Christ, who is after God's own heart. Serving in humblemindedness, not seeking great things, serving in love with many tears and in many trials.

In his ministry he was as faithful as he was Christ-like in his character. He *kept nothing back. He* had not shunned to declare all the counsel of God. The many who profess to be preachers and teachers in our own times and who shun to declare all the counsel of God and keep back certain truths are not the servants of Christ, but they are manpleasers. And elsewhere the Apostle says, "If I were still trying to please man, I would not be a servant[9] of Christ" (Gal 1:10). How often this is done. The second Coming of Christ for the establishment of his Kingdom and the other great prophetic unfoldings connected with this event are often set aside and kept back, though they are an important part of the counsel of God.

Then he did not confine his ministry to a sermon on the Lord's day during the years of his presence in Ephesus, but publicly and from *house to house* he had labored. Nor did he confine his ministry to a certain class of people. He testified to the Jews and to the Greeks repentance towards God, and faith toward our Lord Jesus Christ. Both repentance and faith belong together and are inseparably connected. He preached and taught that Jews and Gentiles were lost and have to take their true places as sinners before God, and trust in the Lord Jesus Christ. When the Gospel is preached, and faith by hearing cometh to the heart, true repentance will be the result.

2. The announcement of his anticipated sufferings and his determination to endure (vs. 22–27).

In the second place we find the announcement of his anticipated sufferings and his determination to endure. Dark forebodings are filling his mind. Going to Jerusalem he is bound in the spirit, which does not mean the Holy Spirit, but his own spirit. The future is dark for him as no revelation has reached him what is to be his fate. But at the same time the Holy Spirit bore witness in every city that bonds and afflictions were in store for him. And yet he pushes on towards Jerusalem. With all the uncertainty about what is to come he possesses the certainty that the beloved saints of Ephesus were to see his face no more. Was he in the Lord's will when he went on in this way in spite of the Holy Spirit's warning? Certainly not. But his whole soul must have been filled with a

---

[8] Or *which was also in Christ Jesus*
[9] Or *slave;* Greek *bondservant*

consuming love and burning desire for his kinsmen, his brethren in Jerusalem. What then if bonds and afflictions were to come upon him? What if he were to share in the city of his fathers some of the sufferings of Christ? His heart longed "that I may know him and the power of his resurrection, and may share his sufferings, becoming like him in his death" (Phil 3:10). And later he could write, "I am already being poured out" (2 Tim 4:6). It is the triumph of faith which breathes in verse 24 of our chapter. Though he had gone on his way in self-will, yet in faith he could say:

> But I do not account my life of any value nor as precious to myself, if only I may finish my course and the ministry that I received from the Lord Jesus, to testify to the gospel of the grace of God (20:24).

Words of faith these are. And faithfully he had labored preaching both the Gospel of Grace and the Kingdom of God, not shrinking from declaring all the counsel of God and therefore he was pure from the blood of all. He had preached the truth in its fullness and completeness and with that the responsibility of the servant ends; but the servant of Christ who does not declare all the counsel of God has a fearful responsibility. Well has one said, there are three kinds of servants: A good Christian and a good workman, such as Paul; A good Christian and a bad workman, himself saved, but his work to be consumed; Then he who seeks to corrupt and destroy the temple of God, whose work as well as himself shall perish. And such evil workmen were even then in existence seeking to corrupt the faith. As long as Paul was in the world his spiritual energy resisted and overcame these evil things. What should come after his departure he makes known by the Spirit of God in the third part of his address.

3. The charge to the elders and the warning (vs. 28–31).

It is a solemn charge the Apostle now delivers. At the same time it is full of instructions. As overseers they were charged with taking heed first to themselves. Later Paul wrote to Timothy, then in Ephesus, "keep a close watch on yourself and on the teaching" (1 Tim 4:16). Only in this way could they discharge their solemn responsibility. The flock is mentioned, meaning the sheep of Christ and the Church of God, to which all the sheep of Christ belong, and over these the elders were overseers and called to feed the church. It is a significant expression "the church of God, which he obtained with his own blood" (20:28). Here the blood of our Lord Jesus Christ, the spotless Lamb, is called "his own blood, the blood of God." How great the cost-price! It was God Himself in his Son, one with Him, who accomplished the work. If we but could think of all those, no matter where they are, redeemed and saved by grace, as the flock and as the assembly of God, which he who is God purchased with his blood, what love and graciousness would energize us and what deep concern we would have towards all!

And then the reason is given why they should take such heed. Verses 29 and 30 contain a prophecy. The Apostle speaks concerning his departure and he does not mention anyone to take his place. All the talk among Ritualists of apostolic succession is a pure invention and worse. The warning is concerning grievous wolves who would enter in among the flock, and concerning false teachers who were to arise in their own midst, speaking perverse things to draw away disciples after them. How abundantly this great prediction has been verified. And never before has it been so evident as now. Wolves in sheep-clothing, with the most damnable heresies like Millennial Dawnism and Christian Science have entered the flock, while from within false leaders have arisen, who propagate the work of Alexander, Hymenaeus and Philetus (1 Tim 1:20; 2 Tim 2:17), and divide the flock. Failure soon appears after God has begun a work. Thus it has been in the past and is so now and will continue till the enemy of God, who stands behind the wolves and the false teachers, is bound. And all this stamps the teaching that the church increases in power and righteousness and leads on towards world-conversion as an untruth. Paul made no such prediction for the church on earth. The truth is that that which lays claim to increased power and expansion is the apostate thing which long ago has abandoned sound doctrine.

4. The final word (vs. 32–35).

In his final word he commends them to God and to the Word of his grace, which is able to build up the individual believer and to give them an inheritance among all them which are sanctified. And blessed be his Name, whatever the apostasy brings, how grievous the wolves may be, how subtle the false teachers with their perverted theories, God and the Word of his Grace abide! Nothing can touch these, and that Word can build us up and will build us up. It is the great minister to the need of our souls, and whenever we turn to it we shall find our need supplied, our faith strengthened, and our spiritual lives quickened. A blessed word to remember in these days. "Now I commend you to God and to the word of his grace, which is able to build you up" (20:32). In the dark days of failure and increasing departure from God, no child of God needs to be in want. Now, more than ever, we may sing, "my cup overflows" (Ps 23:5).

Another personal testimony of this pattern servant of Christ follows. He had coveted no man's silver, or gold, or apparel. He must have held up his hands, when he said, "you yourselves know that these hands ministered to my necessities and to those who were with me" (20:34). And as they looked upon his hands they saw hands roughened by much toil. In this he had given them an object lesson, that they, too, should support the weak, and that they should remember the words of the Lord Jesus, so beautifully illustrated in the Apostle's toil "It is more blessed to give than to receive" (20:35).

This lesson was specially needed in Ephesus where in the heathen worship of Artemis the ministers of the cult obtained great wealth. What a contrast between the luxuriously living, wealth-accumulating priests and temple-servants of the temple of Artemis (Diana) and the humble servant of the Lord, toiling with his own hands! And how this lesson, too, is needed at the present time. The most blessed work on earth, preaching the Gospel and teaching the Word, has been reduced to a profession with a certain income and with fees for service. Charging for such service, which tells out God's unspeakable gift and unfathomable love, is foreign to the teaching of the New Testament. The servant is cast in dependence on his Lord, whom he serves and he will sustain him in all his service. "It is more blessed to give than to receive."[10] He had declared and the true servant of Christ is called upon to share the blessedness of his Lord by spending and being spent, by giving, and helping the weak. A blessed path it is, and blessed, too, because the servant but experiences what a gracious Lord it is whom he serves, who is mindful of him and abundantly supplies all his needs.

---

[10] One of the beatitudes which circulated in the early church apart from those preserved in the Gospels. Being embodied in Acts this one is proven to be genuine.

An affecting farewell scene closes this chapter. He kneeled down and led in prayer. What a prayer it must have been! What an outpouring of the heart in God's presence! They all wept and fell on Paul's neck and kissed him. Their greatest sorrow was that they had heard him say they should see his face no more. And they accompanied him to the ship.

Chapter Twenty-One

The final stages of the journey of the Apostle Paul and his companions to Jerusalem, and what befell him there, are the contents of this interesting chapter.

1. The journey from Miletus to Tyre and Ptolemais (vs. 1–7).

2. In Caesarea (vs. 8–14).

3. The Apostle's Arrival in Jerusalem and his visit to the Temple (vs. 15–26).

4. The Uproar in the Temple. Paul taken prisoner (vs. 27–40).

1. Paul's Journey to Tyre and Ptolemais (vs. 1–7).

And when we had parted from them and set sail, we came by a straight course to Cos, and the next day to Rhodes, and from there to Patara.[1] And having found a ship crossing to Phoenicia, we went aboard and set sail. When we had come in sight of Cyprus, leaving it on the left we sailed to Syria and landed at Tyre, for there the ship was to unload its cargo. And having sought out the disciples, we stayed there for seven days. And through the Spirit they were telling Paul not to go on to Jerusalem. When our days there were ended, we departed and went on our journey, and they all, with wives and children, accompanied us until we were outside the city. And kneeling down on the beach, we prayed and said farewell to one another. Then we went on board the ship, and they returned home.

When we had finished the voyage from Tyre, we arrived at Ptolemais, and we greeted the brothers[2] and stayed with them for one day. (vs. 1–7).

Little needs to be said on the journey itself, for the Holy Spirit gives no record of anything which took place, save the repeated warnings he gave to the Apostle, who in the strongest determination was hastening to reach the chosen goal, Jerusalem. Cos, Rhodes and Patara are mentioned, and from there they took ship to Phoenicia. The landing place in that ancient country was Tyre, where some of the cargo was to be put ashore, and perhaps an additional one was taken aboard, for the destination of the ship was Ptolemais. In Tyre they found a company of disciples and tarried there for seven days. This rather lengthy stay may have been by request of the Apostle, so that they might be enabled to spend a Lord's day with the assembly in Tyre. In Troas (20:6) they also had tarried seven days, and on the first day of the week, as we learned from that chapter, they were engaged in the breaking of bread, remembering the Lord in gathering around his table. Though no statement is made about the Apostle meeting with the believers in Tyre for the same blessed purpose, we can take it for granted that such was the case.

And the Holy Spirit through these disciples warned the Apostle at once that he should not go to Jerusalem. This indeed, was very solemn. If these disciples had spoken of themselves, if it said that they were in anxiety over Paul's journey to that city, one might say that they were simply speaking as men, but the record makes it

---

[1] Some manuscripts add *and Myra*
[2] Or *brothers and sisters*; also verse 17

The Acts of the Apostles

clear that the *Holy Spirit* spoke through them. Could then the Apostle Paul have been under the guidance of that same Spirit in going to Jerusalem? As stated before, the great love for his brethren, his kinsmen, burned in his heart, and so great was his desire to be in Jerusalem that he ignored the voice of the Spirit. The answer which the Apostle gave to their inspired warning is not given, but we know that he did not swerve from his purpose.

Beautiful is the farewell scene in connection with this visit. It even surpasses the farewell of the previous chapter. "And they all brought us on our way, with wives and children," writes the penman, "till we were out of the city; and we kneeled down on the shore and prayed." It is a sweet picture of love. Even the children came along to get the last glimpse of the great man of God, who had tarried in their midst. And what a prayer-meeting it must have been, there on the seashore!

In Ptolemais, which they reached next, the brethren were saluted by them, and they spent one day in their company.

2. In Caesarea (vs. 8–14).

> On the next day we departed and came to Caesarea, and we entered the house of Philip the evangelist, who was one of the seven, and stayed with him. He had four unmarried daughters, who prophesied. While we were staying for many days, a prophet named Agabus came down from Judea. And coming to us, he took Paul's belt and bound his own feet and hands and said, "Thus says the Holy Spirit, 'This is how the Jews[3] at Jerusalem will bind the man who owns this belt and deliver him into the hands of the Gentiles.'" When we heard this, we and the people there urged him not to go up to Jerusalem. Then Paul answered, "What are you doing, weeping and breaking my heart? For I am ready not only to be imprisoned but even to die in Jerusalem for the name of the Lord Jesus." And since he would not be persuaded, we ceased and said, "Let the will of the Lord be done." (vs. 8–14).

40. Caesarea maritima, Roman theatre where Herod Agrippa I received divine accolades. The God-fearer Cornelius was converted in the city of Caesarea.

The journey from Ptolemais to Caesarea (see Fig. 41) was probably made on foot. When they arrived in that city, they found a welcome in the house of one whose name is familiar from the earlier chapters of our book. They entered the house of Philip. As there also was an apostle by the name of Philip (Matt 10:3), the Holy Spirit tells us that it was not the Apostle Philip, but Philip the Evangelist, one of the seven (Acts 6:5).

We had his history and great activity before. The last we read of him was at the close of Chapter 8. After he had been so blessedly used in the conversion of the eunuch, and had been caught away by the Spirit, he was found "at Azotus, and as he passed through he preached the gospel to all the towns until he came to Caesarea" (8:40). Here we find him again twenty years later, settled in Caesarea, with his family. His gift as an Evangelist, no doubt, he exercised throughout all these years. There is no record given of the blessed activity of this servant of the Lord, but in that coming day his labor and the blessed results of this great Evangelist will be manifested, as shall be all the works of the Saints of God.

---

[3] Greek *Ioudaioi* probably refers here to Jewish religious leaders, and others under their influence, in that time.

Special mention is made of the four unmarried daughters of Philip, who had the gift of prophecy. This has puzzled some, because elsewhere it is stated "I do not permit a woman to teach or to exercise authority over a man" (1 Tim 2:12), and that women should be silent in the assembly. It has therefore been stated by some, who press this point in a dogmatic way, that these four virgins had their connection with the Jewish and earthly kingdom. But this is far-fetched. Woman is not excluded from the gifts of the Spirit; the exercise of woman's gift, however, is according to the sphere given to her by God. These four daughters possessed the gift of prophesying, and of teaching, and they also made use of the gift. But did they preach and teach in public? Certainly not. If they exercised their gift it must have been in their sphere, that is, in their home, the house of their father. And when Paul and his companions appeared, nothing is said that these virgins made use of the gift in the presence of these visitors. This in itself is very striking. We desire to quote what another has said on this interesting and timely question:

> There is no reason why a woman should not have this or most other gifts as much as a man. I do not say the same kind of gift always. Surely God is wise and gives suited gifts whether to men or women, or, it may be, I was going to say, to children. The Lord is Sovereign, and knows how, as putting all who now believe in the body of Christ, so also to give them a work suitable to the purposes of his own grace. Certainly he did clothe these four daughters of Philip with a very special spiritual power. They had one of the highest characters of spiritual gift they prophesied. And if they were invested with this power, certainly it was not to be put under a bushel, but to be exercised, the only question is, how.
>
> Now Scripture, if we but be subject, is quite explicit as to this. In the first place, prophecy stands confessedly in the highest rank of teaching. It is teaching. Next, the Apostle himself is the person who tells us that he does not suffer a woman to teach. This is clearly decisive; if we bow to the Apostle as inspired to give us God's mind, we ought to know that it is not the place of a Christian woman to teach. He is speaking on this topic, not in 1 Corinthians 11, but in Chapter 14. He is drawing the line between men and women in I Timothy 2. The latter Epistle forbids the women *as a class* to teach. The other and still closer word in the former Epistle, commands them to be silent in the assembly. At Corinth, apparently, there was some difficulty as to godly order and the right relations of men and women, because the Corinthians, being a people of speculative habits, instead of believing, reasoned about things. It was the tendency of the Greek mind to question everything. They could not understand that, if God had given a woman as good a gift as a man, she was not equally to use it. We can all feel their difficulty. Such reasoners are not wanting now. The fault of it all was, and is, that God is left out. His will was not in the thought of the Corinthians. There was no waiting on the Lord to ascertain what was his mind. Clearly, if he has called the church into being, it cannot but be made for his own glory. He has his own mind and will about the church and he has therefore spread out in his Word how all the gifts of his grace are to be exercised.
>
> Now the passages in 1 Corinthians 14 and in I Timothy 2, appear to me to be perfectly plain as to the relative place of the woman, whatever may be her gift. This may be said to decide only as to one sphere the assembly where the woman, according to Scripture, is precluded from the exercise of her gift. I may say further, that in those days it did not occur to them that women should go forth publicly to preach the Word. Bad as the state of things was in early days, they seem to me to have looked for a greater sense of modesty on the part of women. There is not the slightest doubt that many females with the best intentions have thus preached, as they do still. They, or their friends, defend their cause by appeals to the blessing of God on the one hand, and on the other, to the crying need of perishing sinners everywhere. But nothing can be more certain than that Scripture (and this is the standard) leaves them without the slightest warrant from the Lord for their line of conduct. Public preaching of the Gospel on the part of women is never contemplated in Scripture. It was bad enough for the Corinthians to think that they might speak among the faithful. It might have seemed that in the assembly women had the shelter of godly men; that there they were not

offensively putting themselves forward before all sorts of people in the world, as must be the case in evangelizing. Among the godly they may have imagined a veil, so to speak, drawn over them, more or less. But in modern times the end is supposed to justify the means. Gross as the Corinthians were, I must confess that to my mind the plans of our own day seem even more grievous, and with less excuse for them.[4]

Another one appears, whose name is known to us from the previous record. Agabus, one who had likewise a gift of prophecy, came down from Judea. In chapter 11:27 he stood up and announced that there should be a great dearth. He made this prediction by the Spirit and it of course came true. When he had come he took Paul's girdle and with it bound his own hands and feet and then he said:

> Thus says the Holy Spirit, "This is how the Jews at Jerusalem will bind the man who owns this belt and deliver him into the hands of the Gentiles" (21:11).

Here then another warning was given. It was the last and by far the strongest. Did Agabus really speak by the Spirit? The literal fulfilment of his predictive action furnishes the answer. The whole company, both his fellow travelers and the believers in Caesarea began to beseech him not to go up to Jerusalem. Then came Paul's final declaration: "What are you doing, weeping and breaking my heart? For I am ready not only to be imprisoned but even to die in Jerusalem for the name of the Lord Jesus" (21:13). One cannot but admire the wonderful determination and whole-hearted devotion which breathe in these words of the Apostle. He had indeed set his face like

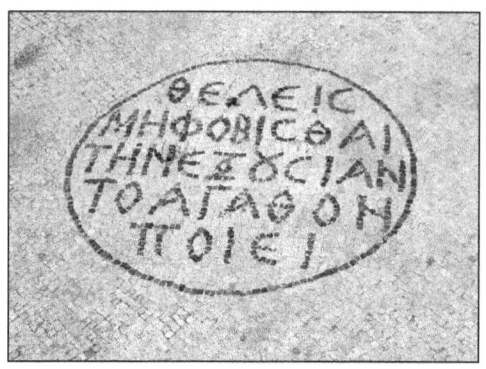

41. One of two mosaics at Caesarea Maritima quoting Romans 13:3. This is the shorter version. The original mosaic is on display at the Kibbutz Sdot Yam Museum.

a flint to go up to Jerusalem, whatever the cost might be. And if the Holy Spirit had so solemnly warned him, and he rejected these warnings, the Lord in his own gracious way over-ruled it all to his own glory and to foreshadow what might be termed "the captivity of the Gospel." God permitted it all for his own wise purpose. He knows the end from the beginning. The blessed Gospel of the Grace and Glory of God committed to the Apostle Paul was soon to be set aside by man and the Judaistic form, that perverted Gospel, to gain the victory. And Paul himself arrested in Jerusalem given over into the hands of the Gentiles and sent to Rome.

"The will of the Lord be done" was the last word spoken before he went up to Jerusalem. And a blessed word it is to remember. The will of the Lord will be accomplished in the lives of his people in spite of all their failures. The whole path of all his people is marked out by Himself. What calm it brings to our troubled hearts if we but remember it always!

3. The Apostle's Arrival in Jerusalem and his Visit to the Temple (vs. 15–26).

After these days we got ready and went up to Jerusalem. And some of the disciples from Caesarea went with us, bringing us to the house of Mnason of Cyprus, an early disciple, with whom

---

[4] Kelly, *Lectures Introductory to the Study of the Acts*, 145. The so-called "Pentecostal people" and other "Holiness sects" ignore the divine injunctions completely, besides teaching positive error like the eradication of the old nature in the believer. Surely the Holy Spirit cannot be there in his fulness, as they claim.

we should lodge.

When we had come to Jerusalem, the brothers received us gladly. On the following day Paul went in with us to James, and all the elders were present. After greeting them, he related one by one the things that God had done among the Gentiles through his ministry. And when they heard it, they glorified God. And they said to him, "You see, brother, how many thousands there are among the Jews of those who have believed. They are all zealous for the law, and they have been told about you that you teach all the Jews who are among the Gentiles to forsake Moses, telling them not to circumcise their children or walk according to our customs. What then is to be done? They will certainly hear that you have come. Do therefore what we tell you. We have four men who are under a vow; take these men and purify yourself along with them and pay their expenses, so that they may shave their heads. Thus all will know that there is nothing in what they have been told about you, but that you yourself also live in observance of the law. But as for the Gentiles who have believed, we have sent a letter with our judgment that they should abstain from what has been sacrificed to idols, and from blood, and from what has been strangled,[5] and from sexual immorality." Then Paul took the men, and the next day he purified himself along with them and went into the temple, giving notice when the days of purification would be fulfilled and the offering presented for each one of them. (vs. 15–26).

It was immediately after those days spent in Caesarea that the Apostle and his companions went up to Jerusalem. As it was before one of the great feasts of Judaism, the road from Caesarea to the City of Jerusalem must have presented a lively picture as large numbers of Jews went up to the feast. Disciples of Caesarea accompanied them, and, as it was almost 70 miles to Jerusalem, the journey had to be made in two days. So they had to lodge in the house of Mnason a Cyprian one of the early disciples. Nothing else is reported of

---

[5] Some manuscripts omit *and from what has been strangled*.

this last stage of the journey to Jerusalem. When they reached their destination at last, they were heartily welcomed by the brethren. With what feeling must the Apostle Paul have entered once more the city of his fathers, which he was to leave as a prisoner! Great are the events, which subsequently took place.

On the day following the company paid a visit to James in whose house all the elders had assembled for the purpose of meeting with Paul and his friends. No doubt they were well informed of his purposed visit to Jerusalem. Where were the apostles? They are not mentioned at all in this account; from which we may conclude that they were absent. And now once more the Apostle relates, what no doubt was dearest to the hearts of James and the elders, what God had wrought through his God-given ministry among the Gentiles. It must have been a very lengthy account; for he rehearsed particularly, "or one by one" the things, which had happened in his great activity. James, however, does not seem to be the spokesman here as he was in the meeting in chapter 15. After Paul had spoken, "they glorified God."

All had progressed nicely up to this point. But now the great crisis is rapidly reached. The meeting had been called in the house of James, and only the elders had been invited for a very good reason. Reports had reached Jerusalem that Paul had taught the Jews among the Gentiles to forsake Moses, and even to deny children the covenant sign, circumcision. Most likely the Judaizing element in the assembly of Jerusalem, the men who were so successfully overcome by the bold arguments of the Apostle at the council in Jerusalem (Acts 15, Gal 2), the men who so strenuously taught, that unless the Gentiles became circumcised, they could not be saved these men were responsible for the rumors. What could be done to convince the multitude that all this was incorrect, that Paul after all was a good Jew? The church in Jerusalem had become strong; its membership numbered myriads (literal translation). But they were in a transition period. They had accepted the Lord Jesus Christ, and yet they held on to the law of Moses. They were all zealous for the Law. They kept all the ordinances of the Law, abstained from certain meats, kept the feast days, went to the temple, made vows, and purified themselves. If this great multitude comes together, say the elders to Paul, they will hear of his arrival. With the accusations made against the Apostle, a great disorder could not be avoided. To discover some way to solve the difficulty and avert the danger, the meeting had assembled in the house of James.

Now the rumors about Paul were indeed true. He had preached the Gospel as it had been given to him by the risen Christ. In that Gospel the law could not be recognized. He had taught the position of the believer in Christ and as such the believing Jew was free from the law. The Epistle to the Romans had been written by him through the Spirit of God several years before. And yet the Lord in his patience had borne with these conditions, which prevailed in Jerusalem.

The fullest teaching on the break which had to come between Christianity and Judaism had not yet been given. The Epistle to the Hebrews furnished this argument and contains the solemn warning of the grave danger of apostasy from the Gospel by clinging to the shadow-things, which are past. To go outside of the camp and bear his reproach is the great exhortation given in that Epistle to these Jewish Christians. No doubt the Apostle Paul wrote that Epistle to his beloved brethren in Jerusalem. His heart was filled with love towards them. In his own soul he knew that all the commands of the law and the law itself had been abolished by the death of Christ. The ordinances had been nailed to the cross. The Holy Spirit foreseeing what would happen had warned him, as we have seen, not to go to Jerusalem. He went to the city and with this he stepped upon dangerous ground. He had left the way into which God had called him, and though it was his all-consuming love for his own brethren which was the motive, he became ensnared by the enemy.

The elders suggest to him that there were four men who had a vow on them. These he should take and purify himself with them as well as pay the charges. This action, they reasoned, would not only demonstrate that the reports were untrue, but that he, the Apostle of Gentiles "live in observance of the law" (21:24). To make this temptation stronger, they re-stated that which had been agreed concerning the status of the believing Gentiles, according to the decision of the church council years ago. All was a most subtle snare. He was by that action to show that, with all his preaching to the Gentiles, he was still a good Jew, faithful to all the traditions of the fathers, and attached to the temple.

Without entering into an examination of what the vow was, and the purifying and offering connected with it, we see the Apostle falling into the snare. He did, as far as the record goes, without a moment's hesitation accept the suggestion of the elders, and for a number of days we see him a visitor to the temple conforming to the customs of the law. Where was prayer and direction from the Lord? Alas, he had gone his own way against the warning voices of the Holy Spirit! And a strange sight it is to see the Apostle Paul back in the temple, going through these dead ceremonies, which had been ended by the death of the cross.

Chapter Twenty-One

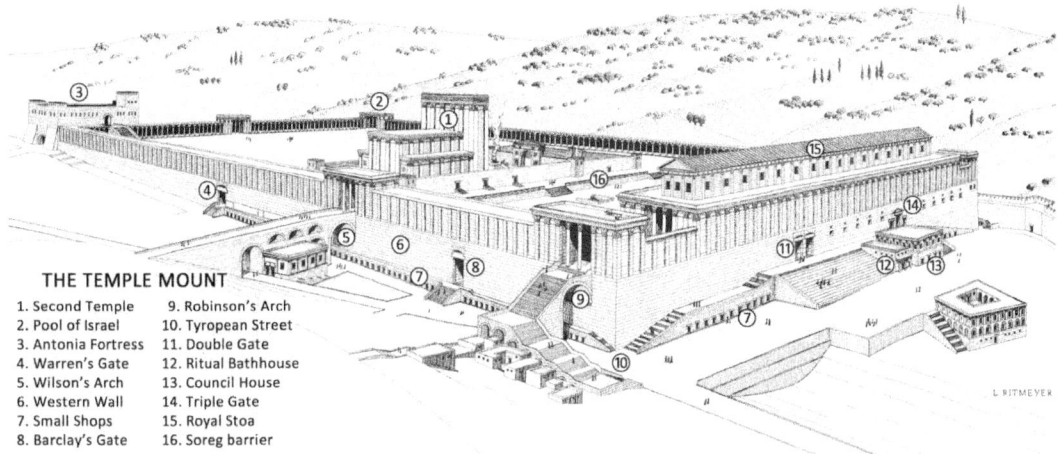

THE TEMPLE MOUNT
1. Second Temple
2. Pool of Israel
3. Antonia Fortress
4. Warren's Gate
5. Wilson's Arch
6. Western Wall
7. Small Shops
8. Barclay's Gate
9. Robinson's Arch
10. Tyropean Street
11. Double Gate
12. Ritual Bathhouse
13. Council House
14. Triple Gate
15. Royal Stoa
16. Soreg barrier

42. Jerusalem, Herod's Temple Mount at the time of Jesus. A reconstruction based on archaeological and historical evidence. This drawing illustrates the Herodian Temple Mount with associated structures and features, as seen from the southwest. This reconstruction is based directly on Leen Ritmeyer's own work at the Temple Mount (© Ritmeyer Archaeological Design. Labels by David E. Graves).

A strange sight to see him, who disclaimed all earthly authority and taught deliverance from the law and a union with an unseen Christ, submitting once more to the elementary things, as he calls them in his Epistle to the Galatians "the beggarly elements"! And has not the whole professing church fallen into the same snare? What the results of this subtle and evil advice were we shall find in the next paragraph.

4. THE UPROAR IN THE TEMPLE: PAUL TAKEN PRISONER (VS. 27–40).

> When the seven days were almost completed, the Jews from Asia, seeing him in the temple, stirred up the whole crowd and laid hands on him, crying out, "Men of Israel, help! This is the man who is teaching everyone everywhere against the people and the law and this place. Moreover, he even brought Greeks into the temple and has defiled this holy place." For they had previously seen Trophimus the Ephesian with him in the city, and they supposed that Paul had brought him into the temple. Then all the city was stirred up, and the people ran together. They seized Paul and dragged him out of the temple, and at once the gates were shut. And as they were seeking to kill him, word came to the tribune of the cohort that all Jerusalem was in confusion. He at once took soldiers and centurions and ran down to them. And when they saw the tribune and the soldiers, they stopped beating Paul. Then the tribune came up and arrested him and ordered him to be bound with two chains. He inquired who he was and what he had done. Some in the crowd were shouting one thing, some another. And as he could not learn the facts because of the uproar, he ordered him to be brought into the barracks. And when he came to the steps, he was actually carried by the soldiers because of the violence of the crowd, for the mob of the people followed, crying out, "Away with him!"
>
> As Paul was about to be brought into the barracks, he said to the tribune, "May I say something to you?" And he said, "Do you know Greek? Are you not the Egyptian, then, who recently stirred up a revolt and led the four thousand men of the Assassins out into the wilderness?" Paul replied, "I am a Jew, from Tarsus in Cilicia, a citizen of no obscure city. I beg you, permit me to speak to the people." And when he had given him permission, Paul, standing on the steps, motioned with his hand to the people. And when there was a great hush, he addressed them in the Hebrew language,[6] saying: (vs. 27–40).

---

[6] Or *the Hebrew dialect* (probably Aramaic).

The Acts of the Apostles

The seven days connected with the vow of these men were almost ended when the Jews, which were in Asia, seeing him in the temple, stirred up all the people and laid hands on him. In all probability Paul was not known to many people in Jerusalem. The Jews who lived in the city may not have known him at all by sight. But the city was filled with many Jews from Asia, that is the province of Asia, and as Ephesian Jews had come to Jerusalem for the feast, he did not escape their notice. They hated him and as they recognized him, they watched him closely and awaited their opportunity to do him harm. He was recognized in the city when a well known Gentile Ephesian, Trophimus, was in his company. They supposed that the Apostle had brought this Gentile Christian in the temple.

The outer court of the temple, which was called the Court of the Gentiles, was open to everybody. Then there was an inner court, which was known by the name of the Court of Israel. This court was separated from the outer court by the middle wall of partition (*soreg* barrier). There were barriers and pillars with inscriptions in Greek and Latin, warning strangers under the penalty of death not to advance into that holy court (see Fig. 43).[7] Inside the barrier was a high wall, which surrounded the inner court, and in this wall were doors (21:30). The eastern part of the Court was reserved for women; then a colonnade ran around the Court of the women (see Fig. 44). In its angles were chambers. One of these was called the House of the Nazarites, where the Nazarites boiled the peace offerings, shaved their heads, and burnt the hair. Here most likely the Jews from Asia discovered the despised and hated Apostle. Now their hour had come to carry out the satanic desire of

43. The Theodotus (priest and synagogue ruler) inscription, discovered by Raymond Weill in Jerusalem in 1914, preventing Gentiles from entering the sacred space (Heb. *soreg*) of the Temple.

putting the Apostle out of the way. So they held him; then with a characteristic phrase "Men of Israel," they cried for help and shouted out their accusation "this is the man who is teaching everyone everywhere against the people (the Jews)and the law and this place" (21:28). This language reminds us of what we read in connection with Stephen, he too had been accused by the Jews in a similar manner. Perhaps in that very moment it all came back to the memory of Paul, for he was present when Stephen stood up to answer the accusations. And even then the words of the Lord, as the Jews seized hold on him, may have come into Paul's heart: "For I will show him how much he must suffer for the sake of my name" (9:16). He had great trials in the past, but now he stood on the threshold of still greater sufferings. But the chief reason these Jews of Asia gave for laying hold on Paul was a false accusation. They charged him of having polluted the temple by bringing Greeks, uncircumcised Gentiles, into that holy place. They had seen him with Trophimus, and took it for granted that Trophimus, and perhaps other Greeks, had followed him into the temple.

A fearful scene followed. The news spread like wildfire. It spread in a very few minutes throughout the temple courts, and to the crowds outside, and with their shoutings and gesticulations they soon

---

[7] Graves, *Biblical Archaeology Vol 1: An Introduction*, 1:206–207.

CHAPTER TWENTY-ONE

attracted others, till the whole city was in an uproar. The name of Paul and temple pollution must have been shouted in every direction. Perhaps some of the older Jews may have even then remembered him as Saul the Pharisee, who so many years ago had been such a prominent figure in Jerusalem. And a great crime it was to defile the temple. Stoning according to their law was the penalty, and that fate seemed to be imminent for Paul. They dragged him out of the temple and the temple guard closed the doors. Then they fell upon him.

They did not dare to stone him in the place where he was; the place outside of the city was reserved for that. So to avoid another pollution of the temple, they began to beat him. They were endeavoring to kill him.

But God watched over his servant. His

44. Model of the Fortress Antonia, a military barracks built by Herod the Great near the Temple Mount and the Pool of Bethesda, in Jerusalem. Although this model displays four towers, Josephus described it as the Tower of Antoinia (*Ant.* 18:4:3). (See Fig 43. No. 3).

life was not in the hands of the mob but in the Lord's own hands, and such is the case with all his people. In connection with the temple buildings was a castle, known by the name, "the fortress of Antonia." It was built upon a very steep rock and connected with the buildings below by stairs. This fortress was occupied by a Roman company of soldiers, a cohort with a chief captain (Greek: *Chiliarch*, commander of a thousand men). The great disturbance in the courts below attracted at once the attention of this officer and he rushed his men to the scene. With soldiers and centurions he came down the stairs, and their appearance brought the beating of Paul to an end.

And the next thing! Two chains are put about the Apostle. Agabus' prophecy is fulfilled. He is a captive now, "the prisoner of the Lord," as later he called himself. Taking the advice of the elders to appease the displeasure of the zealous law-keeping Hebrew Christians, and trying to show that he was a good law-keeping Jew, had led him into this place where he now finds himself.

It was all failure from beginning to end. The object was not reached. And now his great heart filled with love for his brethren, had to begin to learn the sad lesson what the Lord told him "they will not accept your testimony about me" (22:18). As the chains were put up on him, bruised and bleeding, may it then not have dawned upon him that his love for his Jewish brethren had led him in a way which was not the Lord's way?

It is a blessed study to compare the sufferings of Paul, the treatment he received from his brethren according to the flesh, his behavior, with that which happened to the Lord Himself in the days of his flesh. There is a correspondence and it is quite marked. Such a comparison shows the creature weakness and imperfection in Paul, and the absolute perfection of him who, as to his office work, was made perfect through suffering.

The transportation of Paul into the fortress, however, was beset with many difficulties. One cried this and the other that, as the chief captain asked what Paul had done and who he was. The multitude cried again and again, "Away with him," "Away with him," the word which reminds us of another multitude, who rejected the Prince of Life and delivered him into the hands of the Gentiles. So great was the crowd of people that Paul had to be lifted up by the soldiers in order to bring him by the stairway into the fortress on the rock. When about to be led into the castle, Paul addressed the chief captain in Greek. The captain was disappointed in this, for he thought he was a certain Egyptian, who had led four thousand murderers into the desert. Paul gives the Roman officer his pedigree. "I am a Jew, from Tarsus in Cilicia" (21:39) and then requests the privilege of addressing the furious mob. This was permitted and taking a prominent place on the stairs, where he could be seen by all below, and when after beckoning to the people, silence had been secured, he addressed them in Hebrew. The break of the chapter at this point is unfortunate. The next chapter contains the first address of defence of the prisoner Paul.

Chapter Twenty-Two

What a scene it was! On the stairs, midway between the temple court and the fortress, stood the Apostle in chains, his person showing the effects of the beating he had received. Around him were the well-armed Roman soldiers (see Fig. 46), and below the multitude with up-turned faces, still wildly gesticulating and only becoming more silent when they heard the first words from Paul's lips in the Hebrew tongue.[1] We find two sections in this chapter:

1. The Address of the Apostle (vs. 1–21).

2. The Answer from the Mob, and Paul's Appeal to his Roman citizenship (vs. 22–30).

1. The Address of the Apostle (vs. 1–21).

It is the first address in his defence recorded in this book, and his own person and experience is the theme. Seventeen times he uses the word "I," so that we have in his words a sketch of his life. All is well put and shows the great tact and wisdom of the Apostle. We find that the address contains three well-defined parts. He was not permitted to finish his autobiographical statements, but the mob interrupted him, as many years before Stephen's address was cut short.

45. Roman soldier in *lorica segmentata* or *lorica laminata*. Photographed during a show of Legio XV from Pram, Austria.

Paul's Account of himself as a Jew (vs. 1–5).

The accusation against him was that "this is the man who is teaching everyone everywhere against the people and the law and this place" (21:28). This now he tries to meet first of all by the evidence of his past Jewish life. The advice of the elders, too, finds an echo in the opening words of his speech. They had told him that he should prove to the multitude that he walked orderly, keeping the law.

"Brothers and fathers, hear the defense that I now make before you."

---

[1] The Aramaic dialect, which was then universally used among the Jews.

And when they heard that he was addressing them in the Hebrew language,[2] they became even more quiet. And he said:

"I am a Jew, born in Tarsus in Cilicia, but brought up in this city, educated at the feet of Gamaliel[3] according to the strict manner of the law of our fathers, being zealous for God as all of you are this day. I persecuted this Way to the death, binding and delivering to prison both men and women, as the high priest and the whole council of elders can bear me witness. From them I received letters to the brothers, and I journeyed toward Damascus to take those also who were there and bring them in bonds to Jerusalem to be punished. (vs. 1–5).

It was a very wise and tactful utterance with which he began his defense. The crowd below which had used him so roughly and which was ready to murder him, he addressed as "Brothers and fathers." This was bound to secure at once their attention, as well as the use of their own language. But we may see in this conciliatory opening of his address an expression of his graciousness. The words which follow were spoken to show that he had had a true Jewish bringing up, and lived an exemplary Jewish life. First, he gives the fact of his birth outside of the land. Many were thus born and educated away from the homeland, but he was brought up in the City of Jerusalem, thereby showing that he belonged to a very jealous class of Jews, who cared for the religion and customs of the fathers. Furthermore, he had as teacher the great and well-known, as well as highly esteemed, Gamaliel. Gamaliel was a doctor of the Torah, the law, and a great leader of the strictest sect among the Jews, the Pharisees. So the speaker had become a Pharisee and had entered upon a life of the most scrupulous law-keeping as well as obedience to the traditions of the elders.

Next, he bears witness to his own zeal. He "being zealous for God as all of you are this day" (22:3). One can only admire the tactful courtesy of the speaker. He not only spoke of his own zeal for God, but acknowledged the same in his hearers. With these words he even declared the wild scene in which he was so prominently concerned, an expression of their zeal for God. In Romans he had written: "For I bear them witness that they have a zeal for God, but not according to knowledge" (Rom 10:2).

Next, he illustrates that zeal for God, which characterized his career as a Pharisee. Like the assembled mob he had been a persecutor. But he avoids speaking of those he persecuted by name. "I persecuted *this* Way to death" (22:4). All, however, knew what he meant by the expression "this way;" it had for them the meaning of the new sect, which had arisen in Judaism. The same term is used by Paul in Chapter 24:14. And how had he persecuted this new way, the believers in Jesus? Unto death, binding and delivering into prisons both men and women. It was a confession of his persecuting zeal. The same confession we read in the beginning of the Epistle of the Galatians:

> For you have heard of my former life in Judaism, how I persecuted the church of God violently and tried to destroy it. And I was advancing in Judaism beyond many of my own age among my people, so extremely zealous was I for the traditions of my fathers (Gal 1:13-14).

After he had thus briefly referred to the fact that he had been once energized by the same hatred against this way, he appealed to the ecclesiastical authorities as a witness. He referred to the letters, which so many years ago he had received, to persecute the believing Jews in Damascus, the letters which were never delivered by him. May there not have been a few among his hearers, who then remembered the young Pharisee of bygone days, Saul of Tarsus?

---

[2] Or *the Hebrew dialect* (probably Aramaic)
[3] Or *city at the feet of Gamaliel, educated*

The Story of his Conversion (vs. 6-16).

The young Pharisee had disappeared suddenly from the scene, and his persecuting zeal had terminated abruptly. How then had it come about.

> As I was on my way and drew near to Damascus, about noon a great light from heaven suddenly shone around me. And I fell to the ground and heard a voice saying to me, "Saul, Saul, why are you persecuting me?" And I answered, "Who are you, Lord?" And he said to me, "I am Jesus of Nazareth, whom you are persecuting." Now those who were with me saw the light but did not understand [4] the voice of the one who was speaking to me. And I said, "What shall I do, Lord?" And the Lord said to me, "Rise, and go into Damascus, and there you will be told all that is appointed for you to do." And since I could not see because of the brightness of that light, I was led by the hand by those who were with me, and came into Damascus.
>
> And one Ananias, a devout man according to the law, well spoken of by all the Jews who lived there, came to me, and standing by me said to me, "Brother Saul, receive your sight." And at that very hour I received my sight and saw him. And he said, "The God of our fathers appointed you to know his will, to see the Righteous One and to hear a voice from his mouth; for you will be a witness for him to everyone of what you have seen and heard. And now why do you wait? Rise and be baptized and wash away your sins, calling on his name." (vs. 6-16).

The remarkable incident we have already followed in our exposition of the ninth chapter. However, some very interesting details are added here by himself, the former account being the inspired historical record written by Luke. First, we note that it was at noon when the wonderful vision flashed before his eyes. While in Chapter 9 we read of a light that shined from heaven about him, here he tells us that it was a great light, and in Chapter 26:13 Paul informs us that it was "brighter than the sun." In the eleventh verse of our chapter he speaks of it as "glory"; even so it was glory of the risen and ascended Son of God. In Acts 9 we read that the voice of the Lord said to him, "I am Jesus," but here a more detailed account is given by Paul, and from it we learn that the Lord had said, "I am Jesus of Nazareth." As that worthy and blessed Name was mentioned by Paul, what dark and threatening looks must have met his gaze from the up-turned faces! And from his witness they learned that this same Jesus, whom they had rejected, is the Lord, and that he lives in the Glory. Of Ananias, Paul does not speak as a disciple at all, but he calls him "a devout man according to the law" (22:12), who had a good report of all the Jews in Damascus. In all this we have an evidence of the wisdom of Paul. He also avoided the word "Christ," though all knew whom he meant when he speaks of "that Just One." Thus he briefly had described how the Lord, the rejected Jesus of Nazareth, had appeared to him.[5]

The Divine Commission (vs. 17-21).

He next touched upon another episode in his experience. The interesting account he gives here is not recorded n the ninth chapter.

> "When I had returned to Jerusalem and was praying in the temple, I fell into a trance and saw him saying to me, 'Make haste and get out of Jerusalem quickly, because they will not accept your testimony about me.' And I said, 'Lord, they themselves know that in one synagogue after another I imprisoned and beat those who believed in you. And when the blood of Stephen your witness was being shed, I myself was standing by and approving and watching over the garments of

---

[4] Or *hear with understanding*

[5] Some have found a difficulty in the fact that here Paul says that his companions saw the light and heard not the voice, which spake with him. In chapter 9 the record states that they heard the voice. There is no discrepancy here. They did hear the voice, but were not able to understand the words which were spoken. They saw no one; only Paul saw the Lord.

those who killed him.' And he said to me, 'Go, for I will send you far away to the Gentiles.'" (vs. 17-21).

Once more the Lord had appeared to him, while praying in the temple when he was in a trance. In this same temple which stretched out before him, all this had taken place. And what an evidence to them of his sincere character that he had gone to the temple to offer up fervent prayers. He then repeats the words the Lord had spoken to him, "Make haste and get out of Jerusalem quickly, because they will not accept your testimony about me" (22:18). He himself now bound in chains, standing before the Jewish mob, was the living witness to the truth of these words. If he had but remembered those words and had followed completely the divine commission.

At that time his loving heart for his own people had prompted an answer. He told the Lord that he had a peculiar fitness to bear the testimony to his brethren in the beloved city. Did they not know that he had imprisoned and beaten those that believed in Him? When the blood of Stephen, the martyr, was shed, did he not stand by and consent to his death, keeping the raiment of those that slew him? It is beautiful to read these simple words of the intimate conversation Paul carried on with the Lord. And he could tell the Lord all about his sins and hatred against Himself and his own, recount once more the bitter persecutions he had practiced and the part he took in Stephen's death. Here we have a beautiful example of a conscience which has been purged, and knows that all is right. All this Paul relates to prove to them his sincerity as well as love for his kinsmen. The last word the Lord had spoken to him at that time was a word of commission: "go, for I will send you far away to the Gentiles" (22:21). The Lord had therefore called him to be the Apostle of the Gentiles. His defense was complete. He had fully demonstrated that he accusation against him was false, that he loved his people and the Lord Himself had called him to go to the Gentiles.

2. THE ANSWER FROM THE MOB AND PAUL'S APPEAL TO HIS ROMAN CITIZENSHIP (VS. 22-30).

Up to this word they listened to him. Then they raised their voices and said, "Away with such a fellow from the earth! For he should not be allowed to live." And as they were shouting and throwing off their cloaks and flinging dust into the air, the tribune ordered him to be brought into the barracks, saying that he should be examined by flogging, to find out why they were shouting against him like this. But when they had stretched him out for the whips,[6] Paul said to the centurion who was standing by, "Is it lawful for you to flog a man who is a Roman citizen and uncondemned?" When the centurion heard this, he went to the tribune and said to him, "What are you about to do? For this man is a Roman citizen." So the tribune came and said to him, "Tell me, are you a Roman citizen?" And he said, "Yes." The tribune answered, "I bought this citizenship for a large sum." Paul said, "But I am a citizen by birth." So those who were about to examine him withdrew from him immediately, and the tribune also was afraid, for he realized that Paul was a Roman citizen and that he had bound him.

But on the next day, desiring to know the real reason why he was being accused by the Jews, he unbound him and commanded the chief priests and all the council to meet, and he brought Paul down and set him before them. (vs. 22-30).

They were impatient listeners, the storm broke with the word "Gentiles." Another great tumult resulted and the many voices demanded that such a fellow should not live. It was a scene of utmost confusion. All crying, gesticulating wildly, throwing dust in the air, one of the common occurrences when Orientals get excited; they cast off their outer garments to do so.

---

[6] Or *when they had tied him up with leather strips.*

The chief captain seems to have been ignorant of the Aramaic dialect. He gave orders that Paul be now removed into the castle itself and be examined by scourging so that he might find out why they cried so against him. The torture was to be used to make him confess. He was led away, and everything made ready for the cruel treatment, when the prisoner spoke: "Is it lawful for you to flog a man who is a Roman citizen and uncondemned?" (22:25). The centurion reported this to the chiliarch, the chief officer, who at once appeared on the scene. When he discovered that Paul was indeed a Roman by birth, a higher type of Roman citizenship (see Fig. 47) than that which the chief captain had obtained by a great sum, they left their hands off of his person, and even the chiliarch was afraid. It was a highly illegal act to bind a Roman. Paul escaped the awful torture.

Not a few had pointed to this as a prominent failure in the career of the Apostle. According to these critics he made a grave mistake when he pleaded his Roman citizenship; he should have been silent and taken the unjust and cruel treatment without a murmur. If some of these harsh critics of the beloved Apostle were placed in the same condition, what would they do? As one has truly said: "It is easy to be a martyr in

46. Fragment of a Roman military diploma, or certificate of successful military service, granting citizenship to a retiring soldier and the dependents he had with him at the time. The key phrase is "*est civitas eis data*" where *civitas* means citizenship. *CIL* XVI 26 tabula II, Museum Carnuntum, Austria.

theory, and such are seldom martyrs in practice." He had a perfect right to tell the ignorant officers of the law who he was, and thus prevent a flagrant and cruel transgression of the law. And yet his conduct in Philippi was far different. Why did he not announce his Roman citizenship then? The power of the Spirit rested then upon him; it is different here. He is not acting in the liberty and peace of the Spirit, a fact which becomes more apparent in the next chapter, where we see him before the Sanhedrin.

Chapter Twenty-Three

In the last verse of the preceding chapter we read that the chief captain commanded that the chief priests and all the council should gather together. When this was accomplished, Paul was brought down and set before them. We divide the chapter into four sections:

1. Paul before the Sanhedrin (vs. 1–10).

2. The vision of the Lord (v. 11).

3. The plot to kill Paul and its discovery (vs. 12–22).

4. Paul taken to Caesarea (vs. 23–30).

1. PAUL BEFORE THE SANHEDRIN (VS. 1–10).

> And looking intently at the council, Paul said, "Brothers, I have lived my life before God in all good conscience up to this day." And the high priest Ananias commanded those who stood by him to strike him on the mouth. Then Paul said to him, "God is going to strike you, you whitewashed wall! Are you sitting to judge me according to the law, and yet contrary to the law you order me to be struck?" Those who stood by said, "Would you revile God's high priest?" 5And Paul said, "I did not know, brothers, that he was the high priest, for it is written, 'You shall not speak evil of a ruler of your people.'"
>
> Now when Paul perceived that one part were Sadducees and the other Pharisees, he cried out in the council, "Brothers, I am a Pharisee, a son of Pharisees. It is with respect to the hope and the resurrection of the dead that I am on trial." And when he had said this, a dissension arose between the Pharisees and the Sadducees, and the assembly was divided. For the Sadducees say that there is no resurrection, nor angel, nor spirit, but the Pharisees acknowledge them all. Then a great clamor arose, and some of the scribes of the Pharisees' party stood up and contended sharply, "We find nothing wrong in this man. What if a spirit or an angel spoke to him?" And when the dissension became violent, the tribune, afraid that Paul would be torn to pieces by them, commanded the soldiers to go down and take him away from among them by force and bring him into the barracks. (vs. 1–10).

For the last time, the Jewish council is mentioned in this book. Three times before the Sanhedrin had been called together in connection with those who believed in the Lord Jesus (2:5; 5:21 and 6:12–15). Peter and John, the twelve Apostles and Stephen, had to appear before the Sanhedrin and now Paul had to stand in the presence of the same body. Looking straight at the council, Paul did not wait for the formalities connected with the proceedings, but addressed the gathered Sanhedrin as men and brethren. This action shows that he did not consider himself at all an accused criminal. And strange are the words with which he opened his defence: "I have lived my life before God in all good conscience up to this day" (23:1). In this he made a public declaration of his righteousness, which reminds us of his confession as a Pharisee (Phil 3:4–6). This self-justification shows that he was not acting under the leading of the Holy Spirit. This bold language resulted in stirring up the anger of the high priest Ananias, who commanded that the bystanders should smite the Apostle on the mouth. And Paul was not slow to reply with a harsh word, calling the high priest a "whitewashed wall" and demanding of God to smite him. No doubt the high priest was indeed a "whitewashed wall" and fully deserved the judgment from God. But did Paul in speaking thus show the meekness of Him, whose servant he was? If Paul had been in the power of the Spirit and in the knowledge that he was doing the Lord's will, he would not have opened his mouth, nor acted in this hasty manner. However, the utterance he made was fulfilled, for some time later Ananias was assassinated. Paul recovered himself, professing that he did not know the high priest, who had commanded the smiting. The words "I did not know, brothers, that he was the high priest" (23:5), contain an apparent difficulty. The Apostle, so well acquainted with the customs of the council, must have known the high priest, both by the position he occupied and by the dress. Some have suggested that the Apostle was afflicted with a severe eye disease which blurred his vision. But this cannot be fully proven. The word "know" seems to solve the difficulty. This word among the Jews has also the meaning "to acknowledge" or "to make recognition." For instance, it has that meaning in the exhortation "to respect [know] those who labor among you" (1 Thess 5:12). Paul did not know the high priest may therefore mean that he did not want to acknowledge Ananias as the high priest, that he refused to recognize him as such. When Paul said he knew not that it was the high priest, he acknowledged his error he had made in refusing to recognize the president of the council by ignoring him. This seems to solve the difficulty.

The next utterance of the Apostle is still more strange. Once again he addresses the council as men and brethren. Then he cried "I am a Pharisee, a son of Pharisees. It is with respect to the hope and the resurrection of the dead that I am on trial" (23:6). This is the third claim he makes and it shows how far he had drifted. He had claimed being a Jew, then had pleaded his Roman citizenship, and now before the council, he reminds them that he is a Pharisee and the son of a Pharisee. Later from his Roman prison he wrote to the Philippians that he counted this all as dung. He had done so before. Here no doubt is a relapse. The reason which led him to do this was his knowledge that the Sanhedrin was composed of the two warring factions of Judaism, the Sadducees and the Pharisees. With his keen vision and knowledge of the conditions he saw the possible advantage of declaring himself a Pharisee. That might bring them to his side and end the difficulty in which he had become so seriously involved. Besides the confession that he is a prominent Pharisee, he stated the articles of the creed of the Pharisees which were so vigorously opposed by the Sadducees. He mentions "the hope" and "resurrection of the dead," which was really in question. This was a true statement. The hope is the Messianic hope of the coming of the Messiah. He had come in the person of the Lord Jesus Christ and yet he is "the hope"; for he is coming again. The resurrection of the dead is closely connected with Christ and his coming. The Sadducees were the Rationalists, and denied, besides the existence of spirits, the Messianic hope and the resurrection of the dead. A great discussion arose between these two parties. A big commotion followed. Some of the scribes belonging to the Pharisees cried loudly in defence of the prisoner "we find nothing wrong in this man. What if a spirit or an angel spoke to him?" (23:9). The latter sentence was a faint echo of the advice given by Gamaliel. The scene which followed beggars description. The shouting must have been terrific and Paul was in danger of being pulled to pieces by the council mob. Lysias, the chief captain, was obliged to interfere. The soldiers, at his command, came down and rescued Paul and brought him into the castle. The cleverness of Paul had been the means of liberating him from the hands of the Sanhedrin.

2. THE VISION OF THE LORD (V. 11).

> The following night the Lord stood by him and said, "Take courage, for as you have testified to the facts about me in Jerusalem, so you must testify also in Rome." (v. 11).

This is a most gracious and blessed fact, that now the Lord came into this scene of confusion and failure and in greatest tenderness to comfort and cheer his servant. One almost wishes it had pleased the Holy Ghost to give us a more detailed account of Paul in the castle that night and what took place. Two days had passed since the arrest of Paul and they had been eventful days. His body was bruised and full of pain. But how he must have suffered in his spirit! All the warnings frequently uttered by the Spirit of God not to go up to Jerusalem came back to his mind. The failure of having not heeded these warnings must have weighed heavily upon him. And the disappointment he had suffered! It was burning love for his brethren which had led him to Jerusalem and now he had received the fullest evidence that they would not receive his testimony. Thinking of what he had done and failed must have greatly humbled the Apostle. And now he was a prisoner. His career in preaching the Gospel among the Gentiles and Jews had been cut short. No doubt left alone in the castle all these thoughts and others crowded in upon him. There he sought his Lord in Prayer. What a prayer it must have been Paul prayed in the castle! How the tears must have flown as he told the Lord all, confessing his failure and telling him of his disappointment! And then, not an angel, but the Lord, stood by him that night. His loving arms were around his servant. He appeared to cheer him and assure him of his love.

There are three things especially to be noticed in the words of the Lord to Paul. He strengthened him by the encouraging word, "Take courage." In the New Testament this comforting expression is exclusively used by our Lord. And what a meaning it has coming from his lips! "Take courage." Disheartening were Paul's experiences, perplexing his situation, dark and mysterious his future, but the Lord bade him to take courage. What strength must have filled the Apostle's heart as these words came to him! And we too can hear the words of encouragement from our Lord in the midst of our difficulties and failures. He is the same to-day as he was then in that night. With such a Lord at our side we need never to despair.

Then the Lord spoke peace into his humbled breast and calmed all the feelings and questionings which had risen in Paul's mind. How little, Paul may have said to himself, "I told the Jews about my Lord and the Gospel! My testimony was not as faithful as it should have been. But now the Lord tells him that he had testified of him in Jerusalem." What Grace is this! The Lord told him that he had after all borne witness of Him. He did not remind him of his mistakes, his faults, and how he might have avoided them, but he reminds him of his faithfulness. Such is our Lord in his gracious dealings with his servants. All his questionings were ended. He knew all was right between the Lord and himself and that he was under his gracious and loving care. And then the Lord assures him also of future service. He had not yet reached the end of his labors. "You must testify also in Rome" (23:11). Rome then is his goal, which he has to reach as the prisoner of the Lord. How all this must have set him at rest! The Lord was with him and would bring him to Rome. And that Lord is with us and shall guide and provide for his servants. May our hearts be comforted and encouraged by Paul's experience during that night in the castle.

3. THE PLOT TO KILL PAUL AND ITS DISCOVERY (VS. 12–22).

> When it was day, the Jews made a plot and bound themselves by an oath neither to eat nor drink till they had killed Paul. There were more than forty who made this conspiracy. They went to the chief priests and elders and said, "We have strictly bound ourselves by an oath to taste no food till we have killed Paul. Now therefore you, along with the council, give notice to the tribune to bring him down to you, as though you were going to determine his case more exactly. And we are ready to kill him before he comes near."
>
> Now the son of Paul's sister heard of their ambush, so he went and entered the barracks and told Paul. Paul called one of the centurions and said, "Take this young man to the tribune, for he has something to tell him." So he took him and brought him to the tribune and said, "Paul the prisoner called me and asked me to bring this young man to you, as he has something to say to you." The tribune took him by the hand, and going aside asked him privately, "What is it that you have to tell me?" And he said, "The Jews have agreed to ask you to bring Paul down to the council tomorrow, as though they were going to inquire somewhat more closely about him. But do not be persuaded by them, for more than forty of their men are lying in ambush for him, who have bound themselves by an oath neither to eat nor drink till they have killed him. And now they are ready, waiting for your consent." So the tribune dismissed the young man, charging him, "Tell no one that you have informed me of these things." (vs. 12–22).

The conspiracy against Paul reveals the condition of the nation. Jerusalem had indeed become a city of murderers (Isa 1:21). More than forty had made a religious vow that they would kill Paul. The plan is laid and everything ready for its execution. But they had not reckoned with Paul's Lord. He was in his own hands and not in the hands of the Jews or the Gentiles, even as the life of all his servants rests in his omnipotent hand. The plot is discovered. A nephew of Paul was the chosen instrument.

Paul's sister, of whom we have no other knowledge apart from this passage, must have been a person of influence, for the son heard of the secret council and had likewise access into the castle. The chief captain heard of the plot from the lips of the young man and was now deeply concerned about Paul and his safety. This was the result of the knowledge this chief officer had gained, that Paul was a Roman citizen. The record needs no further comment. What now follows is all under his control, who had promised Paul that he would have to witness in Rome for Him.

4. PAUL TAKEN TO CAESAREA (VS. 23–35).

> Then he called two of the centurions and said, "Get ready two hundred soldiers, with seventy horsemen and two hundred spearmen to go as far as Caesarea at the third hour of the night.[1] Also provide mounts for Paul to ride and bring him safely to Felix the governor." And he wrote a letter to this effect:
>
> "Claudius Lysias, to his Excellency the governor Felix, greetings. This man was seized by the Jews and was about to be killed by them when I came upon them with the soldiers and rescued him, having learned that he was a Roman citizen. And desiring to know the charge for which they were accusing him, I brought him down to their council. I found that he was being accused about questions of their law, but charged with nothing deserving death or imprisonment. And when it was disclosed to me that there would be a plot against the man, I sent him to you at once, ordering his accusers also to state before you what they have against him."
>
> So the soldiers, according to their instructions, took Paul and brought him by night to Antipatris. And on the next day they returned to the barracks, letting the horsemen go on with him. When they had come to Caesarea and delivered the letter to the governor, they presented Paul also before him. On reading the letter, he asked what province he was from. And when he learned that he was from Cilicia, he said, "I will give you a hearing when your accusers

---

[1] That is, 9 p.m.

arrive." And he commanded him to be guarded in Herod's praetorium. (vs. 23–35).

The prisoner of the Lord is now delivered into the hands of the Gentiles. A large force of soldiers accompanied Paul for his protection, while horses were also supplied to the Apostle. The danger was great, hence, the great precaution the chief officer, whose name is now mentioned, Claudius Lysias had taken. Could we have read in Paul's own heart we would have seen there the peace of Christ; the words of his Lord still resounded in that faithful and devoted heart "take courage."

The letter of Claudius Lysias to the governor Felix is interesting. It shows how Lysias claims the full credit of having rescued Paul, because he was a Roman. He declares him innocent, yet delivers him into the hands of the governor.

One would also like to know what had become of the forty conspirators. If they were true to their vow not to eat nor to drink till Paul had been killed, they must have starved to death, which, we are sure did not happen. Caesarea is reached in safety and Paul is delivered into the hands of the governor, who promised him a hearing as soon as the accusers would arrive. Jerusalem now laid forever behind him. Rome was before him.

CHAPTER TWENTY-FOUR

The account of the trial of the Apostle Paul before the Governor Felix and how this trial terminated is reported in this chapter.

1. The indictment of Paul (vs. 1–9).

2. The defence of the Apostle (vs. 10–21).

3. How Felix disposed of the case (vs. 22–23).

4. Paul addresses Felix (vs. 24–27).

1. THE INDICTMENT OF PAUL (VS. 1–9).

And after five days the high priest Ananias came down with some elders and a spokesman, one Tertullus. They laid before the governor their case against Paul. And when he had been summoned, Tertullus began to accuse him, saying:

"Since through you we enjoy much peace, and since by your foresight, most excellent Felix, reforms are being made for this nation, in every way and everywhere we accept this with all gratitude. But, to detain[1] you no further, I beg you in your kindness to hear us briefly. For we have found this man a plague, one who stirs up riots among all the Jews throughout the world and is a ringleader of the sect of the Nazarenes. He even tried to profane the temple, but we seized him.[2] By examining him yourself you will be able to find out from him about everything of which we accuse him."

The Jews also joined in the charge, affirming that all these things were so. (vs. 1–9).

If the Jews, after Paul's removal from Jerusalem, had not pressed the case against him, he would have been liberated. As he had gone years ago to Damascus to persecute the Christians there, so now the Jews follow him to Caesarea to accuse him before the Roman governor. They evidently did not lose any time. Only a few days had elapsed when a strong deputation from Jerusalem appeared in Caesarea. The high priest filled with much hatred against Paul had taken it upon himself to come in person. This must have been an unusual occurrence for a person of Ananias' standing to leave Jerusalem. He came not alone but brought with him the elders and a professional Roman lawyer Tertullus. No doubt the scheme of indictment was cleverly laid and the high priest must have counted much on his personal presence and on the eloquence of the hired lawyer. God was left out completely.

The address of Tertullus is characteristically Roman. He pays a flattering tribute to Felix, which however fell on barren ground. That official knew well the hollowness of these compliments. The words Tertullus used against the great man of God are extremely vile and manifest the hiss of the serpent. He "found this man a plague" (24:5), a person of whom society may well be rid of. The indictment contains three counts. First stands a political accusation. This, in presence of the high Roman officer, was of the greatest importance. Any conspiracy against the Roman government was a capital offence. The charge of sedition or treason was thus

---

[1] Or *weary*

[2] Some manuscripts add *and we would have judged him according to our law. /But the chief captain Lysias came and with great violence took him out of our hands,* 8*commanding his accusers to come before you.*

at once laid at the door of the Apostle. The second offence Tertullus brought against Paul was of a religious nature. As ringleader of the Nazarenes, presented by him as a sect of the Jews, he had abetted that which was against the peace of Judaism and introduced not alone a disturbing element, but had transgressed another Roman law, which forbade the introduction of unrecognized religious sects. The third charge was the profanation of the temple. If this last charge could have been proven against Paul the sentence of death would have fallen against him.

The address of Tertullus is most likely not reported in full. There is a difficulty about the words

> and we would have judged him according to our law. But the chief captain Lysias came and with great violence took him out of our hands, commanding his accusers to come before you (24:6-8).

In some of the oldest manuscripts [aleph, A, B] these words are not found; in the manuscripts in which they are found variations occur. The critical school has ruled them out. The chief reason given besides the textual difficulty is because the Jews would not have accused Lysias. We believe the words are genuine and that they belong in the text. If they are omitted the words "By examining him yourself you will be able to find out from him about everything of which we accuse him" must be applied to Paul. But that was against Roman customs that the judge should be referred to the prisoner. If they are not omitted then Tertullus meant that Lysias should himself be examined. Verse 22 settles the difficulty. Felix said that he would delay his decision till Lysias would arrive.

When Tertullus had completed his speech, the Jews, Ananias and his elders fully endorsed the statements of their lawyer.

2. THE DEFENCE OF THE APOSTLE (VS. 10–21).

> And when the governor had nodded to him to speak, Paul replied:
>
> "Knowing that for many years you have been a judge over this nation, I cheerfully make my defense. You can verify that it is not more than twelve days since I went up to worship in Jerusalem, and they did not find me disputing with anyone or stirring up a crowd, either in the temple or in the synagogues or in the city. Neither can they prove to you what they now bring up against me. But this I confess to you, that according to the Way, which they call a sect, I worship the God of our fathers, believing everything laid down by the Law and written in the Prophets, having a hope in God, which these men themselves accept, that there will be a resurrection of both the just and the unjust. So I always take pains to have a clear conscience toward both God and man. Now after several years I came to bring alms to my nation and to present offerings. While I was doing this, they found me purified in the temple, without any crowd or tumult. But some Jews from Asia— they ought to be here before you and to make an accusation, should they have anything against me. Or else let these men themselves say what wrongdoing they found when I stood before the council, other than this one thing that I cried out while standing among them: 'It is with respect to the resurrection of the dead that I am on trial before you this day.'" (vs. 10–21).

For the third time in the history of this book, Paul addresses a Roman officer of high rank, Gallio and Sergius Paulus were the others. His defense is masterly. The Spirit of God helped him now as he faced his cunning accusers and his judge. No flattery is used by him. Any kind of flattery is unworthy of a Christian. The flattering tongue is the serpent's tongue.

> A flattering mouth works ruin (Prov 26:28). . . . A man who flatters his neighbor spreads a net for his feet (Prov 29:5). . . . May the Lord cut off all flattering lips, the tongue that makes great boasts (Ps 12:3).

Paul only refers to the fact that Felix was a judge appointed over the nation for many years. His innocence is apparent in the cheerful manner in which he begins his defence. His address contains: A denial of the first charge; A confession and admission concerning the second, and A complete vindication of the accusation of the temple profanation.

He points first of all to the fact that only twelve days had elapsed since his arrival in Jerusalem and that he did not go there to cause an insurrection against the Roman authorities, but to worship. He did not congregate a crowd. He did not dispute openly (as Stephen did) nor did he incite the Jews in the synagogues or in the city to rebellion. Boldly he asserts that they have no proof whatever against him as a political offender.

But it was different with the second count of Tertullus' indictment. Here he admits the fact that "the Way" which they call heresy, faith in Christ, is his way of worshipping the God of his fathers. But this way did not change his belief in the law and the prophets, as the accusation might have implied. Then he speaks of hope toward God, the resurrection of the dead, both the just and the unjust. He also testifies of his own life and walk as a believer in the way in which he served God. He had used self-discipline to have a conscience void of offence toward God and men. The great truth he held and for which he had been imprisoned, resulted in a righteous life. In a brief word, he speaks of his own love for the nation, and states one of the purposes of his visit to Jerusalem to bring alms and offerings to his nation. How simple, yet masterly, all this was put.

But the last charge had to be refuted. The falsity of what Tertullus had accused him he proves in a few well-chosen words. He had been in the temple, but not to profane it. There was no multitude; there was no tumult from his side. No witnesses were present to substantiate the charge of the profanation of the temple. He even appealed to Ananias and the elders to speak if any evil had been found in him when he had appeared before the Council. He readily owns the statement he had made touching resurrection, the words which precipitated the riot. He had proven the injustice of the charges and by his honest admissions demonstrated his innocence.

3. How Felix Disposed of the Case (vs. 22–23).

> But Felix, having a rather accurate knowledge of the Way, put them off, saying, "When Lysias the tribune comes down, I will decide your case." Then he gave orders to the centurion that he should be kept in custody but have some liberty, and that none of his friends should be prevented from attending to his needs. (vs. 22–23).

Felix had more perfect knowledge of the way. He was acquainted with the truths concerning Christ and with Christianity, though he himself was not walking in the way. He knew that the accusations were not true. He refuses a decision. Justice demanded that Paul should be set at liberty. However, Felix defers it all to the time when Lysias, the chief captain, came to Caesarea. But Lysias never showed up. Paul was kept a prisoner. A second hearing before Felix he never received; but Felix heard Paul, as we read in the concluding paragraph of this chapter.

4. Paul Addresses Felix (vs. 24–27).

> After some days Felix came with his wife Drusilla, who was Jewish, and he sent for Paul and heard him speak about faith in Christ Jesus. And as he reasoned about righteousness and self-control and the coming judgment, Felix was alarmed and said, "Go away for the present. When I get an opportunity I will summon you." At the same time he hoped that money would be given him by Paul. So he sent for him often and conversed with him. When two years had elapsed, Felix was succeeded by Porcius Festus. And desiring to do the Jews a favor, Felix left Paul in prison. (vs. 24–27).

Felix was married three times. His wife,

Drusilla, mentioned here, was a daughter of Herod, that is Agrippa I, who slew James. Drusilla's brother was the Agrippa mentioned in the twenty-sixth chapter of our book. Drusilla had been married to the King of Emesa. She had abandoned him for Felix, and was at that time not yet 20 years old. According to some authorities it was she who expressed the desire to hear the Apostle speak concerning the faith of Christ. No doubt it was mere curiosity, if not to ridicule the servant of the Lord. Where the audience took place is not stated.

Paul knew undoubtedly Felix and Drusilla's history. The prisoner becomes judge. Instead of satisfying their curiosity, he speaks boldly truths concerning righteousness, temperance and judgment to come which uncovered the wicked doings of the pair and touched the conscience of Felix. He trembled as he saw his heart laid bare and got a glimpse of judgment to come. He refused the solemn message and therefore Paul could not present to him the blessed Gospel.

The address of Paul was not completed. Felix broke it off and dismissed the preacher with that familiar excuse, which has led countless souls to eternal ruin, "when I get an opportunity I will summon you" (24:25). He did send often for him and communed with him, but it was not to learn the way of life. He expected a bribe from Paul so that he might purchase his liberty. The Apostle remained a prisoner in Caesarea for two years. No doubt during this time he enjoyed the fellowship of the saints. Besides Luke, Aristarchus, a Macedonian of Thessalonica, was with Paul. We doubt not with the liberty granted to the Apostle he had many opportunities to minister the Word. Perhaps it was during these two years that Luke, the beloved physician, was moved to write the Gospel record which bears his name and which was addressed to Theophilus.

Felix left Paul behind as prisoner, thinking to show the Jews a favor. Porcius Festus became governor in the place of Felix.

Chapter Twenty-Five

Over two years before the history contained in the present chapter transpired, the Lord had spoken to Paul during that memorable night in the castle Antonia, "Take courage, for as you have testified to the facts about me in Jerusalem, so you must testify also in Rome" (23:11). In this chapter we approach the end of this book. Paul appealed to Caesar, and the new governor answered him, "To Caesar you have appealed; to Caesar you shall go" (25:12). After his great speech before King Agrippa, we have the record of the journey, the shipwreck and his arrival in Rome and his presence there. With this the great historical book of the Acts closes.

1. Festus and the Jews. Paul appeals to Caesar (vs. 1–12).

2. King Agrippa visits Festus (vs. 13–22).

3. Paul brought before the King (vs. 23–27).

1. Festus and the Jews. Paul appeals to Caesar (vs. 1–12).

> Now three days after Festus had arrived in the province, he went up to Jerusalem from Caesarea. And the chief priests and the principal men of the Jews laid out their case against Paul, and they urged him, asking as a favor against Paul[1] that he summon him to Jerusalem—because they were planning an ambush to kill him on the way. Festus replied that Paul was being kept at Caesarea and that he himself intended to go there shortly. "So," said he, "let the men of authority among you go down with me, and if there is anything wrong about the man, let them bring charges against him."
>
> After he stayed among them not more than eight or ten days, he went down to Caesarea. And the next day he took his seat on the tribunal and ordered Paul to be brought. When he had arrived, the Jews who had come down from Jerusalem stood around him, bringing many and serious charges against him that they could not prove. Paul argued in his defense, "Neither against the law of the Jews, nor against the temple, nor against Caesar have I committed any offense." But Festus, wishing to do the Jews a favor, said to Paul, "Do you wish to go up to Jerusalem and there be tried on these charges before me?" But Paul said, "I am standing before Caesar's tribunal, where I ought to be tried. To the Jews I have done no wrong, as you yourself know very well. If then I am a wrongdoer and have committed anything for which I deserve to die, I do not seek to escape death. But if there is nothing to their charges against me, no one can give me up to them. I appeal to Caesar." Then Festus, when he had conferred with his council, answered, "To Caesar you have appealed; to Caesar you shall go." (vs. 1–12).

The new governor, Festus, had arrived at Caesarea, and then went up to Jerusalem, the capital of the province. The Jews had not forgotten Paul, though they had not attempted another accusation before Felix, knowing that the case was hopeless. But they made at once an effort with the new governor. No sooner had this official made his appearance in Jerusalem, but the high priest and the chief of the Jews made a report about Paul. Most likely Festus had not even heard of Paul up to that time. Ananias was no longer high priest; Ishmael

---

[1] Greek *him*

Ben Phabi had taken the office. What really took place in Jerusalem, Festus later relates to Agrippa. When Paul was presented to Agrippa, Festus introduced him by saying, "you see this man about whom the whole Jewish people petitioned me, both in Jerusalem and here, shouting that he ought not to live any longer" (25:24). A scene of tumult must have been enacted in Jerusalem when Festus showed himself. The mob clamored for the life of Paul. When they noticed the reluctance of the governor, they concocted another plan. They requested that Paul should be brought to Jerusalem. On the way there they intended to murder him.

Why did not Festus fall in line with this suggestion? When he saw Paul face to face he asked him the question if he would go up to Jerusalem to be judged there. Why then did he not consent to the proposal of the Jews? he knew nothing of the murderous plot against Paul. It was God who kept him from granting the desire of the Jews. That eye which neither sleeps nor slumbers kept watch over Paul as it still does over every child of God. Festus demanded instead that some Jews should come to Caesarea and accuse Paul and he would hear the case. After he had tarried in Jerusalem for over ten days, he returned to Caesarea. Paul then appeared before him for trial and the Jews were there from Jerusalem. But it was a wild scene again. They brought many and grievous complaints against Paul, but they could not prove anything. This failure must have been the source of much excitement. It was then that the same scene which took place in Jerusalem was gone through once more. They cried out that he should not live any longer (v. 24).

But how calm the Apostle stands in the midst of that scene of turmoil. His words are brief and positive. "Neither against the law of the Jews, nor against the temple, nor against Caesar have I committed any offense" (25:8). This shows that the same accusations were brought against him.

Festus remembered the former request of the Jews to have Paul in Jerusalem. To please them he asked Paul if he would go to Jerusalem. He refuses to be delivered to them. If he is an offender, he is ready to die. Then it was when he appealed to Caesar. Did he do wrong? Certainly not. He knew the Lord's will that he had to testify in Rome. Rome was the goal before him. He acted in this according to the will of God. Festus and Agrippa later declared that he might have been set at liberty, if he had not appealed to Caesar. It was not lack of faith Paul exhibited in appealing to Caesar, but an evidence of faith and submission to the will of the Lord. Festus held a meeting with his council and declared, "to Caesar you shall go" (25:12).

2. KING AGRIPPA VISITS FESTUS (VS. 13–22).

Now when some days had passed, Agrippa the king and Bernice arrived at Caesarea and greeted Festus. And as they stayed there many days, Festus laid Paul's case before the king, saying, "There is a man left prisoner by Felix, and when I was at Jerusalem, the chief priests and the elders of the Jews laid out their case against him, asking for a sentence of condemnation against him. I answered them that it was not the custom of the Romans to give up anyone before the accused met the accusers face to face and had opportunity to make his defense concerning the charge laid against him. So when they came together here, I made no delay, but on the next day took my seat on the tribunal and ordered the man to be brought. When the accusers stood up, they brought no charge in his case of such evils as I supposed. Rather they had certain points of dispute with him about their own religion and about a certain Jesus, who was dead, but whom Paul asserted to be alive. Being at a loss how to investigate these questions, I asked whether he wanted to go to Jerusalem and be tried there regarding them. But when Paul had appealed to be kept in custody for the decision of the emperor, I ordered him to be held until I could send him to Caesar." Then Agrippa said to Festus,

"I would like to hear the man myself." "Tomorrow," said he, "you will hear him." (vs. 13–22).

Agrippa and Bernice paid a visit to the new governor. The father of this king was known as Herod Agrippa and died under awful circumstances (ch. 12) in the year 44. When his father died Agrippa was in Rome. He was too young to receive the kingdom of his father Herod. Eight years later, Herod, King of Chalcis, the uncle of Agrippa, died. He had married Agrippa's sister Bernice, and Caesar gave Chalcis to Agrippa. Later Agrippa received the title as king. Agrippa I had left three daughters besides this son-Bernice, Marianne and Drusilla, the wife of Felix. Bernice, who was the wife of her uncle, after his death joined her brother Agrippa in Rome. She married a Celician ruler, but deserted him and joined again her brother, in whose company she paid this visit to Caesarea.

The coming of King Agrippa solved the dilemma of Festus. He knew little of the case, yet he was expected to make in the so-called "letters demissory," a full statement of the case. Agrippa was a Jew and he was also thoroughly Roman, so that Festus could expect help from him in knowing the facts about his prisoner. After the visit had lasted many days, Festus lays the case of Paul before Agrippa. No further comment is needed on the words of Festus. He shows his ignorance as a Roman heathen of the Lord Jesus and his resurrection, when he calls this great event a Jewish superstition. Agrippa then expressed a desire to hear the man and Festus was only too willing to show this favor to the king.

3. PAUL BEFORE THE KING (VS. 23–27).

So on the next day Agrippa and Bernice came with great pomp, and they entered the audience hall with the military tribunes and the prominent men of the city. Then, at the command of Festus, Paul was brought in. And Festus said, "King Agrippa and all who are present with us, you see this man about whom the whole Jewish people petitioned me, both in Jerusalem and here, shouting that he ought not to live any longer. But I found that he had done nothing deserving death. And as he himself appealed to the emperor, I decided to go ahead and send him. But I have nothing definite to write to my lord about him. Therefore I have brought him before you all, and especially before you, King Agrippa, so that, after we have examined him, I may have something to write. For it seems to me unreasonable, in sending a prisoner, not to indicate the charges against him." (vs. 23–27).

The presentation of Paul was made a state occasion. Agrippa and his wicked sister Bernice appeared in royal splendor and all the military and civic officials turned out. It must have been a splendid gathering which had come together in the audience chamber. After they had all entered and taken their places, the rattling of a chain was heard and Paul was led into the presence of the assembled company. What a contrast! Perhaps they looked upon him with pity as they saw the chain. But more pity must have filled the heart of the great servant of Christ as he saw the poor lost souls bedecked with the miserable tinsel of earth. Festus addressed the King and the whole company. He frankly states what troubled him and that he expects the King to furnish the material for the statements he had, as governor, to send to Rome.

Chapter Twenty-Six

So Agrippa said to Paul, "'you have permission to speak for yourself.' Then Paul stretched out his hand and made his defense" (26:1). But his great address before the King is not so much a defence of himself; he speaks of the Lord and his gracious dealings with himself. The Lord's own words concerning Paul are again accomplished. "He is a chosen instrument of mine to carry my name before the Gentiles and kings and the children of Israel" (9:15). He bears now witness to his Name before a King.

1. The Address of the Apostle Paul (vs. 2–23).

2. The Interruption by Festus and the Appeal to the King (vs. 24–29).

3. The Verdict (vs. 30–32).

1. THE ADDRESS OF THE APOSTLE PAUL (VS. 2–23).

This is no doubt the greatest of his addresses. It has several parts.

The Opening Words (vs. 2–3).

> "I consider myself fortunate that it is before you, King Agrippa, I am going to make my defense today against all the accusations of the Jews, especially because you are familiar with all the customs and controversies of the Jews. Therefore I beg you to listen to me patiently. (vs. 2–3).

These are gracious words. Even as he stands in chains the great Apostle counts himself happy. His happiness consisted in the knowledge that he was now privileged to bear witness of his Lord and the Gospel committed to him before such an audience. What an opportunity it was to him and how he rejoiced that he could speak of Him, whom he served. He also honored the King by a brief remark, in which he expressed his delight in speaking before one who was so fully acquainted with Jewish customs and questions.

A Restatement of his Past Life as a Pharisee (vs. 4–11).

> "My manner of life from my youth, spent from the beginning among my own nation and in Jerusalem, is known by all the Jews. They have known for a long time, if they are willing to testify, that according to the strictest party of our religion I have lived as a Pharisee. And now I stand here on trial because of my hope in the promise made by God to our fathers, to which our twelve tribes hope to attain, as they earnestly worship night and day. And for this hope I am accused by Jews, O king! Why is it thought incredible by any of you that God raises the dead?
>
> "I myself was convinced that I ought to do many things in opposing the name of Jesus of Nazareth. And I did so in Jerusalem. I not only locked up many of the saints in prison after receiving authority from the chief priests, but when they were put to death I cast my vote against them. And I punished them often in all the synagogues and tried to make them blaspheme, and in raging fury against them I persecuted them even to foreign cities. (vs. 4–11).

Similar statements we find in his first address as prisoner when he addressed the Jewish multitudes in the temple (22:3–5). Here, however, he enters more into the character of the accusation brought against him. He had lived conscientiously as a Pharisee. As such he had believed and trusted in the hope of the promise made of God to the fathers. The twelve tribes, that is all Israel serving God instantly, expected the realization of this promised hope. This hope is the national one of the nation's future glory and blessing. But it centers in the Person of the Messiah, Christ. He is the hope of Israel, abundantly borne witness to by the Prophets of God, whose testimony concerning the future of Israel is always linked with the Holy One, the Redeemer, and his manifestation in the midst of Israel. Thus Paul establishes the fact that he is one in hope and spirit with the nation in their expectation of the fulfilment of the promises of God. And on account of this hope, he told the King he was accused of the Jews.

At once he touches upon the resurrection of the Lord Jesus Christ. Why should it be thought a thing incredible with you, that God should raise the dead? The whole history of Israel bears witness to the fact, that God can bring life from the dead. The very origin of the nation demonstrates this, for Sarah's womb was a grave and God brought life out of that grave. Many promises of the past vouched for God's power to raise the dead. The nation had this promise that spiritual and national death is to give way to spiritual and national life (Ezek 37:1–15; Hosea 6:1–3). The resurrection of the Lord Jesus Christ proved him to be the Holy One and the Hope of Israel. In this sense Peter speaks of his resurrection.

> Blessed be the God and Father of our Lord Jesus Christ! According to his great mercy, he has caused us to be born again to a living hope through the resurrection of Jesus Christ from the dead (1 Pet 1:3).

The grave of the Lord Jesus was for the disciples the grave of their national hope, but his resurrection from the dead the revival of that hope.

Then once more the Apostle tells of how he persecuted the saints and did many things contrary to the name of Jesus of Nazareth. It is the darkest picture he gives here of himself. He shut up the saints in prison, he voted their death, he punished them in synagogues, he compelled them to blaspheme, he raved against them and even persecuted them in strange cities. And upon that dark background he can now flash forth once more the story of his conversion.

The Heavenly Vision (vs. 12–17).

> In this connection I journeyed to Damascus with the authority and commission of the chief priests. At midday, O king, I saw on the way a light from heaven, brighter than the sun, that shone around me and those who journeyed with me. And when we had all fallen to the ground, I heard a voice saying to me in the Hebrew language,[1] "Saul, Saul, why are you persecuting me? It is hard for you to kick against the goads." And I said, "Who are you, Lord?" And the Lord said, "I am Jesus whom you are persecuting. But rise and stand upon your feet, for I have appeared to you for this purpose, to appoint you as a servant and witness to the things in which you have seen me and to those in which I will appear to you, delivering you from your people and from the Gentiles—to whom I am sending you" (vs. 12–17).

Once more, for the last time in this book, the record of his remarkable experience is given. As we have given an exposition of it before we need not enter into it again. The comparison of the different records will show that they are complementary and not contradictory as often claimed. He tells here especially of the quality of the light which burst from heaven upon him. It was above the brightness of the sun, the glory light of Him, whose members on earth he had persecuted. Some day the same glory will flash forth once more and that future manifestation of the Lord will mark the conversion of the nation. Paul's experience

---

[1] Or *the Hebrew dialect* (probably Aramaic).

is a type of all this. Then he had received his divine commission. He was to be a minister and a witness of things he had seen and he were yet to see. The latter refer to the subsequent revelations he received from the Lord. But his special ministry was to the Gentiles "to whom I am sending you."

The Gospel Message Declared (v. 18).

> "to open their eyes, so that they may turn from darkness to light and from the power of Satan to God, that they may receive forgiveness of sins and a place among those who are sanctified by faith in me." (v. 18).

This may be looked upon as the center of the Apostle's address. Now the proper moment had arrived to state the Gospel message before this company. It is a terse statement of the message which the Lord had committed to him. All the elements of the Gospel are contained in this verse. There is first the condition of man by nature. Eyes, which are blind, in darkness, under the power of Satan. The eyes are to be opened, and through the Gospel man is turned from darkness to light, from the power of Satan to God. In Colossians 1:12 the same is stated. Then the blessings of conversion. Forgiveness of sins and an inheritance. Faith is the means of all this; sanctification, that is separation, in conversion "by faith in me." One wonders if the Holy Spirit even then did not bless the message to some heart and the Grace of God bestowed these blessings upon some believing sinners. It may have been so. The day will make it known.

The Obedience to the Heavenly Vision (vs. 19–23).

> "Therefore, O King Agrippa, I was not disobedient to the heavenly vision, but declared first to those in Damascus, then in Jerusalem and throughout all the region of Judea, and also to the Gentiles, that they should repent and turn to God, performing deeds in keeping with their repentance. For this reason the Jews seized me in the temple and tried to kill me. To this day I have had the help that comes from God, and so I stand here testifying both to small and great, saying nothing but what the prophets and Moses said would come to pass: that the Christ must suffer and that, by being the first to rise from the dead, he would proclaim light both to our people and to the Gentiles." (vs. 19–23).

He had been obedient to the heavenly vision. How else could it be? his whole life was given up in service to Him, whose Glory he had seen, whose Grace had so wonderfully saved him. In verse 20 he sums up the untiring activity of his life and service. He tells King Agrippa in a brief sentence of the murderous attempt of the Jews. Furthermore he gives God the glory for having kept him through the dark experience since his arrest so that he can continue his witnessing. All his teaching and preaching had been in agreement with the testimony of the Prophets. Christ should suffer, rise from the dead and blessing for the people (Jews) and the Gentiles should be the result.

2. THE INTERRUPTION BY FESTUS AND THE APPEAL TO THE KING (VS. 24–29).

> And as he was saying these things in his defense, Festus said with a loud voice, "Paul, you are out of your mind; your great learning is driving you out of your mind." But Paul said, "I am not out of my mind, most excellent Festus, but I am speaking true and rational words. For the king knows about these things, and to him I speak boldly. For I am persuaded that none of these things has escaped his notice, for this has not been done in a corner. King Agrippa, do you believe the prophets? I know that you believe." And Agrippa said to Paul, "In a short time would you persuade me to be a Christian?"[2] And Paul said, "Whether short or long, I would to God that not only you but also all who hear me this day might become such as I am—except for these chains." (vs. 24–29).

---

[2] Or *In a short time you would persuade me to act like a Christian!*

CHAPTER TWENTY-SIX

47. Aerial photo of Caesarea Maritima. 1. King Agrippas' palace, probably the place of Paul's imprisonment. 2. Hippodrome. 3. The theatre.

Festus, the Gentile, ignorant of much what Paul so blessedly declared and yet deeply impressed with the prisoner's eloquent enthusiasm, interrupted him. "You are out of your mind; your great learning is driving you out of your mind" (26:24). Thus the Lord himself had been charged (Mark 3:21; John 10:20).

Paul in a courteous answer tells the startled Festus that his words were not words of a mad man, but words of truth and soberness. The words of a Spirit guided and Spirit filled man are always such. Then Paul turns to the King and appeals to him. The Jewish King knew that the things he had declared were not inventions of a diseased brain but facts. The facts he had related had not taken place in some obscure corner. The King knew of the appearance of Christ, of his death and all the other related events. Perhaps the uneasiness of the King as the matter was directly put before him led to the bold question of the prisoner. The one who was questioned concerning his life now turns questioner. "King Agrippa, do you believe the prophets? I know that you believe" (26:27). The King was thus brought face to face with the important message. Decision is demanded. Could he, the Jewish King, in the presence of such an audience of Jews and Gentiles commit himself? I know that thou believest, was the declaration of the inspired messenger. He could not deny the fact that he did believe the prophets and he would not confess that he accepted the facts as stated by Paul and that he believed.

It was a clever word by which he escaped the difficulty. "In a short time would you persuade me to be a Christian?" (26:28). The meaning is rather "by a little more persuasion you might make me a Christian." No doubt conviction had taken hold on him. In this half mocking way he answers the Apostle. How many after him have acted in the same way and rejected the Grace, which stood ready to save.

And then that great heart of the Apostle Paul, filled with divine, yearning love, bursts forth in a prayer for the convicted King and the whole company. "I would to God that not only you but also all who hear me this day might become such as I am—except for these chains" (26:29). What a memorable event! Paul before Agrippa and divine love pleading through the prisoner of the Lord.

3. THE VERDICT (VS. 30–32).

> Then the king rose, and the governor and Bernice and those who were sitting with them. And when they had withdrawn, they said to one another, "This man is doing nothing to deserve death or imprisonment." And Agrippa said to Festus, "This man could have been set free if he had not appealed to Caesar." (vs. 30–32).

The audience was over, for the King rose up and that was the signal of the breaking up of the company, never to meet thus again. The verdict of a private consultation is "This man is doing nothing to deserve death or imprisonment." Herod Agrippa said to Festus "This man could have been set free if he had not appealed to Caesar." If Paul had not made his appeal to Caesar he might have then be freed. We have seen before that his appeal to Rome was according to the will of the Lord. To Rome then he goes. All is ordered by a gracious Lord.

Chapter Twenty-Seven

The remarkable book now draws to its close. The journey towards Rome and the Apostle's presence in Rome as a prisoner brings us to the end of the record. Shipwreck and the chief actor of the greater part of this book in a prison conclude the story of the early days of the church on earth. Behind the historical account one may easily see the stormy voyage of the professing church; her adversities, tossing about and shipwreck. However, such an application needs caution. It is easy to step into fanciful and far-fetched allegorical teaching. Besides church history, other applications have been made of this narrative. A commentator claims that the keynote to the interpretation is given in verse 34 in the word *salvation*.

> This and cognate words occur seven times in the chapter: *Hope to be saved, ye cannot be saved, to be completely saved*. While the contrary fate is no less richly depicted *injury, loss, throwing away, perish, kill* and *to be cast away*. The history, then, is a parable of the great salvation, by which man is brought through death to life.[1]

We shall not attempt to seek for an outline of church history in the events of this chapter. Here and there we shall touch upon a few lessons suggested by the account of the voyage. The central figure, the prisoner of the Lord, shall occupy us more than anything else. It is said that in all the classical literature there is nothing found which gives so much information of the working of an ancient ship as this chapter does. Even the critics have acknowledged that this chapter:

> bears the most indisputable marks of authenticity. . . . Historical research and inscriptions have confirmed the facts given in this chapter, while the accuracy of Luke's nautical observations is shown by the great help he has given to our understanding of ancient seamanship. None has impugned the correctness of his phrases; on the contrary, from his description contained in a few sentences, the scene of the wreck has been identified.[2]

The whole account is most clearly proven by a work of wide research by James Smith.[3]

We follow then briefly the different stages of the Apostle's journey towards Rome.

1. From Caesarea to Fair Havens (vs. 1–8).

2. The storm at sea and Paul's vision (vs. 9–26).

3. The Shipwreck (vs. 27–44).

1. From Caesarea to Fair Havens (vs. 1–8).

And when it was decided that we should sail for Italy, they delivered Paul and some other prisoners to a centurion of the Augustan Cohort named Julius. And embarking in a ship of Adramyttium, which was about to sail to the ports along the coast of Asia, we put to sea,

---

[1] Rackham, *The Acts of the Apostles*, 478.

[2] Ibid.

[3] James Smith, *The Voyage and Shipwreck of St. Paul: With Dissertations on the Life and Writings of St. Luke* (London, U.K.: Longman, Brown, Green, Longmans, & Roberts, 1856).

accompanied by Aristarchus, a Macedonian from Thessalonica. The next day we put in at Sidon. And Julius treated Paul kindly and gave him leave to go to his friends and be cared for. And putting out to sea from there we sailed under the lee of Cyprus, because the winds were against us. And when we had sailed across the open sea along the coast of Cilicia and Pamphylia, we came to Myra in Lycia. There the centurion found a ship of Alexandria sailing for Italy and put us on board. We sailed slowly for a number of days and arrived with difficulty off Cnidus, and as the wind did not allow us to go farther, we sailed under the lee of Crete off Salmone. Coasting along it with difficulty, we came to a place called Fair Havens, near which was the city of Lasea. (vs. 1–8).

Some time must have elapsed after the memorable speech before Agrippa and the beginning of the journey. Perhaps the certain other prisoners had first to be gathered and then Paul with the others were delivered to a centurion of Augustus' band, named Julius. The great Apostle with all the wealth of divine revelation is now in custody of a Roman officer. From the second verse we learn that besides the beloved physician and inspired author of this book, Luke, Aristarchus was also on board. In chapter 21:18 we learned that he was then also with the Apostle. Later in writing from Rome Paul calls Aristarchus, his fellow prisoner (Col 2:10), which however, does not necessarily mean that he was carried along as a prisoner. Had he been arrested with the Apostle as some have stated, surmising that he was with Paul in the temple, when the mob fell on him, then surely some statements to that effect would have been made before. Julius treated Paul with much leniency. He knew of course the verdict given by Herod Agrippa, that he was not guilty and might have been a free man had he not appealed to Caesar. At Sidon, where they landed, Paul is permitted to visit his friends and to refresh himself. Most likely Paul was in a physically weakened condition so that Julius entreated him to leave the ship. The Lord's gracious and loving care for his faithful servant shines out in this.

How clearly the whole narrative shows that all is in his hands: officers, winds and waves, all circumstances, are under his control. So far all seemed to go well; but contrary winds now trouble the voyagers. The ship is tossed to and fro. If we look upon the ship as a type of the professing church and the little company, headed by Paul, as the true church, then there is no difficulty in seeing the issue. Winds which drive hither and thither trouble those who hold the truth and live in fellowship with the Lord, while the professing church is cast about. Then Myra was reached. Here they took a ship of Alexandria. The expositors who attempt to trace the history of the church in the account see much in this statement. They tell us that it is typical of the professing church's more direct course towards Rome. These different typical applications are often forced. After sailing slowly many days they reached a place called "the fair havens." Then they reached the island of Crete. The place Lasea has been geographically located. But the name of the port was deceptive. "The fair havens" were far from peace and rest, but the place was exposed to the blasts of the winds. There are no fair havens of peace in this present evil age. The fair havens will only be reached when the Lord Jesus Christ returns.

2. THE STORM AT SEA AND PAUL'S VISION (VS. 9–26).

Since much time had passed, and the voyage was now dangerous because even the Fast [4] was already over, Paul advised them, saying, "Sirs, I perceive that the voyage will be with injury and much loss, not only of the cargo and the ship, but also of our lives." But the centurion paid more attention to the pilot and to the owner of the ship than to what Paul said. And because the harbor

---

[4] That is, the Day of Atonement

was not suitable to spend the winter in, the majority decided to put out to sea from there, on the chance that somehow they could reach Phoenix, a harbor of Crete, facing both southwest and northwest, and spend the winter there.

Now when the south wind blew gently, supposing that they had obtained their purpose, they weighed anchor and sailed along Crete, close to the shore. But soon a tempestuous wind, called the northeaster, struck down from the land. And when the ship was caught and could not face the wind, we gave way to it and were driven along. Running under the lee of a small island called Cauda,[5] we managed with difficulty to secure the ship's boat. After hoisting it up, they used supports to undergird the ship. Then, fearing that they would run aground on the Syrtis, they lowered the gear,[6] and thus they were driven along. Since we were violently storm-tossed, they began the next day to jettison the cargo. And on the third day they threw the ship's tackle overboard with their own hands. When neither sun nor stars appeared for many days, and no small tempest lay on us, all hope of our being saved was at last abandoned.

Since they had been without food for a long time, Paul stood up among them and said, "Men, you should have listened to me and not have set sail from Crete and incurred this injury and loss. Yet now I urge you to take heart, for there will be no loss of life among you, but only of the ship. For this very night there stood before me an angel of the God to whom I belong and whom I worship, and he said, 'Do not be afraid, Paul; you must stand before Caesar. And behold, God has granted you all those who sail with you.' So take heart, men, for I have faith in God that it will be exactly as I have been told. But we must run aground on some island." (vs. 9–26).

The late fall had been reached and navigation was then considered a hazardous thing. Nautical instruments were unknown, and other imperfect knowledge was a great drawback to navigation at that time. Little sea trading was done during the late fall and less during the winter months. They waited till sailing had become dangerous.

The fast mentioned which had passed was that of the Day of Atonement. Could we conclude from this statement that Paul and his companions kept the Day of Atonement by fasting? Some believe this, and that the Apostle continued in all the observances of the ceremonial law and even the traditions of the elders. This is incorrect. It was customary to remember these different feasts and holidays simply for the sake of marking time. In this sense it is mentioned here. Most likely a consultation of the commander of the ship and the owner, who was on board, and the centurion, was held, and Paul was present. He gives them a solemn warning and cautions them to beware. This shows his close fellowship with the Lord. In prayer, no doubt, he had laid the whole matter before the Lord and received the answer, which he communicates to the persons in authority. They looked upon it as a mere guess and the centurion rather trusted in the judgment of the captain and the owner.

And here we can think of other warnings given through the great Apostle. Warnings concerning the spiritual dangers, the apostasy of the last days, the perilous times, warnings against the seducing spirits and doctrines of demons. The professing church has forgotten these divinely-given predictions. The world does not heed them. Like these mariners, who believed in their own wisdom and disregarded the warning given, Christendom has paid no attention to these warnings. For this reason the ship is drifting, cast about by every wind of doctrine and rapidly nearing the long predicted shipwreck.

Their aim was to reach Phoenice, another haven of Crete, to put up for the winter. All went well for a time, but suddenly a terrific tempest arose. The hurricane which struck them was known by the name of Euroclydon. The ship was

---

[5] Some manuscripts *Clauda*

[6] That is, the sea-anchor (or possibly the mainsail).

caught in the high seas and driven by the gale. A small island, Clauda, afforded a little shelter. A smaller boat was trailing behind and was now lifted on board. Helps had to be used to undergird the ship and keep it from going to pieces. Still greater danger was ahead. Large sandbanks were nearby. To prevent the stranding they took in the sail and were once more driven by the wind. All this reminds us of the many endeavors from the side of man to keep professing Christendom together. The power gone, because disobedient to the Lord and his word, things are drifting and all kinds of worldly means and helps are employed to keep from sinking. Paul and his companions were conscious of the fact that they were in the hands of the Lord, who made the sea and at whose command the waves and the wind must obey.

Their trouble had just begun. The next day a part of the cargo was cast from the ship to make it lighter. The third day the tackling of the ship followed. The wheat they still kept, for they had need of it. Later even that went (27:38). Sun and stars were hidden for many days; in despair, they abandoned all hope of salvation. Here we may think of the Satanic influences and power, typified by the continued wind, and of the periods of church history when indeed the sun and stars were hidden, when all testimony to Christ and testimony from the side of his people seemed to have ceased.

When despair had reached its heights, Paul appears once more upon the scene. When all was hopeless the prisoner of the Lord spoke the words of hope and cheer. He reminds them first of their refusal and disobedience. What had came upon them was the result of having not heeded the warning. He then assures them that an angel of God had assured him once more that he would have to stand before Caesar; but God had given to him all that sail with him. Only the ship is to go down, the lives of all who sail with him will be preserved. "So take heart, men, for I have faith in God that it will be exactly as I have been told" (27:25). And now they were willing to listen to him. They had to acknowledge their disobedience and believe the message of cheer as it came from the divinely instructed messenger, assuring them of their ultimate salvation.

And so, at least, in part, drifting Christendom can listen to the Apostle Paul, and if the mistake, the wrong course, is acknowledged, the heavenly-sent message is accepted, salvation is assured.

2. THE SHIPWRECK (VS. 27–44).

When the fourteenth night had come, as we were being driven across the Adriatic Sea, about midnight the sailors suspected that they were nearing land. So they took a sounding and found twenty fathoms.[7] A little farther on they took a sounding again and found fifteen fathoms.[8] And fearing that we might run on the rocks, they let down four anchors from the stern and prayed for day to come. And as the sailors were seeking to escape from the ship, and had lowered the ship's boat into the sea under pretense of laying out anchors from the bow, Paul said to the centurion and the soldiers, "Unless these men stay in the ship, you cannot be saved." Then the soldiers cut away the ropes of the ship's boat and let it go.

As day was about to dawn, Paul urged them all to take some food, saying, "Today is the fourteenth day that you have continued in suspense and without food, having taken nothing. Therefore I urge you to take some food. For it will give you strength,[9] for not a hair is to perish from the head of any of you." And when he had said these things, he took bread, and giving thanks to God in the presence of all he broke it and began to eat. Then they all were encouraged and ate some food themselves. (We were in all 276[10]

---

[7] About 120 feet; a fathom (Greek *orguia*) was about 6 feet or 2 meters.

[8] About 90 feet (see previous note).

[9] Or *For it is for your deliverance.*

[10] Some manuscripts *seventy-six*, or *about seventy-six.*

CHAPTER TWENTY-SEVEN

48. Mosaic of a Roman galley, Bardo Museum, Tunisia, 2nd century AD.

persons in the ship.) And when they had eaten enough, they lightened the ship, throwing out the wheat into the sea.

Now when it was day, they did not recognize the land, but they noticed a bay with a beach, on which they planned if possible to run the ship ashore. So they cast off the anchors and left them in the sea, at the same time loosening the ropes that tied the rudders. Then hoisting the foresail to the wind they made for the beach. But striking a reef,[11] they ran the vessel aground. The bow stuck and remained immovable, and the stern was being broken up by the surf. The soldiers' plan was to kill the prisoners, lest any should swim away and escape. But the centurion, wishing to save Paul, kept them from carrying out their plan. He ordered those who could swim to jump overboard first and make for the land, and the rest on planks or on pieces of the ship. And so it was that all were brought safely to land. (vs. 27–44).

How calm the Apostle and his companions must have been after this assurance of their safety. The dreadful wind might continue and the ship drift still further. They knew they were safe, for God had spoken.

---

[11] Or *sandbank*, or *crosscurrent*; Greek *place between two seas*.

Different it was with the crew of the ship. In great distress they feared the coming disaster and cast out four anchors. The shipmen attempted flight by a clever scheme. Paul discovered their plan and said to the Centurion (see Fig. 10) and soldiers, "unless these men stay in the ship, you cannot be saved" (27:31). God had given him all who were in the ship. The work of the sailors was needed when the daybreak came. And the soldiers believed the word of Paul, for they cut the ropes, which set the boat adrift the sailors tried to use.

Then Paul exhorted them to eat. Once more he assured them that not a hair should fall from the head of anyone. Before the whole company, two hundred and seventy-six persons, Paul took bread and gave thanks to God. The Lord had exalted the prisoner and he really stands out as the leader of the distressed company. They all became encouraged by the words and action. All has its lessons. However the meal has nothing to do with the Lord's Supper. It tells us typically how necessary it is that we must feed on the bread of life in the days of

Page | 255

49. View of the Bay of St. Paul, Malta.

danger, the times when everything breaks up.

The details of the account we do not need to follow. The soldiers suggested the killing of the prisoners. The soldiers were responsible for every prisoner with their lives. If some were to escape they would be killed for the neglect. So for this selfish reason they would have killed each prisoner. The Centurion kept them from carrying out this evil purpose. And when the ship went to pieces all escaped safe to land. God was faithful to his promise. God saved, though the ship went into pieces. Even so God is faithful to his promise and all who trust in his ever-blessed Son are saved and safe, and none of them can be lost. The ship, professing Christendom, is breaking up and the ship cannot save.

The story of the journey towards Rome and the shipwreck reveals the acts of the adversary once more. No doubt he would have prevented the Apostle from reaching Rome in fulfillment of the Lord's word and plan. The last attempt was through the soldiers. But none can frustrate God's purposes. Happy are we if we learn that all rests in his hands whose love will never fail and whose power can never diminish. The winds of trial and adversity, the schemes of man and assaults of the enemy must help together in the fulfillment of his own councils. Yea, all things must work together for good to them that love God. The next chapter brings us to the end of the journey and to Rome itself.

Chapter Twenty-Eight

The final stage of the journey to Rome, the Apostle's arrival there and a brief account of how he called the Jews together in a meeting and delivered them an important message, form the ending of this book.

1. In the Island of Melita (vs. 1–10).

2. The arrival in Rome (vs. 11–16).

3. Paul calling the chief of the Jews and his message (vs. 17–29).

4. The Apostle's activity in Rome (vs. 30–31).

1. IN THE ISLAND OF MELTA (VS. 1–10).

After we were brought safely through, we then learned that the island was called Malta. The native people [A] showed us unusual kindness, for they kindled a fire and welcomed us all, because it had begun to rain and was cold. When Paul had gathered a bundle of sticks and put them on the fire, a viper came out because of the heat and fastened on his hand. When the native people saw the creature hanging from his hand, they said to one another, "No doubt this man is a murderer. Though he has escaped from the sea, Justice[B] has not allowed him to live." He, however, shook off the creature into the fire and suffered no harm. They were waiting for him to swell up or suddenly fall down dead. But when they had waited a long time and saw no misfortune come to him, they changed their minds and said that he was a god.

Now in the neighborhood of that place were lands belonging to the chief man of the island, named Publius, who received us and entertained us hospitably for three days. It happened that the father of Publius lay sick with fever and dysentery. And Paul visited him and prayed, and putting his hands on him healed him. And when this had taken place, the rest of the people on the island who had diseases also came and were cured. They also honored us greatly,[C] and when we were about to sail, they put on board whatever we needed. (vs. 1–10).

Melita, which means "*honey*," is the island of Malta. It was even then a prominent place for navigation where many vessels wintered. Luke calls the inhabitants Barbarians, a term used by the Greeks for all peoples who did not speak their language. The wrecked company was not plundered by the people of the island, but instead received much kindness and were made comfortable in the cold rain which fell. Those who apply all this in an allegorical way, find much meaning in this.[D]

It was God who moved the hearts of these islanders to show such hospitality to the shipwrecked company for the sake of his servants. Paul is active even then. The shipwreck and privations must have told on the great man of God physically, yet we see him going about gathering a bundle of sticks for the fire. This labor must have been difficult, since as a prisoner he wore a chain on his hands. A viper, which had been benumbed by the cold and revived by the heat of the fire, fastened on his hand. The

---

[A] Greek *barbaroi* (that is, non–Greek speakers); also verse 4.

[B] Or *justice*

[C] Greek *honored us with many honors*

[D] The shipwreck is often applied allegorically to the wrecking of Christianity by the world under Constantine the Great and in the name of Melita (*Honey*) they see an indication that the professing church supposed then to have reached "the land which flows with milk and honey." But so many other allegorical meanings, many of them forced, are made, that we do not consider such applications at all. The primary meaning of the account is to give us the history of how Paul reached Rome.

serpent did him no harm and he cast it into the fire, where it found a miserable end. We doubt not it was a poisonous viper. This is denied by some critics on the plea that poisonous snakes are not found in the island of Malta. However, that is no proof that such did not exist at that time. The inhabitants of the island expected Paul to fall dead. If it had been a harmless snake, why such an expectation? God's power was manifested in his behalf; it was unquestionably a fulfillment of the promise in Mark 16:18, "they will pick up serpents with their hands; . . . , it will not hurt them." How Satan tried to hinder Paul from reaching Rome; how he attempted to oppose God's will and God's plan! By the murderous Jews, by the storms of the sea, the suggestion of the soldiers to kill the prisoners, and now by the viper Satan tried to frustrate the Lord's plan. But God kept his servant and no harm could come to him. In the same keeping all his people rest. We are safe under Him, our omnipotent Lord.

The viper which fastened on Paul's hand reminds us of Satan, that old serpent. He is a conquered enemy. He attacks us, he will fasten on us wherever he can; we are told to resist the devil and he will have to flee from us. In a believing, conscious union with Christ, all his attacks will prove harmless, till at last Satan shall be bruised under our feet and the serpent will be cast into the Lake of Fire.

Then there was a manifestation of the gracious power of the Lord towards the inhabitants of the island. Publius, the chief man of the island, had shown also much kindness to the apostle and his companions. The father of Publius was severely sick; Paul visited him and after prayer and the laying on of hands he was healed. As this became known, others who were afflicted with diseases came and were healed. The Lord honored his servant and did good to those, who had shown kindness to his own. Along with the healing of diseases, the Apostle must have preached the blessed Gospel.

2. THE ARRIVAL IN ROME (VS. 11–16).

> After three months we set sail in a ship that had wintered in the island, a ship of Alexandria, with the twin gods [E] as a figurehead. Putting in at Syracuse, we stayed there for three days. And from there we made a circuit and arrived at Rhegium. And after one day a south wind sprang up, and on the second day we came to Puteoli. There we found brothers [F] and were invited to stay with them for seven days. And so we came to Rome. And the brothers there, when they heard about us, came as far as the Forum of Appius and Three Taverns to meet us. On seeing them, Paul thanked God and took courage. And when we came into Rome, Paul was allowed to stay by himself, with the soldier who guarded him. (vs. 11–16).

Three months had gone by the winter months, during which navigation was at a standstill. An Alexandrian vessel, which had wintered in the safe harbor of Melita, carried the company towards their destination, Puteoli, the harbor of Rome. This was in the early part of Spring. After landing at Syracuse (Sicily), and tarrying there for three days, they reached Rhegium, in the straits of Messina, and the next day they came to Puteoli, in the Bay of Naples, almost one hundred and forty miles from the city of Rome. In Puteoli, where a large Jewish colony was situated, they found brethren, who entreated them to stop with them for a week. What an oasis of blessing this must have been for the wearied and tired servants of the Lord! One would almost wish it would have pleased the Holy Spirit to give us a fuller account of the blessed fellowship they must have enjoyed together. And so they came to Rome. The brethren in Rome knew in some way of their coming. They came to meet them as far as Appii Forum and the Three Taverns. Most likely two different companies of brethren

---

[E] That is, the Greek gods Castor and Pollux.
[F] Or *brothers and sisters*; also verses 15, 21

are indicated. The first company met them at Appii Forum, some forty miles from Rome, and the second company at the Three Taverns, some ten miles further on. The news of the Apostle's coming must have been conveyed to Rome from Puteoli. Perhaps the two companies represented the Jewish believers and the Gentile Christians, of which the church in Rome was composed. With what anticipation they must have looked forward to seeing the Apostle, whose face they had never seen. His blessed Epistle addressed to the Saints of God in Rome, the Beloved of God, had been in their possession for a number of years and had brought told blessings to their souls. How often they must have read his words, in the beginning of his letter:

> For I long to see you, that I may impart to you some spiritual gift to strengthen you—that is, that we may be mutually encouraged by each other's faith, both yours and mine. I do not want you to be unaware, brothers,^G that I have often intended to come to you (but thus far have been prevented), in order that I may reap some harvest among you as well as among the rest of the Gentiles (Rom 1:11–13).

He had never been in Rome. The Roman assembly was not founded by Paul and certainly not by Peter. The origin of that church is obscure and the Holy Spirit has not given us a history of the beginning of the church in Rome. And now he whom they all loved, whose face they longed to see, was actually on the way to visit Rome. But in a far different way did he come than he expected when he wrote his Epistle. He came as the prisoner of the Lord. What a meeting it must have been!

---

^G Or *brothers and sisters*. The plural Greek word *adelphoi* (translated "brothers") refers to siblings in a family. In New Testament usage, depending on the context, *adelphoi* may refer either to men or to both men and women who are siblings (brothers and sisters) in God's family, the church.

The record tells us that when Paul saw these beloved brethren, who had shown such love to him by meeting him on the way to accompany him to Rome, that he thanked God and took courage. It is evident that he must have been cast down and depressed in his spirit. How many questions must have been upon his mind! Perhaps anxiety concerning the assembly in Rome also weighed upon him he faced difficulties on all sides. But when he saw the brethren and the evidences of their love, the cloud passed and he thanked God and took courage. Anew he cast himself on the Lord, whose faithfulness and power had been so marked in his experience. There is no better way to meet all depression, anxious feeling, difficulties and obstacles, than the way of thanking God and taking courage, which means, confidence in the Lord. After leaving the Three Taverns, the great Appian Way led them for thirty miles across the Campagna to the great city, the city of power, the mistress of the world, the city of the seven hills the mystical

50. Marble relief of a soldier from the Praetorian Guard from Puteoli, Italy, now displayed in the Pergamum Museum, Berlin (Sk 887).

Babylon. In Rome at last. What emotions must have filled the hearts of Paul, Luke and Aristarchus when they entered Rome! It is written in Genesis 12:5, "they set out to go to the land of Canaan. When they came to the land of Canaan." They went forth to go to Rome and to Rome they came. The Lord had brought them safely to their destination.

Julius then delivered the prisoners to his official superior. But Paul is not in the hands of the Romans, but in the hands of the Lord. He guards him. He was permitted to dwell in his own house with a soldier alongside of him.

3. PAUL IN ROME (VS. 17–29).

> After three days he called together the local leaders of the Jews, and when they had gathered, he said to them, "Brothers, though I had done nothing against our people or the customs of our fathers, yet I was delivered as a prisoner from Jerusalem into the hands of the Romans. When they had examined me, they wished to set me at liberty, because there was no reason for the death penalty in my case. But because the Jews objected, I was compelled to appeal to Caesar—though I had no charge to bring against my nation. For this reason, therefore, I have asked to see you and speak with you, since it is because of the hope of Israel that I am wearing this chain." And they said to him, "We have received no letters from Judea about you, and none of the brothers coming here has reported or spoken any evil about you. But we desire to hear from you what your views are, for with regard to this sect we know that everywhere it is spoken against."
>
> When they had appointed a day for him, they came to him at his lodging in greater numbers. From morning till evening he expounded to them, testifying to the kingdom of God and trying to convince them about Jesus both from the Law of Moses and from the Prophets. And some were convinced by what he said, but others disbelieved. And disagreeing among themselves, they departed after Paul had made one statement: "The Holy Spirit was right in saying to your fathers through Isaiah the prophet:
>
> > "Go to this people, and say, 'You will indeed hear but never understand, and you will indeed see but never perceive.' For this people's heart has grown dull, and with their ears they can barely hear, and their eyes they have closed; lest they should see with their eyes and hear with their ears and understand with their heart and turn, and I would heal them."[H]
>
> Therefore let it be known to you that this salvation of God has been sent to the Gentiles; they will listen.[I] (vs. 17–29).

And now it is for the very last time in this book "to the Jew first." The first service the great Apostle rendered in Rome was not in the assembly, but he called the chief of the Jews together. He knew no bitterness in his heart against the Jews. In writing the letter to the Romans he had written,

> I am speaking the truth in Christ—I am not lying; my conscience bears me witness in the Holy Spirit—that I have great sorrow and unceasing anguish in my heart (Rom 9:1–2). . . . Brothers, my heart's desire and prayer to God for them is that they may be saved (10:1).

And now, after all the sad experience he had made, the treatment he had received from his kinsmen, after he had found out their malice and deep hatred, the same love burns in his heart and the same yearning for their salvation possesses him. In Rome he manifests first of all his loving interest in his Jewish brethren. To these leading Jews he testified once more that he was innocent of any wrong doing. Briefly, he rehearsed his whole case and why he had been compelled to appeal to Caesar. For this purpose to talk to them about this matter he had called them. Then most likely he must have lifted his hands, from which the prisoner's chain dangled, and said, "since it is because of the hope of Israel that I am wearing this chain" (28:20). The Jews, however, wanted to hear more from his lips of "But we desire to hear from you what your views are, for with

---

[H] Isaiah 6:9–10

[I] Some manuscripts add verse 29: *And when he had said these words, the Jews departed, having much dispute among themselves.*

regard to this sect we know that everywhere it is spoken against" (28:22). They knew he believed in Christ. A great meeting took place a short time later. Many Jews assembled in Paul's lodging. The meeting lasted from morning till evening. Once more he testified the Kingdom of God to a large company of Jews. He also persuaded them concerning Jesus both out of the laws of Moses and out of the Prophets. What a wonderful message must have came from his lips as he unfolded the prophetic testimony concerning the Messiah in the power of the Spirit of God! But what was the result? Some believed and some believed not. They did not agree amongst themselves. The end of God's gracious way with the Jews is reached. We repeat for the last time, it was to the Jew first. The final crisis is reached. Judgment must now be executed upon the nation and the blindness is now to come, which has lasted so long and will continue till the fullness of the Gentiles is come in (Rom 11:26). Stephen, whose death young Saul had witnessed and approved (8:1), had pronounced judgment upon the nation, in Jerusalem. God's mercy had still waited. Marvelous Grace, which took up the young Pharisee, Saul, and made him the Apostle to the Gentiles! Through him, the chosen instrument, the Lord still sought his beloved Israel, even after Jerusalem had so completely rejected the offered mercy. We have seen how the Apostle's intense love for his brethren had led him back to Jerusalem, though warned repeatedly by the Holy Spirit. And now he is used to give the very last message to the Jews and speak the final word of condemnation. It is interesting to see how the Spirit of God quotes through the Apostle the message of judgment, which was given to Isaiah over 700 years before. How long-suffering God is. What infinite patience and mercy he manifested in dealing with Israel. Isaiah had announced the hardening judgment, and God waited 700 years before it was finally accomplished. Twice before these words from Isaiah 6 are mentioned in the New Testament. In Matthew 13:14–15, they are spoken by our Lord after the people had rejected him and the Pharisees had charged him with driving out the demons by Beelzebub, the prince of demons. They rejected Him, whom the Father had sent. Again, we find the Lord making use of these words at another occasion. In John 12:37–41, they are applied after the full rejection of the Son Himself and his testimony. Here in our passage they are used for the last time. The rejection is now complete and the result is the threatened blindness rests upon the nation. But we must not forget that the Spirit of God had announced all this in the Epistle to the Romans. The eleventh chapter unfolds the Jewish question and assures us that in spite of all this, the blindness of Israel is not permanent. God has not cast away this people, whom he foreknew. He will yet bring the remnant to Himself and forgive them their sins. God's gifts and calling are without repentance.

Paul then announced that the salvation of God is sent to the Gentiles, and they will hear it. This marks the larger beginning of the world-wide proclamation of the Salvation of God among the Gentile races. And what a blessed description of the Gospel we have here, "the Salvation of God"! This still continues. God takes out from the Gentiles a people for his name. Blessed be God for the preaching of the Gospel in regions beyond, and for the blessed members which are added to his body, the church, in Korea, China, India and elsewhere. But the offer of the Salvation of God to the Gentiles will likewise close. Romans 11:18–22 contains the solemn message, one of the great forgotten messages of the Bible. Boasting Gentile Christendom will someday be cut off and the broken off branches will be grafted in again into their good olive tree. The apostasy of Christendom, the wicked

ACTS OF THE APOSTLES

rejection of the Person of Christ, the constant and ever increasing perversion of the Gospel of God are sure signs that a change of dispensations is imminent.

4. THE APOSTLE'S ACTIVITY IN ROME (VS. 30–31).

> He lived there two whole years at his own expense,[J] and welcomed all who came to him, proclaiming the kingdom of God and teaching about the Lord Jesus Christ with all boldness and without hindrance. (vs. 30–31).

A prisoner in Rome and yet active. He preached the Kingdom of God (not of heaven, the Jewish, earthly aspect of it), and ever speaking of that worthy name, that blessed and adorable Person, the Lord Jesus Christ. The ending of the book is sad and it is joyous. Sad to see the great Apostle a prisoner, shut up in Rome with his God-given Gospel. Joyous because the last verse mentions the Lord Jesus Christ and an unhindered ministry of the Gospel. The Book begins with Jerusalem and ends with Rome. It is a prophecy of the course of the professing church. The book closes in an unfinished way, because the acts of Christ, the Spirit of God, and Satan, recorded in this book, are not finished. We hear nothing more of Paul, though we know that from the prison (see Fig. 52) the Holy Spirit of God sent forth through him the blessed Epistles, in which he has been pleased to give us the highest revelation. And how much more might be written on all this!

THE END

51. Mamertine prison (Italian *Carcere Mamertino*; right) in Rome, Italy. The arch of Septimius Severus is on the left. It is believed, by eighth cent. tradition, to be the prison of Peter and Paul during the persecution of Nero (*ca.* A.D. 64–67. Tacitus *Ann.* 15.44; Suetonius *Nero* 35; *1 Clem.* 5:2–5).

J Or *in his own hired dwelling*

Appendix A

CHRONOLOGY OF PAUL'S LIFE

By Daivd E. Graves, PhD.

McRay has described efforts to establish a chronology[A] of the dates for the events of Paul's life as "one of the most baffling problems of New Testament study."[B] Donfried also cautions that:

it must be acknowledged that no matter from what perspective one views the data, *there can be no absolutely definite chronology of this period*; all attempts must be tentative and subject to correction and

---

[A] Thomas H. Campbell, "Paul's 'Missionary Journeys' as Reflected in His Letters," *Journal of Biblical Literature* 74, no. 2 (1955): 80–87; Karl Paul Donfried, "Chronology: New Testament," ed. David Noel Freedman et al., *ABD* (New York, N.Y.: Doubleday, 1996), 1:1012–1013; Rainer Riesner, *Paul's Early Period: Chronology, Mission Strategy, Theology*, trans. Douglas W. Stott (Grand Rapids, Mich.: Eerdmans, 1998); F. F Bruce, *Paul, Apostle of the Heart Set Free* (Grand Rapids, Mich.: Eerdmans, 2000), 318–19; Andrew E. Steinmann, *From Abraham to Paul: A Biblical Chronology* (St. Louis, Miss.: Concordia, 2011).

[B] John McRay, *Paul: His Life and Teaching* (Grand Rapids, Mich.: Baker Academic, 2007), 60.

ACTS OF THE APOSTLES

revision (emphasis added).[C]

However, in determining dates there are certain markers that assist in the chronology of events in the book of Acts:

- Acts 9:25; 2 Cor 11:32: The death of the Nabataean King Aretas IV Philopatris, between AD 37–40,[D] who was the client king of the Romans and whose capital was in Petra, Jordan (Josephus *Ant.* 13.387–92; *J.W.* 1.99–103). Aretas was the father-in-law of Herod Antipas who controlled Galilee and Perea. Antipas was first married to Aretas' daughter Phasaelis but later divorced her (AD 36) to marry his brother Philip's wife Herodias (Matt 14:3–4; Mark 6:17–18; Luke 3:19–20). The divorce caused friction between Aretas and Antipas that led to Aretas invading Antipas' territory, which included Bantanaea, south of Damascus (Josephus *Ant.* 18.109–25; *J.W.* 2.94–95). Aretas' power reached as far north as Damascus, where he appointed an ethnarch (Gr. *ethnarches*, from *ethnos* "nation" + *arkhein* "to rule") over the city.[E] With the accession of the Roman emperor Caligula (AD 37–41), a new policy of tolerance for client kings was proposed and it is assumed that Damascus was not under Nabataean control before AD 37. Campbell concludes:

    > we can claim with some confidence that Aretas did not control the city beyond early 37 C.E....and [it would have been] largely impossible during the reign of Philip over the Decapolis, that is, up to 34 C.E. . . .We know, moreover, that in late 36 C.E. Aretas launched a successful military strike against Antipas, ruler of Galilee.[F]

- Vardaman builds a case based on microletters[G] on the coins of Aretas, for the control of Damascus being passed from Aretas IV to Tiberius after AD 33/34,[H] towards the end of Tiberius' career in AD 37.[I] While it is unlikely that Paul's departure from Damascus (2 Cor 11:32; Acts 9) took place as early as AD 34, the general consensus of scholars is that the events of Acts 9 must have taken place between AD 36 and 37.[J]

[C] Donfried, "Chronology: NT," 1:1017.

[D] Gerald F. Hawthorne, Ralph P. Martin, and Daniel G. Reid, eds., *Dictionary of Paul and His Letters* (Downers Grove, Ill.: InterVarsity, 1993), 117; Lee Martin MacDonald, "Acts," in *The Bible Knowledge Background Commentary: Acts-Philemon*, ed. Craig A. Evans and Isobel A. Combes (Colorado Springs, Colo.: Cook, 2004), 72; E. Jerry Vardaman, "Jesus' Life: A New Chronology," in *Chronos, Kairos, Christos*, ed. Jack Finegan, E. Jerry Vardaman, and Edwin M. Yamauchi (Winona Lake, Ind.: Eisenbrauns, 1989), 72.

[E] Douglas A. Campbell, "An Anchor for Pauline Chronology: Paul's Flight from 'The Ethnarch of King Aretas' (2 Corinthians 11:32-33)," *Journal of Biblical Literature* 121, no. 2 (2002): 281 n. 7; G. W. Bowersock, *Roman Arabia* (Cambridge, Mass.: Harvard University Press, 1998), 65–69; Steinmann, *From Abraham to Paul*, 302.

[F] Campbell, "An Anchor for Pauline Chronology," 296–97.

[G] "Microletters are very samll inscriptions placed on coins and other objects. They are so small that a magnifying glass is required to see them and, in case you may be wondering, magnifying glasses were indeed used in antiquity." Arthur E. Palumbo, *The Dead Sea Scrolls and the Personages of Earliest Christianity* (New York, N.Y.: Algora, 2004), 175.

[H] Emil Schürer, *The History of the Jewish People in the Age of Jesus Christ (175 BC–AD 135)*, ed. G. Vermes, F. Miller, and M. Black, Rev (Edinburgh, U.K.: T&T Clark, 1979), 1:852 n. 25.

[I] Vardaman, "Jesus' Life: A New Chronology," 71–73.

[J] George Ogg, *The Chronology of the Life of Paul* (London, U.K.: Epworth, 1968), 22–23; Robert Jewett, *A Chronology of Paul's Life* (Minneapolis, Minn.: Fortress, 1979), 30–33; Ralph P. Martin, *2 Corinthians*, ed. David A Hubbard and Glenn W Barker, Word Biblical Commentary 40 (Dallas, Tex.: Word Books, 1998), 385–86; Campbell, "An Anchor for Pauline Chronology," 296–97.

- Acts 11:28; Acts 18:2: On January 24th AD 41, Caligula (AD 37–41) was assassinated and Claudius Caesar (AD 41–54) came to the throne (Suetonius *Cl.* 10, 25; Josephus *Ant.* 19.212–20).

- Acts 12:20–23: the death of Herod Agrippa I in AD 44 (Josephus *Ant.* 19.343–50; *J.W.* 2.219).

- Acts 13:6–12: Sergius Paulus was Proconsul of Cyprus in AD 41–54 during the time of Claudius Caesar (Pliny *Nat.* 2.113).

- Acts 24:27; 25:12: Felix's reign as the procurator of Judea was succeeded (Josephus *Ant.* 20.8.7, 9; *J.W.* 2.13.7) by Porcius Festus in about AD 59 (Josephus *J.W.* 2.14.1; *Ant.* 20.8.9–11) until his death in AD 62 when he was succeeded by Lucceius Albinus.[K]

- Paul composed his theological writings between AD 50 and 68.[L]

One must keep in mind as Donfried has reminded us:

> Any attempt to reconstruct the chronology of the NT must be tentative at best. The primary intention of the Gospels and other NT writings is not historical or biographical—they are documents of faith intended to proclaim, teach, and encourage the various early Christian communities.[M]

Köstenberger recommends that the best approach "relies primarily on Paul's letters for the chronology of Paul's life and supplements that chronology with data from Acts."[N] This allows for the possibility that Luke may have arranged some of his material topically.[O] However, the details of the events that Luke provided are none the less historical and accurate.

Date ca. AD	Time of Year	Event
33–36		Paul's conversion in Damascus (Gal 1:12–17; Acts 9:1–25).
36–37		The visit to Arabia and Syria and the return to Damascus for three years (Gal 1:17–18; 2 Cor 11:23–33).
37		The first visit to Jerusalem for two weeks (Acts 9:26–30; Gal 1:18–19).
37–40		The death of Aretas IV Philopatris (Acts 9:25; 2 Cor 11:32).
37–43		Visit to Syria (Antioch Acts 11:26a) and Cilicia (Tarsus; Acts 9:30; Gal 1:21).
41	January	Caligula was assassinated.
41–54		Claudius Caesar's rule (Acts 11:28; Acts 18:2).

[K] F. F. Bruce, *New Testament History*, 2nd ed. (New York, N.Y.: Doubleday, 1980), 345; Joel B Green, "Festus, Porcius (Person)," ed. David Noel Freedman et al., *ABD* (New York, N.Y.: Doubleday, 1992), 794–95.

[L] Darrell L. Bock, *Breaking The Da Vinci Code: Answers to the Questions Everyone's Asking* (New York, N.Y.: Nelson, 2006).

[M] Donfried, "Chronology: NT," 1:1012–1013.

[N] Andreas J. Köstenberger, L. Scott Kellum, and Charles L Quarles, *The Cradle, the Cross, and the Crown: An Introduction to the New Testament* (Nashville, Tenn.: Broadman & Holman Academic, 2009), 397; Campbell, "Paul's 'Missionary Journeys'"; Joseph A. Fitzmyer, "The Pauline Letters and the Lucan Account of Paul's Missionary Journeys," *Society of Biblical Literature Seminar Papers* 27 (1988): 82–89.

[O] L. C. A. Alexander, "Chronology of Paul," ed. Gerald F. Hawthorne, Ralph P. Martin, and Daniel G. Reid, *Dictionary of Paul and His Letters* (Downers Grove, Ill.: InterVarsity, 1993), 115–23.

44		Paul's trip to Antioch (Acts 11:25–26) and the prophet Agabus predicts a great famine which "came to pass in the days of Claudius Caesar" (Acts 11:28).
		James the apostle beheaded and the imprisonment of Peter (Acts 12:1–2).
		The death of Herod Agrippa I (Acts 12:20–23).
45/46		Famine in Judea (Acts 11:28).
46		Second visit to Jerusalem for famine relief.
46–48		First missionary journey (Acts 13:2–14:28).
49		Apostolic conference at Antioch (Acts 15:1–2; Gal 2:12–14). Galatians written.
		Jews expelled from Rome.
50		After 14 years, Paul visits Jerusalem with Barnabas and Titus for a conference (Acts 15:2–29; Gal 2:1).
50–52		Paul's second missionary journey (Acts 15:40–18:23).
50	Spring	Berea, southern Greece and Athens. Paul's arrival in Corinth.
50–51	Autumn	Paul stayed in Corinth for about 1.5 years (Acts 18:1, 5, 11, and 18) then sailed to Caesarea. 1 & 2 Thess were written from Caesarea.
51–52	July	Gallio governed Achaia (Acts 18:12–17).
51	Summer	Paul's trial before Gallio in Achaea (Acts 18:12–17).
52	Passover?	Paul visits Jerusalem for the feast (Acts 18:21–22).
52–60		Felix is Roman procurator in Palestine.
52–53	Winter	Paul spent several months in Antioch, Syria (Acts 18:23).
53–58	Spring	Paul's third missionary Journey (Acts 18:23–21:17). Activity in the churches of Galatia, Asia, Macedonia, and Achaia with special emphasis on the collection of the offering for Jerusalem (Gal 2:10; 1 Cor 16:1–4; 2 Cor 8–9; Rom 15:25–32).
53	Autumn	Paul arrives in Ephesus where he writes 1 Corinthians.
54–68		Nero's reign.
55	Spring	Painful visit to Corinth; Paul sends severe letter ("Corinthians C") by the hand of Titus.
56	Summer	Paul leaves Ephesus after three years (Acts 20:31).
	Autumn	Paul in Troas.
	October	Paul leaves Troas for Macedonia, meets Titus, sends letter of reconciliation ("Corinthians D").
57	Spring	Paul arrives in Corinth where he likely wrote Romans.
	Passover	Paul in Philippi where he likely wrote 2 Corinthians.
	Pentecost	Paul's arrival in Jerusalem with an offering (1 Cor 16:3; Rom 15:25–32).
57–59		Paul was imprisoned by Felix in Caesarea for two years until Festus took over (Acts 23:23–26:32).
59–60	October	Festus took over from Felix as the Roman Procurator of Judea (Acts 24:27–25:1).
60–62		Porcius Festus became procurator of Judea (Acts 24:27; 25:12).

Chronology Of Paul's Life

60		Shipwrecked on Malta (Acts 27:1–28:16).
60–62	Spring	Paul arrived in Rome and was imprisoned where he wrote Ephesians, Colossians, Philemon and Philippians.
62		James the Lord's brother stoned.
64	July	Fire in Rome.
63–67		Paul's trip to Spain and later journeys (Pastoral Epistles).
64/65		1 Timothy and Titus written from Philippi.
66		Jewish rebellion against Rome and Christians in Jerusalem flee.
67		2 Timothy written from Rome.
67–68		Paul beheaded; Peter crucified.

Maps

Map 1: The First Missionary Journey

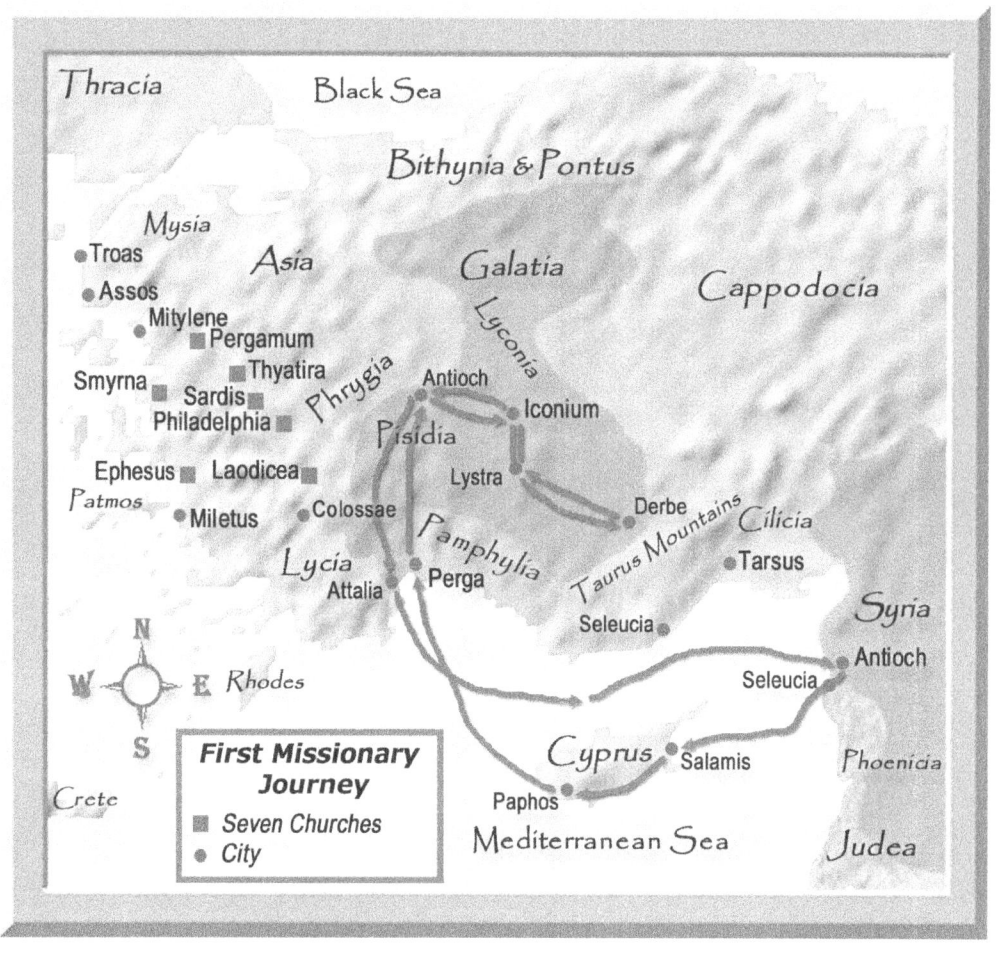

52. **MAP 1**: The First Missionary Journey.

MAP 2: THE SECOND MISSIONARY JOURNEY

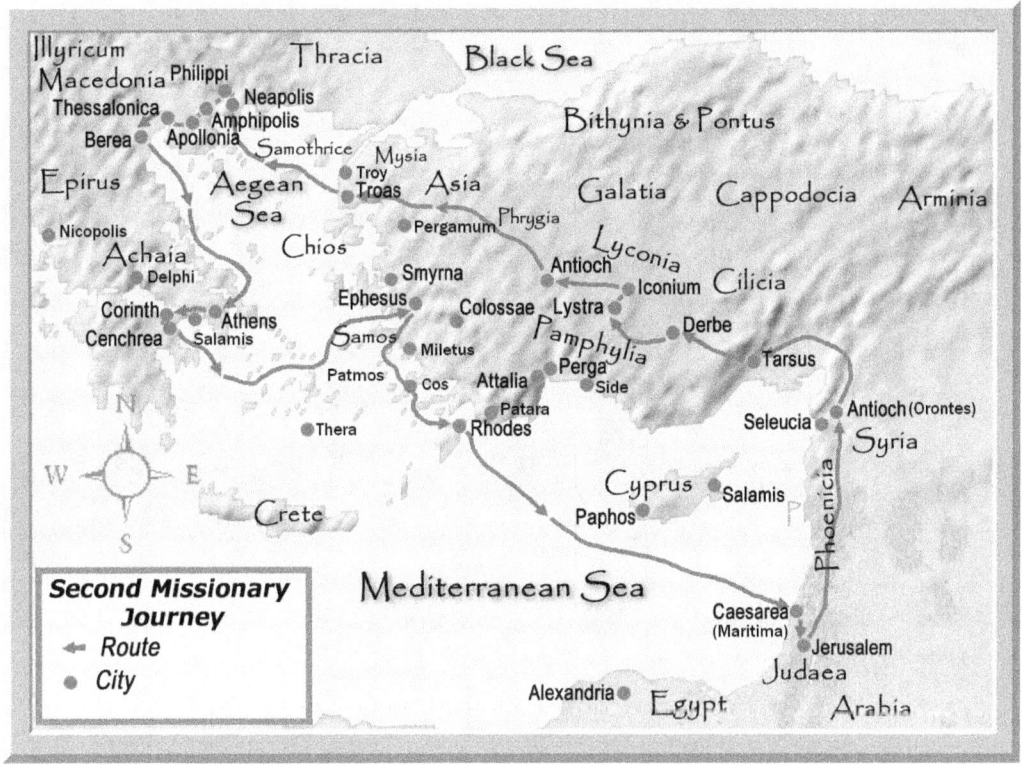

53. **MAP 2:** The Second Missionary Journey.

MAP 3: THE THIRD MISSIONARY JOURNEY AND TRIP TO ROME

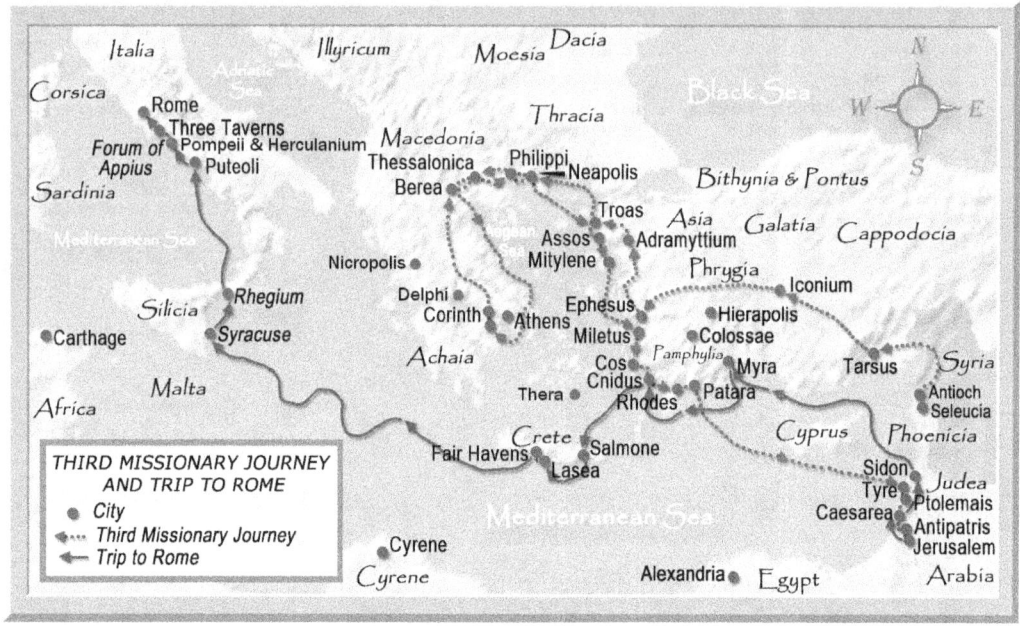

54. **MAP 3**: The Third Missionary Journey and trip to Rome.

BIBLIOGRAPHY

Alexander, L. C. A. "Chronology of Paul." Edited by Gerald F. Hawthorne, Ralph P. Martin, and Daniel G. Reid. *Dictionary of Paul and His Letters*. Downers Grove, Ill.: InterVarsity, 1993.

Alford, Henry. *The New Testament for English Readers*. 2 vols. London, U.K.: Rivingtons, 1863.

Bengel, Johann Albrecht. *Gnomon of the New Testament*. Translated by Andrew Robert Faussett. 3rd ed. Vol. 2. Smith, English & Company, 1860.

Bock, Darrell L. *Breaking The Da Vinci Code: Answers to the Questions Everyone's Asking*. New York, N.Y.: Nelson, 2006.

Bowersock, G. W. *Roman Arabia*. Cambridge, Mass.: Harvard University Press, 1998.

Bruce, F. F. *New Testament History*. 2nd ed. New York, N.Y.: Doubleday, 1980.

Bruce, F. F. *Paul, Apostle of the Heart Set Free*. Grand Rapids, Mich.: Eerdmans, 2000.

Burkill, T. Alec. "The Competence of the Sanhedrim." *Vigiliae Christianae* 10 (1956): 80–96.

Campbell, Douglas A. "An Anchor for Pauline Chronology: Paul's Flight from 'The Ethnarch of King Aretas' (2 Corinthians 11:32-33)." *Journal of Biblical Literature* 121, no. 2 (2002): 279–302.

Campbell, Thomas H. "Paul's 'Missionary Journeys' as Reflected in His Letters." *Journal of Biblical Literature* 74, no. 2 (1955): 80–87.

Cohen, S. J. F. "Crossing the Boundary and Becoming a Jew." *Harvard Theological Review* 82 (1989): 13–33.

Donfried, Karl Paul. "Chronology: New Testament." Edited by David Noel Freedman, Gary A. Herion, David F. Graf, and John David Pleins. *ABD*. New York, N.Y.: Doubleday, 1996.

Evans, Craig A. "Sanhedrin." In *The Eerdmans Dictionary of Early Judaism*, edited by John J. Collins and Daniel C. Harlow, 1193–94. Grand Rapids, Mich.: Eerdmans, 2010.

Fitzmyer, Joseph A. "The Pauline Letters and the Lucan Account of Paul's Missionary Journeys." *Society of Biblical Literature Seminar Papers* 27 (1988): 82–89.

Gaebelein, Arno Clemens. *The Prophet Joel, an Exposition*. New York, N.Y.: Our Hope, 1909.

Grant, Frederick W. *The Numerical Bible: Acts to 2 Corinthians*. 7 vols. New York, N.Y.: Loizeaux Brothers, 1978.

Graves, David E. *Biblical Archaeology: An Introduction with Recent Discoveries That Support the Reliability of the Bible*. Vol. 1. Toronto, Ont.: Electronic Christian Media, 2014.

Green, Joel B. "Festus, Porcius (Person)." Edited by David Noel Freedman, Gary A. Herion, David F. Graf, and John David Pleins. *ABD*. New York, N.Y.: Doubleday, 1992.

Hawthorne, Gerald F., Ralph P. Martin, and Daniel G. Reid, eds. *Dictionary of Paul and His Letters*. Downers Grove, Ill.: InterVarsity, 1993.

Hengel, Martin. "Between Jesus and Paul: The 'Hellenists,' the 'Seven' and Stephen (Acts 6:1–15; 7:54–8:3)." In *Between Jesus and Paul: Studies in the Earliest History of Christianity*, 1–29. Eugene, Ore.: Wipf & Stock, 2003.

Jewett, Robert. *A Chronology of Paul's Life*. Minneapolis, Minn.: Fortress, 1979.

Kelly, William. *Lectures Introductory to the Study of the Acts, the Catholic Epistles, and the Revelation*. London, U.K.: W .H. Broom, 1870.

Kilgallen, John. *The Stephen Speech: A Literary and Redactional Study of Acts 7: 2-53*. AnBib 67. Rome: Pontifical Biblical Institute, 1976.

Köstenberger, Andreas J., L. Scott Kellum, and Charles L Quarles. *The Cradle, the Cross, and the Crown: An Introduction to the New Testament*. Nashville, Tenn.: Broadman & Holman Academic, 2009.

Levison, N. "The Proselyte in Biblical and Early Post-Biblical Times." *Scottish Journal of Theology* 10 (1957): 45–56.

Lightfoot, John. *Horæ Hebraicæ et Talmudicæ*. Translated by Robert Gandell. 4 vols. Oxford, U.K.: Oxford University Press, 1859.

Lightfoot, John, and Robert Gandell. *Horae Hebraicae et Talmudicae: Hebrew and Talmudical Exercitations upon the Gospels, the Acts, Some Chapters of St. Paul's Epistle to the Romans, and the First Epistle to the Corinthians*. 4 vols. Oxford, U.K.: Oxford University Press, 1859.

MacDonald, Lee Martin. "Acts." In *The Bible Knowledge Background Commentary: Acts-Philemon*, edited by Craig A. Evans and Isobel A. Combes, 19–194. Colorado Springs, Colo.: Cook, 2004.

Martin, Ralph P. *2 Corinthians*. Edited by David A Hubbard and Glenn W Barker. Word Biblical Commentary 40. Dallas, Tex.: Word Books, 1998.

McRay, John. *Paul: His Life and Teaching*. Grand Rapids, Mich.: Baker Academic, 2007.

Ogg, George. *The Chronology of the Life of Paul*. London, U.K.: Epworth, 1968.

Palumbo, Arthur E. *The Dead Sea Scrolls and the Personages of Earliest Christianity*. New York, N.Y.: Algora, 2004.

Peterson, Brian. "Stephen's Speech as a Modified Prophetic Rîb Formula." *Journal of Evangelical Theological Society* 57, no. 2 (2014): 351–69.

Porton, Gary G. *The Stranger within Your Gates*. Chicago Studies in the History of Judaism. Chicago, Ill.: The University of Chicago Press, 1994.

Rackham, Richard Belward. *The Acts of the Apostles: An Exposition*. 7th ed. London, U.K.: Methuen & Company, 1901.

Renan, Ernest. *Saint Paul*. Paris, France: Calmann Lévy, 1888.

Riesner, Rainer. *Paul's Early Period: Chronology, Mission Strategy, Theology*. Translated by Douglas W. Stott. Grand Rapids, Mich.: Eerdmans, 1998.

Schürer, Emil. *The History of the Jewish People in the Age of Jesus Christ (175 BC–AD 135)*. Edited by G. Vermes, F. Miller, and M. Black. Rev. 4 vols. Edinburgh, U.K.: T&T Clark, 1979.

Scobie, Charles H. H. "The Use of Source Material in the Speeches of Acts 3 and 7." *New Testament Studies* 25 (1979): 399–421.

Smith, James. *The Voyage and Shipwreck of St. Paul: With Dissertations on the Life and Writings of St. Luke*. London, U.K.: Longman, Brown, Green, Longmans, & Roberts, 1856.

Steinmann, Andrew E. *From Abraham to Paul: A Biblical Chronology*. St. Louis, Miss.: Concordia, 2011.

Sylva, Dennis D. "The Meaning and Function of Acts 7:56–60." *Journal of Biblical Literature* 106 (1987): 261–75.

Vardaman, E. Jerry. "Jesus' Life: A New Chronology." In *Chronos, Kairos, Christos*, edited by Jack Finegan, E. Jerry Vardaman, and Edwin M. Yamauchi, 55–84. Winona Lake, Ind.: Eisenbrauns, 1989.

Watson, Alan. *The Trial of Stephen: The First Christian Martyr*. Athens, Ga.: University of Georgia Press, 1996.

INDEX

1

1 Corinthians   28, 39, 40, 45, 67, 72, 79, 95, 110, 126, 152, 173, 192, 193, 195, 198, 214, 266
1 Kings   46, 90
1 Thessalonians   44, 95, 104, 153, 179, 184, 185, 192, 193, 214, 235

2

2 Thessalonians   73, 98, 137, 184, 185, 192, 214, 266

A

Aaron   26, 80, 89
Abraham   56, 57, 60, 61, 85, 86, 87, 88, 150, 151, 263, 264
Achaia 191, 194, 197, 202, 204, 205, 208, 209, 210, 266
Acts   264, 265, 266, 267
Acts, book of   264
advocate   25
Aeneas   120
Agabus   132, 136, 220, 222, 227, 266
Agora   187
Agrippa   109, 110, 136, 137, 138, 139, 204, 242, 243, 244, 245, 246, 248, 249, 250, 252, 265, 266
Agrippa I   245
Alexander   62, 102, 202, 206, 208, 217
Alexandria   82, 161, 196, 197, 252, 258
Alford, Henry   45, 110, 111, 133, 154, 177, 178, 202
Ananias   69, 70, 71, 72, 94, 107, 110, 113, 114, 115, 231, 234, 239, 240, 241, 243
Andrew   20, 27
Andronicus   107
Anglo-Israel   42
Annas   62
Antioch   22, 79, 81, 123, 132, 133, 134, 135, 136, 137, 142, 143, 144, 146, 148, 149, 152, 154, 155, 158, 159, 160, 161, 162, 163, 167, 168, 169, 171, 174, 191, 195, 196, 213, 265, 266
Antioch in Pisidia   149
Aphrodite   147
Apollo   177
apostle(s)   17, 18, 19, 21, 22, 23, 27, 28, 29, 30, 33, 38, 41, 42, 47, 49, 50, 51, 53, 54, 55, 57, 61, 62, 63, 64, 65, 66, 67, 68, 69, 70, 73, 74, 75, 76, 77, 79, 80, 81, 94, 96, 98, 99, 100, 101, 109, 110, 112, 113, 114, 115, 116, 117, 119, 121, 130, 131, 132, 133,134, 135, 136, 137, 138, 141, 147, 153, 154, 155, 156, 157, 158, 159, 162, 163, 164, 167, 169, 172, 173, 180, 186, 201, 204, 207, 208, 214, 223, 234, 251, 266
apostolic   41, 42, 64, 72, 75, 96, 99, 114, 131, 133, 134, 135, 145, 158, 173, 184, 192, 196, 201, 203, 210, 216
Appian Way   259
Aquila   191, 192, 195, 197, 199, 202
Arabia   117, 171, 264, 265
Arabian(s)   37
Aramaic   225, 229, 230, 233, 247
Areopagite   188, 190
Areopagus   186, 187, 190
Aretas IV   118
Aretas, king   264, 265
Aristarchus   202, 205, 208, 209, 210, 242, 252, 260
Aristotle   186
arrest   53, 61, 62, 63, 66, 70, 74, 82, 107, 138, 204, 236, 248
Artemis   196, 205, 206, 207, 208, 217
ascension   22, 23, 25, 26, 29, 47, 74
Asia   18, 36, 82, 149, 172, 173, 174, 176, 177, 196, 199, 201, 202, 204, 205, 206, 207, 210, 212, 213, 225, 226, 240, 251, 266
Asiarchs   206, 207, 208
Assos   212, 213
Assyrian   67
Athenian(s)   186, 187, 188, 190
Athens   84, 171, 182, 185, 186, 187, 188, 189, 191, 193, 206, 213, 266
atonement   26
Attalia   159, 160
Azotus   102, 104, 220

B

Babel   39
Babylon   89, 260
baptism   24, 29, 32, 48, 50, 72, 98, 100, 103, 104, 114, 129, 131, 134, 150, 152, 157, 177, 181, 193, 197, 199, 200, 201
baptismal regeneration   48

INDEX OF SUBJECTS

baptized   23, 24, 27, 31, 32, 38, 44, 47, 48, 49, 97, 98, 99, 101, 103, 115, 116, 131, 132, 150, 176, 180, 181, 191, 193, 197, 199, 200, 231
Barbarian(s)   156, 181, 189, 190, 257
Bar-Jesus   146, 147
barley   34
Barnabas   20, 38, 68, 69, 70, 71, 110, 117, 119, 132, 134, 135, 136, 137, 140, 142, 143, 144, 145, 146, 148, 153, 154, 156, 157, 158, 159, 160, 161, 162, 164, 165, 166, 167, 168, 169, 170, 171, 209, 266
Barsabas   168
Barsabbas   29, 167
Bartholomew   27
Basilica   22
Beautiful Gate   53, 55
Beelzebub   261
beheaded   266, 267
Berea   171, 182, 185, 186, 209, 210, 266
Berean   185, 209
Bernice   244, 245, 250
Bible   xiii, 17, 28, 46, 48, 49, 60, 80, 81, 108, 109, 114, 117, 147, 165, 182, 185, 199, 204, 261, 264
biographies   265
birth   32, 35, 53, 54, 98, 106, 156, 230, 232, 233
Bithynia   173, 174
blasphemy   74, 82, 94, 154, 193
Blastus   141
blood   17, 32, 42, 51, 58, 75, 76, 81, 94, 95, 96, 108, 118, 120, 122, 126, 138, 164, 167, 168, 189, 191, 211, 213, 216, 223, 231, 232
brethren   19, 27, 28, 48, 58, 86, 87, 88, 106, 116, 119, 127, 132, 136, 138, 140, 149, 151, 155, 163, 168, 169, 170, 172, 181, 184, 186, 195, 196, 202, 205, 210, 216, 220, 223, 224, 227, 232, 234, 235, 236, 258, 259, 260
brother(s)   28, 43, 45, 46, 47, 48, 49, 85, 149, 150, 164, 205, 229, 230, 234, 260

C

Caesar   136, 182, 184, 243, 244, 245, 250, 252, 253, 254, 260, 265, 266
Caesarea   18, 20, 44, 57, 102, 104, 117, 119, 123, 124, 126, 127, 132, 133, 141, 195, 196, 219, 220, 222, 223, 234, 237, 238, 239, 241, 242, 243, 244, 245, 251
Caesarea Maritima   266
Caiaphas   62
Caligula   264, 265
Canaan   85, 86, 150, 260
Candace   101, 103
Capernaum   120
Cappadocia   36, 173
carnal   39
Catholic Epistles   17, 36
Cenchrea   195, 210
centurion   123, 255, 256
Cephas   164, 169, 209
chain(s)   227
Chalcis   245
Chaldeans   85
chariot(s)   101, 103
Chasidim   43
Chios   212
Chrestus   192
Christendom   51, 81, 99, 100, 114, 128, 145, 151, 165, 178, 185, 253, 254, 256, 261
Christian Science   98, 100, 101, 204, 216
Christian(s)   267
Christianity   264
Cilicia   82, 92, 105, 106, 119, 167, 168, 169, 170, 171, 225, 228, 230, 237, 252, 265
circumcision   18, 20, 53, 81, 85, 105, 122, 123, 124, 127, 130, 131, 132, 133, 141, 143, 148, 161, 162, 163, 164, 167, 168, 171, 172, 173, 196, 223
Cities of Refuge   58
citizen   106, 181, 225, 232, 233, 237
citizenship   106, 168, 181, 229, 232, 233, 235
Claudius   106, 135, 136, 191, 192, 194, 237, 238, 265, 266
Claudius Lysias   106, 237, 238
Clement, Epistles of   262
cloud(s)   23, 25, 26, 35, 52, 58, 59, 104, 108, 166, 259
coins   264
Colossians   17, 112, 170, 248, 267
comfort   20, 39, 56, 96, 115, 117, 120, 125, 130, 236
comforter   18, 24, 31
commission   19, 101, 106, 107, 120, 125, 130, 133, 168, 232, 247, 248
conversion   20, 61, 171, 231, 265
Corinth   39, 171, 191, 192, 193, 195, 198, 199, 210, 221, 266
Corinthian   38, 40, 193, 198
Corinthians   29, 32, 38, 39, 40, 49, 50, 85, 95, 103, 106, 109, 110, 152, 159, 170, 171, 173, 179, 191, 192, 193, 195, 198, 204, 211, 214, 221, 264, 266
Cornelius   38, 48, 87, 99, 116, 120, 122, 123, 124, 125, 126, 127, 128, 129, 131, 137, 143, 166, 176, 200
Cos   219
council   20, 62, 65, 66, 70, 74, 75, 76, 77, 78, 79, 82, 83, 84, 86, 88, 89, 90, 91, 92, 93, 96, 106, 119, 133, 143, 163, 164, 165, 167, 168, 171, 172, 173, 196, 207, 209, 223, 224, 230, 232, 234, 235, 237, 240, 243, 244
Council in Jerusalem   162
Cretans   37
Crete   188, 252, 253
Crispus   191, 193, 195
cross   25, 31, 45, 55, 58, 75, 111, 117, 122, 130, 151, 164, 174, 176, 180, 182, 197, 210, 211, 215, 224
crucified   19, 42, 43, 44, 45, 46, 47, 48, 50, 60, 63, 64, 65, 84, 87, 108, 111, 116, 122, 137
crucifixion   42, 45, 57, 267

Cyprus 68, 69, 133, 134, 137, 143, 146, 169, 170, 171, 219, 222, 252, 265
Cyrene 36, 82, 133, 134, 143, 144

D

Damaris 188
Damascus 33, 106, 107, 108, 109, 111, 112, 113, 114, 115, 116, 117, 118, 171, 230, 231, 239, 247, 248, 264, 265
Daniel 25, 26, 43, 63, 67
daughter(s) 42, 220, 221, 245
David 28, 44, 45, 46, 47, 55, 64, 66, 67, 89, 90, 147, 150, 151, 152, 164, 166, 167, 203
Day of the First Fruits 34
death 264, 265, 266
Decapolis 264
Delphi 177
Demas 18
Demetrius 183, 205, 206, 207, 208
demon 92, 97, 177, 178, 203
demon(s) 39, 40, 56, 98, 100, 202, 253, 261
Derbe 155, 156, 158, 159, 171, 172, 209, 210
Deuteronomy 60, 89, 92, 129, 149
Devil 40, 208
Diana 207, 208, 217
Dice 29
Dionysius 188, 190
disciple(s) 23, 24, 25, 27, 28, 29, 31, 33, 34, 37, 38, 43, 47, 50, 62, 63, 64, 66, 67, 71, 76, 77, 79, 81, 82, 99, 105, 107, 113, 115, 116, 117, 119, 120, 134, 136, 138, 144, 153, 154, 158, 159, 160, 164, 191, 196, 197, 199, 200, 201, 205, 208, 209, 210, 211, 213, 216, 219, 222, 223, 247
disease(s) 57, 202, 257, 258
doctrine(s) 17, 19, 23, 41, 48, 81, 101, 253
Dora 124
Dorcas 120
Drusilla 241, 242, 245

E

earthquake 68, 179, 180
edification 39, 168
Egypt 36, 86, 87, 88, 89, 90, 98, 104, 149, 151, 183
Elamites 36
elder(s) 62, 63, 64, 65, 66, 82, 83, 86, 105, 136, 146, 158, 159, 162, 163, 164, 167, 172, 173, 185, 202, 209, 213, 214, 216, 223, 224, 227, 229, 230, 237, 239, 240, 241, 244, 253
Eleazar 76
Elijah 36, 68, 212
Elymas 146, 147, 148, 154, 155, 203
Emesa 242
England 41
Epaphras 18

Ephesians 33, 38, 39, 41, 59, 64, 85, 112, 122, 126, 205, 206, 208, 267
Ephesus 38, 99, 116, 171, 173, 191, 192, 195, 196, 197, 198, 199, 202, 203, 205, 206, 207, 209, 212, 213, 214, 215, 216, 217, 266
Epicurean(s) 186, 187, 188, 189
epilepsy 109
Epistle(s) 17, 28, 41, 50, 58, 67, 80, 91, 100, 112, 116, 150, 159, 172, 184, 185, 191, 192, 193, 195, 214, 215, 262, 267
Erastus 194, 202, 204
Ethiopia 103, 104
Ethiopian 94, 101, 103, 104, 144
Eucharist 50
Eunice 156, 172
eunuch 94, 101, 102, 103, 104, 220
Eutychus 209, 212
evangelist(s) 41, 134, 145, 159, 161, 162, 166, 176, 179, 214
exhortation 21, 39, 50, 67, 135, 149, 153, 168, 181, 209, 224, 235
Exodus 17, 22, 34, 70, 79, 151
Ezekiel 34, 49
Ezra 173, 176

F

Feast of Harvest 34
Feast of Weeks 34
Felix 190, 204, 237, 238, 239, 240, 241, 242, 243, 244, 245, 265, 266
Festus 109, 110, 204, 241, 242, 243, 244, 245, 246, 248, 249, 250, 265, 266
Field of Blood 28
fire 24, 34, 35, 36, 37, 42, 62, 68, 87, 153, 197, 204, 257
flesh 23, 26, 42, 44, 46, 71, 72, 79, 80, 86, 106, 111, 114, 119, 122, 132, 151, 161, 167, 227
flock 41, 70, 128, 213, 216
forgiveness 19, 47, 71, 75, 93, 100, 120, 122, 129, 130, 150, 152, 190, 248
Forum of Appius 258

G

Gaius 159, 193, 202, 205, 208, 209, 210
Galatia 143, 149, 154, 171, 173, 191, 196, 207, 266
Galatians 46, 66, 72, 80, 86, 88, 95, 101, 104, 105, 109, 112, 113, 114, 115, 117, 119, 123, 128, 131, 132, 133, 135, 141, 143, 145, 149, 150, 151, 152, 162, 163, 164, 169, 170, 171, 173, 195, 196, 202, 209, 214, 215, 223, 225, 230, 265, 266
Galilean(s) 36, 37, 65, 76
Galilee 23, 28, 117, 120, 129, 138, 150, 264
Gallio 191, 194, 210, 240, 266
Gamaliel 70, 76, 77, 106, 230, 235
Gauls 149

INDEX OF SUBJECTS

Gaza 101, 102, 103, 104
Gentile(s) 17, 18, 19, 20, 22, 28, 33, 37, 38, 41, 45, 48, 49, 55, 57, 58, 60, 66, 67, 69, 79, 80, 86, 87, 88, 90, 94, 100, 102, 104, 105, 109, 112, 113, 115, 120, 121, 122, 123, 124, 125, 126, 127, 128, 129, 130, 131, 132, 133, 134, 135, 136, 137, 141, 143, 146, 147, 148, 149, 151, 152, 153, 154, 155, 156, 160, 161, 162, 163, 164, 165, 166, 167, 168, 169, 171, 172, 173, 182, 185, 190, 191, 193, 201, 203, 204, 206, 213, 215, 220, 222, 223, 224, 226, 228, 232, 236, 237, 238, 246, 247, 248, 249, 259, 260, 261
gifts 31, 38, 39, 40, 41, 73, 74, 80, 136, 144, 145, 162, 163, 194, 203, 214, 221, 261
glorified 18, 19, 25, 26, 28, 31, 33, 55, 56, 57, 58, 66, 75, 91, 105, 108, 111, 132, 133, 135, 154, 167, 223
glory 18, 23, 25, 26, 31, 35, 36, 46, 47, 57, 68, 82, 83, 85, 86, 88, 89, 90, 91, 93, 95, 96, 107, 108, 109, 110, 111, 112, 113, 116, 117, 142, 197, 204, 222, 231, 248
Gnosticism 101
God-fearer 125
gold 55, 188, 189, 207, 213, 217
Gomorrah 59
gospel 17, 18, 19, 20, 21, 22, 23, 24, 26, 27, 29, 31, 32, 33, 36, 37, 38, 41, 43, 47, 48, 53, 64, 67, 73, 75, 78, 80, 81, 83, 85, 92, 94, 96, 97, 98, 100, 101, 102, 103, 104, 105, 111, 112, 113, 116, 117, 119, 120, 122, 123, 124, 125, 129, 130, 131, 133, 134, 137, 143, 145, 147, 148, 149, 150, 151, 152, 153, 154, 155, 156, 158, 159, 161, 162, 163, 164, 165, 166, 167, 169, 170, 171, 172, 174, 176, 177, 178, 179, 180, 181, 182, 183, 184, 185, 188, 190, 191, 192, 193, 196, 197, 200, 202, 203, 204, 205, 208, 211, 215, 216, 217, 221, 222, 224, 236, 242, 246, 248, 258, 261, 262, 265
governor 109, 118, 173, 189, 237, 238, 239, 240, 242, 243, 245, 250
Grace of God 27, 51, 69, 115, 119, 122, 126, 144, 163, 180, 195, 214, 248
Grecian(s) 79, 80, 81
Greece 266
Greek 25, 34, 37, 38, 42, 44, 56, 57, 63, 66, 74, 79, 81, 85, 97, 103, 104, 106, 111, 112, 117, 128, 129, 133, 144, 147, 150, 153, 156, 157, 163, 165, 166, 172, 174, 175, 177, 180, 182, 185, 186, 187, 188, 189, 191, 194, 199, 205, 206, 207, 208, 209, 215, 220, 221, 225, 226, 227, 228, 243, 254, 255, 257, 258, 259, 264
Greek(s) 32, 106, 109, 133, 134, 135, 155, 182, 183, 184, 186, 189, 190, 191, 192, 194, 195, 201, 202, 213, 214, 215, 225, 226, 257

H

Habakkuk 34, 150, 152
hallucination 109
Handkerchief(s) 202

Haran 85
heaven(s) 23, 25, 26, 32, 33, 34, 35, 36, 37, 41, 47, 55, 58, 60, 63, 66, 67, 68, 69, 71, 83, 89, 90, 91, 104, 107, 108, 109, 110, 111, 112, 117, 120, 125, 126, 127, 132, 133, 143, 153, 156, 158, 159, 162, 167, 180, 181, 184, 187, 189, 200, 231, 247, 262
Hebraism 46
Hebrews 27, 79, 81, 84, 92, 95, 105, 111, 161, 224
Hebrews, Book of 25, 32, 34, 45, 74, 88, 95
Hellenist(s) 79, 82, 84, 96, 117, 133, 161
heretic(s) 76
Hermes 156
Herod 20, 66, 67, 74, 124, 137, 138, 139, 141, 142, 143, 144, 238, 242, 245, 250, 252, 264
Herod Agrippa I 265, 266
Herod Antipas 264
Hillel 76, 106
Holy of Holies 26
Holy Spirit 17, 18, 19, 21, 22, 23, 24, 25, 26, 27, 28, 29, 30, 31, 32, 33, 34, 35, 36, 37, 38, 39, 40, 41, 42, 43, 44, 45, 46, 47, 48, 49, 50, 51, 52, 53, 55, 57, 58, 59, 61, 63, 64, 65, 66, 67, 68, 69, 70, 71, 72, 73, 74, 75, 76, 77, 78, 79, 80, 81, 82, 85, 86, 89, 90, 91, 95, 98, 99, 100, 104, 105, 108, 111, 112, 114, 115, 116, 117, 120, 123, 124, 127, 129, 130, 131, 132, 134, 135, 139, 140, 143, 144, 145, 146, 147, 150, 153, 157, 159, 162, 163, 164, 165, 167, 168, 169, 170, 172, 173, 174, 175, 179, 182, 183, 184, 186, 195, 197, 198, 199, 200, 201, 203, 205, 208, 209, 210, 211, 212, 213, 214, 215, 219, 220, 222, 224, 234, 248, 258, 259, 260, 261, 262
hope 25, 26, 38, 41, 43, 95, 247, 251
Hosea 44, 151, 247
Hymenaeus 202, 217
hypnotism 40

I

Iconium 153, 154, 155, 156, 158, 159, 171, 172
imprisoned 266, 267
imprisonment 18, 20, 61, 137, 139, 205, 213, 237, 250, 266
incarnation 27, 98, 152
Irvingite 41
Isaac xiii, 56, 57, 85, 86, 87
Isaiah 27, 44, 55, 56, 57, 58, 90, 101, 102, 103, 148, 150, 153, 154, 167, 195, 237, 260, 261
Israel 18, 19, 23, 24, 25, 26, 29, 33, 34, 38, 41, 42, 43, 44, 46, 47, 53, 54, 55, 56, 57, 58, 59, 60, 63, 66, 67, 71, 72, 73, 74, 75, 76, 79, 80, 82, 86, 87, 88, 89, 91, 92, 102, 103, 105, 106, 107, 108, 111, 113, 115, 116, 122, 129, 148, 149, 151, 154, 166, 167, 197, 201, 225, 226, 246, 247, 260
Italian 262

J

Jacob 56, 57, 58, 85, 86, 87, 89, 90, 97, 154, 166
jailer 178, 179, 180, 181
James 17, 27, 35, 41, 42, 119, 123, 137, 138, 139, 140, 141, 164, 165, 166, 167, 168, 169, 209, 223, 242, 251, 266, 267
James, Book of 168, 195
James, the son of Alphaeus 27
Jeremiah 44
Jerusalem 18, 19, 20, 22, 23, 24, 26, 27, 28, 29, 31, 36, 37, 41, 42, 43, 44, 51, 52, 54, 59, 62, 65, 68, 69, 73, 75, 76, 78, 79, 82, 90, 94, 95, 96, 98, 99, 100, 101, 102, 103, 106, 107, 110, 112, 113, 114, 115, 116, 117, 118, 119, 120, 122, 123, 129, 130, 132, 133, 134, 135, 136, 137, 138, 141, 142, 143, 148, 149, 150, 151, 153, 161, 162, 163, 164, 165, 167, 168, 169, 170, 171, 172, 173, 195, 196, 199, 204, 205, 209, 212, 213, 215, 219, 220, 222, 223, 224, 225, 226, 227, 230, 231, 232, 236, 237, 238, 239, 240, 241, 243, 244, 245, 246, 248, 260, 261, 262, 265, 266, 267
Jesus 264
Jew(s) 17, 18, 19, 20, 24, 32, 33, 34, 36, 37, 41, 42, 43, 47, 48, 50, 57, 58, 60, 64, 69, 70, 79, 81, 82, 85, 88, 94, 96, 100, 101, 105, 106, 107, 108, 109, 112, 113, 115, 116, 117, 118, 119, 120, 121, 122, 123, 124, 125, 126, 127, 128, 129, 130, 131, 132, 133,134, 136, 137, 138, 139, 143, 146, 147, 148, 149, 150, 151, 152, 153, 154, 155, 156, 158, 161, 162, 164, 166, 168, 170, 172, 173, 176, 178, 182, 183, 184, 185, 186, 188, 190, 191, 192, 193, 194, 195, 196, 197, 198, 200, 201, 202, 204, 206, 208, 209, 210, 213, 214, 215, 220, 222, 223, 224, 225, 226, 227, 228, 229, 230, 231, 232, 235, 236, 237, 239, 240, 241, 242, 243, 244, 245, 246, 247, 248, 249, 257, 258, 260, 261, 266
Jewish 19, 24, 25, 33, 34, 37, 38, 41, 43, 48, 53, 54, 57, 61, 63, 64, 71, 73, 77, 94, 95, 102, 105, 106, 109, 112, 117, 121, 124, 126, 127, 128, 129, 130, 133, 137, 139, 140, 141, 146, 153, 155, 158, 161, 165, 171, 172, 173, 182, 183, 185, 191, 194, 196, 197, 201, 202, 203, 209, 220, 221, 224, 227, 229, 230, 232, 234, 241, 244, 245, 246, 249, 258, 260, 262, 267
Jezebel 177
Joel 42, 43, 44, 175
John 17, 23, 24, 27, 29, 31, 35, 38, 41, 45, 46, 48, 50, 53, 54, 55, 56, 59, 61, 62, 63, 64, 65, 66, 67, 69, 70, 84, 87, 91, 92, 94, 96, 97, 98, 99, 101, 102, 103, 104, 105, 108, 110, 111, 112, 114, 116, 128, 129, 130, 131, 132, 138, 139, 140, 142, 146, 148, 149, 150, 151, 153, 164, 169, 170, 197, 199, 200, 201, 209, 210, 234, 249, 261
John the Baptist 31, 138, 139, 197
Joppa 104, 120, 121, 122, 124, 125, 127, 132
Joseph 29, 68, 85, 86, 87, 88, 89, 95
Josephus, Jewish Antiquities 264, 265
Josephus, Jewish War 264, 265
Joshua 58, 84, 85, 89, 90
Judah 41, 43
Judaism xiii, 63, 81, 105, 124, 128, 148, 151, 153, 161, 187, 197, 204, 223, 224, 230, 235, 240
Judaizer(s) 162, 163, 164, 165, 173, 196, 201, 223
Judas 18, 22, 27, 28, 29, 30, 76, 113, 114, 167, 168, 169, 171
Jude 17, 104
Judea 19, 20, 23, 36, 37, 42, 94, 96, 97, 105, 117, 120, 122, 129, 132, 136, 137, 138, 141, 143, 161, 162, 220, 222, 248, 260, 265, 266
Julius 251, 252, 260
Junia 107
Jupiter 157, 208
Justus 29, 193
Justus, Titius 191

K

Keys of the Kingdom 20
kingdom xiii, 19, 22, 23, 24, 25, 29, 33, 41, 44, 47, 48, 51, 53, 55, 59, 60, 61, 64, 71, 74, 97, 98, 102, 103, 118, 120, 121, 122, 133, 137, 138, 140, 143, 149, 155, 158, 159, 166, 167, 197, 201, 204, 213, 215, 216, 221, 245, 260, 261, 262

L

lame 18, 53, 54, 55, 56, 57, 61, 64, 65, 66, 96, 97, 156
language(s) 36, 37, 38, 157
legion 124
letter 266
Letter(s) 263, 264, 265, 266
Libertines 82
Libya 36
Lightfoot 34, 35, 60, 103, 115
Lord's Supper 50, 51, 144, 211, 255
Lucius 143, 144, 183, 194
Luke 17, 18, 19, 22, 24, 27, 29, 31, 32, 34, 63, 65, 77, 92, 99, 111, 112, 120, 124, 138, 151, 166, 171, 175, 177, 181, 182, 210, 231, 242, 251, 252, 257, 260, 264, 265
Lycaonia 155, 156, 158
Lydda 104, 120
Lystra 94, 155, 156, 158, 159, 171, 172, 185

M

Macedonia 18, 147, 172, 174, 176, 191, 194, 204, 205, 208, 209, 210, 266
Macedonians 176, 205
magistrate(s) 179
Malta 257, 258, 267
Mamertine prison 262
Manaen 143, 144

INDEX OF SUBJECTS

manuscript(s) 78, 89, 96, 101, 104, 120, 142, 150, 167, 168, 169, 201, 203, 206, 211, 212, 213, 219, 223, 239, 240, 253, 254, 260
Marianne 245
Mark 28, 62, 63, 69, 87, 116, 120, 126, 130, 139, 140, 142, 146, 148, 151, 169, 170, 249, 258, 264
martyr(s) 91, 108, 120, 138, 232, 233
martyrdom 79, 84, 94, 137, 138, 139
Martyrdom of Stephen 91
Mary 27, 32, 139, 140, 166
Masada 76
Matthew 19, 27, 28, 29, 33, 59, 63, 64, 148, 203, 261
Matthias 22, 27, 28, 29, 30
Mauro, Philip 40
Medes 36
meditation(s) 27
Melchizedek 25, 26
Mercurius 157
Mercury 156
Mesopotamia 36, 42, 85
Messiah 44, 45, 46, 47, 48, 55, 60, 64, 65, 89, 103, 116, 137, 151, 183, 197, 198, 235, 247, 261
Micah xiv, 44
Midrash 27
Miletus 125, 209, 210, 212, 213, 214, 219
Millennial 23, 46, 104, 216
Millennial Dawnism 98
millennium 59
miracle(s) 19, 36, 37, 41, 54, 55, 56, 65, 66, 72, 74, 75, 78, 82, 88, 93, 95, 97, 98, 109, 117, 119, 120, 122, 132, 140, 157, 165, 197, 202
mission 19, 25, 51, 101, 104, 114, 115, 125, 135
missionary 266
Mitylene 212
Mnason 134, 222, 223
Moloch 89, 90
moon 42, 167
Moses 29, 46, 60, 80, 82, 84, 85, 87, 88, 89, 90, 93, 94, 97, 126, 133, 150, 152, 162, 163, 164, 167, 172, 185, 196, 223, 248, 260, 261
mother 27, 139, 140, 156, 172, 173
Mount of Olives 26, 59

N

Nabataean 264
Nabataeans 118
Nazarene(s) 42, 44, 45, 47, 55, 57, 63, 112, 134, 139, 239, 240
Nazareth 33, 44, 45, 47, 55, 63, 75, 82, 83, 87, 88, 103, 129, 151, 231, 246, 247
Nazarite(s) 226
Nehemiah 46
Nero, Emperor 262, 266
new covenant 211
New Testament 17, 19, 20, 22, 24, 31, 33, 37, 41, 45, 57, 59, 67, 70, 73, 84, 104, 112, 114, 128, 136, 138, 139, 145, 148, 159, 181, 183, 205, 210, 217, 236, 259, 261, 263, 264, 265
Nicanor 79, 81
Nicodemus 45, 87, 95
Nicolaitanes 81
Nicolas 81
Nicolaus 79
Niger 143, 144
Novatus 194
Numbers, Book of 92, 195

O

Occultism 204
Old Testament 22, 24, 26, 30, 33, 34, 36, 43, 44, 45, 53, 55, 59, 74, 85, 92, 116, 129, 158, 165, 166, 183, 192
Olivet 25, 27, 166
Olivet discourse 25, 166
One Body 32
overseer(s) 213, 214, 216

P

Palestine 266
Pamphylia 36, 148, 149, 158, 159, 169, 252
Pantheist 189
Paphos 146, 147, 148, 149
parable(s) 19, 64, 251
Parmenas 79, 81
Parthian(s) 36
Passover 34, 35, 64, 98, 138, 183, 266
pastor(s) 41, 145, 214
Patara 219
patriarch(s) 85, 86
Paul 264, 265, 266, 267
Pauline Epistles 17, 32, 111
peace 24, 81
Pentateuch 17, 149
Pentecost 18, 20, 22, 23, 25, 27, 28, 29, 30, 31, 32, 33, 34, 35, 36, 37, 38, 42, 43, 44, 46, 47, 48, 49, 58, 61, 68, 71, 80, 84, 95, 99, 100, 103, 105, 107, 116, 125, 131, 134, 144, 196, 200, 212, 213, 266
Pentecostal 41, 203, 222
Perea 264
Perga 148, 149, 159, 160
Peter 17, 18, 20, 27, 28, 29, 30, 31, 35, 37, 38, 41, 42, 43, 44, 45, 46, 47, 48, 49, 50, 53, 55, 56, 57, 58, 59, 60, 61, 62, 63, 64, 65, 66, 67, 70, 71, 72, 73, 74, 75, 78, 82, 84, 85, 87, 89, 94, 98, 99, 100, 101, 102, 103, 105, 107, 114, 116, 117, 119, 120, 121, 122, 123, 124, 125, 126, 127, 128, 129, 130, 131, 132, 133, 135, 136, 137, 138, 139, 140, 141, 143, 150, 151, 152, 161, 164, 165, 169, 173, 200, 201, 234, 247, 259, 266, 267
Petra, Jordan 264
Pharaoh 86, 87

Pharisee(s) 64, 76, 82, 83, 86, 92, 94, 105, 106, 107, 108, 111, 113, 115, 116, 119, 133, 162, 163, 187, 227, 230, 231, 234, 235, 246, 261
Philemon 17, 264, 267
Philetus 217
Philip 20, 27, 38, 74, 79, 81, 94, 96, 97, 98, 99, 100, 101, 102, 103, 104, 105, 133, 138, 176, 220, 221, 264
Philippi 18, 44, 57, 117, 124, 126, 171, 172, 174, 176, 177, 179, 181, 184, 193, 203, 209, 210, 233, 266, 267
Philippians 80, 95, 106, 177, 193, 205, 214, 215, 216, 234, 267
Philo 197
Phoenice 133, 137, 163, 253
Phoenicia 133, 162, 219
Phoenician(s) 134, 141
Phrygia 36, 171, 173, 191, 196
Phrygian 155
physician 17, 18, 22, 23, 65, 175, 210, 242, 252
Pierson, Arthur T. 39
Pilate 56, 66, 67, 86, 97, 150
Pisidia 149, 158, 159, 171, 213
Pisidian Antioch 152
Plato 186
Platonism 197
Pliny 103, 173, 194, 265
Pliny the Elder, Natural History 265
Politarch(s) 182, 183, 184
Pontus 36, 173, 191
Pool of Siloam 49
Praetorian Guard 259
prayer(s) 22, 24, 25, 27, 30, 40, 50, 51, 53, 54, 58, 62, 66, 67, 68, 76, 79, 80, 92, 99, 100, 106, 108, 114, 117, 120, 124, 125, 127, 138, 139, 140, 141, 144, 158, 159, 165, 168, 169, 174, 176, 177, 179, 186, 205, 212, 218, 220, 224, 236, 250, 253, 258, 260
preaching 20, 21, 22, 37, 38, 41, 43, 48, 55, 57, 64, 68, 70, 77, 78, 79, 80, 84, 87, 94, 96, 97, 98, 101, 102, 104, 115, 116, 117, 120, 129, 130, 133, 134, 137, 146, 150, 151, 155, 158, 160, 166, 167, 168, 172, 173, 184, 186, 188, 191, 198, 203, 208, 211, 216, 217, 221, 224, 236, 248, 261
Priest(s) 25, 211
priesthood 26, 51, 128, 144
Priscilla 191, 192, 195, 197, 199, 202
prison 20, 50, 64, 66, 74, 75, 76, 77, 94, 95, 96, 105, 106, 112, 114, 119, 138, 139, 140, 178, 179, 180, 181, 205, 230, 235, 241, 246, 247, 251, 262
prisoner(s) 18, 19, 106, 112, 120, 140, 141, 204, 219, 223, 227, 228, 233, 235, 236, 237, 238, 240, 241, 242, 244, 245, 246, 249, 250, 251, 252, 254, 255, 256, 257, 259, 260, 262
Prochorus 79, 81
proconsul(s) 97, 146, 194, 206, 265
promise 18, 23, 26, 27, 31, 32, 35, 46, 47, 48, 49, 53, 56, 58, 59, 73, 85, 86, 87, 88, 122, 125, 126, 152, 165, 181, 200, 246, 247, 256, 258
prophecy 27, 43, 44, 45, 46, 47, 55, 59, 64, 67, 103, 115, 172, 175, 204, 216, 221, 222, 227, 262
prophet(s) 24, 29, 33, 34, 39, 41, 42, 43, 45, 46, 55, 57, 58, 59, 60, 64, 88, 89, 90, 98, 99, 101, 103, 112, 116, 122, 129, 130, 134, 136, 143, 145, 146, 147, 148, 149, 150, 151, 154, 164, 166, 167, 168, 183, 185, 197, 220, 240, 241, 247, 248, 249, 260, 261, 266
proselyte(s) 37, 41, 79, 81, 124, 153, 161
Psalm(s) 25, 28, 29, 42, 47, 49, 67, 68, 72, 104, 152, 183, 217, 240
Ptolemais 219, 220
Publius 257, 258
Puteoli 258
Python 177, 203

R

Rabbi 87
Rackham, Richard Belward 99, 113, 121, 138, 162, 186, 204, 206, 207, 251
Red Sea 88, 89
Redeemer 88, 247
Remphan 90
repentance 19, 48, 49, 53, 58, 60, 61, 65, 73, 75, 84, 91, 100, 120, 129, 132, 133, 150, 151, 152, 190, 197, 199, 200, 213, 215, 248, 261
Rephan 89
resurrection 22, 23, 25, 29, 33, 34, 35, 42, 44, 45, 46, 57, 61, 64, 68, 69, 74, 75, 95, 110, 117, 120, 122, 130, 132, 152, 176, 186, 187, 188, 190, 197, 211, 216, 234, 235, 240, 241, 245, 247
return of Christ 23
Revelation, Book of 17, 26, 35, 36, 41, 81, 97, 104, 108, 128, 130, 166, 177, 180, 210
Rhegium 258
Rhodes 219
risen 18, 19, 24, 28, 29, 31, 41, 50, 51, 69, 105, 109, 111, 117, 128, 130, 135, 140, 210, 224, 231, 236
Ritualism 128, 144
Roman 264, 266
Roman citizen 232
Roman law 95, 141, 180, 194, 240
Roman officer 228, 239, 240, 252
Romans 49, 59, 73, 86, 103, 106, 107, 129, 130, 141, 148, 150, 151, 178, 181, 188, 189, 191, 192, 195, 200, 201, 202, 205, 210, 214, 224, 230, 244, 259, 260, 261, 264, 266
Rome 18, 19, 20, 37, 82, 84, 94, 97, 101, 107, 138, 140, 141, 149, 177, 178, 181, 191, 192, 199, 204, 205, 206, 207, 222, 236, 237, 238, 243, 244, 245, 250, 251, 252, 256, 257, 258, 259, 260, 262, 266, 267, 270

S

Sabbath 27, 43, 149, 150, 151, 153, 161, 164, 167, 176, 182, 183, 191, 192, 210
Sadducee(s) 61, 74, 187, 234, 235
saint(s) 25, 26, 104, 166, 220, 259
Salamis 146
Saloniki 182
Samaria 19, 20, 23, 38, 53, 94, 96, 97, 98, 99, 100, 101, 102, 105, 117, 120, 122, 131, 133, 137, 138, 143, 147, 162, 163, 200
Samaritan(s) 96, 97, 98, 99, 100, 101, 114, 116, 200, 201
Samuel 60, 150
Sanhedrin 62, 63, 64, 65, 92, 94, 101, 106, 233, 234, 235
Sapphira 69, 70, 71, 72
Satan 19, 40, 70, 71, 72, 73, 79, 90, 91, 97, 118, 128, 139, 147, 162, 178, 180, 185, 199, 202, 203, 204, 248, 258, 262
Saul 20, 29, 33, 46, 57, 76, 82, 86, 91, 92, 94, 95, 105, 106, 107, 108, 109, 110, 111, 112, 113, 114, 115, 116, 117, 119, 120, 134, 135, 136, 137, 142, 143, 144, 145, 146, 148, 150, 151, 169, 171, 227, 230, 231, 247, 261
Saviour 18, 26, 32, 75, 111, 147, 151, 178, 181, 200
Sceva 202, 203
school 202, 240
Second Coming 26, 91, 166, 184
second missionary journey 18, 171, 172, 174, 196, 266
Secundus 183, 209, 210
Seleucia 116
Seleucus Nicator 134
Senate 187, 206
Seneca 194
Sennacherib 67
Septuagint (LXX) 85, 165, 166
Sergius Paulus 146, 147, 148, 240, 265
serpent 183, 239, 240, 258
servant(s) 18, 19, 32, 42, 55, 66, 118, 124, 125, 156, 157, 158, 170, 174, 177, 178, 179, 184, 194, 208, 212, 215, 216, 217, 236, 237, 257, 258
sheep 62, 101, 103, 128, 216
Shekinah 25
ship(s) 122, 175, 210, 212, 213, 218, 219, 251, 252, 253, 254, 255, 256, 258
shipwreck(s) 204, 243, 251, 253, 256, 257
Sidon 133, 141, 142, 252
signs 19, 33, 34, 36, 41, 42, 43, 44, 45, 49, 51, 60, 66, 68, 73, 74, 78, 82, 87, 88, 89, 90, 96, 97, 98, 100, 117, 122, 155, 164, 200, 262
Silas 77, 167, 168, 169, 170, 171, 173, 177, 178, 179, 180, 181, 182, 184, 185, 186, 191, 192, 193
Simon Magus 98, 100, 101, 203
Simon, the Zealot 27, 97, 98, 99, 100, 106, 120, 121, 124, 125, 126, 127, 132, 147
Sinai, Mount 36, 68, 87, 88
smoke 42
Socrates 186, 187
Sodom 59
soldier(s) 97, 124, 125, 138, 139, 141, 176, 225, 227, 228, 229, 234, 235, 237, 238, 254, 255, 256, 258, 260
Solomon 25, 61, 73, 89, 90
Solomon's porch 61, 73
Solomon's portico 56, 73
Solomon's temple 25
Son of Consolation 69
Son of God 27, 32, 51, 57, 61, 63, 67, 71, 101, 103, 107, 110, 112, 113, 115, 116, 117, 151, 152, 176, 231
Sopater 183, 209, 210
sorcerer(s) 97, 100, 101, 147, 148, 154
soreg 226
Sosthenes 194, 195
Spain 267
Spiritualism 98, 204
Statius 194
Stephanas 193
Stephen 19, 20, 29, 38, 46, 76, 79, 80, 81, 82, 84, 85, 86, 88, 89, 90, 91, 92, 93, 94, 95, 105, 107, 108, 111, 119, 120, 122, 133, 137, 158, 226, 229, 231, 232, 234, 241, 261
Stoic 186, 188, 189, 194
stoning 227
Strabo 103
Suetonius 97, 192, 262, 265
suffering 17, 22, 25, 61, 67, 77, 86, 94, 96, 114, 118, 138, 154, 158, 179, 227, 261
Sunday 210
supernatural xiii, 19, 40, 74, 159
Sylvanus 185
synagogue(s) 34, 43, 62, 76, 79, 82, 94, 95, 107, 115, 116, 117, 119, 120, 124, 143, 146, 149, 151, 152, 153, 154, 155, 156, 158, 161, 164, 171, 176, 182, 183, 184, 185, 186, 191, 192, 193, 194, 195, 196, 197, 201, 231, 240, 241, 246, 247
Syracuse 258
Syria 97, 167, 168, 169, 170, 171, 195, 209, 210, 219, 265, 266

T

tabernacle 90, 167, 183
Tabitha 120
Tacitus 262
Talmud 27, 36, 103, 106, 138, 185, 203
Tarshish 105
Tarsus 20, 29, 33, 46, 57, 76, 82, 86, 92, 105, 106, 108, 109, 112, 113, 114, 115, 117, 119, 134, 135, 171, 186, 208, 225, 228, 230, 265
teacher(s) 28, 41, 50, 73, 143, 145, 149, 162, 163, 164, 165, 166, 168, 173, 184, 185, 196, 199, 200, 201, 213, 214, 215, 216, 217

temple 27, 50, 51, 53, 54, 55, 56, 61, 62, 64, 74, 75, 77, 84, 86, 90, 93, 96, 100, 119, 147, 156, 157, 195, 196, 205, 206, 207, 208, 216, 217, 219, 222, 223, 224, 225, 226, 227, 229, 231, 232, 239, 240, 241, 243, 244, 246, 248, 252
temple, of Solomon 35
tentmaker 191, 192, 208
Tertullus 239, 240, 241
Thecla 106, 155
Theophany 36
Theophilus 17, 22, 242
Thessalonian 95, 184
Thessalonians 26, 35, 59, 137, 152, 166, 171, 179, 184, 185, 191, 193, 209
Thessalonica 171, 182, 184, 185, 186, 192, 193, 202, 209, 210, 242, 252
Theudas 76
Thomas 27, 108
Thracians 176
Three Taverns 258, 259
Thyatira 176, 177
Tiberius 264
Timon 79, 81
Timothy 18, 73, 109, 149, 154, 156, 159, 170, 171, 172, 173, 177, 185, 186, 191, 192, 193, 195, 202, 204, 209, 210, 216, 221, 267
Titus 159, 163, 202, 266, 267
tomb 25, 45, 46, 55, 86, 117, 150
tongue(s) 25, 34, 35, 36, 37, 38, 39, 40, 41, 44, 72, 78, 100, 109, 110, 115, 131, 157, 180, 194, 199, 200, 201, 229, 240
Torah 34, 106, 183, 230
Transfiguration, Mount of 25
Trinity 18, 26, 32
Troas 18, 171, 173, 174, 209, 210, 211, 212, 219, 266
Trophimus 202, 209, 210, 225, 226
Tychicus 202, 209, 210
Tyrannus, hall of 201, 202
Tyre 133, 141, 142, 219

U

Unknown God 188
Unleavened Bread 138, 209

V

Venus 147
Verna 185
viper 257, 258
virgin 27, 32, 207
Vitellius 97

W

wedding 19
wheat 24, 34, 254, 255
wine xiii, 37, 43, 51, 157, 211
wisdom 39, 88
wolves 216
women 27, 39, 40, 41, 54, 63, 73, 94, 95, 96, 97, 105, 107, 153, 154, 176, 177, 182, 184, 185, 192, 205, 221, 226, 230, 259
wonder(s) 34, 42, 44, 45, 49, 51, 66, 68, 70, 73, 82, 87, 88, 89, 90, 93, 98, 155, 156, 164, 165, 248
worship 39, 85, 89, 101, 103, 128, 137, 138, 144, 158, 161, 167, 173, 176, 178, 183, 187, 188, 194, 205, 207, 210, 211, 217, 240, 241, 246, 253

Z

zealot 112
Zechariah 26, 49, 56, 57, 108
Zeus 156, 157
Zion 56, 68, 103, 152

Also by David E. Graves

Biblical Archaeology Vol. 1: Introduction with Recent Discoveries That Support the Reliability of the Bible, 2014; ISBN-13: 978-1502467072; *Vol. 2: Famous Discoveries That Support the Reliability of the Bible*, 2015 ISBN-13: 978-0-9948060-2-4.

Each year archaeologists discover many new finds at sites throughout the lands of the Bible, but few of them make the news headlines. Revisionist scholars often seek to undermine and downplay the relevance of many of the discoveries, believing that Sodom never existed, the Exodus never happened, Jericho never fell to the Israelites, and David was never a great king. This work challenges the minimalist views by bringing together many of the new discoveries from the last 20 years highlighting the recent finds that are relevant to the claims of the Bible. Experienced archaeologist David Graves has assembled a helpful collection of discoveries that will take you on a journey to:

- Confirm the historicity of the biblical events and people of the past
- Explore the full range of new archaeological discoveries, from pottery, inscriptions, seals, ossuaries, through to coins, manuscripts, and other artifacts
- Present a short history of archaeology, outlining its characteristics and role in Christian apologetics
- Lay out the limitations of archaeology and its methodological fallacies
- Explain the meticulous method of excavation
- Explore the significance of manuscripts for the transmission of the Bible
- Navigate the maze of arguments between the minimalists and maximalists controversy

This insightful book will:

- Illustrate archaeological finds with more than 140 pertinent photographs, maps, charts, and tables
- Include a glossary defining technical archaeological terms
- Provide extensive footnotes and bibliography for future study

This invaluable resource provides an interesting and informative understanding of the cultural and historical background of the Bible illustrated from archaeology. This is an accessible resource intended for laypeople who want to know more about archaeology and the Bible, whether in seminary courses, college classrooms, church groups or personal study.

Also by David E. Graves

The Location of Sodom: Key Facts for Navigating the Maze of Arguments for the Location of the Cities of the Plain., 2016. ISBN 13:978-0-9948060-3-1.

The Bible describes the destruction of Sodom and Gomorrah in Genesis 19 in terms of fire and brimstone falling from heaven. But what actually happened to these cities? Where are they today? Did they survive the cataclysmic destruction? Two archaeological sites have recently been identified as Sodom, but which is the best candidate for the location of Sodom: Tall el-Hammâm, at the northern end of the Dead Sea in the Jordan Valley, or Bâb edh-Dhrâ, at the southern end of the Dead Sea in the Ghor? Trying to navigate the maze of arguments can be a daunting task.

Graves provides a useful tool for readers in their quest for the location of this illusive biblical city. This work provides sixty-two helpful facts grouped together in methodological, hermeneutical, geographical, chronological, archaeological, cataclysmal, and geological chapters, which set the stage for further research and consideration. This work includes the material from the Key Facts for the Location of Sodom Student Edition: Navigating the Maze of Arguments and additional information, including a chapter of the material presented in an article titled "My Journey to Locate the Genesis Pentapolis North of the Dead Sea," additional primary source quotations, and testimonial quotes for both sites.

The advantage of such a book is that it provides a collective source of material for readers that would otherwise take a long time to assemble or otherwise be inaccessible. Numerous detailed maps, charts, tables, and photographs are included which will help facilitate understanding of the unfamiliar terrain of the Dead Sea and Jordan Valley. A glossary defines technical terms, and extensive footnotes, a bibliography, and reference to a large index of subjects and authors provides an invaluable resource to readers for future study.

Also by David E. Graves

Key Themes of the Old Testament: A Survey of Major Theological Themes, 2013. ISBN-13: 978-1478122692; *Key Themes of the New Testament: A Survey of Major Theological Themes,* 2013. ISBN-13: 978-1490922744.

Surveys 12 Old Testament themes written for the undergraduate audience from a themes perspective. The themes include history of the English Bible, biblical revelation, inspiration, transmission of the text, creation context, sovereignty of God, sin and the human condition, protoevangelium, covenant, biblical law, Israelite worship, and prophets.

New Testament Themes covered include the kinds of biblical literature, birth and early years of Jesus, the ministry of Jesus, the death of Jesus, the resurrection and ascension of Jesus, and the founding, development, formation and future of the Church. At over 440 pages and over 100 photos, maps and charts this book will complete the Biblical Themes series.